United Nations
Department of Economic and Social Development
Transnational Corporations and Management Division

United Nations Library on Transnational Corporations
Volume 4

TRANSNATIONAL CORPORATIONS AND BUSINESS STRATEGY

Note

The Transnational Corporations and Management Division (formerly the United Nations Centre on Transnational Corporations) of the United Nations Department of Economic and Social Development serves as the focal point within the United Nations Secretariat for all matters related to transnational corporations and acts as secretariat to the Commission on Transnational Corporations, an intergovernmental subsidiary body of the United Nations Economic and Social Council. The objectives of the work programme are to further the understanding of the nature of transnational corporations and of their economic, legal, social and political effects on home and host countries and in international relations, particularly between developed and developing countries; to secure effective international arrangements aimed at enhancing the contribution of transnational corporations to national development goals and world economic growth; and to strengthen the negotiating capacity of host countries, in particular the developing countries, in their dealings with transnational corporations.

General Disclaimer

United Nations Library on Transnational Corporations

Volume 4

TRANSNATIONAL CORPORATIONS AND BUSINESS STRATEGY

**Edited by Donald J. Lecraw
and Allen J. Morrison**

General editor: John H. Dunning

London and New York
published for and on behalf of the United Nations,
Transnational Corporations and Management Division,
Department of Economic and Social Development

First published 1993
by Routledge
11 New Fetter Lane, London EC4P 4EE

Simultaneously published in the USA and Canada
by Routledge
a division of Routledge, Chapman and Hall, Inc.
29 West 35th Street, New York, NY 10001

Typeset by Leaper & Gard Ltd, Bristol, England
Printed and bound in Great Britain by
Mackays of Chatham PLC, Chatham, Kent

British Library Cataloguing in Publication Data

A catalogue reference for this book is available from the British Library.

ISBN 0-415-08537-3 (Vol. 4)
ISBN 0-415-08554-3 (Set A)
ISBN 0-415-08559-4 (All 20 volumes)

*Library of Congress Cataloging in Publication Data
has been applied for.*

ISBN 0-415-08537-3 (Vol. 4)
ISBN 0-415-08554-3 (Set A)
ISBN 0-415-08559-4 (All 20 volumes)

Contents

Preface

The importance of transnational corporations and the globalization of production are now well recognized. Transnational corporations have become central actors of the world economy and in linking foreign direct investment, trade, technology and finance, they are a driving force of economic growth. Their impact on the economic and social welfare of developed and developing countries is both widespread and critical.

It is one of the functions of the Transnational Corporations and Management Division (formerly the United Nations Centre on Transnational Corporations – the focal point in the United Nations for all issues relating to transnational corporations – to undertake and promote research on transnational corporations to contribute to a better understanding of those firms and their impact. Over the past thirty years, research on this phenomenon has mushroomed, and hundreds of books and reports, as well as thousands of papers, have been published. It is the principal purpose of this twenty-volume *United Nations Library of Transnational Corporations* to distil, summarize and comment on some of the more influential of those writings on the role of transnational corporations in the world economy. In particular, the contributions in the *United Nations Library* deal with four main issues: the determinants of the global activities of transnational corporations, their organizational structures and strategies, their interactions with the economies and legal systems of the countries in which they operate and the policies that governments pursue towards those corporations. The twenty volumes are intended to cover a wide range of topics that embrace economic, organizational and legal issues.

To accomplish that task, the Centre assembled a distinguished group of editors, who were commissioned to select the seminal contributions to their subject areas published over the past twenty to thirty years. They were also asked to prepare comprehensive bibliographies of writings on their subjects for inclusion in the volumes, and state-of-the-art introductions that summarize the development of their subjects, review the most important current issues and speculate about future work. We hope that the result in each case is a volume that provides a succinct, yet comprehensive overview of the subject to which it is devoted.

Broadly speaking, the volumes in this series fall into two categories. First, there are those that address the interaction between the activities of transnational corporations and the environment of which these firms are part. Second, there are those that analyse the internal organization and management of transnational corporations, in response to, or in anticipation of, changes in their external environment. This volume is an example of the second category. In it, two of the leading researchers in the field seek to identify and explain the evolving managerial strategies of transnational corporations and how, in particular, they vary between different kinds of transnational corporations and the industries and countries within which they operate.

The authors show, among other things, that the literature on the management and organization of resources and capabilities owned across national boundaries is a very recent one; researchers are still trying to grapple with the theory and practice of transnational business conduct. At the same time, as the authors point out, a good deal of evidence has accumulated to suggest that, within particular industries and countries, transnational corporations of different sizes and nationalities do pursue distinctive strategies, for example, with respect to sourcing, research and development, product diversification and marketing. Those firm-specific behavioural characteristics must be taken into account by scholars who wish to seek generalized explanations of both the determinants and consequences of activities of transnational corporations.

In the present volume, Donald J. Lecraw, Professor at the School of Business Administration at the University of Western Ontario, Canada, and the Institute Rengembangan Manejemen Indonesia of Baru-Jakarta, and Allen J. Morrison, Assistant Professor at the University of Western Ontario, succinctly guide the reader through the principal literature on the evolving strategy of transnational corporations, and explain why scholars, business persons and politicians are becoming increasingly interested in the impact of such strategy on the globalization of production and markets.

New York, May 1992

Karl P. Sauvant
Chief, Research and
Policy Analysis Branch,
Transnational Corporations
and Management Division

John Dunning
General Editor of
United Nations Library on
Transnational Corporations

Acknowledgements

The editors and publishers would like to thank the following publishers, other organisations and individuals for permission to reprint copyright material: Academy of Management; *California Management Review*, University of California, Berkeley; *The Columbia Journal of World Business Studies*; Joseph Farris; Ed Fisher; Dana Fradon; *Harvard Business Review*, Harvard Business School; Harvard University Press; *Journal of International Business Studies*, University of South Carolina; MIT Sloan School of Management; Pergamon Press; Donald Reilly; John Wiley & Sons.

Acknowledgement is also due to: the Ballinger Publishing Company; and Lexington Books.

Introduction: Transnational Corporations and Business Strategy – The Foundations of an Emerging Field

Donald J. Lecraw and Allen J. Morrison

The compilation of an edited volume on transnational corporations (TNCs) and business strategy is a timely, yet daunting task. The task is made pertinent by the soaring levels of transnational investment and trade in goods, services and technology that has typified the decade of the 1980s. The increasing number and size of TNCs have resulted in the introduction of new forms of competition that challenge and compel even wholly domestic competitors. For the majority of corporations today, the formulation and implementation of business strategy can no longer be separated from concurrent pressures for internationalization: the dichotomy between domestic and international business has been dissolved.

The decade of the 1980s saw large swings in the real exchange rates of major countries, changes in the volume of international trade and shifts in the value, source and destination countries of international capital and foreign direct investment flows. Companies worldwide have endeavoured to respond to those changes by adjusting their strategies and organizational structures to meet better emerging global competition, both threats and opportunities. The decade of the 1990s promises to be no less challenging as trading blocs are formed in Europe, North America and possibly among the Pacific Rim countries, and as the economies of the Central and Eastern European countries are reformed and opened to trade and investment flows.

Over the past decades, TNCs have played a major role in world production, trade, capital flows and technology generation and transfer. There is every prospect that, in the 1990s, their role will increase. In the 1980s, it was estimated that, for the United Kingdom, trade by TNCs accounted for 80 per cent of exports, while for the United States, trade associated with United States-based TNCs accounted for 75 per cent of exports and over 50 per cent of imports. Intra-firm trade by TNCs accounted for over 30 per cent of imports and exports from Japan. Inflows of foreign direct investment (FDI) rose from \$22 billion in 1975 to nearly \$200 billion in 1989.[1] In 1988, it was estimated that there were 600 industrial companies accounting for between 20 per cent and 25 per cent of value added in the production of goods in the market economies of the world.[2]

The present volume focuses on the strategies of a large group of corporations that confront international competitive pressures with operations and investments that cross national boundaries. In order to undertake those operations, TNCs formulate international strategies and, in order to implement them effectively, devise unique organizational structures and control systems. The strategy of a TNC represents a blueprint for action that enables the corporation to achieve particular goals and objectives.[3] Its structure, in contrast, represents the internal organization of tasks, decision-making, power, human resources and so on, that are designed to implement effectively the intended strategy.[4]

A better understanding of the behaviour and impact of TNCs is useful for several groups: for managers of TNCs as they endeavour to maximize the value of their firms through international operations; for the governments of host and home countries of TNCs in their efforts to increase the net benefits TNCs have for their countries; and for those who study national and international economics to understand how economies function, to forecast future developments and to make policy recommendations designed to foster economic development.

Conflicting Perspectives of Transnational Corporation Imperatives

As a field of inquiry, international strategic management is in its infancy. It draws heavily from the two related fields of international business and strategic management, both emerging disciplines in their own right. The challenge for those studying TNC strategies is to synthesize the perspectives of those two disciplines in order to clarify how and why TNCs behave the way they do.

The fields of international business and strategic management have much in common. Both draw on multiple overlapping disciplines including, among others, economics, business management, political science and sociology. Both share a common central theme: the nature of the interaction between the organization and its environment. In strategic management, the design of organizational strategies represents the leveraging of competitive advantages *vis-à-vis* critical environmental opportunities and threats.[5] In a similar manner, international business represents the combination of comparative advantage (through transnational factor endowments) and the market failure of intermediate goods.[6] In both cases, the organization justifies its existence through an ability to differentiate itself from its environment. In the case of international business, however, the environment is more complex as multiple countries represent diverse patterns of demand, government regulation and indigenous competition, both within and among nations.

International business and strategic management are also similar in that they both espouse contrasting perspectives of organizational imperatives. The two perspectives are determinism and behaviouralism. Determinism suggests that organizational activity is founded on rational behaviour according to assessments of internal and external exigencies. In contrast, the behavioural perspective argues that individual decision-makers determine organizational outcomes and that those decision-makers are restricted in their rationality by both personality and a limited knowledge of internal and external exigencies.

The Deterministic Perspective

In international business, a broad range of theories has emerged that is designed to explain various TNC-related phenomena according to different types of market disequilibria, or disparities in the efficiencies of markets. The causes of market disequilibria are a variety of physical, cultural, political, technological and economic factors that separate one market from another. Market disequilibria suggest that, when international markets are not functioning efficiently, opportunities exist to internalize activities thus exploiting inefficiencies while concurrently moving the market towards greater efficiency.[7] As a consequence, market disequilibria and the ability of TNCs to internalize transactions efficiently have been used to explain various forms of TNC activity under certain conditions.

In spite of the clarity of this perspective, little agreement exists over the application of internalization at a particular level of abstraction. Some theories focus on market closing activities at the transaction level within the TNC;[8] some on the TNC itself;[9] while other theories focus on industry structural disequilibria between countries and hence the internationalization of entire industries.[10] While all market disequilibria theories ultimately involve various types of international activities of central importance to the TNC, not all are designed to explain the overall activities of the TNC.[11] They are most useful in understanding the problem of becoming a TNC rather than the strategies of existing TNCs.[12]

From a strategic management perspective, researchers have also developed a host of deterministic theories that attempt to link organizational activities with a variety of contingencies in the external environment of the firm.[13] Fundamental among these is the industrial organization perspective of the competitive environment. According to that perspective, strategy is determined by the match the organization achieves between its distinctive competencies and imperatives arising from the structure of the industry in which it operates.[14] That perspective effectively removes the decision-maker from strategy formulation by suggesting that decision-making is a normative process which results in one best strategy option for the organiz-ation given its external environment.[15]

A common problem with the deterministic perspective of both inter-national business and strategic management researchers is that the approach is largely reductionist. Reductionism suggests that only a few critical relationships are necessary to explain the operations and perform-ance of an entire TNC. In real life applications, the resulting generalization can lead to a loss of predictive power. Related to this problem is the reduction of the decision-maker to a black box. Managers are portrayed as strictly reactive agents for rational organizational outcome. The suggestion is that – irrespective of the unit of analysis – the TNC follows, and cannot determine, environmental opportunities. Reciprocal cause-and-effect relationships are ignored.[16]

Behavioural Perspective

A means of overcoming the limitations of determinism is the behavioural perspective of strategic management and international business. In inter-national business, the behavioural approach attempts to explain both the initiation of international business operations by a firm and the definition of ongoing activities by focusing on the characteristics and opportunities faced by key decision-makers. According to one explanation, managers develop different perspectives of their environment, leading to the adop-tion of ethnocentric, polycentric, or geocentric organizational strategies.[17] In another explanation, it is asserted that overseas investment decisions rarely result from rational, discrete decision-making, but rather stem from an accumulation of opportunity-driven commitments.[18] In this case, it is the voluntaristic decision process of key decision-makers, not determinism, that decides strategic outcome.

A similar perspective has been espoused in strategic management. Here, decision-making has been portrayed as an incremental process that, although intendedly rational, may be highly specific to the individuals involved.[19] A corollary to this perspective allows for comprehensive decision-making but suggests that managers perceive opportunities and threats according to personal value systems, thus resulting in a multitude of strategic choices. Such decision-making allows managers to steer organiz-ations proactively according to personal objectives and assessments.

Both the deterministic and behavioural perspectives shed light on the nature and activity of TNCs. Either may be appropriate, depending on the type of question asked and the assumptions held. Nevertheless, the debate continues with no unifying theory suggested. This continued debate is evi-dence that international strategic management is an emerging field. Throughout the readings that follow, the reader should recognize that while little consensus exists concerning the behavioural or deterministic perspec-tives, the contrast between the perspectives is both intellectually appealing and consistent with the diversity of approaches inherent in international business and strategic management.

Foundations of Transnational Corporation Strategy

The debate between the behavioural and deterministic perspectives has served as a backdrop to the ongoing conceptual developments in the field of international strategic management. International strategic management is fundamentally concerned with the establishment of organizational goals, strategies, structures and evaluative and control mechanisms of an organization.[20] These broad concerns can be further refined into two general themes: strategy *formulation* (including both the process of formulation and the actual strategy content) and strategy *implementation* (including the design of organization structure and the selection of ownership and control systems). In this volume, these two themes provide the structure for the discussion of TNC strategy. TNC strategy refers specifically to the nature of a multi-country business organization's goal-directed activity; it encompasses the development and modification of existing strategy as well as the implementation of the strategy through activities that transcend national boundaries.

By restricting this volume to the formulation and implementation of TNC-related strategies, certain issues relating to the functions and responsibilities of general managers are not addressed. TNC strategies relating to technology generation and transfer, human resources management, business–government relations, international pricing strategy, international production and international finance have been consciously omitted, since to include them would have required a much longer volume and would have detracted from its central thrust: strategic management and TNCs.[21] Other volumes in this series focus on these topics as well as on the broader issues of the role of TNCs in economic development and the influence of TNCs on international trade. The readings in this volume focus more narrowly on the strategic direction of the TNC as determined by general managers.

International Strategy Formulation

The explicit separation of strategy formulation and strategy implementation is a relatively recent phenomenon. Much of the early research on international strategy implicitly recognized the distinction by focusing on the linkage between the strategy of the firm and the organizational structure it uses to implement it. The driving force behind an organizational structure chosen by a TNC was seen to be its strategy.

A. Chandler was one of the principal pioneers in the area of strategy and structure.[22] Chandler's work in the early 1960s played a pivotal role in the development of the emerging fields of strategic management and international business. In his often-cited research, Chandler undertook an in-depth, longitudinal study of the relationship between strategy and structure of 70 of the United States' largest corporations – all ostensibly TNCs. Here, Chandler observed that strategic changes in organizations tended to be followed by changes in organizational structure. He furthermore concluded that organizational change followed a common pattern in the United States TNCs studied. Strategic change commonly followed a four-stage development pattern: first, volume expansion, followed by geographic expansion, vertical integration and finally product diversification. As these firms changed their strategies, structural change soon followed. According to Chandler this relationship between corporate strategy and structure was caused by organizational inefficiency which resulted from the poor fit between evolving strategy and the corporation's historical structure.

Chandler's conceptualization of strategy as broad patterns of organizational behaviour provided much of the foundations for a future stream of research that focused on the strategy formulation process, the content of strategy and the nature of strategy–structure linkages. Most of these contributions were immediately felt in the strategic management field, which in turn served as a foundation for an emerging stream of research on the fit between an organization's strategy and its competitive environment.

Chandler's work had a profound influence on I. Ansoff, another pioneer in the field of strategic management. Ansoff suggested that strategies changed with time because the environment changed. The suggestion here was that the key strategic problem of any corporation was in determining how to match the firm with its environment. In this sense, strategic fit or "matching" was extended from strategy–structure to include strategy–environment. With this recognition of the importance which the environment plays in determining strategy content, Ansoff identified product–market scope as a key component of strategy content.[23] Scope, in this sense, referred to the configuration of the organization's present and planned interactions with its environment and defined which products were offered and in which geographic markets the organization competed. The implication was that strategy could conceptually accommodate unique international dimensions of organizational activity: products and markets could be either domestic or international. Scope in this sense provided the early foundations of the emerging discipline of international strategic management.

The work of Chandler and Ansoff was further expanded in the early 1970s by K. Andrews.[24] Andrews' interests were in developing a comprehensive framework for strategy formulation. According to his framework, strategy formulation involved the consideration of four conditions: the environmental opportunities, threats, risks, etc. facing the organization; the resources and distinctive competencies internal to the organization; the personal values of senior managers; and the non-economic responsibilities of the organization to the society at large. This framework suggested a normative process for strategy formulation that, while developed ostensibly for United States businesses, can be appropriately applied to organizations competing across national boundaries.

The identification of a normative framework for strategy formulation led to a number of attempts to develop a strategic planning framework for TNCs. Perhaps the most noted planning framework is that developed by P. Lorange which is set out in a reading in this volume. Lorange's framework presented the adaptation and integration requirements for TNCs dependent on a variety of organizational types ranging from world-wide product divisions to geographical areas. According to the framework, adaptation to host-country conditions and integration of TNC operations across national borders varied widely according to the type of TNC. Means of balancing the costs and benefits of adaptation versus integration were suggested and included more clearly specifying task direction and adjusting the relative emphasis placed on adaptation and integration during different stages of planning.

Lorange's framework made three important contributions. First, the framework itself provided a normative basis from which TNCs can simplify planning and better utilize their competencies. Second, the framework was built on a classification of TNCs that explicitly recognized and further substantiated the tight linkage between a TNC's strategy and its structure. Third, the framework recognized two broad and conflicting imperatives facing TNCs: adaptation of the organization at the local level to meet host country conditions (i.e., responsiveness) versus international integration of a TNC's activities irrespective of the local environment.[25] That is perhaps the most important contribution of the framework. As described later in the chapter, these imperatives of integration and responsiveness attracted the attention of considerable future research. The focus of this work was on the role the dual imperatives played in determining the relationship between strategy and the TNC's environment.

In spite of the contributions of Lorange's framework it was not intended to capture the nuances of planning in complex organizations. Rather, planning imperatives were related to broad types of TNCs. By the early 1980s, conceptual advances were being made in the strategic management field which provided new comprehensive frameworks of strategic planning. Those advances, as well as contributions from Lorange's earlier work, were recognized by W. Dymsza who developed a "comprehensive, dynamic model of strategic planning" for TNCs.[26] The article by Dymsza, included in this volume, asserts that short-term "operational" planning must be separated from longer term "strategic" planning. Furthermore, strategic and operational planning must be reconciled in the face of multiple levels of decision-making within the organization. In a TNC, planning involves linking decisions made at the subsidiary, business unit, divisional and geographic area levels of analysis. Within these sub-structures, functional activities of marketing, finance, production and so on, all have planning imperatives which must be linked. The suggestion here is that rational, integrated planning based on comprehensive assessments of internal and external imperatives can assist the TNC in its efforts to maximize performance – both in the short and long term.

As was discussed earlier in this chapter, the alternative to a rational, analytical framework is the incremental perspective of strategy formulation. R. Pascale's article is included in this volume as an example of the incremental position. The article by Pascale presented a Japanese perspective of strategy formulation using the example of Honda's movement into the United States market in the late 1950s and early 1960s. Through interviews and secondary data, Pascale provided powerful evidence that organizational change is most appropriately considered as an incremental process. Too often, observers perceive the TNC strictly in terms of strategy, structure or internal control systems. While important, Pascale suggested managing a TNC requires control of six basic "levers": strategy, structure, staff, systems, style and shared values.[27] Only by incrementally balancing all six of these levers will the organization excel in terms of efficiency, responsiveness and innovation.

The part of this book on the strategy formulation process is concluded by Y. Doz's article on international strategic management. The article takes a corporate perspective of decision-making and argues that the hierarchical position of decision-making within a TNC will largely determine the type of strategy pursued. The implication of this viewpoint is that strategy content will be largely determined by the location of decision-making in a TNC.

As background to Doz's article, by the late 1970s the hierarchical nature of strategy was being made more explicit in research studies. A hierarchy of strategy content – extending from the corporate level to the industry-specific business level and finally to the functional level – was implicit in much of the organization theory and strategy research of the 1960s[28] and, by the mid-1970s, had become a central issue in domestic strategy frameworks.[29] The notion of a hierarchy of strategy is that while the corporate level broadly defines the scope of the organization's activities, it is the business level that determines how the organization competes within a given industry environment. Doz was interested in linking this notion that strategic issues are determined at different levels in the TNC with the earlier work of C. Prahalad and P. Lorange on the dual imperative. While Doz's imperatives are political and economic, the linkage with Prahalad's responsiveness and integration imperatives is clear. Using these imperatives, Doz argued that TNC responsiveness implied decentralized decision-making while integration required tight corporate control. As a consequence, environmental imperatives largely dictated strategy content and hence the location of decision-making in TNCs.

International Strategy Content

The recognition of TNC strategy as a hierarchy and the acknowledgment of the importance the environment plays in determining strategy content served as a major impetus for a stream of research examining business conduct within specific types of environmental contexts. The notion that environmental contingencies were critical in determining strategy content spurred considerable interest in characterizing and classifying different environmental contexts.

The work of M. Porter was pivotal in that regard.[30] Porter's perspective was that the primary environment of the TNC was the industry in which it competed. Porter argued that the industry serves as the arena where a TNC determines its competitive strategy and that, if a TNC examined the structural determinants of the industry, strategy formulation would be facilitated. Five structural forces were identified by Porter as fundamental in characterizing an industry: the level of rivalry among existing firms, the bargaining power of suppliers and buyers, the threat of new entrants into the industry and the threat of substitute products or services. Using these five structural forces, Porter developed a classification of generic industries, or common competitive environments. He identified these as fragmented, emerging, mature, declining and global. Within these industries, Porter argued that certain broad patterns of strategic behaviour would be more successful than others.

Encouraged by the broad interest in classifying strategies and industry environments, a series of articles emerged which discussed strategies appropriate for various generic industry contexts.[31] Efforts in international strategy research were naturally focused on better understanding global strategy–industry matches. G. Hamel and C. Prahalad's article, contained in this volume, discussed the complexities of global competition with particular attention focused on differentiating between global competition, a global business and a global company. Global competition refers to the cross-subsidization of national market-share battles; global businesses are those in which the maximum cost efficiency of production requires volume not available in the home market; a global company is one which has established an international distribution system that facilitates the cross-subsidization of key foreign markets.

Research on global strategies and global industries has been typically carried out using the integration-responsiveness framework previously discussed. Among this research is a second article by Porter which is contained in this volume. That later article provided greater detail of the content of integration-responsiveness strategies by developing the configuration–co-ordination framework. That framework built on earlier efforts to conceptualize business activity according to the value-chain concept.[32] The value chain identifies discrete value-creating activities such as incoming logistics, operations and marketing and sales. According to Porter, the essence of TNC strategy could be captured by the international configuration and co-ordination of discrete value-creating activities across national boundaries. Here, configuration refers to the physical positioning of value activities while co-ordination describes the nature of horizontal and vertical linkages along the value chain. According to Porter, global strategies combine concentrated value-activity positioning and tight co-ordination of operations on an international basis.

Further extensions to the integration–responsiveness framework were provided by S. Ghoshal. In the article contained in this volume, Ghoshal extended the conceptualization of strategy–industry linkages by arguing that multiple international strategies may be sustained in the same industry context. Here, Ghoshal expanded the integration–responsiveness framework from strictly the industry unit of analysis to the company level, the functional level and finally the task level. Each of these can be represented in terms of integration and responsiveness. In a global industry, for example, TNCs can compete using widely different patterns of integration or responsiveness; TNC strategy, in turn, can be supported by different patterns of emphasis on integration and responsiveness of marketing, production and so on. The key for a TNC is to determine the best way to leverage existing competencies given critical success factors in the industry.

While much of the research on the content of TNC strategy during the mid-1980s has been couched in terms of integration–responsiveness, not all researchers have viewed the industry as a critical focus of competition. In fact, several observers have argued that TNCs have become preoccupied with competing against other industry-based competitors and that, instead, they should refocus attention on serving the customer in various national markets. One such researcher is K. Ohmae; one of his articles is contained in this volume.

Ohmae suggested that instead of conceptualizing the industry as the competitive environment, the marketplace should be considered the TNC's most critical environment. Largely using Japanese examples, Ohmae argued that international competitiveness is determined not so much by beating the competition as it is by creating customer value. Value can be created by understanding customer needs – what customers are actually buying and will want to buy in the future – in terms of both tangibles and intangibles. As such, customer positioning rather than competitive positioning determines international success.

The final article in this part of the book presents G. Hedlund's discussion of the TNC of the future. According to Hedlund, TNCs will face mounting and concurrent pressures for host-country responsiveness, cost minimization through the international integration of activities and techno-logical excellence. As a consequence, the TNCs of the future will increas-ingly take on the form of a heterarchy – an internationally integrated, horizontal network of linked activities. Natural limits to the globalization of competition will result in the unique patterns of integration in the geo-centric firm.[33] Hedlund's description of the heterarchical TNC of the future also served as the foundation for C. Bartlett and S. Ghoshal's transnational strategy.[34] The transnational strategy – not to be confused with the strategy of TNCs – involves concurrent emphasis on efficiency, responsiveness and organizational learning. In order to meet increasing pressures to balance concurrent demands for local responsiveness and global integration, Hedlund and Bartlett and Ghoshal advocated the development of the "horizontal" organization that learns and responds at the periphery as well as at the centre. The suggested metaphor is the "firm as a brain" where thinking and learning goes on throughout the entire organization.

By linking organizational strategy with structure, Hedlund's article provides a natural transition to a broader discussion of international strategy implementation. Research in this area has focused primarily on two issues: the organizational role in strategy implementation (i.e., the nature of strategy–organizational structure linkages), and unique strategic control issues within a TNC. Those issues are the focus of the next two parts of this chapter.

The Implementation of Strategies: the Role of Organization

Not surprisingly, the history of research in TNC strategy implementation follows closely the previously noted work on strategy formulation. During its early stages, research on strategy implementation focused almost exclu-sively on issues of organizational design and structure. That research indi-cated that changes in strategy typically preceded changes in structure. The normative implication was that performance would be maximized if an organization's structure was patterned after its strategy.

Typical of this work was that carried out at Harvard University during the early 1970s. The work at Harvard focused on clarifying the nature of the linkages between a TNC's diversification strategy and organizational structure; it served as a turning point in research on strategy implemen-tation. Perhaps the most notable research of this period was that of R. Rumelt. Building on the work of his colleagues,[35] Rumelt studied the connection between strategy and structure in 200 Fortune 500 corpor-ations over a 20-year period. Using this United States-based sample, Rumelt concluded that there was a secular trend towards divisionalization among the corporations studied and that corporate success was associated with the matching of organizational strategy and structure. Rumelt also argued that performance outcomes could be maximized if corporations pursued related diversification strategies.[36] A related diversification strategy meant that expansion would be carried out only in areas that were closely associated with the core competencies and existing lines of business of the organization. Rumelt asserted that the preferred organizational structure for implementing this type of strategy was the multidivisional structure.

Rumelt's findings were part of a larger group of Harvard studies that can be broken into two major streams – the European studies[37] and the TNC studies.[38] The European studies found that the trend towards product diversification and the divisionalization of structure transcended national boundaries. Those studies, however, used samples comprised of corporations oriented towards domestic operations. While no doubt many of the organizations had international operations, the findings of diversification and divisionalization could not be categorically extended to TNCs.

The findings that large corporations followed a pattern of diversification came as a blow to a growing body of international business theory. That latter theory suggested that TNCs had certain advantages over domestic firms because of both size and an ability to extend their monopoly power internationally and to exploit international labour markets, thus reducing costs.[39] Size and internationality furnished the TNC with power to invest on a much larger scale, using a longer time horizon than smaller domestic firms. Using this reasoning, many researchers believed that TNCs would come to dominate industries via market closing activities (i.e., through exercising monopoly power). The prediction was that performance would be maximized if corporations did not diversify, but concentrated instead on asserting their monopoly power on an international basis. The Harvard findings confounded these predictions and challenged this theoretical rationale for the TNCs' existence.[40]

During that same period of time, a second stream of research was being carried out at Harvard which focused specifically on the TNC as the unit of analysis. In these studies, a TNC was defined as a business enterprise with manufacturing activities in six or more countries. Of that research on TNC strategy and structure, the work of J. Stopford and L. Wells was the largest and most comprehensive.[41] (The Wells article included in this volume summarizes Stopford and Wells' findings, which were originally published in book form.) Stopford and Wells focused on the influence of various organizational characteristics on the multinational structure in a sample of 187 United States TNCs. The study concluded that when tight control over foreign operations was needed, a strong preference existed for using wholly-owned subsidiaries in strategy implementation. In contrast, joint-venture partners were particularly attractive when local marketing skills were desired. Stopford and Wells observed that when foreign product diversity and foreign sales were low, an international division was the most common structural form. However, because of the likelihood of foreign product proliferation and the probability that foreign sales would grow, Stopford and Wells suggested that the international division was a temporary structural anomaly – to be replaced by either a product or area organization. They also suggested that the geographic or product organizations were transient and would eventually be replaced by a matrix structure. The matrix structure was viewed as particularly appropriate for TNCs that had both a high percentage of foreign sales and a high diversity of products.

An update of the Stopford and Wells study is found in the W. Egelhoff article included in this volume. Egelhoff re-examined Stopford and Wells' findings in a study of the strategy and structure of 34 large United States and European TNCs. He was particularly interested in the status of Stopford and Wells' model, since predictions of widespread movements to matrix structures had not materialized – in spite of the fact that many TNCs had high levels of both foreign sales and foreign product diversity.

Through his research, Egelhoff determined that the relative size of a TNC's foreign manufacturing operations was as important as the diversity of foreign products and percentage of foreign sales in determining structure. By analysing the emphasis of TNCs on these three variables, Egelhoff concluded that when international activities were relatively unimportant to a TNC, the corporation should utilize an international division structure. However, when international strategies were relatively important to the overall TNC, structures needed to be designed to facilitate higher levels of co-ordination and communication. When product diversity in foreign markets was high, world-wide product divisions appeared to be most suitable. When the percentage of foreign manufacturing was high, an area structure appeared to be appropriate. And finally, when both foreign product diversity and percentage of foreign manufacturing were high, a matrix based on world-wide product and area divisions seemed to be most beneficial.

Another well-known study that focused on the structural dimensions of strategy implementation was conducted by J. Daniels, R. Pitts and M. Tretter and is included in this volume. These authors were interested in extending both Stopford and Wells' and Chandler's earlier work by studying the relationship between strategy and structure in 93 large TNCs. In the study, TNC strategy was classified according to low, medium and high levels of diversification, and organizational structure was classified by functional, product, international division and area. In addition to the relationship between diversification strategy and structure, the influence of foreign sales control problems (i.e., ownership structure and integration of operations across national boundaries) on structure were explored. There were four major conclusions from this study: (1) if foreign sales were low in proportion to total sales, most foreign operations were handled by existing product or functional divisions (that contrasts with both Stopford and Wells' and Egelhoff's findings that an international division was most appropriate for minimal international emphasis); (2) functional structures were most appropriate when there was low product diversity (again, that differed with the conclusion of Stopford and Wells and Egelhoff who argued that an international division structure – or an area structure when the percentage of foreign sales are high – would be preferable under these circumstances); (3) increasing dependence on foreign sales provided a major impetus for the adoption of an international division structure (that agrees with previous findings, but only to a limit; at an extreme, neither Stopford and Wells nor Egelhoff found support for that finding); and (4) if international sales surpassed domestic sales, an area structure may be most appropriate (that finding was clearly supported by the previous research).

Clearly, more research is needed in this area. While there is a broad recognition that strategy influences TNC structure, little agreement exists over how strategy – or, for that matter, structure – should be measured. Furthermore, by building almost exclusively on the early work from Harvard, strategy–structure research has become preoccupied with TNC diversification and formal organizational structure. This lack of clarity combined with narrowly focused research is becoming increasingly prob-lematic given that much of the strategy–content research has shifted to the business/division unit of analysis.

Considerable evidence is also mounting that formal organizational struc-tures may be less important than informal structures in strategy implemen-tation. Bartlett's article, included in this volume, indicated that wholesale structural changes were frequently unnecessary and destructive. Rather, changes in internal systems were often sufficient to effect strategy implementation. Internal systems influenced information gathering and communication and consequently played a vital role in decision-making. From this viewpoint, rather than turning to expensive and disruptive organizational changes, managers should focus on changing behaviour through altering reward systems, articulating goals and values and encour-aging organizational flexibility.

Strategic Control and Ownership

One of the arguments advanced by Bartlett was that formal organizational structures cannot and should not be the sole means of achieving organiz-ational control. Strategic control should be designed to achieve a "fit" between the content and process of strategy formulation and implemen-tation.[42] Fit in this sense refers to congruity between an identified strategy – say low-cost exporting – and the implementation of the strategy through, for example, an organizational commitment to cost cutting, efficiency and an effective programme for export promotion. Consequently, control should be both externally oriented (focusing on strategy formulation designed to maximize the fit of the TNC with its environment) and internally oriented (focusing on strategy implementation).

In terms of strategic control, the discussion contained in J. Pfeffer's article, included in this volume, is particularly useful in articulating the interplay between external and internal control. Pfeffer argued that organizations exist within an institutional network including industry members and social/political actors. Within this external network, TNC profits and survival are determined by inter-organizational power. Power can be controlled in a strategically meaningful way through resource exchanges and institutional arrangements with network members. Resource exchanges in essence represent the internalization concept of gaining independence from the external market through the control of tangible and intangible asset flows; institutional arrangements in contrast represent more formal coalition agreements. In a sense, external control involves a "negotiated environment" where coalitions – with social/political actors and other industry members – are essential. The point here is that TNCs are part of (and consequently have at least partial control over) their environments. Because of this degree of control, more effort must be placed on developing political and inter-organizational management skills.

The appropriateness of establishing international coalitions is discussed in the R. Reich and E. Mankin article included here. These authors argued that control issues represented insurmountable obstacles in many transnational coalitions. Japanese partners in particular gained valuable access to process technology while transferring little of long-term value to foreign partners. The short-term orientation of United States TNCs in particular discouraged the installation of adequate technology control mechanisms. Reich and Mankin argued that efforts to improve international competitiveness would be better spent on encouraging within-country coalitions – either involving domestic industry partnerships or business–government agreements – than on establishing technology and marketing-based Japanese/United States coalitions.

In the literature on the establishment of international coalitions, P. Beamish's article stands out because of its review of the characteristics of joint-venture partnerships in high income and developing countries. Beamish focused his discussion on the mitigating influence the activities and policies of national governments have on the structuring of joint-venture partnerships. Through his research, Beamish concluded that instability and managerial dissatisfaction were higher in developing country joint ventures than in joint ventures in high income countries. The suggestion was that when joint ventures were based in developing countries, implementation strategies must be significantly altered.

Notwithstanding the important findings of Beamish's research, the article unfortunately provided only a limited discussion of the different types of strategic partnerships which have become more commonplace in the 1980s. Since the mid-1980s, there has been a growing interest in the design of strategic partnerships consistent with the globalization of competition. A wave of partnerships in such industries as automobiles, aircraft, pharmaceuticals, telecommunications and semiconductors have spurred renewed interest in coalitions as a means of maximizing a TNC's international competitiveness.

J. Killing's article is included in this volume because of its discussion of the role task complexity and organizational complexity play in the formation and management of these types of strategic alliances. The article developed a framework of strategic partnership or alliance types according to the level of operating task and organizational complexity of the alliance. In all, different alliance types were discussed. Unlike Beamish's article, which discussed strategic partnerships across a variety of national settings, Killing's article was written from the perspective of companies in high income countries. It does, however, add considerably to our understanding of the breadth of strategic possibilities in the establishment of alliances.

An extension of the formal control mechanisms established through strategic alliances is the international control associated with parent–subsidiary relationships. At issue here is how much and what type of control a TNC parent can or should exert over a subsidiary. B. Baliga and A. Jaeger's article is included in this volume because of its comprehensive treatment of these issues. They argued that the object of parental control is either subsidiary behaviour or output and that parents can select either bureaucratic or cultural control mechanisms to achieve control. Bureaucratic control is commonly used in Western TNCs and involves the imposition of explicit rules of behaviour. Cultural control, prevalent in Japanese TNCs, relies on more subtle socialization pressures. In addition to the means of achieving control, Baliga and Jaeger identified the types of TNC interdependencies that influence control requirements. Here, the reading provides an excellent extension of organization theory to the context of the TNC.

Conclusions

This introductory chapter has been designed to provide a foundation for further reading on TNC strategy. Although many of the more noteworthy articles in the field are contained in this volume, it has proven impossible to include all those articles that have made significant contributions to this emerging field. Rather, the intention has been to cover the core areas of TNC strategy while recognizing a variety of philosophical differences in conceptualizing international competition. While it has become clear that as yet there is little consensus on the nature or domain of TNC strategy, it should also be clear that almost every perspective is relevant and practicable under particular circumstances.

One objective which was not entirely met was the incorporation of non-North American perspectives of TNC strategy. It should be evident to the reader that this volume has drawn most heavily from North American-based publications. One problem is that the English-speaking academics in Europe or Japan were typically trained in the United States, thereby increasing the likelihood of inheriting North American perspectives on TNCs. Hence, the bulk of articles published in the readily accessible, quality journals are dominated by North American thinking. It is clearly recognized that, most likely, many excellent non-English articles relating to TNC strategy exist; however, unless these articles have been translated, they could not be considered for inclusion in this volume. The reader must be cautioned of the possible bias in the selection and discussion of articles in this volume.

The North American/European foundations of TNC strategy would likely benefit by examining the contributions available from other cultures. Of particular concern is the need for improved TNC strategy frameworks that could account for the rise of new forms of heterarchical competition. Much of the analysis of TNC strategy now involves multiple units of analysis including corporate headquarters, business divisions, subsidiaries and multi-level coalitions. Too much of existing thinking is grounded in the diversification strategies/structure frameworks of the 1970s.

Finally, more research is also needed in broadening conceptualizations of the TNC environment. Domestic strategic management researchers have tended to be preoccupied with strategy–industry linkages while ignoring the political and customer-based aspects of the environment. The importance of understanding non-industry dimensions of the environment is much more critical for TNCs given extensive country-to-country divergence in political and social pressures.[43]

An analysis of TNC strategy ultimately represents a melding of two emerging fields of study: international business and strategic management. The theories, frameworks and classifications developed in each field further our understanding of the strategic behaviour of TNCs. While this chapter has highlighted the dialectical thinking that has characterized TNC strategy (i.e., determinism and behaviouralism, business versus corporate level strategy, formulation versus implementation), the foundations are designed to help researchers and practitioners provide order to the often seemingly random and unstructured activities of TNCs. In the final analysis, multiple forces are at play, both inside the TNC and within its environment. To quote Ralph Waldo Emerson: "Cause and effect, means and ends, seed and fruit cannot be severed; for the effect already blooms in the cause, the end pre-exists in the means, the fruit in the seed".[44] Such is the challenge of characterizing TNC strategy.

Notes

1. UNCTC (1988), *Transnational Corporations in World Development: Trends and Prospects* (United Nations publication, Sales No. E. 88.II.A.7) and UNCTC, "Recent developments related to transnational corporations and international economic relations", E/C.10/1991/2, 51 pp., mimeo.

2. UNCTC (1988), op. cit., p. 16.

3. J. Chrisman, C. Hofer and W. Boulton, "Toward a system for classifying business strategies", *Academy of Management Review*, 13 (1988), pp. 413–428.

4. For an extensive discussion of the dimensions of formal and informal organizational structures see, D. Katz and R. Kahn, *The Social Psychology of Organizations*, 2nd ed. (New York, John Wiley, 1978); P.R. Lawrence and J.W. Lorsch, *Organization and Environment* (Homewood, Ill., Richard D. Irwin, 1967); H. Mintzberg, *The Structuring of Organizations: A Synthesis of the Research* (Englewood Cliffs, N.J., Prentice-Hall, 1979); T. Parsons, *Structure and Process in Modern Societies* (New York, Free Press, 1960); and D. Pugh, D. Hickson and C. Hinings, "An empirical taxonomy of structures of work organizations", *Administrative Science Quarterly*, 14 (1969), pp. 115–126.

5. C.W. Hofer and D. Schendel, *Strategy Formulation: Analytical Concepts* (St. Paul, MN, West Publishing Co., 1978); and M.E. Porter, *Competitive Strategy: Techniques for Analyzing Industries and Competitors* (New York, Free Press, 1980).

6. J.H. Dunning, *International Production and the Multinational Enterprise* (London, Allen and Unwin, 1981); A. Rugman, *Inside the Multinationals: the Economist of Internal Markets* (New York, Columbia University Press, 1981); and D. Teece, "Transaction cost economics and the multinational enterprise", *Journal of Economic Behavior and Organization*, 7 (1986), pp. 21–45.

7. P. Buckley and M. Casson, *The Future of the Multinational Enterprise* (London, Macmillan, 1976); A. Rugman, *Inside the Multinationals: The Economics of Internal Markets* (New York, Columbia University Press, 1981); D. Teece, "Multinational enterprises: market failure and market power considerations", *Sloan Management Review*, 22 (1981); pp. 3–17; D. Teece, "Transaction cost economics and the multinational enterprise", *Journal of Economic Behavior and Organization*, 7 (1986), pp. 21–45; and O.E. Williamson, *Markets and Hierarchies: Analysis and Antitrust Implications* (New York, Free Press, 1975).

8. P. Buckley and M. Casson, *The Future of the Multinational Enterprise* (London, Macmillan, 1976); C. Galbraith and N. Kay, "Towards a theory of multinational enterprise", *Journal of Economic Behavior and Organization*, 7 (1986), pp. 3–19; A. Rugman, *Inside the Multinationals: The Economics of Internal Markets* (New York, Columbia University Press, 1981); and D. Teece, "Transaction cost economics and the multinational enterprise", *Journal of Economic Behavior and Organization*, 7 (1986), pp. 21–45.

9. R. Aliber, "The MNE in a multiple-currency world", in J.H. Dunning, ed. *The Multinational Enterprise* (London, Allen and Unwin, 1971), pp. 49–56; S. Hymer, *The International Operations of National Firms: A Study of Direct Foreign Investment* (originally published as doctoral dissertation in 1960) (Cambridge, Mass., MIT Press, 1976); and C. Kindleberger, *American Business Abroad* (New Haven, Yale University Press, 1969).

10. E. Flowers, "Oligopolistic reaction in European and Canadian direct investment: an ex-post empirical analysis", *Journal of International Business Studies*, 11 (Fall/Winter 1980), pp. 43–55; F. Knickerbocker, *Oligopolistic Reaction and Multinational Enterprise* (Cambridge, Mass., Harvard University, Graduate School

of Business, Division of Research, 1973); K. Kojima, *Direct Foreign Investment: A Japanese Model of Multinational Business Operations* (Beckenham, Croom Helm, 1978); and R. Vernon, "International investments and international trade in the product cycle", *Quarterly Journal of Economics*, 81 (May 1966), pp. 190–207.

11. For a more complete discussion of theory development in international business, see the volume in this series by John H. Dunning.

12. M. Porter, "Changing patterns of international competition", *California Management Review*, 28 (1986), pp. 9–40.

13. C. Hofer, "Toward a contingency theory of business strategy", *Academy of Management Journal*, 18 (1975), pp. 784–810; R. Caves and M. Porter, "From entry barriers to mobility barriers: conjectural decisions and contrived deterrence to new competition", *Quarterly Journal of Economics*, 91 (1977), pp. 241–262; K. Hatten, D. Schendel and A. Cooper, "A strategic model of the U.S. brewing industry, 1952–1971", *Academy of Management Journal*, 21 (1978), pp. 592–610; D. Schendel and G. Patton, "A simultaneous equation model of corporate strategy", *Management Science*, 24 (1978), pp. 1611–1621; H. Christensen and C. Montgomery, "Corporate economic performance: diversification strategy versus market structure", *Strategic Management Journal*, 2 (1981), pp. 327–343; D. Hambrick, "High profit strategies in mature capital goods industries; a contingency approach", *Academy of Management Journal*, 26 (1983), pp. 687–707; and C. Anderson and C. Zeithaml, "Stage of the product life cycle, business strategy, and business performance", *Academy of Management Journal*, 27 (1984), pp. 5–24.

14. C.W. Hofer and D. Schendel, *Strategy Formulation: Analytical Concepts* (St. Paul, MN, West Publishing Co., 1978).

15. Other contingency theories extend this analysis further by arguing that organizations have no autonomy whatsoever in determining strategic direction. Rather, they are "selected" by their environments much the same as biological populations are selected through evolutionary process. For a more complete discussion of the population ecology perspective of organizational activity see, M.T. Hannan and J. Freeman, "The population ecology of organizations", *American Journal of Sociology*, 82 (1977), pp. 929–964; and W.G. Astley and C.J. Fombrun, "Collective strategy: social ecology of organizational environments", *Academy of Management Review*, 8 (1983), pp. 576–587.

16. An excellent discussion of the determinism in strategic management research is found in, L. Bougeois, "Strategic management and determinism", *Academy of Management Review*, 9 (1984), pp. 586–596; P. Hirsch and R. Freidman, "Collaboration or paradigm shift?: economic vs. behavioral thinking about policy", *Academy of Management Proceedings* (1986), pp. 31–35.

17. See, H.V. Perlmutter, "The tortuous evolution of the multinational corporation", *Columbia Journal of World Business* (January–February 1969), pp. 9–18. Ethnocentrism represents the belief that what has worked at home will work best in the foreign country. An ethnocentric corporation will pattern international operations according to home country values, control systems, and so on. Polycentrism describes an organization that is overwhelmed by differences in its operating environment. A polycentric corporation will maintain the independence of host country operations. Geocentrism represents a balance between ethnocentrism and polycentrism. A geocentric corporation seeks to maximize the corporation on global perspective, through a balance of responsiveness and integration.

18. See, Y. Aharoni, *The Foreign Investment Decision Process* (Cambridge, Mass., Harvard Business School, 1966).

19. For a more complete discussion of incremental strategy formulation, see, D. Braybrooke and C. Lindblom, *A Strategy of Decision: Policy Evaluation as a Social*

Process (New York, Free Press, 1970); R. Cyert and J. March, *A Behavioral Theory of the Firm* (Englewood Cliffs, N.J., Prentice-Hall, 1963); J. Kotter, "What effective general managers really do", *Harvard Business Review*, 60 (November–December 1982), pp. 156–167; H. Mintzberg, "Patterns in strategy formation", *Management Science,* 24 (1978), pp. 934–948; and J. Quinn, *Strategies for Change: Logical Incrementalism* (Homewood, Ill., Richard D. Irwin, 1980).

20. See, D. Schendel and C. Hofer, *Strategic Management* (Boston, Little Brown & Co., 1979).

21. On these important issues, see:

On human resource management,
H. Lane and J. DiStephano, *International Management Behavior: From Policy to Practice* (Scarborough, Ont., Nelson, 1988); R. Tung, "Selection and training of personnel for overseas assignments", *Columbia Journal of World Business*, 16 (Winter 1981), pp. 68–78; R. Hayes, "Expatriate selection: insuring success and avoiding failure", *Journal of International Business Studies*, 5 (1974), pp. 25–37; and A. Phatak, *International Dimensions of Management*, 2nd ed. (Boston, PWS-Kent, 1989).

On technology and development transfer,
J. Baranson, *Technology of the Multinational: Corporate Strategy in a Changing World Economy* (Lexington, Mass., Lexington Books, 1978); and W. Gruber, M. Dileep and R. Vernon, "The R & D factor in international trade and international investment of U.S. industries", *Journal of Political Economy*, 75 (February 1967), pp. 20–37.

On transfer pricing strategy,
R. Caves, "International corporations: the industrial economics of foreign investment", *Economica*, 38 (1971), pp. 1–27; T. Horst, "The simple analytics of multinational firm behavior", in M. Connolly and A. Swoboda eds., *International Trade and Money*, (Toronto, University of Toronto Press, 1973), pp. 72–84; and A. Rugman and L. Eden, eds., *Multinationals and Transfer Pricing* (New York, St. Martin's Press, 1985).

On international finance,
R. Bettis, "Modern financial theory, corporate strategy and public policy: three conundrums", *Academy of Management Review*, 11 (1983), pp. 534–549; M. Adler and B. Dumas, "International portfolio choice and corporate finance: a synthesis", *Journal of Finance*, 38 (June 1983), pp. 925–984; and B. Solnik, "International arbitrage pricing theory", *Journal of Finance*, 38 (May 1983), pp. 449–457.

On business–government relations,
S.J. Kobrin, *Managing Political Risk Assessment* (Los Angeles, University of California Press, 1982); M. Fitzpatrick, "The definition and assessment of political risk in international business: a review of the literature", *Academy of Management Review*, 8 (1983), pp. 249–254; and J. Simon, "A theoretical perspective on political risk", *Journal of International Business Studies*, 15 (Winter 1984), pp. 123–143.

On production strategy,
R. Hayes and S. Wheelwright, "The dynamics of process/product life cycles", *Harvard Business Review*, 57 (March–April 1979), pp. 127–136; J. Nakane, J. and R. Hall, "Management specs for stockless production", *Harvard Business Review*, 61 (May–June 1983), pp. 84–91; and W. Skinner, *Manufacturing: The Formidable Competitive Weapon* (New York, John Wiley, 1985).

22. See, A.D. Chandler Jr., *Strategy and Structure: Chapters in the History of*

Industrial Enterprise (Cambridge, Mass., MIT Press, 1962).

23. For a more complete discussion of the definition of organizational scope, see, J. Chrisman, C. Hofer and W. Boulton, "Toward a system for classifying business strategies", *Academy of Management Review*, 13 (1988), pp. 413–428; and C. Hofer and D. Schendel, *Strategy Formulation: Analytical Concepts* (St. Paul, MN, West, 1978).

24. See, K. Andrews, *The Concept of Corporate Strategy* (Homewood, Ill., Richard D. Irwin, 1971).

25. C.K. Prahalad, "The strategic process in a multinational corporation" (unpublished doctoral dissertation, Graduate School of Business Administration, Harvard University, 1975), introduced the concept of integration–responsiveness. Integration–adaptation is a parallel concept which was apparently introduced independently from Prahalad's work.

26. See, W. Dymsza, "Global strategic planning: a model and recent developments", *Journal of International Business Studies*, 15 (Fall 1984), pp. 169–184.

27. Not surprisingly, this list borrows heavily from Peters and Waterman which publicized the idea of multiple levers for success; see T. Peters and R. Waterman, *In Search of Excellence* (New York, Warner Books, 1982).

28. See, for example, S. Tilles, "Strategies for allocating funds", *Harvard Business Review*, 44 (1966), pp. 72–80; P. Blau, "A formal theory of differentiation", *American Sociology Review*, 35 (1970), pp. 201–218; I. Ansoff, *Corporate Strategy: An Analytic Approach to Business Policy for Growth and Expansion* (New York, McGraw-Hill, 1965); and P.R. Lawrence and J.W. Lorsch, *Organization and Environment* (Homewood, Ill., Richard D. Irwin, 1967).

29. See, C.W. Hofer, "Toward a contingency theory of business strategy", *Academy of Management Journal*, 18 (1975), pp. 784–810; and C.W. Hofer and D. Schendel, *Strategy Formulation: Analytical Concepts* (St. Paul, MN, West Publishing Co., 1978).

30. See, M.E. Porter, *Competitive Strategy: Techniques for Analyzing Industries and Competitors* (New York, Free Press, 1980).

31. See, for example:

On strategies in fragmented industries,
G. Dess, "Consensus on strategy formulation and organizational performance: competitors in a fragmented industry", *Strategic Management Journal*, 8 (1987), pp. 259–277; and K. Keels, J. Chrisman, W. Sandberg and D. Schweiger, "A causal model of industry fragmentation" (unpublished manuscript, the University of South Carolina, 1987).

On strategies in mature industries,
C. Zeithaml and L. Fry, "Contextual and strategic differences among mature businesses in four dynamic performance situations", *Academy of Management Journal*, 27 (1984), pp. 841–860; D. Hambrick and S. Scheter, "Turnaround strategies for mature industrial–product business units", *Academy of Management Journal*, 26 (1983), pp. 231–248; and K. Harrigan, "Exit decisions in mature industries", *Academy of Management Journal*, 25 (1986), pp. 707–732.

On strategies in emerging industries,
D. Aaker and G. Day, "The perils of high growth markets", *Strategic Management Journal*, 7 (1986), pp. 409–421; and G. Yip, "Gateways to entry", *Harvard Business Review*, 60 (September–October 1982), pp. 85–92.

On strategies in declining industries,
K. Harrigan, *Strategies for Declining Businesses* (Lexington, Mass., Lexington

Books, 1980); and M.E. Porter, *Competitive Strategy: Techniques for Analyzing Industries and Competitors* (New York, Free Presss, 1980).

32. M.E. Porter, *Competitive Advantage* (New York, Free Press, 1985); B. Kogut, "Designing global strategies: comparative and competitive value added chains", *Sloan Management Review*, 26 (Summer 1985a), pp. 15-28; and B. Kogut, "Designing global strategies: profiting from operational flexibility", *Sloan Management Review*, 26 (Fall 1985b), pp. 27-38.

33. The limits of globalization have been discussed at length by, Y. Doz, "International industries: fragmentation versus globalization", in Bruce Guile and Harvey Brooks, eds., *Technology and Global Industry: Companies and Nations in the World Economy* (Washington, D.C., National Academy Press, 1987), pp. 96-118.

34. C. Bartlett and S. Ghoshal, "Organizing for worldwide effectiveness: the transnational solution", *California Management Review*, 31 (Fall 1988), pp. 54-74.

35. Rumelt's conceptualization of corporate diversification was borrowed from the earlier work by, L. Wrigley, "Divisional autonomy and diversification" (unpublished Ph.D. dissertation, Harvard Business School, 1970).

36. This conclusion was based on Rumelt's observation that corporations that followed a strategy of related diversification had superior performance than did corporations that pursued single product, vertical integration or unrelated diversification strategies. Although this conclusion may have been correct, Rumelt's basis for it was fundamentally flawed. To the extent that firm and industry characteristics determine strategy, following a strategy of related diversifications may not be appropriate for many corporations. See, R. Caves, M. Porter and A. Spence, *Competition in an Open Economy* (Cambridge, Mass., Harvard University Press, 1980); and D. Lecraw, "Performance of transnational corporations in less developed countries", *Journal of International Business Studies*, 14 (Spring/Summer 1983), pp. 15-34.

37. This work includes that of, D. Channon, "Strategy and structure of British enterprise" (unpublished Ph.D. dissertation, Harvard Business School, 1971); G. Pooley-Dyas, "Strategy and structure of the French enterprise" (unpublished Ph.D. dissertation, Harvard Business School, 1972); H. Thanheiser, "Strategy and structure of the German enterprise" (unpublished Ph.D. dissertation, Harvard Business School, 1972); and F.D.J. Pavan, "The Strategy and structure of the Italian enterprise" (unpublished Ph.D. dissertation, Harvard Business School, 1972).

38. This principally includes the work of, J.M. Stopford and L.T. Wells, Jr., *Managing the Multinational Enterprise: Organization of the Firm and Ownership of the Subsidiaries* (New York, Basic Books, 1972); L.G. Franko, *The European Multinationals* (Greenwich, CT, Greylock Press, 1976); and L.G. Franko, *The European Multinationals: A Renewed Challenge to American and British Big Business* (Greenwich, CT, Greylock Press, 1976).

39. This work was championed largely by, S. Hymer, "The efficiency (contradiction) of multinational corporations", *American Economics Review*, 60 (1970), pp. 441-448; and C. Kindleberger, *American Business Abroad: Six Lectures on Direct Investment* (New Haven, CT, Yale University Press, 1969).

40. In explaining why evidence of market closing activity was not found in the United States and Europe; B. Scott, "The industrial state: old myths and new realities", *Harvard Business Review*, 51 (March-April 1973), pp. 133-148, concluded that technological changes led to greater division of labour which resulted in further specialization, and new products which resulted in diversification.

41. J.M. Stopford and L.T. Wells, Jr., *Managing the Multinational Enterprise* (New York, Basic Books, 1972).

42. See, for example, W.G. Egelhoff, "Strategy and structure in multinational corporations" (Paper presented at the Academy of International Business Annual

Meeting, New Orleans, 1980); and P. Lorange, S. Morton and S. Ghoshal, *Strategic Control* (St. Paul, MN, West Publishing Co., 1986).

43. C. Kennedy, "The external environment–strategic planning interface: U.S. multinational corporate practices in the 1980s", *Journal of International Business Studies*, 15 (1983), pp. 99–108; J. Boddewyn, "Political aspects of MNE theory", *Journal of International Business Studies*, 19 (1988), pp. 341–364; J. Kogut and H. Singh, "The effect of national culture on the choice of entry mode", *Journal of International Business Studies*, 19 (1988), pp. 411–432; and J.H. Dunning, "A study of international business: a plea for a more interdisciplinary approach", *Journal of International Business Studies*, 20 (1989), pp. 411–436.

44. Quote taken from Emerson's "Essays: first series compensation, 1841" as reported in B. Atkinson, ed., *The Selected Writings of Ralph Waldo Emerson* (New York, The Modern Library, 1950).

Bibliography

Aaker, D. and G. Day, "The perils of high growth markets", *Strategic Management Journal*, 7 (1986), pp. 409–421.

Adler, M. and B. Dumas, "International portfolio choice and corporate finance: a synthesis", *Journal of Finance*, 38 (May 1983), pp. 449–457.

Aharoni, Y., *The Foreign Investment Decision Process* (Cambridge, Mass., Harvard Business School, 1966).

Aliber, R., "The MNE in a multiple-currency world", in J. Dunning, ed. *The Multinational Enterprise* (London, Allen and Unwin, 1971).

Anderson, C. and C. Zeithaml, "Stage of the product life cycle, business strategy, and business performance", *Academy of Management Journal*, 27 (1984), pp. 5–24.

Andrews K., *The Concept of Corporate Strategy* (Homewood, Ill., Richard D. Irwin, 1971).

Ansoff, I., *Corporate Strategy: An Analytic Approach to Business Policy for Growth and Expansion* (New York, McGraw-Hill, 1965).

Astley, W.G. and C. Fombrun, "Collective strategy: social ecology of organizational environments", *Academy of Management Review*, 8 (1983), pp. 576–587.

Atkinson, B., ed., *The Selected Writings of Ralph Waldo Emerson* (New York, The Modern Library, 1950).

Baranson, J., *Technology and the Multinational: Corporate Strategies in a Changing World Economy* (Lexington, Mass., Lexington Books, 1978).

Bartlett, C. and S. Ghoshal, "Organizing for worldwide effectiveness: the transnational solution", *California Management Review*, 31 (Fall 1988), pp. 54–74.

Bettis, R., "Modern financial theory, corporate strategy and public policy: three conundrums", *Academy of Management Review*, 11 (1983), pp. 534–549.

Blau, P., "A formal theory of differentiation", *American Sociology Review*, 35 (1970), pp. 201–218.

Boddewyn, J., "Political aspects of MNE theory", *Journal of International Business Studies*, 19 (1988), pp. 341–364.

Bourgeois, L., "Strategic management and determinism", *Academy of Management Review*, 9 (1984), pp. 586–596.

Braybrooke, D. and C. Lindblom, *A Strategy of Decision: Policy Evaluation as a Social Process* (New York, Free Press, 1970).

Buckley, P. and M. Casson, *The Future of the Multinational Enterprise* (London, Macmillan, 1976).

Caves, R., "International corporations: the industrial economics of foreign invest-ment", *Economica*, 38 (1971), pp. 1–27.

Caves, R. and M. Porter, "From entry barriers to mobility barriers: conjectural decisions and contrived deterrence to new competition", *Quarterly Journal of Economics*, 91 (1977), pp. 241–262.

Caves, R., M. Porter and A. Spence, *Competition in an Open Economy* (Cambridge, Mass., Harvard University Press, 1980).

Chandler, A.D. Jr., *Strategy and Structure: Chapters in the History of Industrial Enterprise* (Cambridge, Mass., MIT Press, 1962).

Channon, D., "Strategy and structure of British enterprise" (unpublished Ph.D. dissertation, Harvard Business School, 1971).

Chrisman, J., C. Hofer and W. Boulton, "Toward a system for classifying business strategies", *Academy of Management Review*, 13 (1988), pp. 413–428.

Christensen, H. and C. Montgomery, "Corporate economic performance: diversifi-cation strategy versus market structure", *Strategic Management Journal*, 2 (1981), pp. 327–343.

Cyert, R. and J. March, *A Behavioral Theory of the Firm* (Englewood Cliffs, N.J., Prentice-Hall, 1963).

Dess, G., "Consensus on strategy formulation and organizational performance: competitors in a fragmented industry", *Strategic Management Journal*, 8 (1987), pp. 259–277.

Doz, Y., "International industries: fragmentation versus globalization", in Bruce Guile and Harvey Brooks, eds., *Technology and Global Industry: Companies and Nations in the World Economy* (Washington, D.C., National Academy Press, 1987).

Dunning, J., *International Production and the Multinational Enterprise* (London, Allen and Unwin, 1981).

——, "A study of international business: a plea for a more interdisciplinary approach", *Journal of International Business Studies*, 20 (1989), pp. 411–436.

Dymsza, W., "Global strategic planning: a model and recent developments", *Journal of International Business Studies*, 15 (Fall 1984), pp. 169–184.

Egelhoff, W.G., "Strategy and structure in multinational corporations: an information-processing approach", *Administrative Science Quarterly*, 27 (1982), pp. 435–458.

Fitzpatrick, M., "The definition and assessment of political risk in international business: a review of the literature", *Academy of Management Review*, 8 (1983), pp. 249–254.

Flowers, E., "Oligopolistic reaction in European and Canadian direct investment: an ex-post empirical analysis", *Journal of International Business Studies*, 11 (Fall/Winter 1980), pp. 43–55.

Franko, L.G., *The European Multinationals* (Greenwich, CT, Greylock Press, 1976).

Franko, L.G., *The European Multinationals: A Renewed Challenge to American and British Big Business* (Greenwich, CT, Greylock Press, 1976).

Galbraith, C. and N. Kay, "Towards a theory of multinational enterprise", *Journal of Economic Behavior and Organization*, 7 (1986), pp. 3–19.

Gruber, W., M. Dileep and R. Vernon, "The R&D factor in international trade and international investment of U.S. industries", *Journal of Political Economy*, 75 (February 1967), pp. 20–37.

Hambrick, D., "High profit strategies in mature capital goods industries: a contin-gency approach", *Academy of Management Journal*, 26 (1983), pp. 687–707.

Hambrick, D. and S. Scheter, "Turnaround strategies for mature industrial-product business units", *Academy of Management Journal,* 26 (1983), pp. 231–248.

Hannan, M.T. and J. Freeman, "The population ecology of organizations", *American Journal of Sociology,* 82 (1977), pp. 929–964.

Harrigan, K., *Strategies for Declining Businesses* (Lexington, Mass., Lexington Books, 1980).

——, "Exit decisions in mature industries", *Academy of Management Journal,* 25 (1982) pp. 707–732.

Hatten, K., D. Schendel and A. Cooper, "A strategic model of the U.S. brewing industry, 1952–1971", *Academy of Management Journal,* 21 (1978), pp. 592–610.

Hayes, R., "Expatriate selection: insuring success and avoiding failure", *Journal of International Business Studies,* 5 (1974), pp. 25–37.

Hayes, R. and S. Wheelwright, "The dynamics of process/product life cycles", *Harvard Business Review,* 57 (March–April 1979), pp. 127–136.

Hirsch, P. and R. Freidman, "Collaboration or paradigm shift?: economic vs. behavioral thinking about policy", *Academy of Management Proceedings* (1986), pp. 31–35.

Hofer, C., "Toward a contingency theory of business strategy", *Academy of Management Journal,* 18 (1975), pp. 784–810.

Hofer, C. and D. Schendel, *Strategy Formulation: Analytical Concepts* (St. Paul, MN, West Publishing Co., 1978).

Horst, T., "The simple analytics of multinational firm behaviour", in M. Connolly and A. Swoboda, eds., *International Trade and Money* (Toronto, University of Toronto Press, 1973).

Hymer, S., "The efficiency (contradiction) of multinational corporations", *American Economics Review,* 60 (1970), pp. 441–448.

Katz, D. and R. Kahn, *The Social Psychology of Organizations* (2nd ed.) (New York, John Wiley, 1978).

Keels, K., J. Chrisman, W. Sandberg and D. Schweiger, "A causal model of industry fragmentation" (unpublished manuscript, the University of South Carolina, 1987).

Kennedy, C., "The external environment–strategic planning interface: US multinational corporate practices in the 1980s", *Journal of International Business Studies,* 15 (1983), pp. 99–108.

Kindleberger, C., *American Business Abroad: Six Lectures on Direct Investment* (New Haven, CT, Yale University Press, 1969).

Knickerbocker, F., *Oligopolistic Reaction and Multinational Enterprise* (Cambridge, Mass., Harvard University, Graduate School of Business, 1973).

Kobrin, S.J., *Managing Political Risk Assessment* (Los Angeles, University of California Press, 1982).

Kogut, B., "Designing global strategies; comparative and competitive value added chains", *Sloan Management Review,* 26 (Summer 1985a), pp. 15–28.

——, "Designing global strategies; profiting from operational flexibility", *Sloan Management Review,* 26 (Fall 1985b), pp. 27–38.

Kogut, B. and H. Singh, "The effect of national culture on the choice of entry mode", *Journal of International Business Studies,* 19 (1988), pp. 411–432.

Kojima, K., *Direct Foreign Investment: A Japanese Model of Multinational Business Operations* (Beckenham, Croom Helm, 1978).

Kotter, J., "What effective general managers really do", *Harvard Business Review,* 60 (November–December 1982), pp. 156–167.

Lane, H. and J. DiStefano, *International Management Behavior: From Policy to Practice* (Scarborough, Ont., Nelson, 1988).

Lawrence, P. and J. Lorsch, *Organization and Environment* (Boston, Harvard Business School, 1967).

Lecraw, D., "Performance of transnational corporations in less developed countries", *Journal of International Business Studies*, 14 (Spring/Summer 1983), pp. 15–33.

——, "Diversification strategy and performance", *Journal of Industrial Economics*, 33 (1984), pp. 179–198.

Lorange, P., S. Morton and S. Ghoshal, *Strategic Control* (St. Paul, MN, West Publishing Co., 1986).

Mintzberg, H., *The Nature of Managerial Work* (New York, Harper & Row, 1973).

——, *The Structuring of Organizations: A Synthesis of the Research* (Englewood Cliffs, N.J., Prentice-Hall, 1979).

Nakane, J. and R. Hall, "Management specs for stockless production", *Harvard Business Review*, 61 (May–June 1983), pp. 84–91.

Parsons, T., *Structure and Process in Modern Societies* (New York, Free Press, 1960).

Pavan, F., "The strategy and structure of Italian enterprise" (doctoral dissertation, Harvard Business School, Boston, Mass., 1972).

Perlmutter, H.V., "The tortuous evolution of the multinational corporation", *Columbia Journal of World Business* (January–February 1969), pp. 9–18.

Peters, T. and R. Waterman, *In Search of Excellence* (New York, Warner Books, 1982).

Phatak, A., *International Dimensions of Management* (2nd ed.) (Boston, PWS-Kent, 1989).

Pooley-Dyas, G., "Strategy and structure of French enterprise" (unpublished Ph.D. dissertation, Harvard Business School, 1972).

Porter, M.E., *Competitive Strategy: Techniques for Analyzing Industries and Competitors* (New York, Free Press, 1980).

——, *Competitive Advantage* (New York, Free Press, 1985).

——, "Changing patterns of international competition", *California Management Review*, 28 (1986), pp. 9–40.

Prahalad, C.K., "The strategic process in a multinational corporation" (unpublished doctoral dissertation, Graduate School of Business Administration, Harvard University, 1975).

Pugel, T., "Technology transfer and neoclassical theory of international trade", in R. Hawkins and A. Prasad, eds., *Technology Transfer and Economic Development* (Greenwich, CT, JAI Press, 1981).

Pugh, D., D. Hickson and C. Hinings, "An empirical taxonomy of structures of work organizations", *Administrative Science Quarterly*, 14 (1969), pp. 115–126.

Quinn, J., *Strategies for Change: Logical Incrementalism* (Homewood, Ill., Richard D. Irwin, 1980).

Rugman, A., *Inside the Multinationals: The Economics of Internal Markets* (New York, Columbia University Press, 1981).

Rugman, A. and L. Eden, eds., *Multinationals and Transfer Pricing* (New York, St. Martin's Press, 1985).

Rumelt, R., *Strategy, Structure, and Economic Performance* (Boston, Graduate School of Business Administration, Harvard University, 1974).

Schendel, D. and G. Patton, "A simultaneous equation model of corporate strategy", *Management Science*, 24 (1978), pp. 1611–1621.

Schendel, D. and C. Hofer, *Strategic Management* (Boston, Little, Brown & Co., 1979).

Scott, B., "The industrial state: old myths and new realities", *Harvard Business*

Review, 51 (March–April 1973), pp. 133–148.

Simon, J., "A theoretical perspective on political risk", *Journal of International Business Studies*, 15 (Winter 1984), pp. 123–143.

Skinner, W., *Manufacturing: The Formidable Competitive Weapon* (New York, John Wiley, 1985).

Solnik, B., "International abitrage pricing theory", *Journal of Finance*, 38 (May 1983), pp. 449–457.

Stopford, M. and L. Wells, Jr., *Managing the Multinational Enterprise* (New York, Basic Books, 1972).

Teece, D., "Multinational enterprises: market failure and market power considerations", *Sloan Management Review*, 22 (1981), pp. 3–17.

——, "Transaction cost economics and the multinational enterprise", *Journal of Economic Behavior and Organization*, 7 (1986), pp. 21–45.

Thanheiser, H., "Strategy and structure of German enterprise" (unpublished Ph.D. dissertation, Harvard Business School, 1972).

Tilles, S., "Strategies for allocating funds", *Harvard Business Review*, 44 (1966), pp. 72–80.

Tung, R., "Selection and training of personnel for overseas assignments", *Columbia Journal of World Business*, 16 (Winter 1981), pp. 68–78.

Vernon, R., "International investment and international trade in the product cycle", *Quarterly Journal of Economics* 81 (May 1966), pp. 190–207.

Williamson, O., *Markets and Hierarchies: Analysis and Antitrust Implications* (New York, Free Press, 1975).

Wrigley, L., "Divisional autonomy and diversification" (unpublished Ph.D. dissertation, Harvard Business School, 1970).

Yip, G., "Gateways to entry", *Harvard Business Review*, 60 (September–October 1982), pp. 85–92.

Zeithaml, C. and L. Fry, "Contextual and strategic differences among mature businesses in four dynamic performance situations", *Academy of Management Journal*, 27 (1984), pp. 841–860.

PART ONE: Strategy Formulation: Process

1

A Framework for Strategic Planning in Multinational Corporations*

Peter Lorange

*Source: *Long Range Planning* (June 1976), pp. 30–37.

Introduction

Strategic planning in a multinational corporation has a two-fold task: to identify the strategic options most relevant to the corporation and to 'narrow down' these options into the one best plan. Stated this way there is of course nothing fundamentally different between the strategic planning task of a multinational corporation and that of any other large corporation. However, since multinationals offer several complex and distinctively different approaches to organizational design and planning, it is useful to examine some of the problems of strategic planning in the context of the multinationals.

The broad definition of the strategic planning tasks given above has several implications. In order to be able to identify the most relevant strategic options, the corporation needs to *adapt* continuously to the environment. Also, in order to narrow down the strategic options into the one best plan, the corporation must be able to *integrate* its many diverse activities. In this article we shall attempt to clarify the major purposes of planning in the multinationals in terms of adaptation and integration needs.

Given the diversity of settings in which multinationals operate, the adaptation and integration tasks will not be the same for all multinationals. Indeed, the opposite is true; each multinational will be faced with unique adaptation and integration tasks. However, in order for us to develop some generalizations about the adaptation and integration tasks of planning in multinationals, we shall start out by identifying a few multinational corporate archetypes, followed by a discussion of their planning purposes in terms of adaptation and integration. We shall then present some normative propositions about adaptation/integration and the costs of striking a reasonable balance between the two in planning systems.

Empirical findings on long range planning in multinationals reported by others indicate that (a) it is hard to find actual examples of multinationals that in all respects fit into any of the archetypes to be suggested[1] and (b) the formal planning systems of multinationals seem to be much less developed than those we recommend here.[2] However, we do not see this as limiting the value of the arguments to be presented. We intend to propose some fundamental dimensions of planning for multinationals that might be useful to improve the understanding of the planning phenomenon. Obviously the proposed normative framework is not intended for uncritical adaptation in specific cases.

A Taxonomy of Multinational Corporations

We shall distinguish between types of multinational corporations according to the dimensions along which the organization has been structured.[3] There seem to be two dimensions that might dominate the organizational structure: the product dimension, which occurs in companies which have adopted a so-called divisionalized structure, with each division responsible for one class of products; and the geographical area dimension, wherein each division is responsible for carrying out all the corporation's business within a given geographical area.

Complete domination of corporate structure by one dimension can prove to be inefficient. For instance, there might be considerable duplication of effort by having the product divisions operate their own separate organizations in one country. When evolving from such a product structure, the matrix structure might be described as consisting of a *leading* product dimension and a *grown* area dimension.[4]

Alternatively, when evolving out of an area-dominated structure the matrix structure would have a leading area dimension and a grown product dimension.[5]

So we perceive four types of multinationals, depending on the degree of emphasis they put on the product dimension and/or the area dimension. This continuum of multinationals is shown in Figure 1.

It should be stressed that typologizing into four categories is an oversimplification, since we are really dealing with a continuum. Further, dimensions other than product versus area orientation are likely to be considered in a realistic taxonomy of multinational corporations. In an integrated oil company, for instance, the *functional* dimension will typically be prominent, together with the area dimension. Also, the taxonomy adopted does not apply to the early evolutionary stages of corporate internationalization. Thus, much richer and probably also more realistic classifications may conceivably be developed.[6] However, keeping the purpose of this article in mind, little seems to be gained by adopting a more detailed taxonomy of multinationals.

Planning Purposes: Adaptation and Integration Needs

Let us analyze the nature of the requirements for adaptation and integration in each of the four multinational archetypes we are considering.

The Product-Organized Corporation

This corporation will conduct its worldwide activities by means of several divisions, each responsible for carrying out the business strategy for one class of products on a worldwide basis. In terms of *adaptation*, then, each *division* will be responsible for scanning its own business environment. This implies a heavy pressure on each division to adapt to changes in each national market. How should the marketing promotion campaign be laid out for the promotion of a division's products in a particular country? Which models seem particularly worthwhile emphasizing in a given country? The pressures for scanning and adaptation within each worldwide product division will be on monitoring changes in area trends and taking advantage of the resulting opportunities. The major responsibility for carrying out this scanning rests on functional managers within each division. Among the advantages of this form of adaptation will be a basis for the development of strong international plans for each business, which may enjoy the benefits of economies of scales in worldwide product strategies. Among the disadvantages may be the lack of adaptation to diverse geographical area inputs. Potential duplication of efforts by several divisions in interpreting the need for adaptation to the same geographical area may also be a problem.

At the *corporate* level of the product-division type of corporation *adaptation* tasks will center on the 'mix' of the portfolio of divisions. Multinational strategy questions will not be addressed at headquarters, except when reviewing division plans to probe their soundness. Important issues for corporate management are how to adapt to changing patterns of inflation/deflation and/or devaluation/revaluation, and which divisions should receive added/diminished emphasis, given differences in the nature of products, capital intensity, and relative strength in an area that is becoming more/less attractive. At the extreme, these resulting corporate

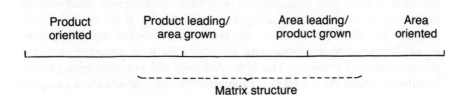

| Product oriented | Product leading/ area grown | Area leading/ product grown | Area oriented |

Matrix structure

Figure 1 The taxonomony of multinational corporations according to relative emphasis on product orientation vs area orientation.

adaptation needs may lead to the triggering of acquisitions, i.e., involvement in new business lines on a worldwide basis, or divestitures, i.e., pullout of a business on a worldwide basis.

The *integrating* task of the worldwide product *division* will be primarily to make sure that the overall activities of the division are consistent. There will be a need to integrate the strategic programs within each product division as well as the various functional activities. On the other hand there will probably be relatively less need for area integration, since that each program and/or function is slated to work independently within the worldwide area. Thus, the main coordination focus will be on each worldwide business line activity.

At the *corporate* level there will be a need to integrate and coordinate the portfolio of worldwide business divisions, emphasizing financial funds flow interrelations among the divisions. Again, any portfolio adjustments resulting from a need for stronger integration will be in modification of the plans of one or more of the product divisions, and not in area coordination directly.

It can be deduced that the formal organization structure itself plays a major role in facilitating the integration task. A major reason for the particular choice of the worldwide product division structure is in fact the need to integrate this type of company's worldwide activities along the product dimension. Thus, the formal organizational chart will typically be a reflection of the integration needs of an organization.[7]

The Geographically Area-Organized Corporation

In order to dichotomize the adaptation needs among the various multinational archetypes as clearly as possible we shall consider the opposite of the product-organized in a number of geographical divisions, each undertaking a relatively broad spectrum of businesses within its own area of the world. We shall first discuss the adaptation needs within each area division, and then consider adaptation challenges at the corporate level.

A primary task for each area *division* will be adapting its product portfolio to the area conditions and determining which products or businesses to emphasize. This will be the main responsibility of the general manager of the division, who will rely to a large extent on his business managers within the area. Thus, each area division will have considerable autonomy in providing environmental scanning data from its part of the world. Headquarters for the area division will probably be staffed with executives mostly from the host country and have broader local expertise than the product-oriented divisions. The latter divisions will probably have general worldwide rather than local geographical expertise and will most likely be staffed with executives from several nations. Divisions of the area-dominated multinational will have the potential for strong geographical area strategies and plans. The biggest disadvantage is probably the lack of adaptation of product strategies to several geographical areas. The adaptive efforts might lead to too much duplication of efforts in production, new product development, etc. among the areas and the risk of too much fragmentation, particularly if the geographical areas are small.

At the *corporate* level the *adaptation* requirements will be related to balancing the portfolio of area divisions. The task will be to assess the long-term health of each area given the composition of products of each division. Given devaluation/revaluation and/or inflation/deflation opportunities and/or threats, corporate will evaluate which products seem to have the best future in various areas and which should be deemphasized; this may lead to changes in the portfolio. The central question will be whether the firm is emphasizing a set of products which result in the best worldwide geographical balance. We shall expect to find a much higher need for international staffing and broad worldwide expertise at the corporate level in the area-dominated multinational than in that which is product-oriented.

There seem to be diametrical differences between the two multinational archetypes in their needs for international competence and staff skills to carry out the adaptation tasks of planning at corporate as well as at divisional levels.[8] This is not surprising since the adaptation needs for the geographical area-organized multinational generally are so different from the adaptation needs of the worldwide product-oriented multinational. The product division will focus on adapting to changing geographical area patterns, the geographical area division to changing business or product opportunities. At the corporate level, too, the adaptation challenges will be fundamentally different, although in both instances the task will be to monitor the balance of the portfolio of divisions according to devaluation/revaluation and/or inflation/deflation patterns. Thus, the adaptation needs for the divisional and corporate levels of the two types of multinationals will be structured along the *opposite* dimension to the one on which the corporation is organized.

The *divisional* level needs for *integration* will focus on pulling together the diverse business activities within the given area. This implies that product policies within the area should be integrated, and that the program and/or functional activities within the area will be coordinated. There will probably be less pressure to integrate the businesses worldwide, though, since each division is responsible for adapting a business or product exclusively to its given area. The *corporate* level will coordinate the several area divisions so that the portfolio may become integrated; portfolio adjustments will probably be in terms of areas, not products. Again, the choice of organizational structure, which in this case is primarily along the area dimension directly reflects the integrative needs of the corporation.

Let us now leave the two extreme positions and consider the matrix structures, which will be faced with adaptation and integration tasks along *both* the product *and* area dimension. Before discussing the adaptation and integration tasks of our two matrix-based archetypes, however, let us review some relevant facts about coordination between the dimensions of a matrix structure. Effective coordination between the matrix dimensions must involve people; managers representing each dimension must get together to share information and work out decisions that take into account the considerations of each dimension. In order to facilitate coordination, then, it seems reasonable to form committees.[9] Staffing of these committees should reflect the matrix dimensions involved, and also be manned with executives from appropriate organizational levels. A major implication of the decentralized organizational structures considered here is that the responsibility for business strategy formulation and implementation as well as the bulk of the action program decisions will be made at the division level. Consequently, it will be at this level that integration of the inputs from the various dimensions will have to take place, as each dimension should influence the way that business strategy decisions are made and carried out. It should be noted that a matrix structure does not imply that representatives from each dimension will have to cooperate in detail to reach decisions at each level of the organization. Rather, the multidimensional cooperation will take place at *one* level, namely through the business coordination committees at the division level. Below this, there will generally be unidimensional reporting to cope with the functional strategy tasks. At the corporate level only the leading dimension will be represented to formulate and implement a portfolio strategy.

Product Leading/Area Grown Matrix Structure

This type of multinational will have a product-dominated organizational structure. However, going all the way along the product dimension with parallel business divisions operating worldwide would mean forfeiture of many of the benefits of being a large multinational and not merely a collection of business division. Thus, the rationale for the matrix structure is the acknowledgement that more than one dimension might be beneficial and a willingness to capitalize on potential economies of scales.

What requirements for *adaptation* face the product leading/area grown matrix structure? The answer is a combination of the adaptation requirements facing the worldwide product division organizations and the geographical area division organizations, but with relatively more emphasis of the factors discussed for the product division organization. Thus, at the divisional level the adaptation requirement will be dominated by changes in the area conditions. However, some emphasis will also be put on assessing changes in the business product dimension within each area. At the corporate level, similarly, adaptation of the portfolio should be primarily a response to area reconsiderations but also for business line reconsiderations.

In this type of corporation, which typically has evolved from a very strong dominance of the product dimension to the present balance, the *integrating* needs will probably not be too different from those of the worldwide product/organized corporation. At the division level the primary integrative concern will be to get the product lines together. However, a secondary concern will be to ensure the product integration in such a way that the areas also are integrated to the largest possible extent. At the corporate level the product dimension will again be the one receiving the most attention for integration, so that the portfolio of worldwide product activities will be coordinated. However, this portfolio will need to be modified to take into account area coordination.

Area Leading/Product Line Grown Matrix Structures

For this last type of matrix structure the opposite of what was the case in the previous section will be the pattern. The *adaptation* requirements of the product dimension will be the most important, both at divisional and corporate levels. However, the area adaptation dimension will also play a role.

The *integrative* needs are likely to be similar to those of the corporation which is geographical area divisionalized. At the divisional as well as the corporate level the area dimension will probably be the one requiring the most integrative attention. This should be modified by the need to integrate the product dimension as well.

Summary Pattern of Adaptation and Integration Requirements

A summary of the adaptation and integration requirements of each of our four multinational archetypes is presented in Table 1. As we see there is a continuing shift in adaptation and integration requirements as we go from

Table 1 Summary of the integration and adaptation planning tasks of the multinational corporations in our taxonomy

Taxonomy of Corporations	Adaptation	Integration
Worldwide Product Divisions	Along Area dimension	Along Product dimension
Product Leading/Area Grown Matrix	Primarily along Area dimension; some along Product dimension	Primarily along Product dimension; some along Area dimension
Area Leading/Product Grown Matrix	Primarily along Product dimension; some along Area dimension	Primarily along Area dimension; some along Product dimension
Geographical Area Divisions	Along Product dimension	Along Area dimension

one organizational extreme to the other. It is important to recognize that the adaptation needs fall into a pattern along a continuum which goes *contrary* to the product/area organizational structure continuum of multinationals, while the integration needs fall along a continuum that goes in the *same* direction as the organization structure. This leads us to our first normative statement, namely that while the *integration task* of planning should be undertaken in such a way that it *follows the organizational structure*, the *adaptation task* should be carried out in a direction *contrary to organizational structure.*

Costs of Planning in Multinationals

In this section we shall consider some of the costs of undertaking planning in each multinational archetype. One might ask whether it would not have been more natural to discuss first the issues of design and implementation of planning systems so that they might fulfill the requirements outlined in the previous section, then to consider the costs associated with the systems design alternatives. It shall turn out, however, that cost considerations may have a major influence on the choice of the planning systems design approach. Thus, by discussing costs of planning at this point, we shall be able to advance a more cost-effective planning systems design approach.

The relative proportion of overall planning costs attributed to the area dimension versus the business dimension of course changes as one moves from the one extreme to the other, as illustrated in Figure 2.

We see that the relative importance of each dimension's planning cost segment will be dependent on the multinational archetype at hand. This, however does not imply that the *absolute* costs of planning remain the same for each archetype. For instance, evolving from a structure with geographic area divisions to a matrix with the area dimension dominated and product dimensions grown, the purpose will be to maintain a planning strength along *both* dimensions. The planning costs of the area dimension will remain more or less the same, and the planning costs of the product dimension will be added. Thus, the nature of the absolute costs of planning implies that Figure 2 will have to be modified, as illustrated in Figure 3.

From Figure 3 one will see that the choice of organizational structure is not a free one, since the planning costs associated with a matrix structure may be substantially higher than for 'extreme' structures dominated by one dimension. Thus, one may conclude that only in instances in which the added benefits accrued by carrying two dimensions outweigh the added costs will the adoption of a matrix structure be justified. Also, the instances in which a matrix planning structure will be justified cost benefit-wise will probably be fewer than commonly anticipated, given the significantly higher than expected planning costs associated with such systems.

Diminishing the Costs of Planning in Matrix Archetypes

Given the obvious potential payoffs of adapting and integrating along more than one dimension, and disregarding the added planning costs, we should discuss the two ways of changing the cost/benefit tradeoff point: increasing the benefits from planning in the matrix archetypes, and decreasing the planning costs of these archetypes. We shall propose a way of decreasing the planning costs which turn out also to increase the benefits of planning.

Keeping in mind that the planning process implies a narrowing down of strategic options which may come about through a series of stages, say objectives-setting, planning, and budgeting, we may ask the following question: Are the adaptation and integration requirements equally important at each stage of progressive narrowing down?

First, we should consider which is the more important purpose of the objectives-setting stage, to ensure adaptation or integration. At this stage the major planning task should be to reexamine the fundamental assumptions for being in business, evaluate opportunities and threats, and consider whether the rationale for the firm's policies is still valid; in other words, where the firm stands relative to the environment. A realistic and effective adaptation to the current environmental conditions is the major concern. Integration, on the other hand, plays a lesser role at the objectives-setting stage.

At the next narrowing down stage, the planning stage, we still have to cater to the need for adaptation. More detailed plans will be developed in order to follow up on the major issues for adaptation to the environment

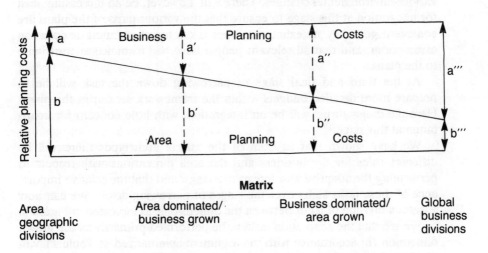

Figure 2 The relative proportion of planning costs attributable to the product dimension vs the area dimension. The a's indicate product dimension cost functions. The b's indicate area dimension cost functions.[10]

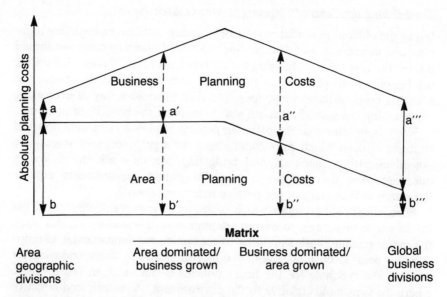

Figure 3 The absolute proportion of planning costs attributable to the product dimension vs the area dimension. The a's indicate product dimension cost functions. The b's indicate area dimension cost functions.

identified in the objectives-setting stage. Typically, there will be the calculation and evaluation of a number of 'what ifs' to assess the effects of various environmental changes. There will, however, be an increasing need for integration at this stage to ensure that the various parts of the plans are consistent, that they are exhaustive when taken together, based on common assumptions, and that all relevant people have had a chance to contribute to the plans.

At the third and final stage of narrowing down the task will be to prepare more detailed budgets within the framework set out in the plans. Here the major thrust will be on integration, with little concern for adaptation at this stage.[11]

We have shown that in each of the matrix archetypes there will be different roles for the business and the area dimensions with respect to performing the adaptive and integrative tasks, and that the relative importance of these tasks shifts over the stages of narrowing down. We can now suggest a division of labor between the dimensions, as indicated in Figure 4.

We see that the adaptation task, to be performed primarily by the grown dimension (in accordance with the argument summarized in Table 1), will play a *relatively* more important role in the early part of the narrowing down process than the integration task to be performed by the leading dimension. Later in the narrowing down process, however, the roles will be

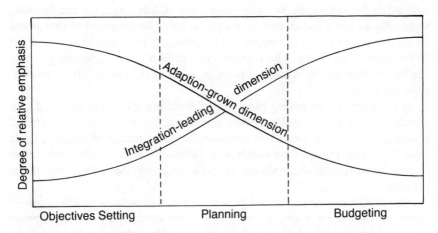

Figure 4 The relative importance of the adaptation function of the grown dimension vs the integration function of the leading dimension at each of the 'narrowing down' stages.

reversed and the leading dimension will be relatively more dominating.

Before discussing the specific implications of this opportunity for division of labor in the planning function of the matrix archetypes, let us emphasize that we are talking about *relative* importance of the tasks of the two dimensions. For instance, in a matrix structure with a mature and strong worldwide product dimension and a recent and weak area dimension the *absolute* importance of the leading dimension may prevail at all stages, although the relative emphasis will nevertheless follow the pattern indicated in Figure 4.

Let us also consider how the planning tasks of our two extreme organizational structures, the worldwide product organization and the area organization, can be interpreted in terms of Figure 4. If neither of these organizational forms has a grown dimension, will the adaptation task be taken care of? Yes, to some extent, since the leading dimension will adapt to environmental changes within relatively narrow limits. However, a lesser need for environmental adaptation will be perceived in a structure organized along one of the two extreme archetype forms. Also, the capacity for environmental adaptation will be much greater in a matrix organization. In fact the environmental adaptation need is probably the major reason for organizing along a matrix structure.

What are some of the implications that the pattern outlined in Figure 4 will have on the division of labor in the execution of the planning function? We see that extensive interaction among executives of the two dimensions of the matrix structure does not have to take place all through the narrowing down process, but only during the middle stage, i.e. the planning stage. An added sense of direction can probably be achieved in that it will be clearer which group of people will be primarily responsible at each stage of the narrowing down. The communication flows of the planning system can be simplified and be more explicit in terms of indicating who is responsible for what.

In addition to improving planning by instilling an added sense of task direction there will probably also be considerable cost savings. The cost of planning in a matrix should be considerably less through division of labor than if the conventional approach were followed, namely full-blown interaction between the dimensions at each stage of the narrowing down process.

This brings us to our second general normative statement, that *costs of planning* should be a major consideration in establishing an *appropriate balance* between adaptation and integration. The relative balance will be skewed towards more integration emphasis and less adaptation emphasis because of the costs associated with planning. However, emphasizing adaptation during the early stages of planning and integration during the later stages will tend to counteract this relative imbalance and will allow for a strengthening of the system's adaptation ability.

Conclusion

We have analyzed the adaptation and integration requirements of several corporations within a taxonomy of multinationals and have come up with a pattern of planning tasks for the multinationals. It turned out that to carry out this planning would be exceedingly expensive for several of the corporations. However, we were able to suggest a way to simplify planning and utilize task specialization. We suggest that this approach might lead to an operational, simplified, more effective, and less expensive planning activity in multinational corporations.

References

1. See Channon, Derek F., Prediction and practice in multinational strategic planning. Paper presented at the *2nd Annual European Seminar on International Business*, European Institute for Advanced Studies in Management (1974).

2. See Schwendiman, John S., International strategic planning: still in its infancy, *Worldwide P & I Planning*, September–October (1971).

3. This section is based heavily on Lorange, Peter, Formal planning in multinational corporations, *Columbia Journal of World Business*, Summer (1973). See also Lorange, Peter, La procedure de planification dans les entreprises multinationals, *Revue Economique et Sociale*, March (1973). Other classifications have

been proposed in Rutenberg David P., Organizational archetypes of a multinational company, *Management Science*, **16** (6) (1970); Perlmutter, Howard V., L'entreprise internationale-Trois conceptions, *Revue Economique et Sociale*, May (1965); and in Robinson, Richard D., *International Business Management*, Chapter 8, Holt, Rinehart & Winston, Inc., New York (1973).

4. Davis has developed the concepts of 'leading' and 'grown' dimensions of matrix structures. See Davis, Stanley M., Two models of organization: unity of command versus balance of power, *Sloan Management Review*, Fall (1974).

5. We shall, however, not imply that the evolution of matrix structures will have to be towards an ultimate equal balance between the two dimensions.

6. See Robinson, R., *op. cit.*

7. See Chandler, Alfred D., *Strategy and Structure*, MIT Press (1962), and Galbraith, Jay, *Designing Complex Organizations*, Addison-Wesley (1973).

8. Some of the differences in staffing patterns for nationals vs. non-nationals of four large European-based multinationals found by Davis, Edstrom and Galbraith support this. See Davis, Harry, Anders Edstrom, and Jay Galbraith, Transfer of managers in multinational organizations, European Institute for Advanced Studies in Management, Working Paper 74–19, Brussels (1974).

9. See Goggin, William, How the multi-dimensional structure works at Dow-Corning, *Harvard Business Review*, January–February (1974). See also Davis, *op. cit.*

10. Galbraith has suggested this exhibit. See Galbraith, Jay R., Matrix Organization Design; How to Combine Functional and Project Forms, *Business Horizons*, Summer (1971) (Exhibit 3), p. 70.

11. See Vancil, Richard F. and Peter Lorange, Strategic planning in diversified corporations, *Harvard Business Review*, January–February (1975), for an approach to a three-step narrowing down of strategic options.

2

A Model and Recent Developments*

William A. Dymsza[†]

*Source: *Journal of International Business Studies* 15 (Fall 1984), pp. 169–183.

Abstract. This article develops a comprehensive, dynamic model of strategic planning for multinational corporations. The model depicts many aspects in MNC strategic planning systems, while recognizing that many variations exist among companies. Within the context of the model and experience of companies, certain approaches to competitive assessment, focusing on strategic issues, portfolio planning, and threat/opportunity analysis, are emphasized. Finally, the article examines recent ways in which MNCs have been fine-tuning their strategic planning to deal with rapidly changing global environments, to meet new competition, and to achieve profitability and other goals.

Introduction

One of the most important developments in management has been the much greater emphasis that multinational companies have placed on strategic planning as a framework for decision making.

Over the years the process of strategic planning has been refined and fine-tuned by multinational companies to make it more significant in decision making. Confronted with rapid—often discontinuous—changes and with greater uncertainty in their business across the world, managements of multinational companies have developed a more analytical framework for planning as a basis for making decisions. These managements want to anticipate and adapt to future changes and uncertainties rather than be victims of them. They want to employ their corporate resources—management, personnel, technologies, business know-how, funds, and other assets—in a more efficient and productive way to attain their corporate objectives. They want to explore global opportunities for profits and service to their consumers, to reduce threats, uncertainties, and exposure to risk, and to achieve greater competitive efficiency, along with profitability objectives around the world. As a result, multinational companies are making greater use of strategic planning as a key management process.

Unique Aspects of International Strategic Planning

Types of Decisions

Even though many aspects of international strategic planning are similar to those of domestic business planning, some important differences do exist, creating uniqueness and complexity. For example, the types of decisions that strategic planning should help a multinational company to make are as follows: In what region and what countries and when should a company expand its international commitments in funds, technology, management, know-how, and personnel? Should it enter a new country? What type of entry should it undertake in countries with opportunities: exporting, licensing, direct investments, management contracts, other arrangements? What are the opportunities/risks in various countries in different modes of entry? In what countries should it expand its existing plants, undertake new investments, make acquisitions? What product adaptations should it make and what new products should it introduce in various countries? To what extent should it change its marketing and product mixes in different countries? What should the company do about exchange risk, political vulnerability, and adverse governmental controls and regulations? Should it disinvest or phase out business in certain countries? Where should it raise funds for its worldwide operations? Should it go into joint ventures with private firms or government enterprises abroad, and under what conditions? What management development programs should it undertake at headquarters and its affiliates abroad?

Differences in International Business Management

The range of choices shown above indicates the complexity of international strategic planning and some of the respects in which the process differs from planning for domestic business. The differences between strategic planning for international business and domestic operations arise from the complexity of undertaking business in foreign countries with different and changing political, regulatory, economic, sociocultural, business, and other environments. Further, risk dimensions in international business vary, often change, and are difficult to ascertain precisely.

Strategic and Operational Planning

Multinational companies engage in 2 basic types of planning: 1) strategic or long-term planning, and 2) operational or tactical planning.[1] Strategic planning, which often involves a time dimension of 3 to 7 years (often 5 years) is the most significant type of planning in establishing the futute directions and major courses of action for the multinational corporation. Strategic planning involves formulation of key objectives and goals for the corporation and its global system of enterprises, including the determination of strategies that allocate corporate resources among units in various countries to achieve the established objectives.

Operational planning, on the other hand, encompasses highly detailed plans, procedures, and budgets for the company and its international units, usually for a period of one or 2 years. The operational plans serve as a framework for day-to-day decision making and also as a basis for the monitoring and control systems. Some multinational companies may also have very long-range plans of 15 to 20 years (for example, to develop new high-technology products); certain petroleum companies may project supply-demand in oil for 2 decades or longer as part of their planning. But the strategic planning with a time period of 3 to 7 years (often 5 years) and the operational planning (usually for a year) constitute the basic types of business planning that are crucial for management of multinational corporations.

It should be emphasized that strategic planning constitutes a major responsibility of top management at headquarters because nothing less than the future of the multinational corporation is at stake; executives of divisions, regional offices, and national subsidiaries are generally also involved. Under operational planning, on the other hand, not only the top but also the middle layer managers and the functional staff of country affiliates, regional offices, and divisions of the corporation participate in the process. The operational plans of all units should be interrelated with the strategic plans and approved by the top management of the multinational corporation.

Model of International Strategic Planning

Figure 1 shows a model for comprehensive strategic planning for multinational corporations.[2] This model starts with a reevaluation of company philosophy, mission, or definition of business and then moves to a managerial audit of the strengths and weaknesses of all units and the total enterprise, an assessment of competition in national markets, and an evaluation and projection of key political, legal, economic, cultural, regulatory, technological, and business factors in major countries and regions. After an

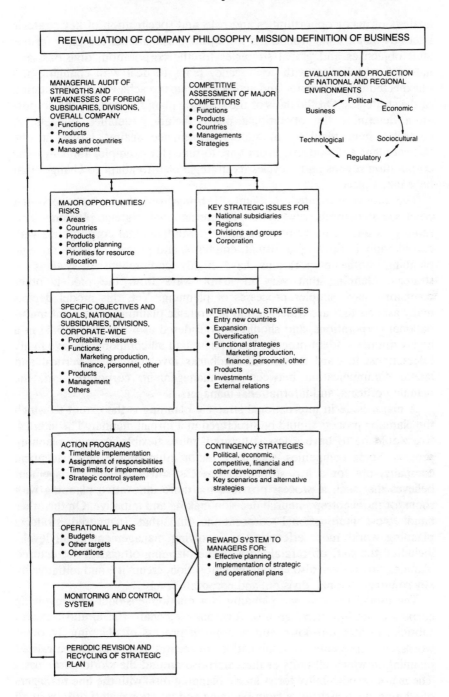

Figure 1 Model for comprehensive strategic planning for MNCs

analysis of major opportunities and risks and specification of key strategic issues by major units around the world, the multinational company formulates objectives and global strategies for the corporation, divisions, and national subsidiaries, with contingency plans to deal with changing and unexpected developments, and action programs to achieve implementation of the strategies. On the basis of the strategic plan, the units of the corporation determine the operational plans, including detailed budgets. A control system regularly monitors performance against targets in the tactical plans and budgets. From time to time (for example, annually), the corporation revises and recycles its strategic plan to adapt to changes that have taken place.

The model presented in Figure 1 brings out the components that comprise a comprehensive system of international strategic planning. This represents one of many possible models. Multinational corporations vary considerably in the scope, format, emphasis, and process of their strategic planning. Some corporations have highly comprehensive systems of strategic planning that vary in major ways from the model; other companies have simpler processes of planning. Yet, this model depicts many aspects that are widely found in strategic planning systems of multinational corporations, and should be considered as a dynamic model in a highly interdependent process. Each phase and all components have many interactions, forward flows, and feedbacks involving much vertical and lateral communication between top management, corporate staff, the planning officers, and international managers.

A major issue in international strategic planning is the extent to which the planning process should be structured in a formal manner. The alternative would be to have a less structured, more flexible strategic planning process. Some companies, such as a major international pharmaceutical company, opt for a less structured process, since the top management believes that such a process provides for more innovative planning with room for more entrepreneurial decision making and initiative. On the other hand, most multinational corporations find that structured strategic planning works more effectively in involving management at all levels, including the staff officers along with the planning officials. A structured planning process can also encourage innovation, creativity, and initiative by key country, regional, division, and corporate levels.

The model for strategic planning is a multidimensional one involving corporate headquarters, groups, divisions, regional offices, and national subsidiaries in a top-down and bottom-up process of planning. In other words, it represents a combination of centralized and decentralized planning in which all units of the enterprise around the world participate. The major responsibility for strategic planning rests with the line managers of all units, with assistance from planning and functional staff officers at all levels. The top management of the multinational corporation, however, has

Figure 2 Major factors in international competitive assessment*

Key resources	Production	Marketing	Management processes—developments
Management • HQ, groups, divisions • National subsidiaries Local Managers • In top, middle positions • National • Subsidiaries Engineering, technical, administrative skilled manpower in major countries Technology • Patents in key countries • Production processes • Product know-how • Effectiveness of R&D Capital and Financial Resources • Global • Regional • Major countries Business Know-how	Physical Capacity • Countries Plants and Equipment • Location • Size and type • Age • Automation Economies of Scale Productivity Global or Regional Rationalization Human Resources • Management, technical workforce • Labor unions • Turnover	Marketing Mix • Divisions • Regions • Countries Products • Product mix • New product introduction • Adaptation of products • Product differentiation Brand Names and Trademarks Market Segmentation Customer Service Distribution • Type • Effectiveness Promotion • Expenditures • Type and media • Effectiveness Price • Type Investment and Expenditures • On various aspects of market development	Organization • Centralization • Decentralization • Line and staff Information and Control System • Accounting system • Computerized systems Strategic and Operational Planning Management Development • Corporate level • Divisions • National subsidiaries Development of National Managers Personnel and Staffing Practices • Experience • Longevity • Turnover • Replacement Reward Systems Corporate Value System

*Key factors in the company are evaluated in relation to major competitors.

the primary responsibility for determining the overall global directions and objectives and for coordinating the strategies of all units worldwide.

This model provides for major flexibility in the needs of companies for integrated or adaptive planning and some balance between the two.[3] Integrated planning involves global unification of functional, product, or other strategies, and centralization of decisions, particularly in production, finance, R&D, and investments. Adaptive planning comprises differentiation and responsiveness to diversity of country environments. Multinational corporations characterized by high technology or rapid technological change, complex sourcing, and high economies of scale often require integrated planning.[4] On the other hand, firms with somewhat limited economies of scale, mature products in the product cycle, and major emphasis on marketing, and those facing diversity in consumer tastes and government regulations need considerable adaptive planning. Most multinational corporations have to achieve some balance between integration and adaptation in their strategic planning and operational decisions.

The strategic planning process and resource allocation based on it can be used as a catalyst to achieve convergence among managers on key decisions and consensus-building among executives whose priorities and perceptions vary widely.[5] It can create pressures for interaction among managers, for convergence of views, and for conflict resolution. A reward system for effective participation in the planning process and for achievements of goals and subgoals fosters such a business climate.

The model also coordinates the international control system with operational and strategic planning of the enterprise and its units around the world. This fosters implementation of strategic and operational plans. Implementation is also fostered by deep involvement of top management in the planning process, dissemination of key aspects of corporate plans, and rewards to managers for effective strategic planning and implementation.

Every aspect of the strategic planning and control process is important in this model; but, because some aspects are well known and because space is limited, the balance of this paper will focus on competitive assessment, strategic issues, portfolio planning, and opportunity/risk analysis, with examples.

Competitive Assessment

The competitive audit assesses actual and potential competition faced by the corporation in countries, regions, and worldwide, particularly in major country markets.[6] The audit involves analysis of industry, technology, product cycle and product development, and of substitute product trends in major markets. The auditing company then identifies major competitors in country markets, their types of operation, their business policies and practices, and their key strengths and weaknesses. The performance of units of the company is compared with that of competitors in matters such as sales growth, share of market, market/expense costs, quality of products, product change and innovation, labor productivity, costs of manufacturing, physical facilities and scale of operations, profit margins, various measures of profitability, and competence of management and personnel. The analysis should also deal with companies that are producing and marketing substitute products and with potential competitors in national markets. Figure 2 shows a comprehensive format for assessment of competition in major countries. Figure 3 shows criteria used by a marketing-oriented multinational company in assessing competitive position in key product/country markets.

Some precise quantitative data about major competitors may be difficult to obtain. With a systematic effort, however, much of the information can be estimated or pieced together from annual reports (required in some countries), and from trade journals, company magazines, statistical analyses, and other sources. The country subsidiaries should maintain systematic information about major competitors, updated for strategic planning purposes.

From such quantitative performance comparisons and exercises of qualitative judgments, the corporation should be able to assess strengths and weaknesses of major competitors in various countries and regions. It should also be able to determine competitive advantages that it has over other companies in specific countries; it should lead from these strengths in its strategies. For example, companies that find they have one or more competitive advantages in proprietary product lines, product design, brand names, advertising, distribution, or manufacturing costs in various countries should emphasize these strengths in determining their strategies. Generally, it is more important to lead with competitive strengths than to allocate resources to overcome weaknesses.

Certain multinational companies try to ascertain the key strategies of major competitors in product/country markets in order to respond to them better. For example, from its competitive assessments, a major diversified electronics company ascertains major competitors in many key product/country markets. Using its competitive information, the company simulates strategic plans for its major competitors as if for its own enterprise. These strategical plans formulated for competitors enable the electronics company to establish more realistic strategic plans to deal with existing and emerging competition in specific country/product markets.[7]

Figure 3 Criteria for assessing competitive position

Factor	Competitive position		
	Strong	Moderate	Weak
Market position	# 1 or # 2	Included in top 6	Not among top 6
Relative market share (percentage)	30 percent or higher	15–30 percent	Less than 15 percent
Relative growth	Exceeds market average growth by 20 percent	±20 percent of market average growth	Lags market average growth rate by 20 percent or more
Relative pricing	High (a leader)	Moderate (a follower)	Low
Cost comparison and productivity per worker	Less cost advantage	About average for industry	High costs
Product quality level	Favorable	Neutral	Unfavorable
Innovation	Market leader—consistently first with new products, new technology, and so on	About even with other competitors	Lags market consistently in new products/services
Marketing strength	Recognized as leader in market	About average for industry	Generally lower than industry
Advertising/promotion activity	High	Moderate	Low
Managerial competence	Favorable	Neutral	Unfavorable
Overall ranking	Strong	Moderate	Weak

Strategic Issues

Some companies require the managers of each country subsidiary, regional office, and division to determine 3 or 4 strategic issues that will have the most significant impact on their business during the planning period. This requires the managements of each unit to analyze profoundly and concentrate on a few key issues. The management should be able to determine such strategic issues from a careful study of their business and analysis of trends in the industry, technology, key environmental factors, competition, and emerging opportunities.

Examples of strategic issues are the following: major new competition emerging in some countries; adverse changes in government and increased political vulnerability; conversely, favorable changes in the regulatory climate in countries with changing governments; requirements for new product innovations and improvements; needed refurbishment of marketing effort, including promotion and distribution; need for development of more competent middle and top local managers in the subsidiary; and emerging increases in raw material costs.

Other strategic issues can emphasize the need to adapt existing products, introduce new products, engage in more effective market segmentation, improve external relations, develop appropriate technology in labor-intensive developing countries, investigate ways to increase labor productivity, improve relations with labor unions, and provide effective incentives for national managers. In the mid-1970s, a major multinational pharmaceutical company shifted to a less structured strategic planning system that emphasized strategic issues at the country, regional, and corporate levels.[8] This led to less structured strategic planning with more management concentration on critical issues affecting the company's future business. The pharmaceutical's operational planning continued to be highly structured and related to its control and monitoring system. Another highly diversified multinational conglomerate, on the other hand, requires its country and product managers to focus on 2 or 3 critical strategic issues in order to establish more realistic goals within the context of the corporation's broad objectives in growth of profits and its style of management—one that fosters confrontation by line and staff managers from headquarters, regions, countries, and products.

Companies that require managers of national subsidiaries, regional officers, and divisions to develop key strategic issues find that such development establishes more focus in their strategic planning on emerging opportunities and threats to business in various areas of the world. The process can also lead to the formulation of more innovative and realistic strategies.

Portfolio Planning and Opportunity/Risk Analysis

From the analysis of key environmental factors in major countries, combined with the managerial and competitive audits and a focus on strategic issues, multinational corporations can generally pinpoint the countries with the most promising opportunities in relation to risk. Many companies have adopted strategic portfolio planning, however, which is a more sophisticated approach to determining priorities for allocation of corporate resources in complex enterprises with a portfolio of businesses.[9] This approach establishes criteria for evaluating, allocating resources to, and planning the future direction of a portfolio of businesses involving a combination of several product lines in a number of countries.

Companies utilizing portfolio planning typically take the following steps:[10]

1) Redefine various businesses as strategic business units (SBUs), often different from the operating units. The SBUs may be defined by product/country market or, occasionally, product/country units.

2) Use a portfolio matrix to determine the attractiveness and competitiveness of SBUs. Common grids are the Boston Consulting Group Market growth/share matrix, the General Electric Industry attractiveness/business position matrix, and the Shell Directional Policy Mix.

3) On the basis of this framework, assign strategic missions to SBUs and allocate resources to each of them over the planning period.

Based upon his survey of more than 300 of the *Fortune* "1000" companies and his other studies, Haspeslagh shows that portfolio planning is widely used by large enterprises in the United States—many of them multinational.[11] According to him the real issue is not which portfolio grid to use, but the definition of strategic business units and assignment of strategic missions to them. Decisions on strategic missions require broad analysis of industry/product characteristics, competitive positions, anticipated responses by major competitors, available financial resources, and interactions with other businesses in the portfolio.[12] Managerial judgments, involving the weighing of significant trade-offs, also play an important part in assignment of strategic missions and allocation of resources.

Most U.S. multinational companies that use portfolio planning define their strategic business units by products in the American and foreign markets. The SBUs for planning commonly differ from the organizational operational units. Thus, these companies encounter problems of coordinating management of the SBUs and the operational units of the enterprise in the United States and in foreign countries. Further, multinational companies encounter some difficulties of integrating the country environmental factors and the product dimensions in determining missions of

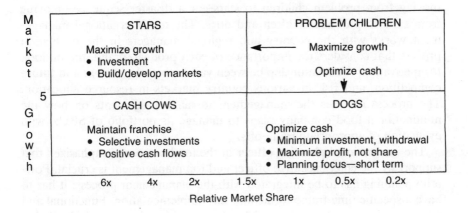

Figure 4 Product/brand grid

SBUs and allocation of resources to them. As multinational companies gain experience with portfolio planning and integrate it into strategic planning and management, however, they find that it becomes an effective managerial process.

An Example of Portfolio Planning in a Multinational Food Company

Portfolio planning can be illustrated by a brief example of the Boston Consulting Group matrix used since 1977 by a major multinational food company's international operations.[13]

The food corporation defines its strategic business units by product brands in international markets. As shown in the Product Grid in Figure 4, the position of each strategic business unit is evaluated in a 4-box matrix based upon relative market share and market growth. This establishes the business units as: 1) stars and candidates for investment and building markets; 2) cash cows to maintain the franchise for selective investments and positive cash flows; 3) problem children to watch carefully; and 4) dogs, to optimize cash, minimize investment, maximize profit rather than share of market, and consider for possible divestment. This portfolio planning process provides a role for each product/brand in country markets and results in a means of allocating resources, clarifying priorities, and fostering communications.

The portfolio management of the multinational food company is more sophisticated than may appear on the surface. The company evaluates the performance of SBUs (products/brands in country markets) in the past, present, and future. It engages in forecasting future market growth and market share of SBUs using computerized models, with alternative assumptions. As shown in Figures 5 and 6, the management attempts to ascertain whether the SBUs are going to experience a success sequence—

moving from problem children to stars—or a disaster sequence—moving from stars to problem children and dogs. The top international management works with the country and regional managers in the evaluation process that considers the importance of each product/brand, the outlook for innovation, the relationship between various brands, current and future competition, and risk in various country markets in resource allocation. The process requires the management to make judgements on how the multinational food company plans to manage its portfolio of SBUs, with evaluation of appropriate trade-offs.

The international planning officer of the food company emphasized that support by the chief executive officer and top management is crucial. Portfolio planning has to be integrated with the management process; it has to have a specific time frame for actions and implementation. Functional and educational support are essential, along with patience and flexibility. Further, the top management has to have an effective system of strategic review and control of performance.

Some companies experience difficulties in coordinating portfolio planning for their domestic and overseas units as a result of major differences in country characteristics and variations in risk. Managers can also encounter difficulties in resource allocation to SBUs where facilities and resources are shared among SBUs. Further, portfolio planning may not be

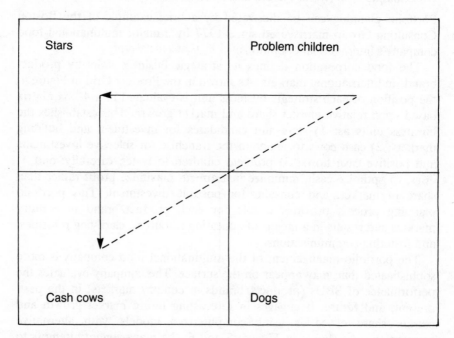

Figure 5 Success sequence

suitable for many new international activities or for those that require a period of nurturing before explosive growth takes place.

Example of a Multinational Corporation's Threat and Opportunity Analysis on a Country Basis

A major diversified multinational electronics company initiated a joint international planning project between corporate strategic planning staff and the international division in the late 1970s to propose changes in the strategic planning process for the corporate and strategic business unit, with the objective of developing strategic plans that would be more responsive to fast-changing environmental and competitive forces.[14] The electronics company wanted to ensure a better matching of country opportunities and needs with SBU strengths and needs. A key aspect of this project was a threat and opportunity analysis of major countries, based upon a number of criteria of political, economic, regulatory, and competitive environments. For each country, the project group developed an environmental profile, a profile of company participation, and specific opportunities and threats by product/country markets and type of involvement—along with corporate response options.

For example, in 1977 the project group made quantitative impact estimates of potential losses in sales, based upon identifying major threats on a

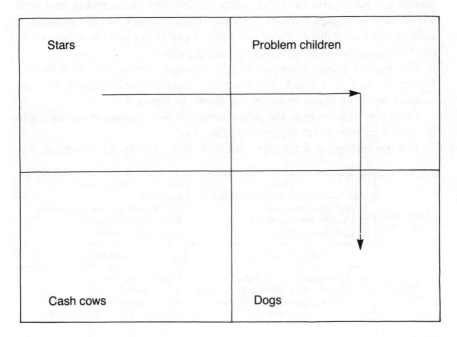

Figure 6 Disaster sequence

country-by-country and product-by-product basis for 1982. These estimates reflected the probability of occurrence, considering the significance
of projected sales and assuming no effective counter-strategies.

On the other side of the coin, with respect to opportunity analysis, the
project group identified opportunities from all sources on the country-by-
country and product-by-product basis. It estimated incremental opportunities—the additional sales that the electronics company was expected to
attain in 1982 over and above current plans and/or opportunities that had
already been identified. The estimates were considered to be rough, as they
were restricted to major opportunities and were highly discounted to reflect
corporate capabilities. Because incremental opportunities were conducted
on a country-by-country basis, the estimates understated regional opportunities that were available through regional coverage and rationalization in
certain areas, such as, the EEC. They also did not consider possible incremental opportunities through synergism.

From this study, the project group concluded that the company should
plan more effectively for risk containment and opportunity exploitation.
This required new emphasis on defensive strategic thrusts because of the
changed international outlook. The name of the game in strategic planning
was going to involve more international risk management—establishing
priorities for investments, potential investment limits by countries, more
stringent risk assessment of new ventures, and synergistic contingency
planning. Finally, the electronic corporation's top management and staff
would have to engage in more corporate-level overviews of the company's
current and future involvement in a limited number of key countries and to
establish priorities in the strategic planning process.

The project group proposed a new strategic vocabulary, as shown in
Figure 7, and a 9-block Incremental Opportunity/Defensive Posture
matrix classifying major countries, as shown in Figure 8.

From the 9-box matrix, the major countries were classified according to
the new vocabulary that designated priorities.

The protect/grow countries received first priority in planning; the

	Risk	Response
Defensive posture	1) High-risk countries 2) Medium-risk countries 3) Low-risk countries	A defensive posture—to protect A manage risk situation A posture to monitor
	Opportunities	Classification
Opportunity orientation	1) High incremental opportunities 2) Medium incremental opportunities 3) Low incremental opportunities	A growth country An enhance country A hold country

Figure 7 Strategic vocabulary

management risk/grow countries and protect/enhance countries were given second priority. One of the conclusions from these priorities was that the multinational electronics corporation needed to bring the total strength of the company to bear on its international business, in a combination of exploiting opportunities and defending its positions. In order to do this, it should establish early positions in high-growth country markets; it should shift resources to nations with the greatest potential, particularly nations with undeveloped human and natural resources. The electronics company's future business in these nations should include not only permanent export participation, but also licensing, low-risk direct investment, and types of joint ventures. Corporate strategic planning would play an important part in this process, in conjunction with the international division, the global product divisions, the strategic business units, and the country managements.

The threat/opportunity analysis added an important dimension to the global strategic planning of the electronics company. This process in itself, however, did not enable the management of the company to foresee and develop strategies to deal with the consequences of certain major political and economic changes that emerged in the late 1970s and the early 1980s—such as, the rise of the radical, Moslem government in Iran, the declining income of the OPEC countries, and rising foreign debt of many developing countries in Latin America and elsewhere nor did this process correctly ascertain changes in growth patterns in many countries as a result of the severe economic recession in the 1980s.

The electronics company found that it had to improve its forecasting of political, economic, and competitive changes to utilize effectively its threat/opportunity analysis in its strategic planning. Further, it had to engage in more contingency planning, in action programs that assigned specific responsibilities to managers for follow-through and implementation, and in more effective strategic and operational controls.

With rapid and unforeseen changes taking place in many areas, a number of other multinational companies have been utilizing early warning systems—focusing on key indicators—which they relate to contingency plans and action programs. This has enabled some multinationals to adapt more readily to major environmental changes in a timely fashion. Nevertheless, early warning systems do not necessarily alert multinational companies to critical emerging problems in major countries and to environmental changes and discontinuities.

All in all, the threat/opportunity analysis shown above provides a systematic way for the multinational corporation and its international, product and SBU managements to undertake more effective international risk management in the strategic planning process. However, the system requires sophisticated forecasting, comprehensive evaluation of key environmental factors and sound management judgment. It also requires periodic reevaluation, along with comprehensive assessments of future

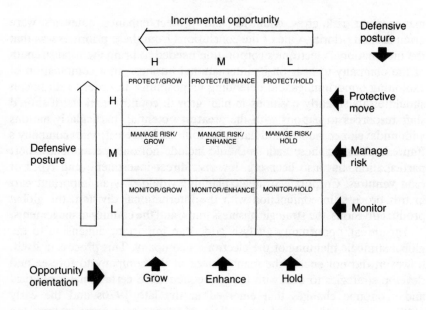

Figure 8 Incremental opportunity/defensive posture matrix

political risk, socio-economic changes, competitive developments, contingency planning, and effective strategic and operational control.

Recent Trends and Concluding Comments

The emphasis of many multinational companies on competitive assessment, strategic issues, portfolio planning, and opportunity risk analysis—as shown in this discussion and examples—fits within the context of the comprehensive model of global strategic planning outlined at the beginning of this paper. This generalized model shows many aspects of global strategic planning that U.S. and European multinationals utilize for their global management, although many variations exist. These companies have been developing strategic planning systems that fit their business requirements, including their country and product involvement, customer orientation, style of management, and corporate culture.

Faced with increased change and uncertainty and a more competitive international environment, multinational companies have been fine-tuning their strategic planning systems. A number of them have been moving into more integrative planning in order to rationalize utilization of resources on a global basis. Another trend has been to develop more formalized strategic planning with line and staff managerial involvement at headquarters, regional, and country levels. These companies have often utilized computerized forecasting models, expanded use of portfolio planning to determine resource allocation to SBUs, engaged in more rigorous assessment of actual and potential competition in country/product markets, developed strategies that emphasize productivity improvement and cost reductions of all units around the world, and planned longer-term investments in modernizing plants, research and development, marketing programs, and management development. Through portfolio planning and hard-headed management, multinational companies have striven to increase their return on investments by concentrating on their profitable and promising product lines and divesting country and product operations that have not been achieving their earnings goals or that do not fit within their long-term company mission or definition of their business. These companies have given more attention to international risk management and exploitation of their unique advantages.

On the other hand, some multinational companies have moved to somewhat less structured and more flexible strategic planning. For example, a major pharmaceutical company and other multinational companies emphasize global strategic issues, innovative planning, and entrepreneurial initiatives. Several multinationals have different time dimensions and formats for business planning by headquarters, divisions, and country affiliates. A major diversified electronics company—long a leader in global management by strategic planning—has shifted away from highly sophisticated, time-consuming models developed by its corporate strategic planning staff. This company, with a new chief executive officer, has substantially reduced its planning staff and has concentrated its strategic planning on key high technology businesses in which the company is a leader, on more down-to-earth portfolio planning to allocate resources in order to obtain rate of return earnings goals, on divestment of business that does not fit the corporate mission, and on development of more entrepreneurship in management. Whether companies have engaged in more or less structured strategic planning, they have required line managers at all levels to assume major responsibility in the process.

With the increased competition from Japanese multinational companies, a major issue is the emphasis of U.S. companies on longer-range strategic management versus bottom-line profitability results from year-to-year operations. Some scholars have maintained that Japanese enterprises have a longer-term managerial perspective, whereas U.S. multinational and other companies, despite strategic plans, place primary emphasis upon the operational plans, budgets, and rate of return results in the short term. Many U.S. managers of country subsidiaries, regional offices, divisions, and other units believe that they will be evaluated primarily by their profitability results annually rather than by their involvement in and implementation of strategic plans. Further, bonuses, incentive programs, and advancement in the corporate hierarchy are often based upon short-term profitability achievements.

Such an orientation, despite major emphasis upon strategic planning by managers at all levels, does not foster longer-term strategic management. Yet, the author's studies show that many top managements of multinational corporations have placed emphasis on longer-term planning of the future directions of their global enterprises and on achieving some balance between longer-term and short-term results. But in some cases, what may be required is more effective strategic controls and positive incentives for effective strategic planning and implementation at the subsidiary, regional, division, and corporate levels in order to emphasize management by strategic planning globally.

This paper has presented a generalized model of global strategic planning and various approaches to competitive assessment, strategic issues, portfolio planning, and opportunity/risk analysis in business planning by multinational companies. Recent trends show that multinational corporations continue to strive to devise strategic and operational planning and control systems that will enable them to manage their international and domestic business more effectively in an era of rapid, sometimes discontinuous, changes.

Notes

† William A. Dymsza has served as Editor-in-Chief of JIBS since 1975 and is a Fellow of the Academy of International Business. Dr. Dymsza has been an advisor to the OECD and the United Nations and has written widely on international management.

1. For more elaborate discussion of international strategic and operational planning, see George A. Steiner and Warren M. Cannon, *Multinational Corporate Planning* (New York: Macmillan Co., 1966). Chapter 1; Derek F. Channon, *Multinational Strategic Planning* (New York: Amacom, 1978); and William A. Dymsza, *Multinational Business Strategy* (New York: McGraw-Hill, 1972), Chapters 3, 4.

2. For other models and discussion, see William H. Davidson, *Global Strategic Management* (New York: John Wiley & Sons, 1982), Chapter 8.

3. See R. F. Vancil and Peter Lorange, "Strategic Planning in Diversified Companies," *Harvard Business Review*, January–February 1975, pp. 81–90.

4. W. H. Davidson, *Global Strategic Management*, p. 317.

5. See Yves Doz and C. K. Prahalad, "Patterns of Strategic Control within Multinational Corporations," *Journal of International Business Studies*, this issue.

6. For a more comprehensive discussion, see D. F. Channon, *Multinational Strategic Planning*, pp. 73–76.

7. Information obtained in personal interview with an official on the Strategic Planning Staff of the electronics company.

8. Information about the planning of the pharmaceutical and multinational conglomerate was obtained in personal interviews with officers of the companies.

9. See D. F. Channon, *Multinational Strategic Planning*, Chapter 4.

10. See Philippe Haspeslagh, "Portfolio Planning: Uses and Limits," *Harvard*

Business Review, January–February 1982, pp. 58–73.

11. Ibid., pp. 61–62.

12. Ibid., pp. 61–63, 65–66.

13. This example of portfolio planning by international operations of the multinational food company was provided by the strategic planning officer at a meeting of the American Management Association.

14. This example is based upon a paper given to the author by an official after personal interviews at company headquarters.

3

The Real Story Behind Honda's Success*

Richard T. Pascale

*Source: *California Management Review* XXVI (Spring 1984), pp. 47–72.

Perspective One: The Honda Effect

At face value, "strategy" is an innocent noun. Webster defines it as the large-scale planning and direction of operations. In the business context, it pertains to a process by which a firm searches and analyzes its environment and resources in order to 1) select opportunities defined in terms of markets to be served and products to serve them, and 2) makes discrete decisions to invest resources in order to achieve identified objectives.[1]

But for a vast and influential population of executives, planners, academics, and consultants, strategy is more than a conventional English noun. It embodies an implicit model of how organizations should be guided and consequently, preconfigures our way of thinking. Strategy formulation 1) is generally assumed to be driven by senior management whom we expect to set strategic direction; 2) has been extensively influenced by empirical models and concepts; and 3) is often associated with a laborious strategic planning process that, in some companies, has produced more paper than insight.

A $500-million-a-year "strategy" industry has emerged in the United States and Europe comprised of management consultants, strategic planning staffs, and business school academics. It caters to the unique emphasis that American and European companies place upon this particular aspect of managing and directing corporations.

Words often derive meaning from their cultural context. *Strategy* is one such word and nowhere is the contrast of meanings more pronounced than between Japan and the United States. The Japanese view the emphasis we place on "strategy" as we might regard their enthusiasm for Kabuki or sumo wrestling. They note our interest not with an intent of acquiring similar ones but for insight into our peculiarities. The Japanese are somewhat distrustful of a single "strategy," for in their view any idea that focuses attention does so at the expense of peripheral vision. They strongly believe that *peripheral vision* is essential to discerning changes in the customer, the technology or competition, and is the key to corporate survival over the long haul. They regard any propensity to be driven by a single-minded strategy as a weakness.

The Japanese have particular discomfort with strategic concepts. While they do not reject ideas such as the experience curve or portfolio theory outright they regard them as a stimulus to perception. They have often ferreted out the "formula" of their concept-driven American competitors and exploited their inflexibility. In musical instruments, for example, (a mature industry facing stagnation as birthrates in the U.S. and Japan declined), Yamaha might have classified its products as "cash cows" and gone on to better things (as its chief U.S. competitor, Baldwin United, had done). Instead, beginning with a negligible share of the U.S. market, Yamaha plowed ahead and destroyed Baldwin's seemingly unchallengeable dominance. YKK's success in zippers against Talon (a Textron division) and Honda's outflanking of Harley-Davidson (a former AMF subsidiary) in the motorcycle field provide parallel illustrations. All three cases involved American conglomerates, wedded to the portfolio concept, that had classified pianos, zippers, and motorcycles as mature businesses to be harvested rather than nourished and defended. Of course, those who developed portfolio theory and other strategic concepts protest that they were never intended to be mindlessly applied in setting strategic direction. But most would also agree that there is a widespread tendency in American corporations to misapply concepts and to otherwise become strategically myopic—ignoring the marketplace, the customer, and the problems of execution. This tendency toward misapplication, being both pervasive and persistent over several decades, is a phenomenon that the literature has largely ignored.[2] There is a need to explicitly identify the factors that influence how we conceptualize strategy—and which foster its misuse.

Honda: The Strategy Model

In 1975, Boston Consulting Group presented the British government its final report: *Strategy Alternatives for the British Motorcycle Industry*. This 120-page document identified two key factors leading to the British demise in the world's motorcycle industry:

- market share loss and profitability declines, and
- scale economy disadvantages in technology, distribution, and manufacturing.

During the period 1959 to 1973, the British share of the U.S. motorcycle industry had dropped from 49 percent to 9 percent. Introducing BCG's recommended strategy (of targeting market segments where sufficient production volumes could be attained to be price competitive) the report states:

The success of the Japanese manufacturers originated with the growth of their domestic market during the 1950s. As recently as 1960, only 4 percent of Japanese motorcycle production was exported. By this time, however, the Japanese had developed huge production volumes in small motorcycles in their domestic market, and volume-related cost reductions had followed. This resulted in a highly competitive cost position which the Japanese used as a springboard for penetration of world markets with small motorcycles in the early 1960s.[3]

The BCG study was made public by the British government and rapidly disseminated in the United States. It exemplifies the necessary (and I argue, insufficient) strategist's perspective of

- examining competition primarily from an intercompany perspective,
- at a high level of abstraction,
- with heavy reliance on micro-economic concepts (such as the experience curve).

Case writers at Harvard Business School, UCLA, and the University of Virginia quickly condensed the BCG report for classroom use in case discussions. It currently enjoys extensive use in first-term courses in Business Policy.

Of particular note in the BCG study, and in the subsequent Harvard Business School rendition, is the historical treatment of Honda.

The mix of competitors in the U.S. motorcycle market underwent a major shift in the 1960s. Motorcycle registrations increased from 575,000 in 1960 to 1,382,000 in 1965. Prior to 1960 the U.S. market was served mainly by Harley-Davidson of U.S.A., BSA, Triumph and Norton of U.K. and Moto-Guzzi of Italy. Harley was the market leader with total 1959 sales of $16.6 million. After the second world war, motorcycles in the U.S.A. attracted a very limited group of people other than police and army personnel who used motorcycles on the job. While most motorcyclists were no doubt decent people, groups of rowdies who went around on motorcycles and called themselves by such names as "Hell's Angels," "Satan's Slaves" gave motorcycling a bad image. Even leather jackets which were worn by motorcyclists as a protective device acquired an unsavory image. A 1953 movie called "The Wild Ones" starring a 650cc Triumph, a black leather jacket and Marlon Brando gave the rowdy motorcyclists wide media coverage. The stereotype of the motorcyclist was a leather-jacketed, teenage trouble-maker. Honda established an American subsidiary in 1959—American Honda Motor Company. This was in sharp contrast to other foreign producers who relied on distributors. Honda's marketing strategy was described in the 1963 annual report as "With its policy of selling, not primarily to confirmed motorcyclists but rather to members of the general public who had never before given a second thought to a motorcycle...." Honda started its push in the U.S. market with the smallest, lightweight motorcycles. It was superior to the lightweight being sold by Sears, Roebuck in America at that time. It had a three-speed transmission, an automatic clutch, five horsepower (the American cycle only had two and a half), an electric starter and step through frame for female riders. And it was easier to handle. The Honda machines sold for under $250 in retail compared with $1,000–$1,500 for the bigger American or British machines. Even at that early date Honda was probably superior to other competitors in productivity.

By June 1960 Honda's Research and Development effort was staffed with 700 designers/engineers. This might be contrasted with 100 engineers/draftsmen employed by ... (European and American competitors). In 1962 production per man-year was running at 159 units, (a figure not reached by Harley-Davidson until 1974). Honda's net fixed asset investment was $8170 per employee ... (more than twice its European and American competitors). With 1959 sales of $55 million Honda was already the largest motorcycle producer in the world.

Honda followed a policy of developing the market region by region. They started on the West Coast and moved eastward over a period of four-five years. Honda sold 2,500 machines in the U.S. in 1960. In 1961 they lined up 125 distributors and spent $150,000 on regional advertising. Their advertising was directed to the young families, their advertising theme was "You Meet the Nicest People on a Honda." This was a deliberate attempt to dissociate motorcycles from rowdy, Hell's Angels type people.

Honda's success in creating demand for lightweight motorcycles was phenomenal. American Honda's sales went from $500,000 in 1960 to $77 million in 1965. By 1966 the market share data showed the ascendancy of Japanese producers and their success in selling lightweight motorcycles.

Starting from virtually nothing in 1960, the lightweight motorcycles had clearly established their lead.[4]

	U.S. Market Share (%)
Honda	63
Yamaha	11
Suzuki	11
Harley-Davidson	4
BSA/Triumph and others	11

Quoting from the BCG report:

> The Japanese motorcycle industry, and in particular Honda, the market leader, present a [consistent] picture. The basic philosophy of the Japanese manufacturers is that high volumes per model provide the potential for high productivity as a result of using capital intensive and highly automated techniques. Their marketing strategies are therefore directed towards developing these high model volumes, hence the careful attention that we have observed them giving to growth and market share.

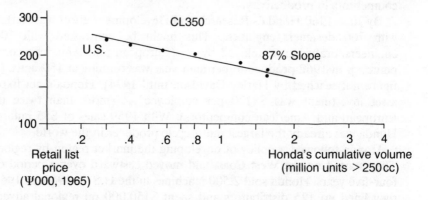

Source: BCG "Strategy Alternatives for the British Motorcycle Industry".

> The overall result of this philosophy over time has been that the Japanese have now developed an entrenched and leading position in terms of technology and production methods.... The major factors which appear to account for the Japanese superiority in both these areas are ... (specialized production systems, balancing engineering and market requirements, and the cost efficiency and reliability of suppliers).[5]

As evidence of Honda's strategy of taking position as low cost producer and exploiting economies of scale, other sources cite Honda's construction in 1959 of a plant to manufacture 30,000 motorcycles per month well ahead of existing demand at the time. (Up until then Honda's most popular models sold 2,000–3,000 units per month.)[6]

The overall picture depicted by the quotes above exemplifies the "strategy model." Honda is portrayed as a firm dedicated to being the low price producer, utilizing its dominant market position in Japan to force entry into the U.S. market, expanding that market by redefining a leisure class ("Nicest People") segment, and exploiting its comparative advantage via aggressive pricing and advertising. Richard Rumelt, writing the teaching note for the UCLA adaptation of the case states: "The fundamental contribution of BCG is not the experience curve per se but the ever-present assumption that differences in cost (or efficiency) are the fundamental components of strategy."[7]

The Organizational Process Perspective

On September 10, 1982, the six Japanese executives responsible for Honda's entry into the U.S. motorcycle market in 1959 assembled in Honda's Tokyo headquarters. They had gathered at my request to describe in fine grain detail the sequence of events that had led to Honda's ultimate position of dominance in the U.S. market.[8] All were in their sixties; three were retired. The story that unfolded, greatly abbreviated below, highlights miscalculation, serendipity, and organizational learning—counterpoints to the streamlined "strategy" version related earlier.

Any account of Honda's successes must grasp at the outset the unusual character of its founder, Sochiro Honda and his partner, Takeo Fujisawa. Honda was an inventive genius with a large ego and mercurial temperament, given to bouts of "philandering" (to use his expression).[9] In the formative stages of his company, Honda is variously reported to have tossed a geisha out a second-story window,[10] climbed inside a septic tank to retrieve a visiting supplier's false teeth (and subsequently placed the teeth in his mouth),[11] appeared inebriated and in costume before a formal presentation to Honda's bankers requesting financing vital to the firm's survival (the loan was denied),[12] hit a worker on the head with a wrench,[13] and stripped naked before his engineers to assemble a motorcycle engine.[14]

Post-war Japan was in desperate need of transportation. Motorcycle manufacturers proliferated, producing clip-on engines that converted bicycles into makeshift "mopeds." Honda was among these but it was not until he teamed up with Fujisawa in 1949 that the elements of a successful enterprise began to take shape. Fujisawa provided money as well as financial and marketing strengths. In 1950 their first D type motorcycle was introduced. They were, at that juncture, participating in a fragmented industry along with 247 other manufacturers. Other than its sturdy frame, this introductory product was unnoteworthy and did not enjoy great commercial success.[15]

Honda embodied a rare combination of inventive ability and ultimate self-confidence. His motivation was not primarily commercial. Rather, the company served as a vehicle to give expression to his inventive abilities. A successful company would provide a resource base to pursue, in Fujisawa's words, his "grandiose dream." Fujisawa continues, "There was no end to his pursuit of technology."[16]

Fujisawa, in an effort to save the faltering company, pressed Honda to abandon their noisy two-stroke engine and pursue a four-stroke design. The quieter four-stroke engines were appearing on competitive motorcycles, therefore threatening Honda with extinction. Mr. Honda balked.

But a year later, Honda stunned Fujisawa with a breakthrough design that doubled the horsepower of competitive four-stroke engines. With this innovation, the firm was off and putting, and by 1951 demand was brisk.[17] There was no organization, however, and the plant was chaotic.[18] Strong demand, however, required early investment in a simplified mass production process. As a result, *primarily* due to design advantages, and secondarily to production methods, Honda became one of the four or five industry leaders by 1954 with 15 percent market share.[19]

For Fujisawa, the engine innovation meant increased sales and easier access to financing. For Mr. Honda, the higher horsepower engine opened the possibility of pursuing one of his central ambitions in life—to race his motorcycle and win. Winning provided the ultimate confirmation of his design abilities. Racing success in Japan came quickly. As a result, in 1959 Honda raised his sights to the international arena and committed the firm to winning at Great Britain's Isle of Man—the "Olympics" of motorcycle racing. Again, Honda's inventive genius was called into play. Shifting most of the firm's resources into this racing effort, Honda embarked on studies of combustion that resulted in a new configuration of the combustion chamber that doubled horsepower and halved weight. Honda leapfrogged past European and American competitors—winning in one class, then another, winning the Isle of Man manufacturer's prize in 1959 and sweeping the first five positions by 1961.[20]

Fujisawa, throughout the fifties, sought to turn Honda's attention from his enthusiasm with racing to the more mundane requirements of running an enterprise. By 1956, as the innovations gained from racing had begun to pay off in vastly more efficient engines, Fujisawa pressed Honda to adapt this technology for a commercial motorcycle.[21] Fujisawa had a particular segment in mind. Most motorcyclists in Japan were male and the machines were used primarily as an alternative form of transportation to trains and buses. There were, however, a vast number of small commercial establishments in Japan that still delivered goods and ran errands on bicycles. Trains and buses were inconvenient for these activities. The purse-strings of these small enterprises were controlled by the Japanese wife—who resisted buying conventional motorcycles because they were expensive, dangerous, and hard to handle. Fujisawa challenged Honda: Can you use what you've learned from racing to come up with an inexpensive, safe-looking motorcycle that can be driven with one hand (to facilitate carrying packages).[22]

In 1958, the Honda 50cc Supercub was introduced—with an automatic clutch, three-speed transmission, automatic starter, and the safe, friendly look of a bicycle (without the stigma of the outmoded mopeds). Owing almost entirely to its high horsepower but *lightweight 50cc engine* (not to production efficiencies), it was affordable. Overnight, the firm was over-whelmed with orders. Engulfed by demand, they sought financing to build a new plant with a 30,000 unit per month capacity. "It wasn't a speculative investment," recalls one executive. "We had the proprietary technology, we had the market, and the demand was enormous."[23] (The plant was completed in mid-1960.) Prior to its opening, demand was met through makeshift, high cost, company-owned assembly and farmed-out assembly through subcontractors.[24] By the end of 1959, Honda had skyrocketed into first place among Japanese motorcycle manufacturers. Of its total sales that year of 285,000 units, 168,000 were Supercubs.[25]

Fujisawa utilized the Supercub to restructure Honda's channels of distribution. For many years, Honda had rankled under the two-tier distribution system that prevailed in the industry. These problems had been exacerbated by the fact that Honda was a late entry and had been carried as secondary line by distributors whose loyalties lay with their older manufacturers. Further weakening Honda's leverage, all manufacturer sales were on a consignment basis.

Deftly, Fujisawa had characterized the Supercub to Honda's distributors as "something much more like a bicycle than a motorcycle." The traditional channels, to their later regret, agreed. Under amicable terms Fujisawa began selling the Supercub directly to retailers—and primarily through bicycle shops. Since these shops were small and numerous (approximately 12,000 in Japan), sales on consignment were unthinkable. A cash-on-delivery system was installed, giving Honda significantly more leverage over its dealerships than the other motorcycle manufacturers enjoyed.[26]

The stage was now set for exploration of the U.S. market. Mr Honda's racing conquests in the late fifties had given substance to his convictions about his abilities. While still heavily occupied by the Isle of Man, success fueled his quest for new and different challenges.

To the onlooker from Japan, the American market was vast, untapped, and affluent. In addition, Honda had experimented with local Southeast Asian markets in 1957–58 with little success. With little disposable income and poor roads, total Asian exports had reached a meager 1,000 units in 1958.[27] The European market, while larger, was heavily dominated by its own name brand manufacturers, and the popular mopeds dominated the low price, low horsepower end. Spurred in part by ambition and in part by a process of deduction, Fujisawa and Honda focused attention on the United States.

Two Honda executives—the soon-to-be named president of American Honda, Kihachiro Kawashima and his assistant—arrived in the U.S. in late 1958. [Mr. Kihachiro Kawashima subsequently became Executive Vice President of Honda Motor Co., Ltd. Japan.] Their itinerary: San Francisco, Los Angeles, Dallas, New York, and Columbus. Mr. Kawashima recounts his impressions:

My first reaction after travelling across the United States was: How could we have been so stupid as to start a war with such a vast and wealthy country! My second reaction was discomfort. I spoke poor English. We dropped in on motorcycle dealers who treated us discourteously and in addition, gave the general impression of being motorcycle enthusiasts who, secondarily, were in business. There were only 3,000 motorcycle dealers in the United States at the time and only 1,000 of them were open five days a week. The remainder were open on nights and weekends. Inventory was poor, manufacturers sold motorcycles to dealers on consignment, the retailers provided consumer financing; after-sales service was poor. It was discouraging.

My other impression was that everyone in the United States drove an automobile—making it doubtful that motorcycles could ever do very well in the market. However, with 450,000 motorcycle registrations in the U.S. and 60,000 motorcycles imported from Europe each year it didn't seem unreasonable to shoot for 10 percent of the import market. I returned to Japan with that report.

In truth, we had no strategy other than the idea of seeing if we could sell something in the United States. It was a new frontier, a new challenge, and it fit the "success against all odds" culture that Mr. Honda had cultivated. I reported my impressions to Fujisawa—including the seat-of-the-pants target of trying, over several years, to attain a 10 percent share of U.S. imports. He didn't probe that target quantitatively. We did not discuss profits or deadlines for breakeven. Fujisawa told me if anyone could succeed, I could and authorized $1 million for the venture.

The next hurdle was to obtain a currency allocation from the Ministry of Finance. They were extraordinarily skeptical. Toyota had launched the Toyopet in the U.S. in 1958 and had failed miserably. "How could Honda succeed?" they asked. Months went by. We put the project on hold. Suddenly, five months after our application, we were given the go-ahead—but at only a fraction of our expected level of commitment. "You can invest $250,000 in the U.S. market," they said, "but only $110,000 in cash." The remainder of our assets had to be in parts and motorcycle inventory.

We moved into frantic activity as the government, hoping we would give up on the idea, continued to hold us to the July 1959 start-up timetable. Our focus, as mentioned earlier, was to compete with the European exports. We knew our products at the time were good but not far superior. Mr. Honda was especially confident of the 250cc and 305cc machines. The shape of the handlebar on these larger machines looked like the eyebrow of Buddha, which he felt was a strong selling point. Thus, after some discussion and with no compelling criteria for selection, we configured our start-up inventory with 25 percent of each of our four products—the 50cc Supercub and the 125cc, 250cc, and

305cc machines. In dollar value terms, of course, the inventory was heavily weighted toward the larger bikes.

The stringent monetary controls of the Japanese government together with the unfriendly reception we had received during our 1958 visit caused us to start small. We chose Los Angeles where there was a large second and third generation Japanese community, a climate suitable for motorcycle use, and a growing population. We were so strapped for cash that the three of us shared a furnished apartment that rented for $80 per month. Two of us slept on the floor. We obtained a warehouse in a run-down section of the city and waited for the ship to arrive. Not daring to spare our funds for equipment, the three of us stacked the motorcycle crates three high—by hand, swept the floors, and built and maintained the parts bin.

We were entirely in the dark the first year. We were not aware the motorcycle business in the United States occurs during a seasonable April-to-August window—and our timing coincided with the closing of the 1959 season. Our hard-learned experiences with distributorships in Japan convinced us to try to go to the retailers direct. We ran ads in the motorcycle trade magazine for dealers. A few responded. By spring of 1960, we had forty dealers and some of our inventory in their stores—mostly larger bikes. A few of the 250cc and 305cc bikes began to sell. Then disaster struck.

By the first week of April 1960, reports were coming in that our machines were leaking oil and encountering clutch failure. This was our lowest moment. Honda's fragile reputation was being destroyed before it could be established. As it turned out, motorcycles in the United States are driven much farther and much faster than in Japan. We dug deeply into our precious cash reserves to air freight our motorcycles to the Honda testing lab in Japan. Throughout the dark month of April, Pan Am was the only enterprise in the U.S. that was nice to us. Our testing lab worked twenty-four-hour days bench testing the bikes to try to replicate the failure. Within a month, a redesigned head gasket and clutch spring solved the problem. But in the meantime, events had taken a surprising turn.

Throughout our first eight months, following Mr. Honda's and our own instincts, we had not attempted to move the 50cc Supercubs. While they were a smash success in Japan (and manufacturing couldn't keep up with demand there), they seemed wholly unsuitable for the U.S. market where everything was bigger and more luxurious. As a clincher, we had our sights on the import market—and the Europeans, like the American manufacturers, emphasized the larger machines.

We used the Honda 50s ourselves to ride around Los Angeles on errands. They attracted a lot of attention. One day we had a call from a Sears buyer. While persisting in our refusal to sell through an intermediary, we took note of Sears's interest. But we still hesitated to push the 50cc bikes out of fear they might harm our image in a heavily macho market. But when the larger bikes started breaking, we had no choice. We let the 50cc bikes move. And surprisingly, the retailers who wanted to sell them weren't motorcycle dealers, they were sporting goods stores.

The excitement created by the Honda Supercub began to gain momentum. Under restrictions from the Japanese government, we were still on a cash basis. Working with our initial cash and inventory, we sold machines, reinvested in inventory, and sunk the profits into additional inventory and advertising. Our advertising tried to straddle the market. While retailers continued to inform us that our Supercub customers were normal everyday Americans, we hesitated to target toward this segment out of fear of alienating the high margin end of our business— sold through the traditional motorcycle dealers to a more traditional "black leather jacket" customer.[28]

Honda's phenomenal sales and share gains over the ensuing years have been previously reported. History has it that Honda "*redefined*" the U.S. motorcycle industry. In the view of American Honda's start-up team, this was an innovation they backed into—and reluctantly. It was certainly not the strategy they embarked on in 1959. As late as 1963, Honda was still working with its original Los Angeles advertising agency, its ad campaigns straddling all customers so as not to antagonize one market in pursuit of another.

In the spring of 1963, an undergraduate advertising major at UCLA submitted, in fulfillment of a routine course assignment, an ad campaign for Honda. Its theme: You Meet the Nicest People on a Honda. Encouraged by his instructor, the student passed his work on to a friend at Grey Advertising. Grey had been soliciting the Honda account—which with a $5 million a year budget was becoming an attractive potential client. Grey purchased the student's idea—on a tightly kept nondisclosure basis. Grey attempted to sell the idea to Honda.[29]

Interestingly, the Honda management team, which by 1963 had grown to five Japanese executives, was badly split on this advertising decision. The President and Treasurer favored another proposal from another agency. The Director of Sales, however, felt strongly that the Nicest People campaign was the right one—and his commitment eventually held sway. Thus, in 1963, through an inadvertent sequence of events, Honda came to adopt a strategy that directly identified and targeted that large untapped segment of the marketplace that has since become inseparable from the Honda legend.[30]

The Nicest People campaign drove Honda's sales at an even greater rate. By 1964, nearly one out of every two motorcycles sold was a Honda. As a result of the influx of medium income leisure class consumers, banks and other consumer credit companies began to finance motorcycles—shifting away from dealer credit, which had been the traditional purchasing mechanism available. Honda, seizing the opportunity of soaring demand for its products, took a courageous and seemingly risky position. Late in 1964, they announced that thereafter, they would cease to ship on a consignment basis but would require cash on delivery. Honda braced itself for revolt. While nearly every dealer questioned, appealed, or complained, none relinquished his franchise. In one fell swoop, Honda shifted the power relationship from the dealer to the manufacturer. Within three years, this would become the pattern for the industry.[31]

The "Honda Effect"

The preceding account of Honda's inroads in the U.S. motorcycle industry provides more than a second perspective on reality. It focuses our attention on different issues and raises different questions. What factors permitted two men as unlike one another as Honda and Fujisawa to function effectively as a team? What incentives and understandings permitted the Japanese executives at American Honda to respond to the market as it emerged rather than doggedly pursue the 250cc and 305cc strategy that Mr. Honda favored? What decision process permitted the relatively junior sales director to overturn the bosses' preferences and choose the Nicest People campaign? What values or commitment drove Honda to take the enormous risk of alienating its dealers in 1964 in shifting from a consignment to cash? In hindsight, these pivotal events all seem ho-hum common sense. But each day, as organizations live out their lives without the benefit of hindsight, few choose so well and so consistently.

The juxtaposed perspectives reveal what I shall call the "Honda Effect." Western consultants, academics, and executives express a preference for oversimplifications of reality and cognitively linear explanations of events. To be sure, they have always acknowledged that the "human factor" must be taken into account. But extensive reading of strategy cases at business schools, consultants' reports, strategic planning documents as well as the coverage of the popular press, reveals a widespread tendency to overlook the process through which organizations experiment, adapt, and learn. We tend to impute coherence and purposive rationality to events when the opposite may be closer to the truth. How an organization deals with miscalculation, mistakes, and serendipitous events *outside its field of vision is often crucial to success over time.* It is this realm that requires better understanding and further research if we are to enhance our ability to guide an organization's destiny.

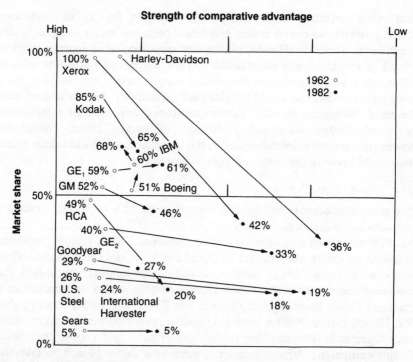

Markets defined as follows: Xerox: plain copiers; Harley-Davidson: motorcycles; Kodak: photographic film; IBM: mainframe computers; GE (General Electric)$_1$: generators; GE$_2$: electrical appliances (refrigerators); GM: passenger cars; Boeing: commercial widebody jet aircraft; RCA: color TVs; Goodyear: OEM tires; U.S. Steel: finished steel; International Harvester: farm tractors; Sears: mass-market retailing.

Figure 1 Market share and comparative advantage trends in thirteen key industries, 1962–1982

Perspective Two: Shifts in the Nature of Competition

The "microeconomic" and "miscalculation" models focus on different factors and attribute success to different causal events. Both perspectives are valuable; which one is more valuable depends, in part, on the environment in which an organization finds itself. Which view of reality is most appropriate in the environmental context of the eighties?

Two decades ago, American companies were, with rare exception, the flagships of the world's industrial armada. Across a diverse range of products and services, one found dominant American companies, each a world leader in its industry, each having carved out a seemingly impregnable strategic enclave. In twenty years, this picture has changed.

Let us consider the extent and nature of this change. Beginning with the

Department of Commerce's list of twenty major industries, eliminating those industries heavily regulated (e.g., transportation (railroads and airlines), utilities, banking); those industries selling primarily to government (e.g., defense and aerospace); and those industries where competition is primarily of a regional rather than a national nature (e.g., construction, food chains). We are left with thirteen industries within which firms compete on a national and often international basis and whose success is primarily self-determined (i.e., not heavily dependent upon geographical advantages or governmental regulation). Identifying the leading firm in each of these industries based on *Fortune* 500 rankings, we can trace their movements over the past twenty years—1962 through 1982—in terms of market share positions and gains or losses in comparative advantage. These provide the coordinates for Figure 1.

Individual companies focus on changes *within* their industrial environment. When we aggregate across industries, we observe trends impacting upon all participants. Figure 1 reveals that nine of the leading firms declined both in share and competitive advantage. Two additional companies lost competitive advantage while retaining parity in share. Only Boeing and IBM gained along the market share and competitive advantage dimensions. What factors account for this deterioration in competitive position over the past twenty years?

The early sixties was, above all, a period of industrial expansion. The Index of Industrial Production registered a 15.6 percent *increase* from 1960 to 1963, compared with a *decrease* of 9.1 from 1979 to 1982.[32] In nearly all sectors, there were increases in primary demand enabling participants to grow without doing so at one another's expense. Interest rates were low (prime rates averaging 4.5 percent in 1961, as compared with an average 18.87 percent in 1981), and investors embraced risks in their determination to capitalize on the optimism of the times. Technological change fuelled continual product and process innovation with the result that productivity increases followed almost effortlessly. Table 1 summarizes these and other factors.

Another ingredient important in securing a firm's competitive position was technological advantage. Bell Laboratories's patents for the first transistors guaranteed a seven-year strategic haven during which time it exploited high margins and recouped its investments. Xerox copiers and IBM's 360 enjoyed much the same competitive respite as did, in one form or another, nearly every other industrial leader. However, patents and proprietary process technology preserve advantage as long as the players of an industrial family honor the rules. This was to change as competition shifted from the domestic to the international arena.

The international pecking order of the sixties (that is, one nation's standing in relation to others), was determined by factors largely separate from the industrial sphere. National status was dependent on military

Table 1 Dramatic changes over two decades undermine secure market position

	Environmental shifts	
	From (1960s)	*To (1980s)*
Growth rates	• Rapid growth in most industries with room for most serious competitors	• Slowed growth or stagnation; squeezing incremental growth out of competition
Nature of competition	• Oligopolistic competitors in most industries	• Encroachment of international rivals
	• Primary focus on domestic markets and competitors	• Focus on international competition • Domestic scale economies finance penetration pricing in overseas markets
	• Implicit "rules" shared by domestic competitors foster stability	• New competitors each playing by different rules (e.g., niche vs. scale strategies) force continued innovation, price cutting, quality improvements all resulting in competitive instability
Expressions of nationalism	• National status dependent on military, technological leadership and level of involvement in international diplomatic dialogue	• The "new mercantilism" • International status and domestic prosperity linked to trade expansionism
	• Internal domestic focus	• Focus on international trade and economic linkages among trading partners
Economic environment	• Expansionistic, low interest/rates	• Stable or contracting economic climate
	• Risk seeking investor climate	• High interest rates • Risk adverse investor climate in most industries
	• Inflation	
Technology	• Rapid technological changes with numerous products early in life cycle	• Slowed technological change in many industries • Maturing products

Table 1 (continued)

	Environmental shifts	
	From (1960s)	*To (1980s)*
	• Patents serve to protect technological advantage with secure domestic	• Fierce international competitive surveillance and "reverse engineering" dilute patent protection and rapidly equalize technological advance
IMPLICATIONS:	• Few secure enclaves. • Changing rules. • Intense competition from international rivals.	• Relative stability, security.

strength, technological leadership (measured by Nobel prizes and mega-feats such as space shots), Olympic gold medals, and a country's centrality in the world geopolitical dialogue. NATO, not GNP, was the dominant acronym at the time.

The environment fostered set piece competition. To oversimplify, oligopolistic competitors focused primarily on domestic markets, participants shared implicit rules. These factors fostered competitive stability—abundantly the case in automotive manufacturing and consumer electronics. That is not to say that some industries, such as steel, had not begun to encounter competitive pressures. But relatively speaking, from the post-war period through the mid-sixties, a strategic enclave, once established was defended with comparative ease.

The arts of war have been forever at the mercy of changing armaments; technology changes faster than beliefs. Each leap—from arrow to rifle to infrared seeking missile—renders an era of military knowledge obsolete and imposes a painful reexamination and transition. Military science is the kin of managerial science. The stable industrial world culminating in the sixties was accompanied by a body of managerial beliefs which in the hindsight of the eighties, endowed us with the tactics of Gallipoli in a theater more akin to Vietnam.

The perceived nature of competition in the sixties made strategy the king of management functions. Conceptual rather than operational thinking prevailed, giving impetus to management consulting firms armed with matrices, experience curves, and other microeconomic paraphernalia. Business schools proliferated as did courses emphasizing the quantitative sciences in an era when success was secured via bold-stroke actions rather than nuance. Qualitative refinements in organizational process and operations management were frosting on the managerial cake. The danger, as our military analogue implies, is that such beliefs, once internalized, tend to persist beyond their time—even when environmental circumstances render them inappropriate.

In the late sixties, research at Harvard Business School exposed an industrial anomaly that has proven a precursor of our times.[33] The major home appliance industry (refrigerators, stoves, dishwashers, washers, and dryers) was revealed to defy the conventional wisdom of market behaviour. Dominated by large oligopolistic competitors (Sears, General Electric, Westinghouse) the industry's most profitable participants were its smaller firms (such as Maytag). Whereas other oligopolistic markets fostered stability and protection for their dominant members, in this topsy-turvy industry, the large manufacturers (e.g., G.E.) were squeezed on one hand by continual price pressures from retailers (e.g., Sears) and on the other by the continuing technological innovation of small manufacturers (e.g., Tappan and Maytag). The consumer was the prime beneficiary: quality increased, technological innovation blossomed, and prices in real dollars remained steady or declined.

The explanation for this harsh competitive behavior lay in the asymmetry of the participants. Sears, a mass retailer, competed via price leadership; G.E., the manufacturer, competed on quality leadership, innovation parity, and required market share to support its production economies; smaller survivors lived by their technological wits and innovated in order to keep G.E. and Sears at bay. (By achieving sufficient product differentiation, they were able to justify higher margins.)

Enter the 1980s

We have read, ad nauseam, about the industrial climate of this decade, of the iron law of economic stagnation by which one firm's gain is via another's loss. We have read, too, of higher interest rates and more conservative investors. These are no doubt contributing factors. But in addition, slower technological change in many industries has been accompanied by intense competitive surveillance and rapid technological transfer. Particularly across international boundaries, patent protection is mitigated by reverse engineering and outright infringement. As a result, technology is rapidly equalized.

Another powerful, but often underemphasized, factor in these environmental shifts, is the increasing centrality of the "new mercantilism." National status and, indeed, a nation's domestic prosperity are linked directly to trade. Balance of payments, exchange rates, GNP growth, and unemployment are all inextricably intertwined. Heightened national self-interest has placed the spotlight on the success of each country's contestants in key industries. One firm's competitive response is thus linked to a coordinated national response—involving diplomatic exchanges, threats of trade sanctions, central bank behavior, and protective domestic pricing.

In aggregate, the forces depicted have drastically reshaped competitive activity. Most importantly, they have transformed a great many stable and secure domestic markets into battle zones that more closely resemble the major home appliance example cited earlier. International competitors seem more prone to play by different rules. Some invest to achieve scale economies, some for quality leadership, others for price leadership, still others pursue a niche strategy stressing innovation. Under these circumstances, there is no impregnable stategic stance. As in the home appliance example, every participant, in order to survive, behaves in a way that destabilizes his counterparts. Innovators achieve a breakthrough, draw off customers, and start a share swing. To avoid losing share, the most cost efficient producer must follow, rendering his existing product and process technology obsolete. The low price strategy of still another player, content to follow in technology, creates a cost/price squeeze on the rest ... forcing further innovation and the cycle repeats itself.

Survival for all but the most favored players requires a new competitive response and new organizational capabilities. For those remaining in the upper left-hand corner of Figure 1, defense of the status quo is sufficient. (IBM and Boeing, for example, seem to need to do no more than what they have always done.) For those with high share and weakening competitive advantage, the microeconomic concepts of scale efficiencies are highly applicable. (Insofar as price is *the* key success factor, being larger and re-investing to sustain low price position assures continued success.) As long as a firm's position remains secure, much of what the old strategy model prescribes still obtains.

But for the vast majority of the firms charted in Figure 1, the shift is down scale, with weakening share position and weakening competitive advantage. For these firms, future success is more dependent on flexibility. In particular, three organizational factors become important:

- operational efficiency
- incremental product improvements, and
- the capacity to sense opportunity and execute an effective response.

For most of the firms in Figure 1, these are the key success factors for the eighties. Older, generalized ways of thinking about strategy must expand to adequately grapple with this new challenge.

Perspective Three: The Case for Multiple Perspectives

The argument developed thus far is as follows: first, traditional biases favor analytical and microeconomic tools shaping corporate strategy. Secondly, strategy alone, even if more broadly defined, is not adequate to achieve the levels of innovation and responsiveness that competition in the eighties demands. This is not to assert that management thinking has been solely limited to formulations of strategy alone. In fact, if we pick up *Business Week, Forbes,* or *Fortune* the odds are high stories about efforts to change or turnaround will focus on not one but three "essentials": a new *strategy,* a *reorganization* to fit the strategy, and a new or rejuvenated *system* to track the factors meriting central attention.

We need a still broader framework. A 1972 study comparing a dozen Japanese subsidiaries in the United States with a dozen American counter-parts produced a surprising finding: the Japanese firms had no monopoly on high productivity. In fact, a near-equal mix of Japanese and American firms shared these honors.[34] When the high performing firms (regardless of national ownership) were aggregated, they were found to share much in common. Most notably, they explicitly focused on more than strategy, structure, and systems:

- they paid conscious and concrete attention to management style and had devised ways of transforming style from the intangible realm of personality into a pragmatic instrument of executive direction;
- they did not relegate the hiring and socialization of new employees to a haphazard process governed by personnel departments: instead these firms shared amazing commonality in the step-by-step process through which they welded employees into a productive and committed work-force; and
- they paid attention to the firm's overarching value system, linking its relationship to employees, customer, and society as a whole.

In sum, in addition to 1) strategy, 2) structure, and 3) systems, the high performing firms paid equal attention to 4) style, 5) staff (i.e., their human resources), and 6) shared values. Their use of all *six* of these levers, and their ability to get them all to mesh together, contributed centrally to squeezing more out of their organizations in terms of innovations, respon-siveness, and operational efficiency. Let us examine each dimension in sequence.

Perspective # 1: Strategy

An earlier section has addressed the shortcomings of the narrowly defined microeconomic strategy model. The Japanese avoid this pitfall by adopting a broader notion of "strategy." In our recent awe of things Japanese, most Americans forget that the original products of the Japanese automotive manufacturers badly missed the mark. Toyota's Toyopet was square, sexless, and mechanically defective. It failed miserably, as did Datsun's first several entries into the U.S. market. More recently, Mazda miscalculated badly with its first rotary engine and nearly went bankrupt. Contrary to myth, the Japanese did not from the onset embark on a strategy to seize the high-quality small car market. They manufactured what they were accustomed to building in Japan and tried to sell it abroad. Their success, as any Japanese automotive executive will readily agree, did not result from a bold insight by a few big brains at the top. On the contrary, success was achieved by senior managers humble enough not to take their initial strategic positions too seriously. What saved Japan's near-failures was the cumulative impact of "little brains" in the form of salesmen and dealers and production workers, all contributing incrementally to the quality and market position these companies enjoy today. Middle and upper management saw their primary task as guiding and orchestrating this input from below rather than steering the organization from above along a predetermined strategic course.

The Japanese don't use the term "strategy" to describe a crisp business definition or competitive master plan. They think more in terms of "strategic accommodation," or "adaptive persistence," underscoring their belief that corporate direction evolves from an incremental adjustment to unfolding events. Rarely, in their view, does one leader (or a strategic planning group) produce a bold strategy that guides a firm unerringly. Far more frequently, the input is from below. It is this ability of an organization to move information and ideas from the bottom to the top and back again in continuous dialogue that the Japanese value above all things. As this dialogue is pursued, what in hindsight may be "strategy" evolves. In sum, "strategy" is defined as "all the things necessary for the successful functioning of organization as an adaptive mechanism." Skillful use of the other levers help make adaptation possible.

Perspective # 2: Organizational Structure

For many American managers, reorganizing is the ultimate quick fix. Rearrange the boxes; never mind whether you change behavior inside the boxes.

There is no contention here that how one clusters various activities in an organization is unimportant to getting work done. The problem is, as with *any* of the other six factors taken in isolation, organizational structure is necessary but insufficient. The Coca-Cola Company spent the decades of the 1960s and 1970s in a continuous state of reorganization. The field force was decentralized, matrixed, recentralized. Pepsi-Cola steadily gained ground. Not until the eighties, under steadier guidance and with meticulous attention given to support *systems*, field management *style*, recruitment and training of *staff*, and *shared values*, did Coca-Cola begin to recapture its leadership against its major competitor.

Organizational fads, especially in rapid succession of one another, are a strong indicator of naiveté. No survey of American enterprise over the past two decades could fail to notice the succession of structural fads that have come and gone, each promoting itself as the optimum solution. There was functional organization, then the decentralization of the fifties and sixties, followed by the matrix format of the late sixties and seventies—organizational equivalents of a face-lift—and often just as cosmetic. These solutions almost always failed to live up to expectations. The boxes changed but most everything else stayed the same.

One's ability to get things done in corporations seldom depends upon one's job description and formal authority alone. A great part of one's efficacy stems from knowledge, proven track record, reputation and the trust and confidence of others. These factors are especially important at the *interfaces* between one's job and someone else's. No matter how well conceived an organization is structured, these interfaces between functions exist and successful managers build bridges across them with informal relationships. When a reorganization occurs it destroys these relationships. Not surprisingly, organizations then require six to eighteen months for its members to reestablish new interfaces. Frequent reorganizations are very traumatic as they continually disrupt these essential networks before they become fully rooted.

Reorganization is like open heart surgery—sometimes it is necessary. But if a patient can contain a heart ailment through adequate rest, regular exercise, and by not smoking, it is preferable to the risks of the operating table. Organizations would do well to use other mechanisms to get their existing structure to work whenever possible—rather than resorting too quickly to a structural remedy.

The structural "lever" encounters a fatal flaw in that it imposes a two-dimensional way of thinking upon a phenomenon that cannot be captured in two dimensions. The givens of organizations are ambiguity, uncertainty, imperfection, and paradox. Structural remedies, by their unambiguous two-dimensional nature, impose a falsehood—organizational charts:

- suggest a clarity in reporting relationships that, in fact, retain significant elements of interpersonal *ambiguity*;
- announce finite changes that are, in fact, the outcome of an *uncertain* stream of events;
- suggest mechanistic linkages that deny systemic and interpersonal *imperfections*; and
- by the very act of representing *one* organizational solution (rather than another) deny an inherent *paradox*—that paradox being that today's solution to how one organizes, however appropriate, sows the seeds for the next generation of problems.

Structural solutions are simply not fine enough instruments in and of themselves to assure these delicate tradeoffs. To succeed, structure requires reinforcement from the other managerial factors.

Perspective # 3: Systems

Systems pertain to such things as forms and computer printouts, to how information flows up, down, and across the hierarchy of an organization. Systems to a large extent prescribe how communication occurs—and as a result, tend to configure how appropriately and quickly an organization can respond. Senior management can revise a strategy by a simple decree. Likewise, a structural reorganization is readily conceived and announced. But systems often remain unchanged. Stop to consider the forms we fill in, the reports we receive and promulgate, the incentive systems that reward us, and the procedures that guide us and regulate our lives. Systems condition us like mice in a maze; they gobble up an enormous portion of our discretionary energies. They are not chic, they are not pretty, they're not fast in how they work or how they change. (In fact, their maintenance in organizations is regarded as a low-status activity.) But systems insidiously and powerfully influence how people spend their lives at work each day.

"Hard copy" systems focus on things written in ink on paper—procedures that are written down, computer printouts, tables of numbers, forms, and so forth. In addition, all organizations have informal systems, that is, unwritten understandings that employees internalize about "how business gets done around here." Every organization has unwritten habits and routines. Two important ones are systems for conflict resolution and meeting formats. All organizations evolve rules about how one deals with conflict. In some organizations, it is dealt with openly and directly; in others it is handled in a roundabout way. Likewise, most organizations develop acceptable patterns for meetings. Informal rules provide guidelines as to who talks, who listens, whether presentations are formal monologues or informal dialogues, whether presenters use models and data with lots of analysis, whether they focus on the competition, market assumptions, or the bottom line. Informal systems also determine who gets mentored and the legitimate avenues for favoritism. Informal criteria are usually the first to signal fast-track candidates. These largely unseen and unwritten rules account for a great deal.

The Japanese culture pays attention to informal systems. A great many of the most important rules are implicit. There are rituals for bowing and for who has to bow most deeply, for gift giving, and for eating. Japanese life, to a much greater extent than is true in the Western world, is regulated by these unwritten rituals. As a result, survival in Japanese society requires a certain degree of astuteness at perceiving these unwritten rules. This contributes to the ability of Japanese managers to read the unwritten rules of their organization as clearly as most Westerners can read a balance sheet. Not surprisingly, they expect the informal rules to mesh with the formal ones. In most American organizations, we are far less conscious of whether this meshing occurs and, as a result, many of our formal systems are undermined by the informal ones. In summary, fuller and more meticulous attention to both formal and informal systems is a precondition to improved organizational functioning.

Perspective # 4: Style

A manager's style breathes life into strategy and systems. Regrettably, most readers equate style with certain personality traits. Once so defined, "style" is relegated to the idiosyncratic and intangible domain of psychology.

A most useful way of thinking about style is to equate it to how a manager allocates time and attention. Henry Mintzberg once researched the managerial span of attention.[36] The average length of time spent on any one thing is nine minutes. Management time is chaotic, fragmented, and filled with interruptions. This is the nature of managerial work. Nonetheless, from that chaos subordinates perceive a pattern, whether intended or not. Subordinates observe how bosses allocate their time, what issues really capture their attention, and from this they interpolate what the boss really cares about.

The three most powerful mechanisms for conveying time and attention messages are within an arm's length of where one sits each day. One of them is the in-basket, another is the telephone, and the third is one's calendar. What goes into the pending tray and yellows with age and what items get turned around immediately? What things get circled, and what comments are written in the margins? Is the "metamessage" of style—cost? quality? budget overruns? new product innovation? The people down the line read these messages with uncanny accuracy.

Consider the telephone. Who gets calls? Who doesn't? What question does the boss ask? What behavior is complimented? What draws criticisms, and what doesn't draw comments at all? What is the cumulative pattern that derives from the way the boss uses the phone?

Lastly the calendar. Who gets in, and who's screened out? When the boss is outside the office, where is he—with the controllers, customers, on the production line?

In aggregate, the calendar, the in-basket, and the telephone tell us a lot about one's style. "Style" defined as symbolic behavior provides every manager with a potent lever of influence and we need not transform our personalities to use it. The effective employment of this managerial lever results from nothing less or more than the self-discipline to allocate our time and attention to *do* what we *say* our priorities are.

Perspective # 5: Staff

There is a set of consistent steps that organizations go through to develop a cadre of committed and productive employees. IBM and Procter & Gamble, each in very different ways, do this well. First of all, they target malleable applicants just beginning or very early in their careers. They invest in careful selection. They avoid overselling the candidate and hiding blemishes. They allow the applicant to see rather clearly what the firm is like, permitting applicants to deselect themselves. In addition, of course, the firm plays its part in screening out those who don't fit the mold.

Socialization process begins in the trenches. No employee skips this step. One needs to learn the territory via immersion in the basics of the industry. It's like the infantry: one has to learn to shoot a gun, dig a foxhole, and hit a target.

Next comes coherent, frequently spaced, and predictable rewards. IBM sets quotas that 80 percent of its sales force can reach, then provides detailed and frequent performance reviews to stretch each candidate beyond to reach his own potential. At IBM, almost everyone on the marketing side has to be able to sell computers and keep the customer happy; one doesn't get promoted otherwise, no matter how good one is at other things. Procter & Gamble establishes a six-rung performance ladder that every successful professional candidate is expected to climb within the first two years. The reward systems are unambiguous and generally unbeatable. This clarity and impartiality, it should be noted, derives from *systems* measures and incentives that are honed for simplicity. At P&G it's: What have you done for market share? What are you doing for profits? At IBM it's: What have you sold? Is the customer satisfied?

Nothing enforces reward systems as powerfully as social leverage. Every high performing firm in the sample had periodic get-togethers in which results were reviewed across one's peer group: The boss would start with one person, ask for his report or result and go around the circle. It creates a powerful incentive. The participant finding himself at the bottom one week is powerfully motivated to avoid that embarrassment the next.

We have noted that socialization is sparked by a shared boot camp experience among a cadre of carefully selected young employees. It is strengthened by the social lever of peer comparisons and group norms and reinforced by reward systems that establish unequivocal standards of performance. Yet a fourth support derives from reinforcing folklore. Every organization has a folklore about watershed events or actions. Odds are high, if we listen carefully, that employees can summarize in one or two pithy sentences the essence of what they interpret the folklore to be. When the moral of the stories are inconsistent with what management is striving to achieve, folklore breeds cynicism and a wait-and-see attitude. Folklore acts as a guiding theory of how the firm really works. As such, it powerfully influences how employees respond to management's initiatives.

Last among the determinants of a coherent and committed staff is the availability of consistent role models. There is no more powerful way for instructing younger members of an organization than role models who present a consistent picture of what a person needs to be like to be a winner. Amazingly, many organizations leave role models to chance. The result is a mixed and confusing picture: one promotion seems related to people skills; another seems to underscore office politics; still another honors a reclusive financial wizard. There is no clear pattern. No training program in existence can instruct more powerfully than consistent role models.

Effective socialization requires consistency and meticulous attention to all the ingredients we have discussed. When managed carefully, it promotes behavioral congruence and cohesiveness. For some, this smacks of an Orwellian nightmare. For others it is ho-hum common sense. Nonetheless, most organizations do it very badly, and our outstanding organizations tend to do it well.

The socialization process described is found in most self-sustaining Japanese, American, and European companies. Its primary dividend is the coherence it provides about "how we do business around here." As such, it greatly enhances the strategic process by facilitating the dialogue up and down the hierarchy. Senior managers who shared the same socialization process and common career experiences as those in the field, can communicate with the field in a kind of shorthand. Remember: organizational responsiveness relies on effective communication with minimum politics and the minimal friction loss resulting from conflicting agendas. A meticulous socialization process directly serves this objective.

Perspective # 6: Shared Values[37]

Shared values refer to the overarching value system that ties the purposes of the corporation to the customer, society, and higher order human values. They do not pertain to economic goals such as profit, sales, R.O.I., or market share. For example, IBM's Thomas Watson once stated: "We must be prepared to change all the things we are in order to remain competitive in the environment, but we must never change our three basic beliefs: 1) Respect for the dignity of the individual, 2) Offering the best customer service in the world, and 3) Excellence." In a similar vein, AT&T's value system has for ninety years emphasized 1) "Universal" service, 2) Fairness in handling personnel matters, 3) A belief that work should be held in balance with commitments to one's family and community, and 4) Relationships (i.e., from one manager to another). These four factors are deemed essential in getting things done in a large highly structured company. What makes IBM's or AT&T's value systems so important is that they are not empty slogans. They are deeply internalized. It is hard to talk to an employee of one of these organizations at any length before they surface in one way or another.

What does a strong set of shared values accomplish? It provides a kind of "magnetic north" for an organization which keeps it true to its commitments to employees, the customer, and society. The problem with secular economic values is that their ends often justify inappropriate means: in order to achieve sales or R.O.I. objectives an executive may cut corners on customer service or treat employees in a capricious manner. Having a "magnetic north" helps define the permissible range of behavior in such circumstances. It acts as a kind of a "tie breaker," assisting an employee in making a close call, tilting him or her in the direction that the boss would want taken even though the boss isn't there to personally guide the decision.

Employment involves a social contract as well as a contract prescribing the exchange of labor for capital. In many Western organizations, that contract, while never explicit, often assumes little trust by either party in the other. If the only basis for the relation of company and employee is an instrumental one, it should not be surprising that many people in our organizations do what they must do to get their paycheck but little more. Shared values that concern themselves with the development and wellbeing of employees establish the moral context for this social contract. If such shared values are consistently honored, then employees tend to identify more fully with the company. They see the firm's interest and their own as more congruent and tend to invest themselves more fully in the organization.

Most consultants will confirm that they have been called in to solve a client's problem only to discover in the course of conducting interviews that someone in the client organization already had the solution. But because communication channels were blocked, or, more often, because the individual with the good idea was "turned off" and convinced that the organization wouldn't listen, no initiative was taken. The potential initiator hesitated to invest himself, in the last analysis, because trying is linked to caring, and history had taught him that the firm was not worth caring that much about. We begin to see here the direct connection between shared values and an organization's ability to tap into the "little brains."

Without a doubt, the most significant outcome of the way Japanese organizations manage themselves is that they are better at getting employees to be alert, to look for opportunities to do things better, and to strive by virtue of each small contribution to make the company succeed. It is like building a pyramid or watching a colony of ants: thousands of "little people" doing "little" things, *all with the same basic purpose*, can move mountains.

A recent study of product innovation in the scientific instruments and tool machinery industries indicates that 80 percent of all product innovations are initiated by the customer.[38] The majority of ideas doesn't flow from R&D labs down but from the customer up. To be sure, customers don't do the actual inventing, but their inquiries and complaints plant the seeds for improvements. Given these statistics, it matters a lot whether a company's sales force and others operating out at the tentacles of its field system are vigilant. They need to be open to new ideas *and* willing to initiate within their organization. Here is a key to success of many Japanese companies. We saw this occurring at American Honda. Staying alert and taking entrepreneurial initiative were major tenets of the Honda value system. The Japanese executives at American Honda could count on the fact that if they "erred" in these directions, they were acting as top management would want them to.

To be sure, the case for shared values can be overstated. Self-sustaining firms tend to have a *style* of management that is open to new ideas, ways of handling *staff* that encourage innovation, *systems* that are customer focused and that reward innovation, *skills* at translating ideas into action and so forth. But the ideas don't flow unless the employee *believes* in the corporation and identifies enough with its purposes to "give up" his good ideas. Further, any of us who work in organizations knows how hard they are to move. One has to *really* believe an organization *cares* in order to invest the energy and effort needed to help it change. Such commitment derives from shared values. And if we look at outstanding American firms that have a sustained track record of keeping up with or ahead of competition, we see this to be the case. Hewlett-Packard, Procter & Gamble, 3M, Boeing, Caterpillar are examples. Each has a highly developed value system that causes its employees to identify strongly with the firm. Perhaps the intense loyalty that these firms inspire is just an interesting idiosyncrasy. I believe, on the contrary, that this bond of shared values is fundamental to all of the rest. It is probably the most underpublicized "secret weapon" of great self-sustaining companies.

Conclusion

The intent of the "strategy model" has always been to assess the relationship of a firm with its environment, and identify the key elements of the managerial mix that are relevant to an effective organizational response. Given this charter to view the firm and its environment as an organic whole, our challenge is to develop a more adequate model. The central contention of this paper is that six dimensions are better than one or two or even three. Strategy, structure, and systems are not enough.

A multiple perspective disciplines us against the cognitive and perceptual biases that produce the "Honda Effect." It keeps us honest by drawing us into the interior of organization, forcing us to focus on the fine grain details that drive an effective strategic process. So doing, we learn how each of the S dimensions goes back in history—how the *strategies* that have been attempted, the firm's history of *reorganizations,* the *systems* that have been layered one upon another, the different *styles* of former leaders, and so forth—how each contributes to the legacy of what the firm is today and what stands in the way of moving it forward. Finally, attention to multiple dimensions causes us to grapple with the interdependence of each—that neither strategy nor structure nor any of the factors stands alone. Change efforts that shift only one or two of the factors and leave the remainder alone almost always fail. Only when we move on the multiple fronts across all six factors do we achieve lasting change. This has powerful implications for diagnosis and for practice.

References

1. Joseph L. Bower, *Managing the Resource Allocation Process*, Division of Research, Graduate School of Business Administration, Harvard University, Cambridge, Massachusetts, 1970, pp. 7–8.

2. A recent set of articles have begun to address this problem. See R. H. Hayes and W. J. Abernathy, "Managing Our Way to Economic Decline," *Harvard Business Review* (July/August 1980), p. 67; see also R. H. Hayes, and J. G. Garvin, "Managing As If Tomorrow Mattered," *Harvard Business Review* (May/June 1982), p. 71.

3. Boston Consulting Group, *Strategy Alternatives for the British Motorcycle Industry*, Her Majesty's Stationery Office, London, 30 July 1975, p. XIV.

4. D. Purkayastha, "Note on the Motorcycle Industry—1975," 9-578-210, Harvard Business School, Cambridge, Massachusetts, Rev. 1/81, p. 5, 10, 11, 12.

5. Boston Consulting Group, *Strategy Alternatives*, p. 59; also p. 40.

6. Tetsuo Sakiya, *Honda Motor: The Men, The Management, The Machines* (Tokyo, Japan: Kadonsha International, 1982), p. 119.

7. Richard P. Rumelt, "A Teaching Plan for *Strategy Alternatives for the British Motorcycle Industry*," *Japanese Business: Business Policy*, The Japan Society, New York, NY (1980), p. 2.

8. Anon. *Honda: A Statistical View*, Overseas Public Relations Department of Honda Motor Co., Ltd., Tokyo, Japan (1982), p. 11.

9. Tetsuo Sakiya, "The Story of Honda's Founders," *Asahi Evening News*, June 1–August 29, 1979, Series #19, Series #12; also Series #10, Series #2 and 3.

10. Interviews with Honda executives, Tokyo, Japan, July 1980.

11. Sakiya, *Honda Motor*, p. 69; also Sakiya, "Honda's Founders," Series #4.

12. Sakiya, "Honda's Founders," Series #7 and 8.

13. Sakiya, *Honda Motor*, p. 72.

14. Sakiya, "Honda's Founders," Series #2.

15. Sakiya, *Honda Motor*, pp. 65–69; Sakiya, "Honda's Founders," Series #6.

16. Sakiya, *Honda Motor*, p. 73.

17. Ibid, pp. 71–72.

18. Ibid, p. 71.

19. Data provided by Honda Motor Company, Tokyo, Japan, September 10–12, 1982.

20. Sakiya, "Honda's Founders," Series #11.

21. Ibid, Series #13; also Sakiya, *Honda Motor*, p. 117.

22. Sakiya, "Honda's Founders," Series #11.

23. Richard T. Pascale, Interviews with Honda executives, Tokyo, Japan, September 10, 1982.

24. Ibid.

25. Data provided by Honda Motor Company.

26. Pascale interviews.

27. Ibid.

28. Ibid.

29. Ibid.

30. Ibid.

31. Ibid.

32. The U.S. Federal Reserve Board's "Index of Industrial Production," based on 235 different data series, registered a 15.6% increase (from 66.2 to 76.5) from 1960 to 1963 compared with a 9.1% decrease (from 152.5 to 138.6) from 1979 to 1982.

33. Michael Hunt, "Strategy in the Electric Appliance Industry" (Unpublished Ph.D. dissertation, Harvard Graduate School of Business Administration, Cambridge, Massachusetts, 1971). Also see Michael Hunt, "Teaching Note on the Home Appliance Series," Harvard Graduate School of Business Administration, Cambridge, Massachusetts, 1971.

34. Richard T. Pascale, and A.G. Athos, *The Art of Japanese Management* (New York, NY: Simon & Schuster, 1981).

35. Development of the managerial implications of structure, systems, style, and staff draw heavily on the ideas of Thomas J. Peters. Also see R. H. Waterman, T. J. Peters, and J. R. Phillips, "Structure Is Not Organization," *Business Horizons,* No. 80302 (June 1980).

36. Henry Mintzberg, *The Nature of Managerial Work* (New York, NY: Harper & Row, 1973).

37. Much of this material on shared values is built upon the ideas of Anthony G. Athos. See Pascale and Athos, *The Art of Japanese Management.*

38. Eric von Hippel, "Users as Innovators, *Technology Review* (January 1978) pp. 31–39.

4

Strategic Management in Multinational Companies[*]

Yves L. Doz[†]

[*]Source: *Sloan Management Review*, 21 (Winter 1980), pp. 27–46.

The evolution of multinational companies (MNCs) over the last decade has been characterized by a growing conflict between the requirements for economic survival and success (the *economic* imperative) and the adjustments made necessary by the demands of host governments (the *political* imperative). The lowering of trade barriers and the substantial economies of scale still available in many industries combined with vigorous competition from low cost exporters push the MNCs toward the integration and rationalization of their activities among various countries.[1] Yet, the very international interdependence created by freer trade and MNC rationalization make individual countries more vulnerable to external factors and their traditional domestic economic policies less effective.[2] As a result, most governments turn more and moe to specific sectorial policies implemented through direct negotiations with the companies involved and through incentives tailored to them.[3] Both the economic and political imperatives thus take on increasing importance in the management of the multinationals.

This article, based on intensive field research of the management processes in about a dozen MNCs, analyzes *strategies and administrative processes* used by MNCs to reconcile the conflicting economic and political imperatives. Findings are presented in four sections. First, MNC strategies to respond to the dual imperatives are described and contrasted. Second, conditions under which MNCs are likely to find one or another strategy most suitable for individual businesses are reviewed. Third, the interaction between strategies and the nature of internal management processes is analyzed. Fourth, implications for the management of inter-dependencies between businesses in diversified multinationals are outlined. In the conclusion, means to increase the overall managerial capability of the company are explored.

Multinational Strategies

Faced with the conflict between the economic and political imperatives within a business, MNCs can respond in several ways. Some companies clearly respond first to the economic imperatives, and follow a worldwide (or regional)[4] business strategy where the activities in various countries are integrated and centrally managed. Other companies forgo the economic benefits of integration and let their subsidiaries adjust to the demands of their host government (as if they were national companies), thus clearly giving the upper hand to the political imperative. Finally, some companies try to leave their strategy unclear and reap benefits from economic integration and political responsiveness, in turn, or find compromises between the two. These three strategies are described in this section.

Worldwide Integration Strategy

Some companies choose to respond to the economic imperative and improve their international competitiveness. For companies that already have extensive manufacturing operations in several countries, the most attractive solution is to integrate and rationalize their activities among these countries. Individual plants are to provide only part of the product range (but for sales in all subsidiaries), thereby achieving greater economies of scale.[5] Plants can also be specialized by stages in the production process, and can be located in various countries according to the cost and availability of production factors for each stage (energy, labor, raw materials, skills).[6] Texas Instruments's location of labor-intensive semiconductor finishing activities in Southeast Asia, or Ford's and GM's Europe-wide manufacturing rationalization, as well as their investments in Spain, illustrate this integration strategy.

Extensive transshipments of components and finished products between subsidiaries located in different countries result from such a strategy. Integration also involves the development of products acceptable on a worldwide basis. The "world car" concept pushed by GM, Ford, and Japanese exporters is an example of this approach. The driving principle of this integration strategy is the reduction of unit costs and the capture of large sales volumes; in industries where economies of scale are significant and not fully exploited within the size of national markets, it can bring sizable productivity advantages. For instance, Ford's unit direct manufacturing costs in Europe were estimated to be well below those of national competitors supplying a comparable car range. In industries where dynamic economies of scale are very strong (such as semiconductors), the cost level differences between such leaders as Texas Instruments and smaller national firms were significant. Similarly, IBM was believed to have costs significantly lower than its competitors.[7]

Where integration brought substantial cost advantages over competitors, the integrated firms could allocate part of the benefits from their higher internal efficiency to incur "good citizenship" costs in the host countries, and still remain competitive with non-integrated firms. Some companies had a policy of full employment, balanced internal trade among countries, and performance of R&D in various countries. Such a policy may lead to less than optimal decisions, in a short-term financial sense, as it has some opportunity costs (for instance, the location of new plants and research centers in countries where a company sells more than it buys, instead of in low wage or low manufacturing cost countries). However, such a policy may also be the key to host countries' long-term acceptance of companies as leading worldwide corporations.

The benefits of integration not only enable the MNC to be better tolerated thanks to its ability to incur higher good citizenship costs, but integration itself can be seen as making expropriation less likely in developing countries.[8] Integration provides more bargaining power to MNCs for ongoing operations and also makes extreme solutions to conflicts with host governments (such as expropriation) into outcomes where both the host country and the MNC stand to lose.

A well-articulated, worldwide integration strategy also simplifies the management of international operations by providing a point of view on the environment, a framework to identify key sources of uncertainties, and a purpose in dealing with them. The worldwide integration strategy can guide managers in adopting a *proactive* stance. The simplicity of the driving principle of the integration strategy also makes a consistent detailed strategic planning process possible, as it provides a unifying focus to the various parts of the organization. This process both guides the implementation of strategy and provides for its refinement and evolution over time.

National Responsiveness Strategy

Some companies forgo the potential benefits of integration and give much more leeway to their subsidiaries to respond to the political imperative by having them behave almost as if they were national companies. Yet, the affiliation of subsidiaries to a multinational company can bring them four distinct advantages over purely national competitors. These advantages are:

1. The pooling of financial risks;
2. The spreading of research and development costs over a larger sales volume (than that of local competitors) without the difficulties involved in licensing transactions;
3. The coordination of export marketing to increase overall success in export markets;
4. The transfer of specific skills between subsidiaries (e.g., process technology or merchandising methods).

In this approach, each subsidiary remains free to pursue an autonomous economic or political strategy nationally as its management sees fit, given the situation of the national industry. In industries where the government plays a key role (nuclear engineering and electrical power, for instance), national strategies are primarily political; in industries where other local factors are important sources of differentiation (e.g., food processing), but where government plays a less prominent role, strategies are economic.[9]

In a nationally responsive MNC, the resources, know-how, or services of the headquarters (or of other subsidiaries) are called upon only when the subsidiary management finds them helpful. Little central influence is exercised on the subsidiaries. The nationally responsive MNC, as a whole, has no strategy, except in a limited sense (Brown Boveri's technical excellence, for instance), and the strategy is usually not binding: subsidiaries follow it only when they see it in their own interest. Manufacturing is usually done on a local-for-local basis, with few intersubsidiary transfers. Coordination of R&D and avoidance of duplications are often difficult, particularly when host governments insist upon R&D being carried on locally on specific projects for which government support is available (new telecommunication technologies or microelectronics, for instance).

Administrative Coordination Strategy

Rejecting both clear-cut strategic solutions to the conflict between the economic and political imperatives offered by worldwide integration and national responsiveness, MNCs can choose to live with the conflict and look for structural and administrative adjustments instead of strategic solutions. Such adjustments are aimed at providing some of the benefits of both worldwide (or regional) integration and national responsiveness.

The strategy (literally) is to have no set strategy, but to let each strategic decision be made on its own merits and to challenge prior commitments. Individual decisions thus do not fit into the logic of clear goals, the reasonableness of which is tested against a comprehensive analysis of the environment and an assessment of the organization's capabilities. Strategy is not the search for an overall optimal fit, but a series of limited adjustments made in response to specific developments, without an attempt to integrate these adjustments into a consistent comprehensive strategy.[10]

The need for such adjustments emerges when new uncertainties are identified. These uncertainties can offer opportunities (e.g., the possibility to invest in a new country) or threats (e.g., the development of new technologies by competitors), or lend themselves to conflicting interpretation (the willingness of a government to grant R&D subsidies, but with some local production requirements). Instead of taking a stable proactive stance vis-à-vis the environment and relying on the chosen strategy to provide a framework within which to deal with sources of uncertainties and to make specific decisions as the need arises, companies using administrative coordination absorb uncertainties and try to resolve conflicts internally each time new uncertainties question prior allocations of strategic resources. In short, strategy becomes unclear, shifting with the perceived importance of changes in the economic or political environment, and it may become dissolved into a set of incremental decisions with a pattern which may make sense only *ex post.* Administrative coordination does not allow strategic planning: we are farther from the "timed sequence of conditional moves" representing the usual goal of strategic planning and much closer to public administration where issues get shaped, defined, attended to, and resolved one at a time in a "muddling through" process that never gives analytical consideration to the full implications of a step.[11]

By adopting such an internally flexible and negotiable posture, administratively coordinated companies make themselves more accessible to government influence, and become Janus-faced. On certain issues and at certain points in time, a view consistent with worldwide rationalization will prevail, in other cases national responsiveness will prevail, and in many cases some uneasy blend of the two will result. Some of the central control of the subsidiaries so critical in multinational integration is abandoned, making it easier for subsidiaries to cooperate with powerful partners such as government agencies or national companies on specific projects. Because commitments of resources are not all made consistently over time, and as the company is not likely to be very rationalized (given the role accorded to host governments' demands), excess resources are not likely to allow for large costs of good citizenship. In short, compared with multinational integration; *administrative coordination trades off internal efficiency for external flexibility.* Whereas multinational integration seeks to provide the organization with enough economic power for success, administrative coordination seeks to provide the flexibility needed for a constantly adjusted coalignment of the firm with the more powerful factors in the environment and with the most critical sources of uncertainty.[12] Acceptability to host governments derives from flexibility.

The Three Strategies Compared

Both the worldwide (or regional) integration strategy and the national responsiveness strategy correspond to clear tradeoffs between the economic and the political imperatives. Integration demonstrates a clear preference for the economic imperative; the MNC attempts to fully exploit integration's potential for economic performance and shows willingness to incur large citizenship costs in exchange for being allowed to be very different from national companies. Conversely, national responsiveness minimizes the difference between the MNC and national companies, and thus minimizes the acceptability problems. It expresses a clear sensitivity to the political imperative, at the expense of economic performance. The economic advantages of multinationality are confined to a few domains:

financial risks, amortization of R&D costs, export marketing, and skill transfers among the subsidiaries.

Administrative coordination, because it aims at a constantly fluctuating balance between the imperatives, is an ambiguous form of management. There is a constant tension within the organization between the drive for economic success based on clear economic strategy, and the need to consider major uncertainties springing from the political imperative. The following comment, made by a senior manager in an administratively coordinated MNC, illustrates the tension:

> In the long run we risk becoming a collection of inefficient, government-subsidized national companies unable to compete on the world market. Yet, if we rationalize our operations, we lose our preferential access to government R&D contracts and subsidies. So we try to develop an overall strategic plan that makes some competitive sense, and then bargain for each part of it with individual governments, trying to sell them on particular programs that contribute to the plan as a whole. Often we have to revise or abandon parts of our plan for lack of government support.

Markets, Competition, Technology, and Strategy

In thinking about which type of strategy may suit a particular MNC or an individual business within a diversified MNC, it is important to consider the markets being served, the competition being faced, and the technology being used by the firm. The argument will focus on products and industries for which multinational integration pressures are significant, leaving aside products for which national taste differences (food), high bulk to value added ratio (furniture), dependence on perishable products (food), small optimal size (garments and leather goods), or other such factors usually make rationalization unattractive or unfeasible.

Market Structure and Competition

The range of possible multinational strategies depends upon the structure of the world market in terms of customers and barriers to trade. First, for some products (such as electrical power systems or telecommunications equipment), the technology and economies of production would very strongly suggest global rationalization, but political imperatives are so strong as to prevent it. The international trade volumes, either captive within MNCs or in toto, for telecommunications equipment or power systems are extremely low.[13] In developed countries theoretically committed to free trade, restrictions come through monopoly market power of government-controlled entities — Post, Telegraph, Telephone

(PTT), for instance — or through complex legislation and regulation that create artificial market differentiation. EEC regulations on trucks, officially designed for safety and road degradation reasons, effectively create barriers to entry for importers. In a similar way, inspection regulations for equipment (including the parts and components) purchased by state agencies in many European countries, effectively make it difficult to incorporate imported components into end products sold to the state.

In developing countries, market access restrictions are more straightforward. Under such conditions of restricted trade and controlled market access, worldwide strategic integration is obviously difficult. Often, the very nature of the goods, their strategic importance, as well as characteristics such as bulky, massive equipment produced in small volumes for a few large customers, reinforce the desire on the part of governments to control suppliers closely.[14]

Second, at another extreme, there are some goods that are traded quite freely, whose sales do not depend on location of manufacture or nationality of the manufacturer, and for which economies of scale beyond the size of national markets are significant. In such industries the only viable strategy is worldwide (or regional) integration. This is the strategy followed by all volume car manufacturers in Europe, led by Ford and General Motors but also including such national champions as Fiat, Renault, or Volkswagen. Smaller companies are adopting a specialization strategy by moving out of the price-sensitive volume market and serving the world market from a single location (BMW, Daimler Benz).

Third, and most interesting, are businesses (such as computers or semiconductors) whose markets are partly government-controlled and partly internationally competitive. In such businesses the market is split between customers who select their suppliers on economic grounds and customers that are state-owned or state-influenced and evidence strong preference for some control over their suppliers. Products, such as computers or integrated circuits, are of sufficient strategic and economic importance for host governments to try to have some control over their technology and their production.[15] In such industries governments try to restrict the strategic freedom of all multinationals and show great willingness to reward flexibility. Honeywell, for instance, was liberally rewarded for agreeing to create a joint venture between its French subsidiary and Compagnie Internationale pour l'Informatique, the ailing leader of the French computer industry. In addition to favored access to the French state-controlled markets, the joint venture received substantial grants and research contracts.

In these industries where both the economic and political imperatives are critical, multinationals face the most difficult choice between various possible strategies. Some companies may choose to integrate their operations multinationally, and some may choose to decentralize their operations to better match the demands of individual governments and benefit from their support and assistance. Still others may not make a clear strategic commitment and may instead resort to administrative coordination.

Yet, this choice is likely to look significantly different to various MNCs according to their competitive posture within their industry. In broad terms, *firms with the largest overall shares of the world market are likely to find integration more desirable.* There are several reasons for this choice.

Benefits of Integration. First, still assuming that there are unexploited economies of scale, large firms can achieve lower costs through integration than can smaller firms. The company with the largest overall share of the world market can become the low cost producer in an industry by integrating its operations, thus making life difficult for smaller competitors. Conversely, smaller firms (with significant market shares in only a few countries) can remain cost competitive so long as larger competitors do not move to regional or worldwide integration. Firms that integrate across boundaries in a market that is partly price competitive and partly government-controlled, can expect to gain a larger share of the price competitive market and confine smaller competitors to segments protected by governments that value flexibility and control more than lower prices.[16]

Influence. Second, one can hypothesize that larger firms can have more influence on their environment than smaller ones, and thus find it more suitable to centralize strategic decision making and ignore some of the uncertainty and variety in the environment.[17] In particular, larger firms can take a tougher stance vis-à-vis individual governments when needed, and woo them with higher costs of good citizenship. How much integrated firms may be willing to give to host governments as costs of citizenship to maintain strategic integration may vary substantially. One can argue that a leading integrated firm in a partly government controlled market with no comparable direct competitor (IBM, for instance), may be willing to provide a lot to host countries in order to maintain its integration. Conversely, when keen worldwide competition takes place among integrated companies of comparable strength (e.g., Texas Instruments, Motorola, and Fairchild), the economic imperative becomes much more demanding for each of them, and none may be willing to be accommodating for fear that the others would not match such behavior. In short, the following proposition can be made: *the more one integrated firm is submitted to direct competition from other integrated companies, the less it will be willing to provide host governments, except in exchange for profitable nonmatchable moves.*

The implications of this proposition in terms of public policy toward industry structure are significant. At the regional or worldwide level it raises the issue of whether to encourage competition, or to favor the emergence of a single integrated leading MNC and then bargain with that company on the sharing of revenues. Similarly, a significant industrial policy issue at the national level is whether to encourage competition, or to provide a single multinational with the opportunity for a profitable nonmatchable move.[18]

Conversely, smaller firms (such as Honeywell in comparison with IBM) could draw only lesser benefits from rationalization and had to be extremely flexible in dealing with the uncertainties represented by host governments. Thus, *smaller firms are likely to find administrative coordination more suitable and will enlist host governments' support and subsidies to compete against leading MNCs.* Market access protection, financial assistance, or both can be the only way for these smaller firms — multinational or not — to keep a semblance of competitiveness. In the same way that firms in competitive markets can differentiate their products (or even their strategy) to avoid competing head on against larger firms, firms in these markets under partial government control differentiate their strategy by trading off central control over their strategy for government protection. The willingness of governments to trade off economic efficiency for some amount of political control, as well as the importance of short-term social issues (chiefly employment protection) make such strategic differentiation possible.[19]

For smaller MNCs such differentiation usually involves forgoing integration and letting host governments gain a say in strategic decisions affecting the various subsidiaries. Yet, because the MNC still attempts to maintain some competitiveness in market segments not protected by governments, it is likely to find administrative coordination — despite the ambiguity and managerial difficulty it involves — the least evil.

Finally, national companies can attempt to achieve some economies of scale through interfirm agreements for the joint manufacture of particular components (car engines) or product lines (Airbus A300). Over time, national companies can move to develop a globally integrated system. A case in point is Volkswagen, whose U.S.-assembled "Rabbits" incorporate parts from Brazil, Germany, and Mexico. Where free trade prevails among developed countries, as in the automobile industry, this may be the only suitable strategy for national companies.

In summary, one can hypothesize a relationship between the extent of government control over (and limits to) international trade in an industry, the relative international market share of a firm active in that industry, and the type of strategy it adopts. In industries where free trade prevails, all competitors are expected to have to follow a worldwide (or regional) integration strategy. In industries in which governments take a keen interest, but where they control the markets only partly, and where formal free trade prevails (computers, for instance), all three strategies are likely to coexist within an industry. Finally, in industries where the political imperatives prevail and whose markets are mostly state-controlled, all competitors can be expected to adopt a national responsiveness strategy.

Data supporting the relationship summarized above are presented graphically in Figure 1. It shows the results of the in-depth study of six industries where the economic and the political imperatives strongly conflict. However, one word of caution is necessary here: the patterns shown can only represent the *preferred* strategy of a company. Most companies will have deviant subsidiaries, because within a given industry trade restrictions vary among countries. The figure was built from data in Western Europe, and assumes that in a given industry, trade restrictions are about the same for all countries. That may be approximately true within Western Europe, but is obviously false in other regions. For instance, Ford's European operations achieve integration at the regional level; Ford's other international subsidiaries are much more isolated by tough local content restrictions (for instance, in Latin America). In passing, it may be hypothesized that companies with substantial operations in numerous countries (within the same industry) break them up into regional management units when they face wide differences in the conditions of trade among the regions. Obviously, the value added of products with respect to their weight or bulk also plays a role in limiting worldwide integration in a few industries where the value added per unit of weight is very high, and economies of scale and/or factor cost differences among regions are substantial (e.g., microelectronics).

Technology

Technology is usually seen as an important variable in the interface between MNCs and host governments. The introduction by MNCs of many innovative high technology products and the high market shares they still enjoy in their sales create much tension with host governments. Major industries, such as computers, microelectronics, or aerospace, remain dominated by U.S. multinationals. In tensions between economic and political imperatives within an industry, technology then plays a key role. MNCs that control the technology of specific industries have more power in bargaining with governments and also create technology barriers to competition from national firms. Often the minimal scale requirements increase so rapidly in high technology industries as to make it almost impossible for national firms to catch up.[20]

Technology, Trade, and Strategic Integration.

Higher technology products are likely to correspond to free trade. First, there is ample evidence that MNCs most often introduce their innovations in their home markets first.[21] So long as the new technology is not adopted by many countries, freer trade is likely to prevail for newer products than

Figure 1 Customers, market shares, and multinational strategies

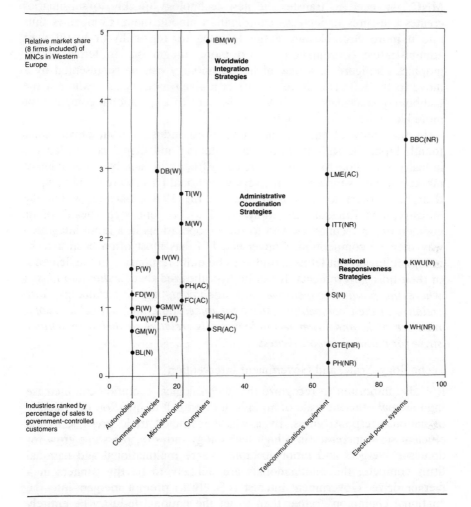

Legend:

1. Types of Strategies
are indicated next to company initials:
W: Worldwide (or regional) integration
AC: Administrative coordination
NR: National responsiveness
N: National company

2. Company Names
are represented by initials:

P	= Peugeot S.A.
FD	= Ford of Europe
R	= Renault
VW	= Volkswagen
GM	= General Motors
BL	= British Leyland
DB	= Daimler Benz

IV	= IVECO
F	= Ford
TI	= Texas Instruments
M	= Motorola
PH	= Philips
FC	= Fairchild
IBM	= International Business Machines
HIS	= Honeywell Information Systems
SR	= Sperry Rand
LME	= LM Ericsson
ITT	= International Telegraph & Telephone
S	= Siemens
GTE	= General Telephone & Electronics
BBC	= Brown Boveri
KWU	= Kraftwerk Union
WH	= Westinghouse

for older ones. Second, during the technology diffusion process within the MNC, the need to transfer the new technology quickly to subsidiaries creates pressures to increase coordination among them. Companies thus find it more desirable and easier to integrate regionally or to tilt their administrative coordination toward more integration. In terms of the graphics of Figure 1, a new higher technology can be represented by a move to the left. The move can affect a given industry as a whole if the technology is available to all MNCs but not to any national company, or more likely the move can be firm-specific.

In the study of the telecommunications industry, both moves were found. First, the shift to electronic switching and digital coding led the industry as a whole to be characterized by freer trade and by the opening of markets to new suppliers, as the various national PTTs were deciding upon their first orders for new equipment in the 1970s. Second, within the industry, LM Ericsson has always tried to be "one step ahead" of its competitors in technology, and to run its operations in a more integrated way than its competition. Conversely, ITT has most often been a technology follower, but let its subsidiaries be quite responsive to the demands of their host governments. It can be hypothesized that, *within an industry where the political imperatives are significant, higher technology firms (relative to their competitors) strive for integration, and can achieve some measure of it, and lower technology firms (relative to their competitors) strive for national responsiveness.*

Technology, Scale, and Government Intervention

It is also important to recognize that technological evolution can increase the minimal efficient scale of an industry and call to question the viability of national responsiveness. Even where restricted trade prevails, as the efficient scale increases in a high technology industry, pressures grow for domestic mergers and rationalization. Where multinational and national firms compete, the multinationals are unlikely to be the winners in a merger drive. Government interest is likely to prompt mergers into the "national champion" rather than to let the national industry be entirely controlled from outside. A national responsiveness strategy, i.e., a rather autonomous national subsidiary, makes such mergers into a national champion easier for the government to implement.

The examples of the French electrical power industry and telecommunications equipment in France and Great Britain tend to confirm the above analysis. In the case of electrical power systems, the transition from fossil fuel boilers to nuclear steam supply not only led to higher minimal efficient scale in the manufacture of turbogenerators, but also increased the interests of host governments in the industry. Two distinct effects were thus combined: minimal size increase and governments' greater interest in the technology itself.[22]

The Influence of Technology

This leaves us with less than a full understanding of the role of technology in the interface between MNCs and host governments in developed countries. On the one hand, for a given industry, a move to higher technology and new products can permit a firm (or all firms in an industry if they have access to the new technology) to be more multinationally integrated and centrally managed than it would otherwise be. There is some unclear causal relationship here, as integration is made possible by higher technology but is also required to facilitate technology transfer within the MNC.[23] On the other hand, it seems that very high technologies become extremely important in developed countries and prompt governments to try to narrowly control their development and use. Also, the move to higher technology often results in larger minimal efficient scale. This scale can be used by integrated multinationals to defend their market shares and attack smaller or less integrated firms, e.g., in microelectronics. In industries where trade is restricted, the government's usual responses are mergers into an emerging "national champion" first, and development of multinational government-sponsored programs second.

In both cases multinationals do not stand to benefit. This was clearly the case in electrical power systems. Telecommunications equipment was more ambiguous. Some countries were moving toward national consolidation (Brazil, France, the UK), and in others new electronic technology resulted in more open markets (Australia, South Africa, Spain, and several small European countries). Electronic technologies obviously increased the importance of the industry, yet provided opportunities to more integrated firms (e.g., LM Ericsson) or national firms with a distinctive technology (e.g., CIT Alcatel). When technology increases both the pressures to integrate within the industry and the interest governments take in the industry, either integration within MNCs across boundaries or integration within a country through government-directed mergers can prevail.

Managerial Implications

In practice, it is important to an MNC, or to executives running individual businesses in diversified multinationals, to recognize those changes in market openness, industry structure, and technology of an industry that foreshadow a need to change the overall strategy. Two simple examples are illuminating. Until the mid-1970s, General Motors ran its international operations as a collection of nationally responsive autonomous subsidiaries. With the globalization of the industry and the rationalization and integration of key competitors (mainly Ford), this posture became untenable. The strongest of the subsidiaries, Adam Opel in Germany, was able to hold its own in Europe, competing as a national company. But other subsidiaries, particularly Vauxhall in the U.K., were severely hurt. In 1975, General Motors started to bring the various subsidiaries together more closely through a series of administrative changes. By 1978, these moves resulted in an administrative coordination approach where numerous contradictions and ambiguities emerged. GM Overseas Operations' top management considered such administrative coordination as a transitional stage toward global integration. Many GMOO managers, however, felt that contradictions between the lingering desire for national subsidiaries' responsiveness and the emerging worldwide integration needs would not be easily resolved. In any case, the company had missed several precious years and had to struggle hard to remain competitive in Europe.

Conversely, in the late 1960s, Westinghouse was looking for acquisitions in the European electrical power system industry. It hoped to expand its business in Europe quickly, thanks to its light water nuclear reactor technology that was emerging as a clear technological winner over indigenous European technologies. To "better" manage its European operations, Westinghouse moved to a worldwide product group structure, aiming at multinational integration. At the same time, as we have seen, the increased minimal scale of the industry, the strategic importance of nuclear-related technologies, and the failure of Europe's own efforts in commercial reactors all combined to increase government sensitiveness about the industry. The discrepancy between the national responsiveness demanded by governments and what Westinghouse appeared willing to provide resulted in tensions in Belgium, France, and Germany, a substantial scale-down of Westinghouse's European expansion plans, and a shift in its strategy. In 1975, a former president of Westinghouse's Power Group commented to the author: "Our basic policy (for nuclear engineering and power plant sales) is to do it in whatever way a country would require." Yet, Westinghouse had probably lost the one opportunity to become a lasting factor in the European power system industry.

Choice of Strategy and Management Process

We have seen that both worldwide (or regional) integration and national responsiveness lead to relatively straightforward management processes that are grounded in a clear strategy and a clear-cut delineation of head-quarters' and subsidiaries' roles and responsibilities. Yet, the relative managerial simplicity both these strategies offer has an opportunity cost: it makes specific adjustment to the varying demands of governments difficult, and may prevent the company from entering certain businesses or certain countries. Such limitations make administrative coordination attractive as a way to increase the MNC's flexibility in finding balances between the economic and the political imperatives that match more closely the specific conditions of a given business in a given country. It is important to recognize that both worldwide integration and national responsiveness almost represent ideal polar opposites. Some MNCs are likely not to wish (or be able) to exercise a clear choice, and thus find themselves improvising compromises through some process of administrative coordination.

In particular, when the political imperative is significant, its very nature makes clear-cut analytical choices impossible. Contrary to the economic imperative, information on the political imperative is most often indirect and not controllable centrally. When a subsidiary manager claims that his plans rest on the word of local intermediaries or on his relationships with national government officials, it is difficult, at best, for managers at head-quarters to determine the soundness of his assumptions. The fact that the government's public logic is often quite different from the reality of the situation and from actual policy-making processes, makes it even more difficult for corporate or regional managers to understand the situation. As a result, top management's inability to reach an analytical choice on decisions involving the political imperative leads to adaptive coalitional decision making in which the firm internalizes tensions and uncertainties and tries to incorporate them into its decision-making process.

Decision Processes and Administrative Coordination

On any particular strategic decision, the company is trying to reach a satis-factory compromise given past decisions and past commitments of resources. Decisions cannot be left to either the subsidiary or the regional (or global) headquarters levels. They have to be reached by some group that collectively captures contradictions in the environment, internalizes them, and resolves them through contention, coalition, and consensus. Individual managers, representing different interests within the company and approaching questions from different points of view, are left to take sides on decisions according to how they perceive problems and how they prefer to deal with sources of uncertainty. In short, the question of deciding "what is right" becomes linked to that of "who is right" and "whose views are favored." Top management, instead of providing the inspiration for a strategic design and managing its implementation, shifts to a new role of deciding how to make decisions: who should be represented, with which voice, on which decisions. Top management can also provide some limits: would such decisions represent too wide a departure from the usual to be accepted? Choices on how to reach decisions can still be guided by a sense of which decisions, or which classes of decisions, should be made with integration as a priority, and which should be made with responsiveness as a priority. The way to convey such sense of priority is not to decide in substance on specific decisions (except when irreconcilable conflicts occur) but to act on the way in which decisions are made, to influence the making and undoing of specific coalitions or to help the shift of coalitions among decisions.

Managing Dependencies

How can top management achieve such influence? Primarily by keeping control of dependencies between subunits competing for power and by regulating the game they pursue. Strategic and operational dependencies can be used to determine who, in the long run, has power over which class of decisions or what functions. For instance, the subsidiaries can be made dependent on the corporate headquarters or on domestic product divisions for key components or for process technology. Conversely, the domestic divisions can be dependent on subsidiaries for export sales. A central difficulty of this approach is the divisiveness introduced within the company by managing dependencies through arm's-length power relationships. Top management also has to develop some integrative forces (for instance, through training, career paths, and compensation) to balance these divisive forces and preserve some sense of corporate identity and loyalty.

Over the long run, successful administrative coordination thus hinges on the maintenance of a balance between divisive and integrative forces that reflects a structure of dependencies among subunits. Careful control of the dependencies between national subsidiary managers, and product unit managers through the use of functional managers and administrative managers, was found to provide top management tools for maintaining such a balance.

Functional Managers. The substantive expertise of functional managers is needed by supporters of multinational integration as well as by supporters of national responsiveness. Managers preferring multinational integration still depend upon functional managers and "the field" (in various countries) to achieve such integration. Conversely, national managers depend on support from functional and administrative headquarters staff and product divisions even though they try to pursue national responsiveness strategies. Because the power of functional managers is based on needed expertise, they may preserve a relatively uncommitted posture between multinational integration and national responsiveness.

Yet functional managers, over time, can develop a functional logic that is aligned to either national responsiveness or worldwide integration. Manufacturing staffs, for instance, can develop a logic that calls for integration and rationalization or for flexible local plants serving separate national markets. Within each function, of course, further distinctions can develop. For instance, rationalized component plants and local-for-local end-product plants can be favored, or distribution channels can be perceived as very different, whereas similar advertising can be used. By influencing corporate functional managers directly in the development of their preference for integration or responsiveness, and by then bringing them to throw their weight to particular issues and not to others, top management can develop a repertoire of intervention methods on the making of particular decisions.

Administrative Managers. Administrative procedures and the managers in charge of them can also be used by top management to maintain the tension between integration and responsiveness. To begin with, the formal structure usually provides a dominant orientation. Even when this structure is a matrix, it is usually complemented by fairly elaborate administrative procedures and guidelines that provide a dominant orientation by defining who is responsible for what and whether it is a primary or a secondary responsibility. Various devices, such as committees and task forces that cut across the formal structure, can be used to bring about changes in perception or to reach actual decisions. Planning processes can also be designed so that integration and responsiveness are considered. For instance, a contention process can exist between subsidiaries and product divisions (e.g., LM Ericsson). Interestingly, IBM had such a system very formalized and well developed among its regions and product groups, and between them and corporate functional staffs. Measurement systems can be set so that managers will see it as their duty to call to top management's attention "excessive" integration, autonomy, or responsiveness (e.g., GTE[24] or GM). Personal reward and punishment systems may be designed to reinforce tensions or ease them according to the measurement criteria and yardsticks used. Management of career paths can also be used to provide multiple views and facilitate coordination.

Administrative staff managers, and the way they design and run their administrative systems, provide top management with the same type of leverage as functional managers. One can expect the controller to strive for uniformity of accounting practices and comparability of results worldwide, opposing differentiation between subsidiaries. Personnel management, on the other hand, can either favor uniformity of pay scales and benefits worldwide, or leave this decision to subsidiaries. The way in which the administrative function develops its own operating paradigm[25] can be managed so that its specific procedures support responsiveness or integration.

Dangers of Administrative Coordination

Even with the potential offered by functional and administrative managers for managing administrative coordination effectively, certain drawbacks are inescapable. In particular, administrative coordination may lead to strategic paralysis, fragmentation, or bureaucratization.

Strategic Paralysis. The willingness to respond to environmental changes when the environment is intrinsically ambiguous and contradictory is likely to lead to strategic paralysis. Students of ambiguous situations where several environments are relevant to decisions have stressed the danger of paralysis created by giving relatively equal power to managers most sensitive to different aspects of the environment.[26] Not using a stable pattern of resource commitment over time, according to spelled out goals, may lead to considerable waste and overall failure. It is fascinating to see that, in an environment where IBM is a strong leader, the agreements on the merger between C2I and Honeywell Bull in France spelled out a substantive strategy to avoid the risk of strategic paralysis. On the other hand, one could draw numerous examples of strategic paralysis from very refined, stable administrative coordination processes.[27]

Strategic Fragmentation. Administrative coordination involves the use of dependencies and the management of power, which create divisive forces. In the absence of a strategic design, the management groups' loyalty must be maintained lest managers' frustrations lead to increasingly disjointed and partial decisions and to fragmentation. Cultural identity is often a means to circumvent these divisive forces. For instance, all top managers at LM Ericsson come from the same Stockholm telecommunications engineering school; the whole top management of Philips remains Dutch and has gone through the same formative experiences. Similarly, strong cultural identity facilitates the foreign expansion of Japanese companies.

Bureaucratization. Managers faced with very uncertain situations and power relationships may be tempted to reduce their perceived uncertainties. By developing bureaucratic procedure to cope with uncertainties, managers will gain power for themselves. Bureaucratic procedure also creates uncertainties for other members of the organization.[28] This leads to bureaucratization and lack of sensitivity to the outside environment. More time is spent on infighting than on external action.

Even assuming that administrative coordination does not lead to strategic paralysis, fragmentation, or bureaucracy, it remains an expensive way to run a business. The internal management process, with its multiple negotiations and complex coalitional processes, consumes much managerial energy and time, and can slow down decision processes considerably. It can also lead to "horse trading" and more suboptimal decisions than would be warranted by the situation at hand.

Should administrative coordination be avoided wherever possible, then? The answer is probably yes, but with the qualifications developed in the first part of this article. When free trade prevails and competitors follow a worldwide integration strategy, a clear choice should be made between committing enough resources to a business and divestment. In industries where governments evince interest, administrative coordination seems, at best, to be a way for the weaker, smaller international companies to stay in certain industries (Honeywell in data processing, Philips in integrated circuits). In industries where trade is restricted, the alternative is between national responsiveness and administrative coordination. For technology leaders within their industry, administrative coordination makes sense, as it can possibly provide for easier technology transfer, and host governments can accept such coordination as a price for receiving the technology.

Strategy in the Diversified Multinational[29]

So long as the several businesses of the multinational rely on the same strategy, the overall corporate management task is not greatly complicated by business diversity. Texas Instruments uses one extreme posture which applies the same semiconductor business logic and global integration framework across the board to all of its businesses.

Another extreme would be a multinational conglomerate adopting a purely financial approach and letting each business develop its own business logic independently. Yet, in most cases, such simple solutions as that of Texas Instruments or the multinational conglomerate are not applicable: the various businesses of the diversified multinational straddle several adaptation patterns and are interdependent. This raises the issues of strategic and administrative differentiation among the businesses, and of managing the interdependencies among differentiated businesses.

Differentiation and Interdependencies

Difficulties develop when the various businesses of a multinational straddle several adaptation patterns; some are most suitably managed through global strategic integration, others through administrative coordination, and still others through national responsiveness. It usually happens that, because of a history of dominance in one business, one pattern is preferred and applied across the board. For instance, Brown Boveri was slow to recognize that its industrial businesses, particularly small motors and breakers, would be faced with worldwide competition following the EEC trade liberalization. When competition came, Brown Boveri was even slower to react, because the logic of the whole organization and the energy of top management were geared to success in the government-controlled, restricted trade power system and heavy electrical equipment businesses.

In a similar vein, after World War II, Philips had strong national organizations and weak worldwide product groups coordinating its activities. With freer trade (following the development of the EEC), moves were made to increase the power of product divisions and to foster integration in similar businesses between national organizations. This led to a balanced product-geography-function matrix that faced great difficulties in businesses where administrative coordination did not fit well. Businesses, such as TV picture tubes or standard semiconductors, did not achieve full integration at a regional (color TV) or global (semiconductors) level, and telecommunications equipment did not enjoy sufficient national autonomy to achieve responsiveness comparable to that of competitors.

An obvious response to the difficulties faced by Brown Boveri or Philips is to differentiate the management among product lines, letting each find the appropriate balance between the economic and the political imperatives.

Yet, extensive interdependencies among businesses would usually make this management differentiation difficult. Interdependencies are of several types. They can involve common technologies among several businesses. For instance, magnetic tape technology at Philips served several product groups: data systems, instrumentation, medical products, professional recording, and audio consumer products. Interdependencies can also derive from vertical integration. The bulk of Philips's electronic component production was transferred internally to be incorporated into Philips's end products; still Philips also wanted to compete on the open market for semiconductors. Interdependencies are also market related, with different products sold to the same customers. IBM's Data Processing Complex's and General Business Group's system offerings overlap at the lower end of medium systems and compete against each other for the same orders. Finally, when products are sold to government-controlled customers, interdependencies may become political. Brown Boveri was commonly told: "We are willing to import your power stations, but what about you creating an export-oriented motor plant in one of our depressed areas to generate employment and offset the trade deficit that importing your power stations would create?"

It is important to recognize the difference in nature between internal interdependencies (common technology, joint production, vertical integration) and external ones (same customers, host governments, and so forth). When interdependencies are internal, the choice of how to relate businesses (from pure arm's length to joint administration) can be made by management. When interdependencies are external, such choice is usually imposed by external agents. The terms under which to coordinate component and TV set production could be decided internally in Philips. However, the Belgian Government's orders for Philips's computers were conditional upon the maintenance of Philips's employment levels in Belgium. The consumer product groups, whose internal interdependencies with the computer group were negligible, but who had high cost factories they wanted to close down in Belgium, suffered from the deal. Allegedly, this problem played some role in Philips's decision to withdraw from the mainframe computer business entirely.

Managing Interdependencies

The central tradeoff in the examples presented above is that between strategic and administrative clarity for individual businesses (i.e., enabling clear choices to be made between worldwide integration and national responsiveness), and the complexity of managing interdependencies.

Developing some clarity usually involves selectivity in the management of interdependencies. It is important to recognize that, within a diversified multinational, the relative importance of various interdependencies may change over time as the "critical factors"[30] in the strategy of a business evolve. ITT was able to revise frequently the formal structure of its European operations to respond to changes in the relative importance of interdependencies. The basic method used by ITT was to organize itself into several product groups worldwide. Each of these was managed somewhat differently: the Automotive Group (auto parts and accessories) and the Microelectronics Group, for instance, were pursuing worldwide integration strongly, whereas the Telecommunications Equipment Group stuck to its national responsiveness strategy. The Business Systems Group pursued regional integration in Europe. Individual businesses could be moved among these groups as warranted by competitive, technological, and government intervention changes. In the mid-1970s, ITT moved the private telephone exchange switching product line from the Telecommunications Equipment Group to the Business Systems Group, where it joined other office equipment. The successful adaptation of electronic switching technology to private exchange and the penetration of the private exchange market by such aggressive, integrated firms as IBM had shifted the key dependency from technology (Telecommunications Equipment Group) to marketing (Business Systems Group). In a similar vein, when ITT adopted worldwide strategic integration for its microelectronics business, it spun off the telecommunication-related components to the Telecommunications Equipment Group. Also ITT decreased the interdependencies between microelectronics and telecommunications in order to achieve a clear strategy for each business.

The development of clarity for Brown Boveri and Philips was more difficult than for ITT. Because they were less widely diversified (most of their products were related), they could not reduce any interdependencies easily. Yet some of their businesses were subject to worldwide product standardization and price competition (for instance, radios at Philips and motors at BBC), and others were more affected by regional or national differences (power systems at BBC, hi-fi at Philips). These different competitive conditions led to divergent strategic directions among businesses.

An approach to interbusiness coordination, under such circumstances, that is being tried by several companies, is the use of corporate functional staff in conjunction with planning committees. At Brown Boveri, corporate marketing staffs coordinated the activities of the various national subsidiaries product line by product line. It was between various members of the corporate marketing staffs that tradeoffs between businesses could be made and the interdependencies could be managed. Assisting the corporate marketing staff in the strategic coordination of each business were several levels of committees. Some of these committees were functional and others were product-oriented. Functional committees could coordinate certain types of interdependencies among technologies and markets of several product groups. Other committees regrouped product division managers of the different subsidiaries and were in charge of managing the regional integration/national responsiveness tradeoffs. Unfortunately, the committees often lacked the consensus necessary for action, as each member adopted a parochial view.

Faced with similar problems, IBM gave operating units the right to formally take issue with the plans of other operating units ("nonconcurrence" in IBM's internal language) that would impact their activities adversely. Through this approach IBM was able to force subunits to consider interdependencies in their planning and budgeting process and to reach a joint solution before their plans could be approved. Top management could also take the initiative of presenting key strategic issues that would require co-ordination between subunits as "focus issues" to be dealt with explicitly in the planning process.[31] Other companies also sometimes pulled key interdependencies of great strategic importance out of the regular structure: Brown Boveri, for instance, established a separate nuclear policy committee with the task of managing all interdependencies relating to nuclear energy.

Despite the efforts described above, the management of interdependencies raises difficult issues. Because costs and benefits of interdependencies lend themselves to ambiguous conflicting interpretations, interdependencies provide a rich arena for power plays and coalition bargaining. While particular coalition configurations seem endless in their variety, they add to the task of strategic management. Furthermore, coalitions often involve external agents. For instance, individual managers can rely on their government to establish linkages among product groups. It is not uncommon for alliances to develop, at least tacitly, between host governments and subsidiaries to decrease the dependence of the subsidiary on headquarters and to develop "binding" commitments with the government.

Faced with such difficulties, the MNC corporate management level is likely to strive for administrative uniformity across businesses. Yet, unless all businesses can be successful with the same strategic logic, some degree of differentiation between businesses remains necessary. In short, uniformity is impossible when businesses straddle several adaptation patterns. Uniformity is possible on some aspects (financial reporting and measurement at ITT, for instance), provided that great leeway for differentiation is left to other aspects. Yet, to avoid cognitive overload at the corporate management level, there are strong pressures toward administrative uniformity, thus making the substance of decisions at the business unit level accessible to the corporate level in a common format. Such administrative pressure for uniformity may prevent the appropriate strategic differentiation among businesses and the development of strategic clarity. These necessary strategic and administrative differentiations suggest that it is usually not possible to maintain unitary corporate office dealing with the substance of decisions. Similarly, a diversified multinational needs (beyond the divisionalized form) a corporate office that only manages selected aspects of the operations and influences decision processes while leaving room for differentiation among businesses — unless all follow the same worldwide integration strategy.

As a concluding note for this section, it may be hypothesized that the complex multinational structures, usually called matrix (or grid) and mixed types, represent an attempt by diversified MNCs to respond to the problems of combining the development of a strategy for each business with the need to manage interdependencies between businesses. Thus, they are not aberrant or transitory structural stages only. Matrix structures correspond to the corporate desire to manage interdependencies among businesses while allowing strategic integration to develop. Mixed structures correspond to a clear differentiation and separation between businesses that follow different adaptation patterns.

Conclusion — Combining Strategic Clarity and Administrative Coordination?

The most difficult tradeoff for the diversified MNC is the one between clarity at the business level (multicountry integration or national responsiveness) and the benefits derived from operating and strategic interdependencies between businesses. The added complexity, compared to domestic diversified companies, of coping with broader environmental variety, makes the management of interdependencies less straightforward and more difficult.

Some simplification can be obtained by limiting and buffering interdependencies. For instance, at LM Ericsson, the national subsidiaries were dependent upon the center for components and technology, but the center could be severed from any subsidiary without great difficulty. Interdependencies between subsidiaries were negligible. Japanese companies usually adopted similar approaches to manage their joint ventures abroad. Philips was treating its semiconductor acquisition in the U.S., Signetics, differently from its European operations, leaving much strategic freedom to the company. So both operating and strategic interdependencies can be structured in such a way as to minimize the need for managing them. There is a tradeoff between the complexity of managing many interdependencies and the joint benefits they bring.

One way companies have tried to order the above tradeoff is to manage simultaneously along several dimensions. For instance, as the Dow Chemical matrix was becoming unbalanced, the operating responsibilities moved toward area executives, thus providing regional integration across vertically interdependent businesses at the area level (Europe, Far East, etc.). Yet, a Corporate Product Department was created with veto power over strategic resource allocation and control over interdependencies between areas.[32] Administrative systems were used by Dow to provide autonomy for regional strategic integration, except for the planning and resource allocation process that was used to check strategic integration and keep the autonomy of areas within bounds.

In an even more discriminating way, IBM's strategic planning process provided for functions, product lines, and areas (or countries) to be managed jointly in a cohesive process. At various stages during the process, inputs and control points were set up so that both the need for integration in relevant units (that differed between functions, businesses, and areas of the world) and the administrative coordination needed between interdependent businesses were recognized, in turn, and conflicts were resolved through a contention process.

ITT was not only letting different businesses develop their own strategies, but also used the various management levels differently. Regional headquarters controlled product and business strategies, but their weight, compared to that of national subsidiary managers, varied considerably from one business to another. The overall planning process was managed from worldwide product group headquarters in New York. Finally, measurement, control, and evaluation were corporate level responsibilities.

More research is needed to conceptualize adequately the responses of these companies. However, these companies illustrate very sophisticated methods for providing both strategic integration and administrative coordination according to the needs for strategic focus and operating or strategic interdependencies between subunits.

References

†The author is indebted to the Associates and the Division of Research of the Harvard Business School for providing support for the research on which this article is based. The author is most grateful to Joseph L. Bower and C. K. Prahalad for their encouragement, insights, and suggestions. The ideas presented in this article are drawn from a book in preparation, *Multinational Strategic Management: Economic and Political Imperatives.*

1. See, for instance, L. G. Franko, *The European Multinationals* (Stamford, CT: Greylock, Inc., 1976).

2. See, for instance: J. Dunning and M. Gilman, "Alternative Policy Prescriptions," in *The Multinational Enterprise in a Hostile World,* ed. Curzon and Curzon

(London: Macmillan & Co., 1977); R. Vernon, *Storm over the Multinationals* (Cambridge, MA: Harvard University Press, 1977); R. Vernon, *Sovereignty at Bay* (New York: Basic Books, 1971).

3. See, for instance, C. Stoffaes, *La Grande Menace Industrielle* (Paris: Calmann-Levy, 1977).

4. Some authors have opposed worldwide and regional management within MNCs. See J. M. Stopford and L. T. Wells, Jr., *Managing the Multinational Enterprise* (New York: Basic Books, 1972).

The evidence in the companies studied suggests that in either case a business strategy responding to the economic imperative underlies regional or worldwide management. Which strategy is preferred in a particular company depends upon cost analysis based primarily on difference in factor costs, freight rates, and barriers to trade between various countries and regions of the world. In terms of responsiveness to individual country policies, there is little difference between regional and worldwide management. See L. G. Franko, *Joint Venture Survival in Multinational Corporations* (New York: Praeger, 1972).

5. See Y. Doz, "Managing Manufacturing Rationalization within Multinational Companies," *Columbia Journal of World Business,* Fall 1978.

6. See R. Vernon, "The Location of Economic Activity," in *Economic Analysis and the Multinational Corporation,* ed. Dunning (London: Allen and Unwin, 1974).

7. Ford's costs are estimated by the author from various industry interviews. For many product families, experience curve models suggested unit cost levels in smaller European firms equal to several times the costs in such firms as Texas Instruments for integrated circuits or Motorola for discrete semiconductors. Exact figures are not public, but their significance can be deduced from the Boston Consulting Group and Mackintosh publications. Large losses among European national semiconductor companies and private communications about losses in Philips's or Siemens's semiconductor businesses support the same point. See P. Gadonneix, "Le Plan Calcul" (DBA diss., Harvard Business School, 1974).

8. See: D. G. Bradley, "Managing against Expropriation," *Harvard Business Review,* July–August 1977, pp. 75–83; B. D. Wilson, "The Disinvestment of Foreign Subsidiaries by U.S. Multinational Companies" (DBA diss., Harvard Business School, 1979).

9. For political strategies, see: J. Zysman, *Political Strategies for Industrial Order* (Berkeley, CA: University of California Press, 1976); Y. Doz, *Government Control and Multinational Strategic Management* (New York: Praeger, 1979). For economic strategies, see U. Wiechmann, "Integrating Multinational Marketing Activities," *Columbia Journal of World Business,* Winter 1974. Wiechmann studied intensively the food and beverage industries.

10. For a comprehensive treatment of strategy as an optimal fit between environmental opportunities and threats and the organizational strengths and weaknesses (consistent with the personal values of top management and the social responsibilities of the corporation), see: K. R. Andrews, *The Concept of Corporate Strategy* (Homewood, IL: Dow Jones Irwin, 1971); D. Braybrooke and C. E. Lindblom, *A Strategy of Decision* (New York: The Free Press, 1963).

11. On strategic planning, see, for example: G. A. Steiner, *Top Management Planning* (New York: Macmillan, 1966); H. I. Ansoff, *Corporate Strategy* (New York: McGraw-Hill, 1965); P. Lorange and R. F. Vancil, eds., *Strategic Planning Systems* (Englewood Cliffs, NJ: Prentice-Hall, 1977).

On "muddling through," see: Braybrooke and Lindblom (1963); R. Cyert and J. March, *A Behavioral Theory of the Firm* (Englewood Cliffs, NJ: Prentice-Hall,

1963); J. D. Steinbruner, *The Cybernetic Theory of Decision* (Princeton: Princeton University Press, 1974).

12. For instance, see S. M. Davis and P. R. Lawrence, *Matrix* (Reading, MA: Addison-Wesley, 1977).

13. See: N. Jéquier, *Les Télécommunications et l'Europe (Geneva: Centre d'Etudes Industrielles, 1976); J. Surrey, World Market for Electric Power Equipment* (Brighton, England: SPRI, University of Sussex, 1972).

14. See O. Williamson, *Markets and Hierarchies: Analysis and Antitrust Implications* (New York: The Free Press, 1975).

15. Y. S. Hu, *The Impact of U.S. Investment in Europe* (New York: Praeger, 1973); N. Jéquier, "Computers," in *Big Business and the State*, ed. R. Vernon (Cambridge, MA: Harvard University Press, 1974).

16. There is ample evidence of this phenomenon in the computer and micro-electronics industries. See: E. Sciberras, *Multinational Electronic Companies and National Economic Policies* (Greenwich, CT: JAI Press, 1977); "International Business Machines: Can the Europeans Ever Compete?" *Multinational Business,* 1973, pp. 37–46.

17. For a discussion of strategic decision making and environmental uncertainty, see E. Rhenman, *Organization Theory for Long-Range Planning* (New York: John Wiley & Sons, 1973).

18. See F. T. Knickerbocker, *Oligopolistic Reaction and Multinational Enterprise* (Boston: Harvard Business School Division of Research, 1973).

19. For a discussion of strategic differentiation and competition in a domestic oligopoly, see R. Caves and M. Porter, "From Barrier to Entry to Barrier to Mobility," *Quarterly Journal of Economics,* May 1977.

20. For instance, see Vernon (1977), chap. 3. The evolution of industries such as nuclear power or aerospace is revealing. As the technology for a given product (e.g., light water nuclear reactors or bypass turbofan jet engines) becomes more wide-spread, the bargaining power of MNCs is eroded. See H. R. Nau, *National Politics and International Technology* (Baltimore, MD: Johns Hopkins University Press, 1974); For lesser developed countries, see N. Fagre and L. T. Wells, "Bargaining Power of Multinationals and Host Governments" (Mimeo, 14 July 1978).

On increasing economies of scale, for instance, see M. S. Hochmuth, "Aero-space," in *Big Business and the State*, ed. R. Vernon (Cambridge, MA: Harvard University Press, 1974).

21. Innovations in mature products are an occasional exception. They are some-times introduced in the most competitive market. For instance, Sony introduced several innovations in the U.S. before introducing them in Japan. Yet many other Sony innovations were first introduced in Japan. For a summary, see Vernon (1977), chap. 3.

22. See Doz (1979). For recent evidence, see "ITT Fights U.K. Bid for Plessey Control of STC," *Electronic News*, 23 October 1978, p. 4.

On electrical power, see: B. Epstein, *The Politics of Trade in Power Plants* (London: The Atlantic Trade Center, 1972). Central Policy Review Staff, *The Future of the United Kingdom Power Plant Manufacturing Industry* (London: Her Majesty's Stationery Office, 1976); Commission des Communautés Européenes, *Situation et Perspective des Industries des Gros Equipements Electromécaniques et Nucléaires liés à la Production d'Energie de la Communauté* (Brussels: CEE, 1976).

For related data on the U.S., see I. Bupp, Jr. and J. C. Derian, *Light Water: How the Nuclear Dream Dissolved* (New York: Basic Books, 1978).

23. See J. Behrman and H. Wallender, *Transfers of Manufacturing Technology*

within Multinational Enterprises (Cambridge, MA: Ballinger, 1976).

24. For a detailed analysis of GTE and LM Ericsson's administrative mechanisms, see Doz (1979).

25. Used here in the sense given by Steinbruner (1974), as the simplifying logic used by a particular function to reduce complexity in its environment by focusing on a few key parameters and taking cybernetic decisions based on them.

26. See: Davis and Lawrence (1977); C. K. Prahalad, "The Strategic Process in a Multinational Company" (D.B.A. diss., Harvard Business School, 1975).

27. See C. K. Prahalad and Y. Doz, "Strategic Change in the Multidimensional Organization" (Harvard Business School-University of Michigan Working Paper, October 1979).

28. See: M. Crozier, *The Bureaucratic Phenomenon* (Chicago: University of Chicago Press, 1964); D.J. Hickson et al., "A Strategic Contingencies' Theory of Intra-organizational Power," *Administrative Science Quarterly* 2 (1971): 216–229.

29. This section draws upon Y. Doz and C.K. Prahalad, "Strategic Management in Diversified Multinationals," in *Functioning of the Multinational Corporation in the Global Context*, ed. A. Negandhi (New York: Pergamon Press, forthcoming).

30. Taken here in the sense of Barnard's "strategic factors" or Selznick's "critical factor."

See: C. L. Barnard, *The Functions of the Executive* (Cambridge, MA: Harvard University Press, 1938); P. Selznick, *Leadership in Administration* (New York: Harper & Row, 1957).

31. See A. Katz, "Planning in the IBM Corporation" (Paper submitted to the TIMS-ORSA Strategic Planning Conference, New Orleans, February 16–17, 1977).

32. See S. M. Davis, "Trends in the Organization of Multinational Corporations," *Columbia Journal of World Business*, Summer 1976, pp. 59–71.

Information on Dow Chemical came from the *1976 Annual Report* and the author's interviews.

PART TWO: Strategy Formulation: Content

5

Do you Really Have a Global Strategy?*

Gary Hamel and C.K. Prahalad

*Source: *Harvard Business Review*, 28 (1985), pp. 139–148.

The threat of foreign competition preoccupies managers in industries from telecommunications to commercial banking and from machine tools to consumer electronics. Corporate response to the threat is often misdirected and ill timed–in part because many executives don't fully understand what global competition is.

They haven't received much help from the latest analysis of this trend. One argument simply emphasizes the scale and learning effects that transcend national boundaries and provide cost advantages to companies selling to the world market.[1] Another holds that world products offer customers the twin benefits of the low-cost and high-quality incentives for foreign customers to lay aside culture-bound product preferences.[2]

According to both of these arguments, U.S. organizations should "go global" when they can no longer get the minimum volume needed for cost efficiency at home and when international markets permit standardized marketing approaches. If, on the other hand, they can fully exploit scale benefits at home and their international export markets are dissimilar, U.S. executives can safely adopt the traditional, country-by-country, multinational approach. So while Caterpillar views its battle with Komatsu in global terms, CPC International and Unilever may safely consider their foreign operations multidomestic.

After studying the experiences of some of the most successful global competitors, we have become convinced that the current perspective on global competition and the globalization of markets is incomplete and misleading. Analysts are long on exhortation – "go international" – but short on practical guidance. Combine these shortcomings with the prevailing notion that global success demands a national industrial policy, a docile work force, debt-heavy financing, and forbearing investors, and you can easily understand why many executives feel they are only treading water in the rising tide of global competition.

World-scale manufacturing may provide the necessary armament, and government support may be a tactical advantage, but winning the war against global competition requires a broader view of global strategy. We will present a new framework for assessing the nature of the worldwide challenge, use it to analyze one particular industry, and offer our own practical guidelines for success.

Thrust and Parry

As a starting point, let's take a look at what drives global competition. It begins with a sequence of competitive action and reaction:

An aggressive competitor decides to use the cash flow generated in its home market to subsidize an attack on markets of domestically oriented foreign competitors.

The defensive competitor then retaliates – not in its home market where the attack was staged – but in foreign markets where the aggressor company is most vulnerable.[3]

An an example, consider the contest between Goodyear and Michelin. By today's definitions, the tire industry is not global. Most tire companies manufacture in and distribute for the local market. Yet Michelin, Goodyear, and Firestone are now locked in a fiercely competitive–and very global–battle.

In the early 1970s, Michelin used its strong European profit base to attack Goodyear's American home market. Goodyear could fight back in the United States by reducing prices, increasing advertising, or offering dealers better margins. But because Michelin would expose only a small amount of its worldwide business in the United States, it has little to lose and much to gain. Goodyear, on the other hand, would sacrifice margins in its largest market.

Goodyear ultimately struck back in Europe, throwing a wrench in Michelin's money machine. Goodyear was proposing a hostage trade. Michelin's long-term goals and resources allowed it to push ahead in the United States. But at least Goodyear slowed the pace of Michelin's attack and forced it to recalculate the cost of market share gains in the United States. Goodyear's strategy recognized the international scope of competition and parried Michelin's thrust.

Manufacturers have played out this pattern of cross-subsidization and international retaliation in the chemical, audio, aircraft engine, and computer industries. In each case international cash flows, rather than international product flows, scale economies, or homogeneous markets, finally determined whether competition was global or national. (For a detailed explanation, see the sub-section entitled "What is cross-subsidization?")

The Goodyear vs. Michelin case helps to distinguish among:

Global competition, which occurs when companies cross-subsidize national market share battles in pursuit of global brand and distribution positions.

Global businesses, in which the minimum volume required for cost efficiency is not available in the company's home market.

Global companies, which have distribution systems in key foreign markets that enable cross-subsidization, international retaliation, and world-scale volume.

Making a distinction between global competition and a global business is important. In traditionally global businesses, protectionism and flexible manufacturing technologies are encouraging a shift back to local manufacturing. Yet competition remains global. Companies must distinguish between the cost effectiveness based on off-shore sourcing and world-scale plants and the competitive effectiveness based on the ability to retaliate in competitors' key markets.

Identifying the Target

Understanding how the global game is played is only the first step in challenging the foreign competitor. While the pattern of cross-subsidization and retaliation describes the battle, world brand dominance is what the global war is all about. And the Japanese have been winning it.

In less than 20 years, Canon, Hitachi, Seiko, and Honda have established worldwide reputations equal to those of Ford, Kodak, and Nestlé. In consumer electronics alone, the Japanese are present in or dominate most product categories.

Like the novice duck hunter who either aims at the wrong kind of bird or shoots behind his prey, many companies have failed to develop a well-targeted response to the new global competition. Those who define international competitiveness as no more than low-cost manufacturing are aiming at the wrong target. Those who fail to identify the strategic intentions of their global competitors cannot anticipate competitive moves and often shoot behind the target.

To help managers respond more effectively to challenges by foreign companies, we have developed a framework that summarizes the various global competitive strategies (see the *Exhibit* on p. 127). The competitive advantages to be gained from location, world-scale volume, or global brand distribution are arrayed against the three kinds of strategic intent we have found to be most prevalent among global competitors: (1) building a global presence, (2) defending a domestic position, and (3) overcoming national fragmentation.

Using this framework to analyze the world television industry, we find

Japanese competitors building a global presence, RCA, GE, and Zenith of the United States defending domestic dominance, and Philips of the Netherlands and CSF Thomson of France overcoming national fragmentation. Each one uses a different complement of competitive weapons and pursues its own strategic objectives. As a result, each reaps a different harvest from its international activities.

Loose Bricks

By the late 1960s, Japanese television manufacturers had built up a large U.S. volume base by selling private-label TV sets. They had also established brand and distribution positions in small-screen and portable televisions – a market segment ignored by U.S. producers in favor of higher margin console sets.

In 1967, Japan became the largest producer of black-and-white TVs; by 1970, it had closed the gap in color sets. While the Japanese first used their cost advantages primarily from low labor costs, they then moved quickly to invest in new process technologies, from which came the advantages of scale and quality.

Japanese companies recognized the vulnerability of competitive positions based solely on labor and scale advantages. Labor costs change as economies develop or as exchange rates fluctuate. The world's low-cost manufacturing location is constantly shifting: from Japan to Korea, then to Singapore and Taiwan. Scale-based cost advantages are also vulnerable, particularly to radical changes in manufacturing technology and creeping protectionism in export markets. Throughout the 1970s, Japanese TV makers invested heavily to create the strong distribution positions and brand franchises that would add another layer of competitive advantage.

Making a global distribution investment pay off demands a high level of channel utilization. Japanese companies force-fed distribution channels by rapidly accelerating product life cycles and expanding across contiguous product segments. Predictably, single-line competitors have often been blind-sided, and sleepy product-development departments have been caught short in the face of this onslaught. Global distribution is the new barrier to entry.

By the end of the decade, the Japanese competitive advantage had evolved from low-cost sourcing to world-scale volume and worldwide brand positions across the spectrum of consumer electronic products.

RCA at Home

Most American television producers believed the Japanese did well in their market simply because of their low-cost, high-quality manufacturing systems. When they finally responded, U.S. companies drove down costs, began catching up on the technology front, and lobbied heavily for government protection.[4] They thought that was all they had to do.

Exhibit A global competitive framework

	Build global presence	Defend domestic dominance	Overcome national fragmentation
1965	Access volume		
		Response lag	Response lag
1970	Redefine cost-volume relationships		
		Match costs	
1975	Cross-subsidize to win the world		Reduce costs at national subsidiary
		Amortize world-scale investments	
1980	Contiguous segment expansion		Rationalize manufacturing
		Gain retaliatory capability	
1985			Shift locus of strategic responsibility
1990			

Some could not even do that; the massive investment needed to regain cost competitiveness proved too much for them and they left the television industry. Stronger foreign companies purchased others.

Those that remained transferred labor-intensive manufacturing offshore and rationalized manufacturing at home and abroad. Even with costs under control, these companies (RCA, GE, and Zenith) are still vulnerable because they do not understand the changing nature of Japanese competitive advantage. Even as American producers patted themselves on the back for closing the cost gap, the Japanese were cementing future profit foundations through investment in global brand positions. Having conceived of global competition on a product-by-product basis, U.S. companies could not justify a similar investment.

Having conceded non-U.S. markets, American TV manufacturers were powerless to dislodge the Japanese even from the United States.

While Zenith and RCA dominated the color TV business in the United States, neither had a strong presence elsewhere. With no choice of competitive venue, American companies had to fight every market share battle in the United States. When U.S. companies reduced prices at home, they subjected 100% of their sales volume to margin pressure. Matsushita could force this price action, but only a fraction of it would be similarly exposed.

We do not argue that American TV manufacturers will inevitably succumb to global competition. Trade policy or public opinion may limit foreign penetration. Faced with the threat of more onerous trade sanctions or charges of predatory trade tactics, global competitors may forgo a fight to the finish, especially when the business in question is mature and no longer occupies center stage in the company's product plans. Likewise, domestic manufacturers, despite dwindling margins, may support the threatened business if it has important interdependencies with other businesses (as, for example, in the case of Zenith's TV and data systems business). Or senior management may consider the business important to the company's image (possible motivation for GE) for continuing television production.

The hope that foreign companies may never take over the U.S. market, however, should hardly console Western companies. TVs were no more than one loose brick in the American consumer electronics market. The Japanese wanted to knock down the whole wall. For example, with margins under pressure in the TV business, no American manufacturer had the stomach to develop its own videocassette recorder. Today, VCRs are the profitability mainstay for many Japanese companies. Companies defending domestic positions are often shortsighted about the strategic intentions of their competitors. They will never understand their own vulnerability until they understand the intentions of their rivals and then reason back to potential tactics. With no appreciation of strategic intent, defensive-minded competitors are doomed to a perpetual game of catch-up.

Loose Bricks in Europe, too

Philips of the Netherlands has become well known virtually everywhere in the world. Like other long-standing MNCs, Philips has always benefited from the kind of international distribution system that U.S. companies lack. Yet our evidence suggests that this advantage alone is not enough. Philips has its own set of problems in responding to the Japanese challenge.

Japanese color TV exports to Europe didn't begin until 1970. Under the terms of their licensing arrangements with European set makers, the Japanese could export only small-screen TVs. No such size limitation existed for Japanese companies willing to manufacture in Europe, but no more than half the output could be exported to the rest of Europe. Furthermore, because laws prohibited Japanese producers from supplying finished sets for private-label sale, they supplied picture tubes. So in 1979, although Europe ran a net trade deficit of only 2 million color televisions, the deficit in color tubes was 2.7 million units. By concentrating on such volume-sensitive manufacturing, Japanese manufacturers skirted protectionist sentiment while exploiting economies of scale gained from U.S. and Japanese experience.

Yet just as they had not been content to remain private-label suppliers in the United States, Japanese companies were not content to remain component suppliers in Europe. They wanted to establish their own brand positions. Sony, Matsushita, and Mitsubishi set up local manufacturing operations in the United Kingdom. When, in response, the British began to fear a Japanese takeover of the local industry, Toshiba and Hitachi simply found U.K. partners. In moving assembly from the Far East to Europe, Japanese manufacturers incurred cost and quality penalties. Yet they regarded such penalties as an acceptable price for establishing strong European distribution and brand positions.

If we contrast Japanese entry strategies in the United States and Europe, it is clear that the tactics and timetables differed. Yet the long-term strategic intentions were the same and the competitive advantage of Japanese producers evolved similarly in both markets. In both Europe and the United States, Japanese companies found a loose brick in the bottom half of the market structure – small-screen portables. And then two other loose bricks were found – the private-label business in the United States and picture tubes in Europe.

From these loose bricks, the Japanese built the sales volume necessary for investment in world-scale manufacturing and state-of-the-art product development; they gained access to local producers, who were an essential source of market knowledge. In Europe, as in the United States, Japanese manufacturers captured a significant share of total industry profitability with a low-risk, low-profile supplier strategy; in so doing, they established a platform from which to launch their drive to global brand dominance.

Regaining Cost Competitiveness

Philips tried to compete on cost but had more difficulties than RCA and Zenith. First, the European TV industry was more fragmented than that of the United States. When the Japanese entered Europe, twice as many European as American TV makers fought for positions in national markets that were smaller than those in the United States.

Second, European governments frustrated the attempts of companies to use offshore sources or to rationalize production through plant closings, lay-offs, and capacity reassignments. European TV makers turned to political solutions to solve competitive difficulties. In theory, the resulting protectionism gave them breathing space as they sought to redress the cost imbalance with Japanese producers. Because they were still confined to marginal, plant-level improvements, however, their cost and quality gap continued to widen. Protectionism reduced the incentive to invest in cost competitiveness; at the same time, the Japanese producers were merging with Europe's smaller manufacturers.

With nearly 3 million units of total European production in 1976, Philips was the only European manufacturer whose volume could fund the automation of manufacturing and the rationalization of product lines and components. Even though its volume was sufficient, however, Philips's tube manufacturing was spread across seven European countries. So it had to demonstrate (country by country, minister by minister, union by union) that the only alternative to protectionism was to support the development of a Pan-European competitor. Philips also had to wrestle with independent subsidiaries not eager to surrender their autonomy over manufacturing, product development, and capital investment. By 1982, it was the world's largest color TV maker and had almost closed the cost gap with Japanese producers. Even so – after ten years – rationalization plans are still incomplete.

Philips remains vulnerable to global competition because of the difficulties inherent in weaving disparate national subsidiaries into a coherent global competitive team. Low-cost manufacturing and international distribution give Philips two of the critical elements needed for global competition. Still needed is the coordination of national business strategies.

Philips's country managers are jealous of their autonomy in marketing and strategy. With their horizon of competition often limited to a single market, country managers are poorly placed to assess their global vulnerability. They can neither understand nor adequately analyze the strategic intentions and market entry tactics of global competitors. Nor can they estimate the total resources available to foreign competitors for local market share battles.

Under such management pressure, companies like Philips risk responding on a local basis to global competition. The Japanese can "cherry pick" attractive national markets with little fear that their multinational rival will retaliate.

What is Cross-subsidization?

When a global company uses financial resources accumulated in one part of the world to fight a competitive battle in another, it is pursuing a strategy we call "cross-subsidization." Contrary to tried-and-true MNC policy, a subsidiary should not always be required to stand on its own two feet financially. When a company faces a large competitor in a key foreign market, it may make sense for it to funnel global resources into the local market share battle, especially when the competitor lacks the international reach to strike back.

Money does not always move across borders, though this may happen. For a number of reasons (taxation, foreign exchange risk, regulation) the subsidiary may choose to raise funds locally. Looking to the worldwide strength of the parent, local financial institutions may be willing to provide long-term financing in amounts and at rates that would not be justified on the basis of the subsidiary's short-term prospects. One note of caution: if competitors learn of your subsidiary's borrowing needs, you may reveal strategic intentions by raising local funds and lose an element of competitive surprise.

Cross-subsidization is not dumping. When a company cross-subsidizes it does not sell at less than the domestic market price. Rather than risk trade sanctions, the intelligent global company will squeeze its competitor's margins just enough to dry up its development spending and force corporate officers to reassess their commitment to the business.

With deteriorating margins and no way of retaliating internationally, the company will have little choice but to sell market share. If your competitor uses simple portfolio management techniques, you may even be able to predict how much market share you will have to buy to turn the business into a "dog" and precipitate a sell-off. In one such case a beleaguered business unit manager, facing an aggressive global competitor, lobbied hard for international retaliation. The corporate response: "If you can't make money at home, there's no way we're going to let you go international!" Eventually, the business was sold.

The Strategic Imperative

International companies like General Motors and Philips prospered in the fragmented and politicized European market by adopting the "local face" of a good multinational citizen. Today Philips and other MNCs need a global strategic perspective and a corresponding shift in the locus of strategic responsibility away from country organizations. That need conflicts with escalating demands by host governments for national responsiveness. The resulting organizational problems are complex.

Nevertheless, companies must move beyond simplistic organizational views that polarize alternatives between world-product divisions and country-based structures. Headquarters will have to take strategic responsibility in some decision areas; subsidiaries must dominate in others. Managers cannot resolve organizational ambiguity simply by rearranging lines and boxes on the organization chart. They must adopt fundamentally new roles.

National subsidiaries can provide headquarters with more competitive intelligence and learn about world competitors from the experiences of other subsidiaries. They must fight retaliatory battles on behalf of a larger strategy and develop information systems, decision protocols, and performance measurement systems to weave global and local perspectives into tactical decisions. Rather than surrender control over manufacturing, national subsidiaries must interact with the organization in new and complex ways.

Such a realignment of strategic responsibility takes three steps:

(1) Analyze precisely the danger of national fragmentation.
(2) Create systems to track global competitive developments and to support effective responses.
(3) Educate national and headquarters executives in the results of analysis and chosen organization design.

This reorientation may take as long as five years. Managing it is the hardest challenge in the drive to compete successfully.

A New Analysis

Managers must cultivate a mind-set based on concepts and tools different from those normally used to assess competitors and competitive advantage.

For example, the television industry case makes clear that the competitive advantage from global distribution is distinct from that due to lower manufacturing costs. Even when they don't have a cost advantage, competitors with a global reach may have the means and motivation for an attack on nationally focused companies. If the global competitor enjoys a high price level at home and suffers no cost disadvantage, it has the means to cross-subsidize the battle for global market share.

Price level differences can exist because of explicit or implicit collusion that limits competitive rivalry, government restrictions barring the entry of new companies to the industry, or differences in the price sensitivity of customers.

The cash flow available to a global competitor is a function of both total costs and realized prices. Cost advantages alone do not indicate whether a company can sustain a global fight. Price level differences, for example, may provide not only the means but also the motivation for cross-subsidization.

If a global competitor sees a more favorable industry growth rate in a foreign market populated by contented and lazy competitors, who are unable or unwilling to fight back, and with customers that are less price sensitive than those at home, it will target that market on its global road. Domestic competitors will be caught unaware.

The implications for these strictly domestic companies are clear. First, they must fight for access to their competitors' market. If such access is unavailable, a fundamental asymmetry results. If no one challenges a global competitor in its home market, the competitor faces a reduced level of rivalry, its profitability rises, and the day when it can attack the home markets of its rivals is hastened. That IBM shares this view is evident from its pitched battle with Fujitsu and Hitachi in Japan.

Global competitors are not battling simply for world volume but also for the cash flow to support new product development, investment in core technologies, and world distribution. Companies that nestle safely in their home beds will be at an increasing resource (if not at a cost) disadvantage. They will be unable to marshal the forces required for a defense of the home market.

Not surprisingly, Japanese MNCs have invested massively in newly industrializing countries (NICs). Only there can European and American companies challenge Japanese rivals on a fairly equal footing without sacrificing domestic profitability or facing market entry restrictions. The failure of Western organizations to compete in the NICs will give the Japanese another uncontested profit source, leaving U.S. and European companies more vulnerable at home.

New Concepts

Usually, a company's decision whether to compete for a market depends on the potential profitability of a particular level of market share in that country. But the new global competition requires novel ways of valuing market share; for example:

Worldwide cost competitiveness, which refers to the minimum world market share a company must capture to underwrite the appropriate manu-facturing-scale and product-development effort.

Retaliation, which refers to the minimum market share the company needs in a particular country to be able to influence the behavior of key global competitors. For example, with only a 2% or 3% share of the foreign market, a company may be too weak to influence the pricing behavior of its foreign rival.

Home country vulnerability, which refers to the competitive risks of national market share leadership if not accompanied by international distribution. Market leadership at home can create a false sense of security. Instead of granting invincibility, high market share may have the opposite effect. To the extent that a company uses its market power to support high price levels, foreign comptitors – confident that the local company has little freedom for retaliation – may be encouraged to come in under the price umbrella and compete away the organization's profitability.

Critical National Markets

Most MNCs look at foreign markets as strategically important only when they can yield profits in their own right. Yet different markets may offer very different competitive opportunities. As part of its global strategy, an organization must distinguish between objectives of (1) low-cost sourcing, (2) minimum scale, (3) a national profit base, (4) retaliation against a global competitor, and (5) benchmarking products and technology in a state-of-the-art market. At the same time, the company will need to vary the ways in which it measures subsidiary performance, rewards managers, and makes capital appropriations.

Product Families

Global competition requires a broader corporate concept of a product line. In redefining a relevant product family – one that is contiguous in distribution channels and shares a global brand franchise – an organization can, for example, scrutinize all products moving through distribution channels in which its products are sold.

In a corollary effort, all competitors in the channels can be mapped against their product offerings. This effort would include a calculation of the extent of a competitor's investment in the distribution channel, including investment in brand awareness, to understand its motivation to move across segments. Such an analysis would reveal the potential for segment expansion by competitors presently outside the company's strategic horizon.

Scope of Operations

Where extranational-scale economies exist, the risks in establishing world-scale manufacturing will be very different for the company that sells abroad only under license or through private labels, compared with the company that controls its own worldwide distribution network. Cost advantages are less durable than brand and distribution advantages. An investment in world-scale manufacturing, when not linked to an investment in global distribution, presents untenable risks.

In turn, investments in worldwide distribution and global brand franchises are often economical only if the company has a wide range of products that can benefit from the same distribution and brand investment. Only a company that develops a continuous stream of new products can justify the distribution investment.

A company also needs a broad product portfolio to support investments in key technologies that cut across products and businesses. Competitors with global distribution coverage and wide product lines are best able to justify investments in new core technologies. Witness Honda's leadership in engine technology, a capability it exploits in automobiles, motorcycles, power tillers, snowmobiles, lawnmowers, power generators, and so forth.

Power over distribution channels may depend on a full line. In some cases, even access to a channel (other than on a private-label basis) depends on having a "complete" line of products. A full line may also allow the company to cross-subsidize products in order to displace competitors who are weak in some segments.

Investments in world-scale production and distribution, product-line width, new product development, and core technologies are interrelated. A company's ability to fully exploit an investment made in one area may require support of investments in others.

Resource Allocation

Perhaps the most difficult problem a company faces in global competition is how to allocate resources. Typically, large companies allocate capital to strategic business units (SBUs). In that view, an SBU is a self-contained entity encompassing product development, manufacturing, marketing, and technology. Companies as diverse as General Electric, 3M, and Hewlett-Packard embrace the concept. They point to clear channels of management accountability, visibility of business results, and innovation as the main benefits of SBU management. But an SBU does not provide an appropriate frame of reference to deal with the new competitive milieu.

In pursuing complex global strategies, a company will find different ways to evaluate the geographic scope of individual business subsystems—manufacturing, distribution, marketing, and so on. The authority for resource allocation, then, needs to reside at particular points in the organization for different subsystems, applying different criteria and time horizons to investments in those subsystems.

Global competition may threaten the integrity of the SBU organization for several reasons. A strong SBU-type organization may not facilitate investments in international distribution. To justify such investments, especially in country markets new to the company, it may have to gain the commitment of several businesses who may not share the same set of international priorities.

Even if individual SBUs have developed their own foreign distribution capability, the strategic independence of the various businesses at the country level may make it difficult to cross-subsidize business segments or undertake joint promotion. The company loses some of the benefits of a shared brand franchise.

Companies may have to separate manufacturing and marketing subsystems to rationalize manufacturing on a local-for-global or local-for-regional basis. Economic and political factors will determine which subsidiaries produce which components for the system. In such a case, a company may coordinate manufacturing globally even though marketing may still be based locally.

Companies might also separate the responsibility for global competitive strategy from that for local marketing strategy. While national organizations may be charged with developing some aspects of the marketing mix, headquarters will take the lead role in determining the strategic mission for the local operation, the timing of new product launches, the targeted level of market share, and the appropriate level of investment or expected cash flow.

Geography-based Organizations

For the company organized on a national subsidiary basis, there is a corollary problem. It may be difficult to gain commitment to global business initiatives when resource allocation authority lies with the local subsidiary. In this case, the company must ensure that it makes national investments in support of global competitive positions despite spending limits, strategic myopia, or the veto of individual subsidiaries.

Finally, the time limit for investments in global distribution and brand awareness may be quite different from that required for manufacturing-cost take-out investments. Distribution investments usually reflect a long-term commitment and are not susceptible to the same analysis used to justify "brick and mortar" investments.

New Strategic Thought

Global companies must have the capacity to think and act in complex ways. In other words, they may slice the company in one way for distribution investments, in another for technology, and in still another for manufacturing. In addition, global competitors will develop varied criteria and analytical tools to justify these investments.

In our experience, few companies have distinguished between the intermediate tactics and long-run strategic intentions of global competitors. In a world of forward-thinking competitors that change the rules of the game in support of ultimate strategic goals, historical patterns of competition provide little guidance. Executives must anticipate competitive moves by starting from new strategic intentions rather than from precooked generic strategies.

It is more difficult to respond to the new global competition than we often assume. A company must be sensitive to the potential of global competitive interaction even when its manufacturing is not on a global scale. Executives need to understand the way in which competitors use cross-subsidization to undermine seemingly strong domestic market share positions. To build organizations capable of conceiving and executing complex global strategies, top managers must develop the new analytic approaches and organizational arrangements on which our competitive future rests.

Notes

1. See Thomas Hout, Michael E. Porter, and Eileen Rudden, "How Global Companies Win Out," HBR September-October 1982, p. 98.

2. See Theodore Levitt, "The Globalization of Markets," HBR May-June 1983, p. 92.

3. See Craig M. Watson, "Counter-Competition Abroad to Protect Home-Markets," HBR January-February 1982, p. 40.

4. See John J. Nevin, "Can U.S. Business Survive Our Japanese Trade Policy?" HBR September-October 1978, p. 165.

6

Changing Patterns of International Competition*

Michael E. Porter[†]

*Source: *California Management Review*, XXVIII (Winter 1986), pp. 9–40.

When examining the environmental changes facing firms today, it is a rare observer who will conclude that international competition is not high on the list. The growing importance of international competition is well recognized both in the business and academic communities, for reasons that are fairly obvious when one looks at just about any data set that exists on international trade or investment. Exhibit 1, for example, compares world trade and world GNP. Something interesting started happening around the mid-1950s, when the growth in world trade began to significantly exceed the growth in world GNP. Foreign direct investment by firms in developing countries began to grow rapidly a few years later, about 1963.[1] This period marked the beginning of a fundamental change in the international competitive environment that by now has come to be widely recognized. It is a trend that is causing sleepless nights for many business managers.

There is a substantial literature on international competition, because the subject is far from a new one. A large body of literature has investigated the many implications of the Heckscher-Ohlin model and other models of international trade which are rooted in the principle of comparative advantage.[2] The unit of analysis in this literature is the country. There is also considerable literature on the multinational firm, reflecting the growing importance of the multinational since the turn of the century. In examining the reasons for the multinational, I think it is fair to characterize this literature as resting heavily on the multinational's ability to exploit intangible assets.[3] The work of Hymer and Caves among others has stressed the role of the multinational in transferring know-how and expertise gained in one country market to others at low cost, and thereby offsetting the unavoidable extra costs of doing business in a foreign country. A more recent stream of literature extends this by emphasizing how the multinational firm internalizes transactions to circumvent imperfections in various intermediate markets, most importantly the market for knowledge.

Exhibit 1 Growth of world trade

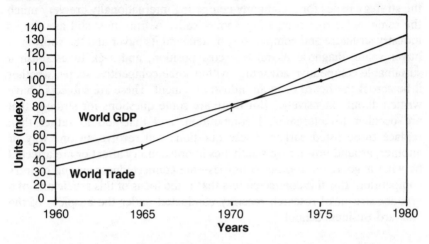

Source: United Nations, *Statistical Yearbooks*

There is also a related literature on the problems of entry into foreign markets and the life cycle of how a firm competes abroad, beginning with export or licensing and ultimately moving to the establishment of foreign subsidiaries. Vernon's product cycle of international trade combines a view of how products mature with the evolution in a firm's international activities to predict the patterns of trade and investment in developed and developing countries.[4] Finally, many of the functional fields in business administration research have their branch of literature about international issues—e.g., international marketing, international finance. This literature concentrates, by and large, on the problems of doing business in a foreign country.

As rich as it is, however, I think it is fair to characterize the literature on international competition as being limited when it comes to the choice of a firm's international strategy. Though the literature provides some guidance for considering incremental investment decisions to enter a new country, it provides at best a partial view of how to characterize a firm's overall international strategy and how such strategy should be selected. Put another way, the literature focuses more on the problem of becoming a multinational than on strategies for established multinationals. Although the distinction between domestic firms and multinationals is seminal in a literature focused on the problems of doing business abroad, the fact that a firm is multinational says little if anything about its international strategy except that it operates in several countries.

Broadly stated, my research has been seeking to answer the question: what does international competition mean for competitive strategy? In particular, what are the distinctive questions for competitive strategy that are raised by international as opposed to domestic competition? Many of the strategy issues for a company competing internationally are very much the same as for one competing domestically. A firm must still analyze its industry structure and competitors, understand its buyer and the sources of buyer value, diagnose its relative cost position, and seek to establish a sustainable competitive advantage within some competitive scope, whether it be across-the-board or in an industry segment. These are subjects I have written about extensively.[5] But there are some questions for strategy that are peculiar to international competition, and that add to rather than replace those listed earlier. These questions will revolve, in one way or another, around how a firm's activities in one country affect or are affected by what is going on in other countries—the connectedness among country competition. It is this connectedness that is the focus of this article and of a broader stream of research recently conducted under the auspices of the Harvard Business School.[6]

Patterns of International Competition

The appropriate unit of analysis in setting international strategy is the industry, because the industry is the arena in which competitive advantage is won or lost. The starting point for understanding international competition is the observation that its pattern differs markedly from industry to industry. At one end of the spectrum are industries that I call *multidomestic*, in which competition in each country (or small group of countries) is essentially independent of competition in other countries. A multidomestic industry is one that is present in many countries (e.g., there is a consumer banking industry in Sri Lanka, one in France, and one in the U.S.), but in which competition occurs on a country-by-country basis. In a multidomestic industry, a multinational firm may enjoy a competitive advantage from the one-time transfer of know-how from its home base to foreign countries. However, the firm modifies and adapts its intangible assets to employ them in each country and the outcome is determined by conditions in each country. The competitive advantages of the firm, then, are largely specific to each country. The international industry becomes a collection of essentially domestic industries—hence the term multidomestic." Industries where competition has traditionally exhibited this pattern include retailing, consumer packaged goods, distribution, insurance, consumer finance, and caustic chemicals.

At the other end of the spectrum are what I term *global* industries. The term global—like the word "strategy"—has become overused and perhaps under-understood. The definition of a global industry employed here is an industry in which a firm's competitive position in one country is significantly influenced by its position in other countries.[7] Therefore, the international industry is not merely a collection of domestic industries but a series of linked domestic industries in which the rivals compete against each other on a truly worldwide basis. Industries exhibiting the global pattern today include commercial aircraft, TV sets, semiconductors, copiers, automobiles, and watches.

The implications for strategy of the distinction between multidomestic and global industries are quite profound. In a multidomestic industry, a firm can and should manage its international activities like a portfolio. Its subsidiaries or other operations around the world should each control all the important activities necessary to do business in the industry and should enjoy a high degree of autonomy. The firm's strategy in a country should be determined largely by the circumstances in that country; the firm's international strategy is then what I term a "country-centered strategy."

In a multidomestic industry, competing internationally is discretionary. A firm can choose to remain domestic or can expand internationally if it has some advantage that allows it to overcome the extra costs of entering and competing in foreign markets. The important competitors in multidomestic industries will either be domestic companies or multinationals with stand-alone operations abroad—this is the situation in each of the multidomestic industries listed earlier. In a multidomestic industry, then, international strategy collapses to a series of domestic strategies. The issues that are uniquely international revolve around how to do business abroad, how to select good countries in which to compete (or assess country risk), and mechanisms to achieve the one-time transfer of know-how. These are questions that are relatively well developed in the literature.

In a global industry, however, managing international activities like a portfolio will undermine the possibility of achieving competitive advantage. In a global industry, a firm must in some way integrate its activities on a worldwide basis to capture the linkages among countries. This will require more than transferring intangible assets among countries, though it will include it. A firm may choose to compete with a country-centered strategy, focusing on specific market segments or countries when it can carve out a niche by responding to whatever local country differences are present. However, it does so at some considerable risk from competitors with global strategies. All the important competitors in the global industries listed earlier compete worldwide with coordinated strategies.

In international competition, a firm always has to perform some functions in each of the countries in which it competes. Even though a global competitor must view its international activities as an overall system, it has still to maintain some country perspective. It is the balancing of these two perspectives that becomes one of the essential questions in global strategy.[8]

Causes of Globalization

If we accept the distinction between multidomestic and global industries as an important taxonomy of patterns of international competition, a number of crucial questions arise. When does an industry globalize? What exactly do we mean by a global strategy, and is there more than one kind? What determines the type of international strategy to select in a particular industry?

An industry is global if there is some competitive advantage to integrating activities on a worldwide basis. To make this statement operational, however, we must be very precise about what we mean by "activities" and also what we mean by "integrating." To diagnose the sources of competitive advantage in any context, whether it be domestic or international, it is necessary to adopt a disaggregated view of the firm. In my newest book, *Competitive Advantage*, I have developed a framework for doing so, called the value chain.[9] Every firm is a collection of discrete activities performed to do business that occur within the scope of the firm—I call them value activities. The activities performed by a firm include such things as salespeople selling the product, service technicians performing repairs, scientists in the laboratory designing process techniques, and accountants keeping the books. Such activities are technologically and in most cases physically distinct. It is only at the level of discrete activities, rather than the firm as a whole, that competitive advantage can be truly understood.

A firm may possess two types of competitive advantage: low relative cost or differentiation—its ability to perform the activities in its value chain either at low cost or in a unique way relative to its competitors. The ultimate value a firm creates is what buyers are willing to pay for what the firm provides, which includes the physical product as well as any ancillary services or benefits. Profit results if the value created through performing the required activities exceeds the collective cost of performing them. Competitive advantage is a function of either providing comparable buyer value to competitors but performing activities efficiently (low cost), or of performing activities at comparable cost but in unique ways that create greater buyer value than competitors and, hence, command a premium price (differentiation).

The value chain, shown in Figure 1, provides a systematic means of displaying and categorizing activities. The activities performed by a firm in any industry can be grouped into the nine generic categories shown. The labels may differ based on industry convention, but every firm performs these basic categories of activities in some way or another. Within each category of activities, a firm typically performs a number of discrete activities which are particular to the industry and to the firm's strategy. In service, for example, firms typically perform such discrete activities as installation, repair, parts distribution, and upgrading.

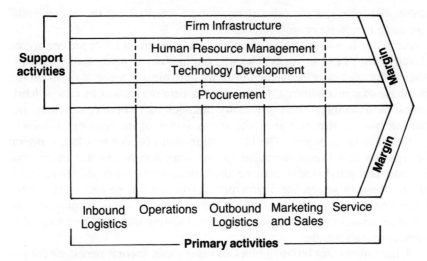

Figure 1 The value chain

The generic categories of activities can be grouped into two broad types. Along the bottom are what I call *primary* activities, which are those involved in the physical creation of the product or service, its delivery and marketing to the buyer, and its support after sale. Across the top are what I call *support* activities, which provide inputs or infrastructure that allow the primary activities to take place on an ongoing basis.

Procurement is the obtaining of purchased inputs, whether they be raw materials, purchased services, machinery, or so on. Procurement stretches across the entire value chain because it supports every activity—every activity uses purchased inputs of some kind. There are typically many different discrete procurement activities within a firm, often performed by different people. Technology development encompasses the activities involved in designing the product as well as in creating and improving the way the various activities in the value chain are performed. We tend to think of technology in terms of product or manufacturing process. In fact, every activity a firm performs involves a technology or technologies which may be mundane or sophisticated, and a firm has a stock of know-how about how to perform each activity. Technology development typically involves a variety of different discrete activities, some performed outside the R&D department.

Human resource management is the recruiting, training, and development of personnel. Every activity involves human resources, and thus human resource management activities cut across the entire chain. Finally, firm infrastructure includes activities such as general management, accounting, legal, finance, strategic planning, and all the other activities decoupled from specific primary or support activities but that are essential to enable the entire chain's operation.

Activities in a firm's value chain are not independent, but are connected through what I call linkages. The way one activity is performed frequently affects the cost or effectiveness of other activities. If more is spent on the purchase of a raw material, for example, a firm may lower its cost of fabrication or assembly. There are many linkages that connect activities, not only within the firm but also with the activities of its suppliers, channels, and ultimately its buyers. The firm's value chain resides in a larger stream of activities that I term the value system. Suppliers have value chains that provide the purchased inputs to the firm's chain; channels have value chains through which the firm's product or service passes; buyers have value chains in which the firm's product or service is employed. The connections among activities in this vertical system also become essential to competitive advantage.

A final important building block in value chain theory, necessary for our purposes here, is the notion of *competitive scope.* Competitive scope is the breadth of activities the firm employs together in competing in an industry. There are four basic dimensions of competitive scope:

- *segment* scope, or the range of segments the firm serves (e.g., product varieties, customer types);
- *industry* scope, or the range of industries the firm competes in with a coordinated strategy;
- *vertical* scope, or what activities are performed by the firm versus suppliers and channels; and
- *geographic* scope, or the geographic regions the firm operates in with a coordinated strategy.

Competitive scope is vital to competitive advantage because it shapes the configuration of the value chain, how activities are performed, and whether activities are shared among units. International strategy is an issue of geographic scope, and can be analyzed quite similarly to the question of whether and how a firm should compete locally, regionally, or nationally within a country. In the international context, government tends to have a greater involvement in competition and there are more significant variations among geographic regions in buyer needs, although these differences are matters of degree.

International Configuration and Coordination of Activities

A firm that competes internationally must decide how to spread the activities in the value chain among countries. A distinction immediately arises between the activities labeled downstream on Figure 2, and those labeled upstream activities and support activities. The location of downstream activities, those more related to the buyer, is usually tied to where the buyer

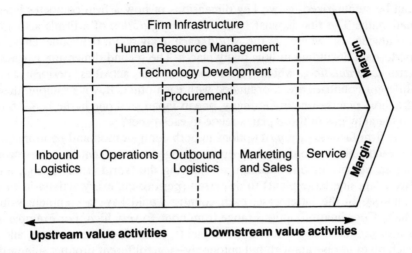

Firm Infrastructure					
	Human Resource Management				
	Technology Development				
	Procurement				
Inbound Logistics	Operations	Outbound Logistics	Marketing and Sales	Service	

Upstream value activities   **Downstream value activities**

Figure 2 Upstream and downstream activities

is located. If a firm is going to sell in Japan, for example, it usually must provide service in Japan and it must have salespeople stationed in Japan. In some industries it is possible to have a single sales force that travels to the buyer's country and back again; some other specific downstream activities such as the production of advertising copy can also sometimes be done centrally. More typically, however, the firm must locate the capability to perform downstream activities in each of the countries in which it operates. Upstream activities and support activities, conversely, can at least conceptually be decoupled from where the buyer is located.

This distinction carries some interesting implications. The first is that downstream activities create competitive advantages that are largely country-specific: a firm's reputation, brand name, and service network in a country grow out of a firm's activities in that country and create entry/mobility barriers largely in that country alone. Competitive advantage in upstream and support activities often grows more out of the entire system of countries in which a firm competes than from its position in any one country, however.

A second implication is that in industries where downstream activities or buyer-tied activities are vital to competitive advantage, there tends to be a more multidomestic pattern of international competition. In industries where upstream and support activities (such as technology development and operations) are crucial to competitive advantage, global competition is more common. In global competition, the location and scale of these potentially footloose activities is optimized from a worldwide perspective.[10]

The distinctive issues in international, as contrasted to domestic, strategy

can be summarized in two key dimensions of how a firm competes internationally. The first is what I term the *configuration* of a firm's activities
worldwide, or where in the world each activity in the value chain is
performed, including in how many places. The second dimension is what I
term *coordination*, which refers to how like activities performed in
different countries are coordinated with each other. If, for example, there
are three plants—one in Germany, one in Japan, and one in the U.S.—how
do the activities in those plants relate to each other?

A firm faces an array of options in both configuration and coordination
for each activity. Configuration options range from concentrated (performing an activity in one location and serving the world from it—e.g., one
R&D lab, one large plant) to dispersed (performing every activity in each
country). In the latter case, each country would have a complete value
chain. Coordination options range from none to very high. For example, if
a firm produces its product in three plants, it could, at one extreme, allow
each plant to operate with full autonomy—e.g., different product standards
and features, different steps in the production process, different raw
materials, different part numbers. At the other extreme, the plants could be
tightly coordinated by employing the same information system, the same
production process, the same parts, and so forth. Options for coordination
in an activity are typically more numerous than the configuration options
because there are many possible levels of coordination and many different
facets of the way the activity is performed.

Figure 3 lists some of the configuration issues and coordination issues
for several important categories of value activities. In technology development, for example, the configuration issue is where R&D is performed: one
location? two locations? and in what countries? The coordination issues
have to do with such things as the extent of interchange among R&D
centers and the location and sequence of product introduction around the
world. There are configuration issues and coordination issues for every
activity.

Figure 4 is a way of summarizing these basic choices in international
strategy on a single diagram, with coordination of activities on the vertical
axis and configuration of activities on the horizontal axis. The firm has to
make a set of choices for each activity. If a firm employs a very dispersed
configuration—placing an entire value chain in every country (or small
group of contiguous countries) in which it operates, coordinating little or
not at all among them—then the firm is competing with a country-centered
strategy. The domestic firm that only operates in one country is the
extreme case of a firm with a country-centered strategy. As we move from
the lower left-hand corner of the diagram up or to the right, we have
strategies that are increasingly global.

Figure 5 illustrates some of the possible variations in international
strategy. The purest global strategy is to concentrate as many activities as

Figure 3 Configuration and coordination issues by category of activity

Value activities	Configuration issues	Coordination issues
Operations	• Location of production facilities for components and end products	• Networking of international plants • Transferring process technology and production know-how among plants
Marketing and sales	• Product line selection • Country (market) selection	• Commonality of brand name worldwide • Coordination of sales to multinational accounts • Similarity of channels and product positioning worldwide • Coordination of pricing in different countries
Service	• Location of service organization	• Similarity of service standards and procedures worldwide
Technology development	• Number and location of R&D centers	• Interchange among dispersed R&D centers • Developing products responsive to market needs in many countries • Sequence of product introductions around the world
Procurement	• Location of the purchasing function	• Managing suppliers located in different countries • Transferring market knowledge • Coordinating purchases of common items

possible in one country, serve the world from this home base, and tightly coordinate those activities that must inherently be performed near the buyer. This is the pattern adopted by many Japanese firms in the 1960s and 1970s, such as Toyota. However, Figures 4 and 5 make it clear that there is no such thing as one global strategy. There are many different kinds of global strategies, depending on a firm's choices about configuration and coordination throughout the value chain. In copiers, for example, Xerox has until recently concentrated R&D in the U.S. but dispersed other activities, in some cases using joint-venture partners to perform them. On dispersed activities, however, coordination has been quite high. The Xerox brand, marketing approach, and servicing procedures have been quite

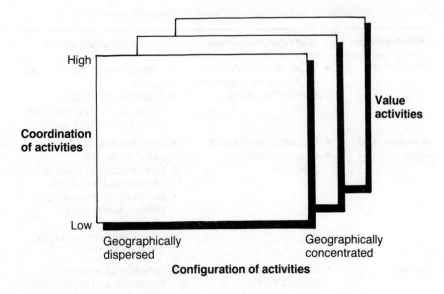

Figure 4 The dimensions of international strategy

standardized worldwide. Canon, on the other hand, has had a much more concentrated configuration of activities and somewhat less coordination of dispersed activities. The vast majority of support activities and manufacturing of copiers have been performed in Japan. Aside from using the Canon brand, however, local marketing subsidiaries have been given quite a bit of latitude in each region of the world.

A global strategy can now be defined more precisely as one in which a firm seeks to gain competitive advantage from its international presence through either concentrating configuration, coordination among dispersed activities, or both. Measuring the presence of a global industry empirically must reflect both dimensions and not just one. Market presence in many countries and some export and import of components and end products are characteristic of most global industries. High levels of foreign investment or the mere presence of multinational firms are not reliable measures, however, because firms may be managing foreign units like a portfolio.

Configuration/Coordination and Competitive Advantage

Understanding the competitive advantages of a global strategy and, in turn, the causes of industry globalization requires specifying the conditions in which concentrating activities globally and coordinating dispersed activities leads to either cost advantage or differentiation. In each case, there are structural characteristics of an industry that work for and against globalization.

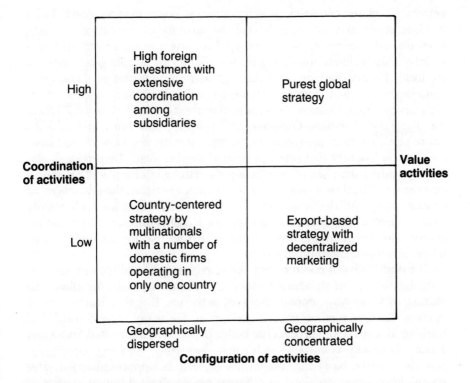

Figure 5 Types of international strategy

The factors that favor concentrating an activity in one or a few locations to serve the world are as follows:

- economies of scale in the activity;
- a proprietary learning curve in the activity;
- comparative advantage in where the activity is performed; and
- coordination advantages of co-locating linked activities such as R&D and production.

The first two factors relate to *how many* sites an activity is performed at, while the last two relate to *where* these sites are. Comparative advantage can apply to any activity, not just production. For example, there may be some locations in the world that are better places than others to do research on medical technology or to perform software development. Government can promote the concentration of activities by providing subsidies or other incentives to use a particular country as an export base, in effect altering comparative advantage—a role many governments are playing today.

There are also structural characteristics that favor dispersion of an activity to many countries, which represent concentration costs. Local product needs may differ, nullifying the advantages of scale or learning from one-site operation of an activity. Locating a range of activities in a country may facilitate marketing in that country by signaling commitment to local buyers and/or providing greater responsiveness. Transport, communication, and storage costs may make it inefficient to concentrate the activity in one location. Government is also frequently a powerful force for dispersing activities. Governments typically want firms to locate the entire value chain in their country, because this creates benefits and spill-overs to the country that often go beyond local content. Dispersion is also encouraged by the risks of performing an activity in one place: exchange-rate risks, political risks, and so on. The balance between the advantages of concentrating and dispersing an activity normally differ for each activity (and industry). The best configuration for R&D is different from that for component fabrication, and this is different from that for assembly, instal-lation, advertising, and procurement.[11]

The desirability of coordinating like activities that are dispersed involves a similar balance of structural factors. Coordination potentially allows the sharing of know-how among dispersed activities. If a firm learns how to operate the production process better in Germany, transferring that learning may make the process run better in plants in the United States and Japan. Differing countries, with their inevitably differing conditions, provide a fertile basis for comparison as well as opportunities for arbi-traging knowledge, obtained in different places about different aspects of the business. Coordination among dispersed activities also potentially improves the ability to reap economies of scale in activities if subtasks are allocated among locations to allow some specialization—e.g., each R&D center has a different area of focus. While there is a fine line between such forms of coordination and what I have termed configuration, it does illustrate how the way a network of foreign locations is managed can have a great influence on the ability to reap the benefits of any given configuration of activities. Viewed another way, close coordination is frequently a partial offset to dispersing an activity.

Coordination may also allow a firm to respond to shifting comparative advantage, where shifts in exchange rates and factor costs are hard to fore-cast. Incrementally increasing the production volume at the location currently enjoying favorable exchange rates, for example, can lower overall costs. Coordination can reinforce a firm's brand reputation with buyers (and hence lead to differentiation) through ensuring a consistent image and approach to doing business on a worldwide basis. This is particularly likely if buyers are mobile or information about the industry flows freely around the world. Coordination may also differentiate the firm with multinational buyers if it allows the firm to serve them anywhere and in a consistent way. Coordination (and a global approach to configuration) enhances leverage with local governments if the firm is able to grow or shrink activities in one country at the expense of others. Finally, coordination yields flexibility in responding to competitors, by allowing the firm to differentially respond across countries and to respond in one country to a challenge in another.

Coordination of dispersed activities usually involves costs that differ by form of coordination and industry. Local conditions may vary in ways that may make a common approach across countries suboptimal. If every plant in the world is required to use the same raw material, for example, the firm pays a penalty in countries where the raw material is expensive relative to satisfactory substitutes. Business practices, marketing systems, raw material sources, local infrastructures, and a variety of other factors may differ across countries as well, often in ways that may mitigate the advantages of a common approach or of the sharing of learning. Governments may restrain the flow of information required for coordination or may impose other barriers to it. The transaction costs of coordination, which have recently received increased attention in domestic competition, are vitally important in international strategy.[12] International coordination involves long distances, language problems, and cultural barriers to communication. In some industries, these factors may mean that coordination is not optimal. They also suggest that forms of coordination which involve relatively infrequent decisions will enjoy advantages over forms of coordination involving on-going interchange.

There are also substantial organizational difficulties involved in achieving cooperation among subsidiaries, which are due to the difficulty in aligning subsidiary managers' interests with those of the firm as a whole. The Germans do not necessarily want to tell the Americans about their latest breakthroughs on the production line because it may make it harder for them to outdo the Americans in the annual comparison of operating efficiency among plants. These vexing organizational problems mean that country subsidiaries often view each other more as competitors than collaborators.[13] As with configuration, a firm must make an activity-by-activity choice about where there is net competitive advantage from coordinating in various ways.

Coordination in some activities may be necessary to reap the advantages of configuration in others. The use of common raw materials in each plant, for example, allows worldwide purchasing. Moreover, tailoring some activities to countries may allow concentration and standardization of other activities. For example, tailored marketing in each country may allow the same product to be positioned differently and hence sold successfully in many countries, unlocking possibilities for reaping economies of scale in production and R&D. Thus coordination and configuration interact.

Configuration/Coordination and the Pattern of International Competition

When benefits of configuring and/or coordinating globally exceed the costs, an industry will globalize in a way that reflects the net benefits by value activity. The activities in which global competitors gain competitive advantage will differ correspondingly. Configuration/coordination determines the ongoing competitive advantages of a global strategy which are additive to competitive advantages a firm derives/possesses from its domestic market positions. An initial transfer of knowledge from the home base to subsidiaries is one, but by no means the most important, advantage of a global competitor.[14]

An industry such as commercial aircraft represents an extreme case of a global industry (in the upper right-hand corner of Figure 4). The three major competitors in this industry—Boeing, McDonnell Douglas, and Airbus—all have global strategies. In activities important to cost and differentiation in the industry, there are compelling net advantages to concentrating most activities and coordinating the dispersed activities extensively.[15] In R&D, there is a large fixed cost of developing an aircraft model ($1 billion or more) which requires worldwide sales to amortize. There are significant economies of scale in production, a steep learning curve in assembly (the learning curve was born out of research in this industry), and apparently significant advantages of locating R&D and production together. Sales of commercial aircraft are infrequent (via a highly skilled sales force), so that even the sales force can be partially concentrated in the home country and travel to buyers.

The costs of a concentrated configuration are relatively low in commercial aircraft. Product needs are homogenous, and there are the low transport costs of delivering the product to the buyer. Finally, worldwide coordination of the one dispersed activity, service, is very important— obviously standarized parts and repair advice have to be available wherever the plane lands.

As in every industry, there are structural features which work against a global strategy in commercial aircraft. These are all related to government, a not atypical circumstance. Government has a particular interest in commercial aircraft because of its large trade potential, the technological sophistication of the industry, its spillover effects to other industries, and its implications for national defense. Government also has an unusual degree of leverage in the industry: in many instances, it is the buyer. Many airlines are government owned, and a government official or appointee is head of the airline.

The competitive advantages of a global strategy are so great that all the successful aircraft producers have sought to achieve and preserve them. In addition, the power of government to intervene has been mitigated by the fact that there are few viable worldwide competitors and that there are the enormous barriers to entry created in part by the advantages of a global strategy. The result has been that firms have sought to assuage government through procurement. Boeing, for example, is very careful about where it buys components. In countries that are large potential customers, Boeing seeks to develop suppliers. This requires a great deal of extra effort by Boeing both to transfer technology and to work with suppliers to assure that they meet its standards. Boeing realizes that this is preferable to compromising the competitive advantage of its strongly integrated world-wide strategy. It is willing to employ one value activity (procurement) where the advantages of concentration are modest to help preserve the benefits of concentration in other activities. Recently, commercial aircraft competitors have entered into joint ventures and other coalition arrangements with foreign suppliers to achieve the same effect, as well as to spread the risk of huge development costs.

The extent and location of advantages from a global strategy vary among industries. In some industries, the competitive advantage from a global strategy comes in technology development, although firms gain little advantage in the primary activities so that these are dispersed around the world to minimize concentration costs. In other industries such as cameras or videocassette recorders, a firm cannot succeed without concentrating production to achieve economies of scale, but instead it gives subsidiaries much local autonomy in sales and marketing. In some industries, there is no net advantage to a global strategy and country-centered strategies dominate—the industry is multidomestic.

Segments or stages of an industry frequently vary in their pattern of globalization. In aluminum, the upstream (alumina and ingot) stages of the industry are global businesses. The downstream stage, semifabrication, is a group of multidomestic businesses because product needs vary by country, transport costs are high, and intensive local customer service is required. Scale economies in the value chain are modest. In lubricants, automotive oil tends to be a country-centered business while marine motor oil is a global business. In automotive oil, countries have varying driving standards, weather conditions, and local laws. Production involves blending various kinds of crude oils and additives, and is subject to few economies of scale but high shipping costs. Country-centered competitors such as Castrol and Quaker State are leaders in most countries. In the marine segment, conversely, ships move freely around the world and require the same oil everywhere. Successful competitors are global.

The ultimate leaders in global industries are often first movers—the first firms to perceive the possibilities for a global strategy. Boeing was the first global competitor in aircraft, for example, as was Honda in motorcycles, and Becton Dickinson in disposable syringes. First movers gain scale and learning advantages which are difficult to overcome. First mover effects are particularly important in global industries because of the association between globalization and economies of scale and learning achieved through worldwide configuration/coordination. Global leadership shifts if industry structural change provides opportunities for leapfrogging to new products or new technologies that nullify past leaders' scale and learning—again, the first mover to the new generation/technology often wins.

Global leaders often begin with some advantage at home, whether it be low labor cost or a product or marketing advantage. They use this as a lever to enter foreign markets. Once there, however, the global competitor converts the initial home advantage into competitive advantages that grow out of its overall worldwide system, such as production scale or ability to amortize R&D costs. While the initial advantage may have been hard to sustain, the global strategy creates new advantages which can be much more durable.

International strategy has often been characterized as a choice between worldwide standardization and local tailoring, or as the tension between the economic imperative (large-scale efficient facilities) and the political imperative (local content, local production). It should be clear from the discussion so far that neither characterization captures the richness of a firm's international strategy choices. A firm's choice of international strategy involves a search for competitive advantage from configuration/coordination throughout the value chain. A firm may standardize (concentrate) some activities and tailor (disperse) others. It may also be able to standardize and tailor at the same time through the coordination of dispersed activities, or use local tailoring of some activities (e.g., different product positioning in each country) to allow standardization of others (e.g., production). Similarly, the economic imperative is not always for a global strategy—in some industries a country-centered strategy is the economic imperative. Conversely, the political imperative is to concentrate activities in some industries where governments provide strong export incentives and locational subsidies.

Global Strategy vs. Comparative Advantage

Given the importance of trade theory to the study of international competition, it is useful to pause and reflect on the relationship to the framework I have presented to the notion of comparative advantage. Is there a difference? The traditional concept of comparative advantage is that factor-cost or factor-quality differences among countries lead to production of products in countries with an advantage which export them elsewhere in the world. Competitive advantage in this view, then, grows out of *where* a firm performs activities. The location of activities is clearly one source of potential advantage in a global firm. The global competitor can locate activities wherever comparative advantage lies, decoupling comparative advantage from its home base or country of ownership.

Indeed, the framework presented here suggests that the comparative advantage story is richer than typically told, because it not only involves production activities (the usual focus of discussions) but also applies to other activities in the value chain such as R&D, processing orders, or designing advertisements. Comparative advantage is specific to the *activity* and not the location of the value chain as a whole.[16] One of the potent advantages of the global firm is that it can spread activities among locations to reflect different preferred locations for different activities, something a domestic or country-centered competitor does not do. Thus components can be made in Taiwan, software written in India and basic R&D performed in Silicon Valley, for example. This international specialization of activities within the firm is made possible by the growing ability to coordinate and configure globally.

At the same time as our framework suggests a richer view of comparative advantage, however, it also suggests that many forms of competitive advantage for the global competitor derive less from *where* the firm performs activities than from *how* it performs them on a worldwide basis; economies of scale, proprietary learning, and differentiation with multinational buyers are not tied to countries but to the configuration and coordination of the firm's worldwide system. Traditional sources of comparative advantage can be elusive and slippery sources of competitive advantage for an international competitor today, because comparative advantage frequently shifts. A country with the lowest labor cost is overtaken within a few years by some other country—facilities located in the first country then face a disadvantage. Moreover, falling direct labor as a percentage of total costs, increasing global markets for raw materials and other inputs, and freer flowing technology have diminished the role of traditional sources of comparative advantage.

My research on a broad cross-section of industries suggests that the achievement of sustainable world market leadership follows a more complex pattern than the exploitation of comparative advantage per se. A competitor often starts with a comparative advantage-related edge that provides the basis for penetrating foreign markets, but this edge is rapidly translated into a broader array of advantages that arise from a global approach to configuration and coordination as described earlier. Japanese firms, for example, have done a masterful job of converting temporary labor-cost advantages into durable systemwide advantages due to scale and proprietary know-how. Ultimately, the systemwide advantages are further reinforced with country-specific advantages such as brand identity as well as distribution channel access. Many Japanese firms were fortunate enough to make their transitions from country-based comparative advantage to global competitive advantage at a time when nobody paid much attention to them and there was a buoyant world economy. European and American competitors were willing to cede market share in "less desirable" segments such as the low end of the producer line, or so they thought. The Japanese translated these beachheads into world leadership by broadening their lines and reaping advantages in scale and proprietary technology. The Koreans and Taiwanese, the latest low labor cost entrants to a number of industries, may have a hard time replicating Japan's success, given slower growth, standardized products, and now alert competitors.

Global Platforms

The interaction of the home-country conditions and competitive advantages from a global strategy that transcend the country suggest a more complex role of the country in firm success than implied by the theory of comparative advantage. To understand this more complex role of the country, I define the concept of a *global platform*. A country is a desirable global platform in an industry if it provides an environment yielding firms domiciled in that country an advantage in competing globally in that particular industry.[17] An essential element of this definition is that it hinges on success *outside* the country, and not merely country conditions which allow firms to successfully master domestic competition. In global competition, a country must be viewed as a platform and not as the place where all a firm's activities are performed.

There are two determinants of a good global platform in an industry, which I have explored in more detail elsewhere.[18] The first is comparative advantage, or the factor endowment of the country as a site to perform particular activities in the industry. Today, simple factors such as low-cost unskilled labor and natural resources are increasingly less important to global competition compared to complex factors such as skilled scientific and technical personnel and advanced infrastructure. Direct labor is a minor proportion of cost in many manufactured goods and automation of non-production activities is shrinking it further, while markets for resources are increasingly global, and technology has widened the number of sources of many resources. A country's factor endowment is partly exogenous and partly the result of attention and investment in the country.

The second determinant of the attractiveness of a country as a global platform in an industry are the characteristics of a country's demand. A country's demand conditions include the size and timing of its demand in an industry, factors recognized as important by authors such as Linder and Vernon.[19] They also conclude the sophistication and power of buyers and channels and the product features and attributes demanded. Local demand conditions provide two potentially powerful sources of competitive advantage to a global competitor based in that country. The first is *first-mover advantages* in perceiving and implementing the appropriate global strategy. Pressing local needs, particularly peculiar ones, lead firms to embark early to solve local problems and gain proprietary know-how. This is then translated into scale and learning advantages as firms move early to compete globally. The other potential benefit of local demand conditions is a baseload of demand for product varieties that will be sought after in international markets. These two roles of the country in the success of a global firm reflect the interaction between conditions of local supply, the composition and timing of country demand, and economies of scale and learning in shaping international success.

The two determinants interact in important and sometimes counter-intuitive ways. Local demand and needs frequently influence private and social investment in endogenous factors of production. A nation with oceans as borders and dependence on sea trade, for example, is more prone to have universities and scientific centers dedicated to oceanographic education and research. Similarly, factor endowment seems to influence local demand. The per capita consumption of wine is highest in wine-growing regions, for example.

Comparative disadvantage in some factors of production can be an advantage in global competition when combined with pressing local demand. Poor growing conditions have led Israeli farmers to innovate in irrigation and cultivation techniques, for example. The shrinking role in competition of simple factors of production relative to complex factors such as technical personnel seem to be enhancing the frequency and importance of such circumstances. What is important today is unleashing innovation in the proper direction, instead of passive exploitation of static cost advantages in a country which can shift rapidly and be overcome. International success today is a dynamic process resulting from continued development of products and processes. The forces which guide firms to undertake such activity thus become central to international competition.

A good example of the interplay among these factors is the television set industry. In the U.S., early demand was in large screen console sets because television sets were initially luxury items kept in the living room. As buyers began to purchase second and third sets, sets became smaller and more portable. They were used increasingly in the bedroom, the kitchen, the car, and elsewhere. As the television set industry matured, table model and portable sets became the universal product variety. Japanese firms, because of the small size of Japanese homes, cut their teeth on small sets. They dedicated most of their R&D to developing small picture tubes and to making sets more compact. In the process of naturally serving the needs of their home market, then, Japanese firms gained early experience and scale in segments of the industry that came to dominate world demand. U.S. firms, conversely, cut their teeth on large-screen console sets with fine furniture cabinets. As the industry matured, the experience base of U.S. firms was in a segment that was small and isolated to a few countries, notably the U.S. Japanese firms were able to penetrate world markets in a segment that was both uninteresting to foreign firms and in which they had initial scale, learning, and labor cost advantages. Ultimately the low-cost advantage disappeared as production was automated, but global scale and learning economies took over as the Japanese advanced product and process technology at a rapid pace.

The two broad determinants of a good global platform rest on the interaction between country characteristics and firms' strategies. The literature on comparative advantage, through focusing on country factor endowments, ignoring the demand side, and suppressing the individual firm, is most appropriate in industries where there are few economies of scale, little proprietary technology or technological change, or few possibilities for product differentiation.[20] While these industry characteristics are those of many traditionally traded goods, they describe few of today's important global industries.

The Evolution of International Competition

Having established a framework for understanding the globalization of industries, we are now in a position to view the phenomenon in historical perspective. If one goes back far enough, relatively few industries were global. Around 1880, most industries were local or regional in scope.[21] The reasons are rather self-evident in the context of our framework. There were few economies of scale in production until fuel-powered machines and assembly-line techniques emerged. There were heterogeneous product needs among regions within countries, much less among countries. There were few if any national media—the *Saturday Evening Post* was the first important national magazine in the U.S. and developed in the teens and twenties. Communicating between regions was difficult before the telegraph and telephone, and transportation was slow until the railroad system became well developed.

These structural conditions created little impetus for the widespread globalization of industry. Those industries that were global reflected classic comparative advantage considerations—goods were simply unavailable in some countries (who then imported them from others) or differences in the availability of land, resources, or skilled labor made some countries desirable suppliers to others. Export of local production was the form of global strategy adopted. There was little role or need for widespread government barriers to international trade during this period, although trade barriers were quite high in some countries for some commodities.

Around the 1880s, however, were the beginnings of what today has blossomed into the globalization of many industries. The first wave of modern global competitors grew up in the late 1880s and early 1900s. Many industries went from local (or regional) to national in scope, and some began globalizing. Firms such as Ford, Singer, Gillette, National Cash Register, Otis, and Western Electric had commanding world market shares by the teens, and operated with integrated worldwide strategies. Early global competitors were principally American and European companies.

Driving this first wave of modern globalization were rising production scale economies due to advancements in technology that outpaced the growth of world economy. Product needs also became more homogenized in different countries as knowledge and industrialization diffused. Transport improved, first through the railroad and steamships and later in trucking. Communication became easier with the telegraph then the telephone. At the same time, trade barriers were either modest or overwhelmed by the advantages of the new large-scale firms.

The burst of globalization soon slowed, however. Most of the few industries that were global moved increasingly towards a multidomestic pattern—multinationals remained, but between the 1920s and 1950 they often evolved towards federations of autonomous subsidiaries. The principal reason was a strong wave of nationalism and resulting high tariff barriers, partly caused by the world economic crisis and world wars. Another barrier to global strategies, chronicled by Chandler,[22] was a growing web of cartels and other interfirm contractual agreements. These limited the geographic spread of firms.

The early global competitors began rapidly dispersing their value chains. The situation of Ford Motor Company was no exception. While in 1925 Ford had almost no production outside the U.S., by World War II its overseas production had risen sharply. Firms that became multinationals during the interwar period tended to adopt country-centered strategies. European multinationals, operating in a setting where there were many sovereign countries within a relatively small geographical area, were quick to establish self-contained and quite autonomous subsidiaries in many countries. A more tolerant regulatory environment also encouraged European firms to form cartels and other cooperative agreements among themselves, which limited their foreign market entry.

Between the 1950s and the late 1970s, however, there was a strong reversal of the interwar trends. As Exhibit 1 illustrated, there have been very strong underlying forces driving the globalization of industries. The important reasons can be understood using the configuration/coordination dichotomy. The competitive advantage of competing worldwide from concentrated activities rose sharply, while concentration costs fell. There was a renewed rise in scale economies in many activities due to advancing technology. The minimum efficient scale of an auto assembly plant more than tripled between 1960 and 1975, for example, while the average cost of developing a new drug more than quadrupled.[23] The pace of technological change has increased, creating more incentive to amortize R&D costs against worldwide sales.

Product needs have continued to homogenize among countries, as income differences have narrowed, information and communication has flowed more freely around the world, and travel has increased.[24] Growing similarities in business practices and marketing systems (e.g., chain stores) in different countries have also been a facilitating factor in homogenizing needs. Within countries there has been a parallel trend towards greater market segmentation, which some observers see as contradictory to the view that product needs in different countries are becoming similar. However, segments today seem based less on country differences and more on buyer differences that transcend country boundaries, such as demographic, user industry, or income groups. Many firms successfully employ global focus strategies in which they serve a narrow segment of an industry worldwide, as do Daimler-Benz and Rolex.

Another driver of post-World War II globalization has been a sharp reduction in the real costs of transportation. This has occurred through innovations in transportation technology including increasingly large bulk carriers, container ships, and larger, more efficient aircraft. At the same time, government impediments to global configuration/coordination have been falling in the postwar period. Tariff barriers have gone down, international cartels and patent-sharing agreements have disappeared, and regional economic pacts such as the European Community have emerged to facilitate trade and investment, albeit imperfectly.

The ability to coordinate globally has also risen markedly in the postwar period. Perhaps the most striking reason is falling communication costs (in voice and data) and reduced travel time for individuals. The ability to coordinate activities in different countries has also been facilitated by growing similarities among countries in marketing systems, business practices, and infrastructure—country after country has developed supermarkets and mass distributors, television advertising, and so on. Greater international mobility of buyers and information has raised the payout to coordinating how a firm does business around the world. The increasing number of firms who are multinational has created growing possibilities for differentiation by suppliers who are global.

The forces underlying globalization have been self-reinforcing. The globalization of firms' strategies has contributed to the homogenization of buyer needs and business practices. Early global competitors must frequently stimulate the demand for uniform global varieties; for example, as Becton Dickinson did in disposable syringes and Honda did in motorcycles. Similarly, globalization of industries begets globalization of supplier industries—the increasing globalization of automotive component suppliers is a good example. Pioneering global competitors also stimulate the development and growth of international telecommunication infrastructure as well as the creation of global advertising media—e.g., *The Economist* and *The Wall Street Journal.*

Strategic Implications of Globalization

When the pattern of international competition shifts from multidomestic to global, there are many implications for the strategy of international firms.

While a full treatment is beyond the scope of this paper, I will sketch some of the implications here.[25]

At the broadest level, globalization casts new light on many issues that have long been of interest to students of international business. In areas such as international finance, marketing, and business-government relations, the emphasis in the literature has been on the unique problems of adapting to local conditions and ways of doing business in a foreign country in a foreign currency. In a global industry, these concerns must be supplemented with an overriding focus on the ways and means of international configuration and coordination. In government relations, for example, the focus must shift from stand-alone negotiations with host countries (appropriate in multidomestic competition) to a recognition that negotiations in one country will both affect other countries and be shaped by possibilities for performing activities in other countries. In finance, measuring the performance of subsidiaries must be modified to reflect the contribution of one subsidiary to another's cost position or differentiation in a global strategy, instead of viewing each subsidiary as a stand-alone unit. In battling with global competitors, it may be appropriate in some countries to accept low profits indefinitely—in multidomestic competition this would be unjustified.[26] In global industries, the overall system matters as much or more than the country.

Of the many other implications of globalization for the firm, there are two of such significance that they deserve some treatment here. The first is the role of *coalitions* in global strategy. A coalition is a long-term agreement linking firms but falling short of merger. I use the term coalition to encompass a whole variety of arrangements that include joint ventures, licenses, supply agreements, and many other kinds of interfirm relationships. Such interfirm agreements have been receiving more attention in the academic literature, although each form of agreement has been looked at separately and the focus has been largely domestic.[27] International coalitions, linking firms in the same industry based in different countries, have become an even more important part of international strategy in the past decade.

International coalitions are a way of configuring activities in the value chain on a worldwide basis jointly with a partner. International coalitions are proliferating rapidly and are present in many industries.[28] There is a particularly high incidence in automobiles, aircraft, aircraft engines, robotics, consumer electronics, semiconductors and pharmaceuticals. While international coalitions have long been present, their character has been changing. Historically, a firm from a developed country formed a coalition with a firm in a lesser-developed country to perform marketing activities in that country. Today, we observe more and more coalitions in which two firms from developed countries are teaming up to serve the world, as well as coalitions that extend beyond marketing activities to encompass activities throughout the value chain.[29] Production and R&D coalitions are very common, for example.

Coalitions are a natural consequence of globalization and the need for an integrated worldwide strategy. The same forces that lead to globalization will prompt the formation of coalitions as firms confront the barriers to establishing a global strategy of their own. The difficulties of gaining access to foreign markets and in surmounting scale and learning thresholds in production, technology development, and other activities have led many firms to team up with others. In many industries, coalitions can be a transitional state in the adjustment of firms to globalization, reflecting the need of firms to catch up in technology, cure short-term imbalances between their global production networks and exchange rates, and accelerate the process of foreign market entry. Many coalitions are likely to persist in some form, however.

There are benefits and costs of coalitions as well as difficult implementation problems in making them succeed (which I have discussed elsewhere). How to choose and manage coalitions is among the most interesting questions in international strategy today. When one speaks to managers about coalitions, almost all have tales of disaster which vividly illustrate that coalitions often do not succeed. Also, there is the added burden of coordinating global strategy with a coalition partner because the partner often wants to do things its own way. Yet, in the face of copious corporate experience that coalitions do not work and a growing economics literature on transaction costs and contractual failures, we see a proliferation of coalitions today of the most difficult kind—those between companies in different countries.[30] There is a great need for researching in both the academic community and in the corporate world about coalitions and how to manage them. They are increasingly being forced on firms today by new competitive circumstances.

A second area where globalization carries particular importance is in *organizational structure*. The need to configure and coordinate globally in complex ways creates some obvious organizational challenges.[31] Any organization structure for competing internationally has to balance two dimensions; there has to be a *country* dimension (because some activities are inherently performed in the country) and there has to be a *global* dimension (because the advantages of global configuration/coordination must be achieved). In a global industry, the ultimate authority must represent the global dimension if a global strategy is to prevail. However, within any international firm, once it disperses any activities there are tremendous pressures to disperse more. Moreover, forces are unleashed which lead subsidiaries to seek growing autonomy. Local country managers will have a natural tendency to emphasize how different their country is and the consequent need for local tailoring and control over more activities in the value chain. Country managers will be loath to give up control over activities or how they are performed to outside forces. They will also frequently paint an ominous picture of host government concerns about local content and requirements for local presence. Corporate incentive systems frequently encourage such behavior by linking incentives narrowly to subsidiary results.

In successful global competitors, an environment is created in which the local managers seek to exploit similarities across countries rather than emphasize differences. They view the firm's global presence as an advantage to be tapped for their local gain. Adept global competitors often go to great lengths to devise ways of circumventing or adapting to local differences while preserving the advantages of the similarities. A good example is Canon's personal copier. In Japan, the typical paper size is bigger than American legal size and the standard European size. Canon's personal copier will not handle this size—a Japanese company introduced a product that did not meet its home market needs in the world's largest market for small copiers! Canon gathered its marketing managers from around the world and cataloged market needs in each country. They found that capacity to copy the large Japanese paper was only needed in Japan. In consultation with design and manufacturing engineers, it was determined that building this feature into the personal copier would significantly increase its complexity and cost. The decision was made to omit the feature because the price elasticity of demand for the personal copier was judged to be high. But this was not the end of the deliberations. Canon's management set out to find a way to make the personal copier saleable in Japan. The answer that emerged was to add another feature to the copier—the ability to copy business cards—which both added little cost and was particularly valuable in Japan. This case illustrates the principle of looking for the similarities in needs among countries and in finding ways of creating similarities, not emphasizing the differences.

Such a change in orientation is something that typically occurs only grudgingly in a multinational company, particularly if it has historically operated in a country-centered mode (as has been the case with early U.S. and European multinationals). Achieving such a reorientation requires first that managers recognize that competitive success demands exploiting the advantages of a global strategy. Regular contact and discussion among subsidiary managers seems to be a prerequisite, as are information systems that allow operations in different countries to be compared.[32] This can be followed by programs for exchanging information and sharing know-how and then by more complex forms of coordination. Ultimately, the reconfiguring of activities globally may then be accepted, even though subsidiaries may have to give up control over some activities in the process.

The Future of International Competition

Since the late 1970s, there have been some gradual but significant changes in the pattern of international competition which carry important implications for international strategy. Our framework provides a template with which we can examine these changes and probe their significance. The factors shaping the global configuration of activities by firms are developing in ways which contrast with the trends of the previous thirty years. Homogenization of product needs among countries appears to be continuing, though segmentation within countries is as well. As a result, consumer packaged goods are becoming increasingly prone toward globalization, though they have long been characterized by multidomestic competition. There are also signs of globalization in some service industries as the introduction of information technology creates scale economies in support activities and facilitates coordination in primary activities. Global service firms are reaping advantages in hardware and software development as well as procurement.

In many industries, however, limits have been reached in the scale economies that have been driving the concentration of activities. These limits grow out of classic diseconomies of scale that arise in very large facilities, as well as out of new, more flexible technology in manufacturing and other activities that is often not as scale sensitive as previous methods. At the same time, though, flexible manufacturing allows the production of multiple varieties (to serve different countries) in a single plant. This may

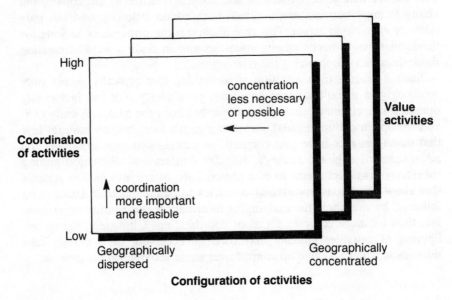

Figure 6 Future trends in international competition

encourage new movement towards globalization in industries in which product differences among countries have remained significant and have blocked globalization in the past.

There also appear to be some limits to further decline in transport costs, as innovations such as containerization, bulk ships, and larger aircraft have run their course. However, a parallel trend toward smaller, lighter products and components may keep some downward pressure on transport costs. The biggest change in the benefits and costs of concentrated configuration has been the sharp rise in protectionism in recent years and the resulting rise in nontariff barriers, harkening back to the 1920s. As a group, these factors point to less need and less opportunity for highly concentrated configurations of activities.

When we examine the coordination dimension, the picture looks starkly different. Communication and coordination costs are dropping sharply, driven by breathtaking advances in information systems and telecommunication technology. We have just seen the beginning of developments in this area, which are spreading throughout the value chain.[33] Boeing, for example, is employing computer-aided design technology to jointly design components on-line with foreign suppliers. Engineers in different countries are communicating via computer screens. Marketing systems and business practices continue to homogenize, facilitating the coordination of activities in different countries. The mobility of buyers and information is also growing rapidly, greasing the international spread of brand reputations and enhancing the importance of consistency in the way activities are performed worldwide. Increasing numbers of multinational and global firms are begetting globalization by their suppliers. There is also a sharp rise in the computerization of manufacturing as well as other activities throughout the value chain, which greatly facilitates coordination among dispersed sites.

The imperative of global strategy is shifting, then, in ways that will require a rebalancing of configuration and coordination. Concentrating activities is less necessary in economic terms, and less possible as governments force more dispersion. At the same time, the ability to coordinate globally throughout the value chain is increasing dramatically through modern technology. The need to coordinate is also rising to offset greater dispersion and to respond to buyer needs.

Thus, today's game of global strategy seems increasingly to be a game of coordination—getting more and more dispersed production facilities, R&D laboratories, and marketing activities to truly work together. Yet, widespread coordination is the exception rather than the rule today in many multinationals, as I have noted. The imperative for coordination raises many questions for organizational structure, and is complicated even more when the firm has built its global system using coalitions with independent firms.

Japan has clearly been the winner in the postwar globalization of competition. Japan's firms not only had an initial labor cost advantage but the orientation and skills to translate this into more durable competitive advantages such as scale and proprietary technology. The Japanese context also offered an excellent platform for globalization in many industries, given postwar environmental and technological trends. With home market conditions favoring compactness, a lead in coping with high energy costs, and a national conviction to raise quality, Japan has proved a fertile incubator of global leaders. Japanese multinationals had the advantage of embarking on international strategies in the 1950s and 1960s when the imperatives for a global approach to strategy were beginning to accelerate, but without the legacy of past international investments and modes of behavior.[34] Japanese firms also had an orientation towards highly concentrated activities that fit the strategic imperative of the time. Most European and American multinationals, conversely, were well established internationally before the war. They had legacies of local subsidiary autonomy that reflected the interwar environment. As Japanese firms spread internationally, they dispersed activities only grudgingly and engaged in extensive global coordination. European and country-centered American companies struggled to rationalize overly dispersed configurations of activities and to boost the level of global coordination among foreign units. They found their decentralized organization structures—so fashionable in the 1960s and 1970s—to be a hindrance to doing so.

As today's international firms contemplate the future, Japanese firms are rapidly dispersing activities, due largely to protectionist pressures but also because of the changing economic factors I have described. They will have to learn the lessons of managing overseas activities that many European and American firms learned long ago. However, Japanese firms enjoy an organizational style that is supportive of coordination and a strong commitment to introducing new technologies such as information systems that facilitate it. European firms must still overcome their country-centered heritage. Many still do not compete with truly global strategies and lack modern technology. Moreover, the large number of coalitions formed by European firms must overcome the barriers to coordination if they are not to prove ultimately limiting. The European advantage may well be in exploiting an acute and well-developed sensitivity to local market conditions as well as a superior ability to work with host governments. By using modern flexible manufacturing technology and computerizing elsewhere in the value chain, European firms may be able to serve global segments and better differentiate products.

Many American firms tend to fall somewhere in between the European and Japanese situations. Their awareness of international competition has risen dramatically in recent years, and efforts at creating global strategies are more widespread. The American challenge is to catch the Japanese in a variety of technologies, as well as to learn how to gain the benefits of co-ordinating among dispersed units instead of becoming trapped by the myths of decentralization. The changing pattern of international competition is creating an environment in which no competitor can afford to allow country parochialism to impede its ability to turn a worldwide position into a competitive edge.

References

† This article grows out of the seventh lecture in a series of lectures on Strategy and Organization for Individual Innovation and Renewal, sponsored by the Transamerica Chair, School of Business Administration, University of California at Berkeley. March 15, 1985.

1. United Nations Center on Transnational Corporations, *Salient Features and Trends in Foreign Direct Investment* (New York, NY: United Nations, 1984).

2. For a survey, see R.E. Caves and Ronald W. Jones, *World Trade and Payments*, 4th ed. (Boston, MA: Little, Brown, 1985).

3. There are many books on the theory and management of the multinational, which are too numerous to cite here. For an excellent survey of the literature, see R.E. Caves, *Multinational Enterprise and Economic Analysis* (Cambridge, England: Cambridge University Press, 1982).

4. Raymond Vernon, "International Investment and International Trade in the Product Cycle," *Quarterly Journal of Economics*, Vol. 80 (May 1966):190-207. Vernon himself, among others, has raised questions about how general the product cycle pattern is today.

5. Michael E. Porter, *Competitive Strategy: Techniques for Analyzing Industries and Competitors* (New York, NY: The Free Press, 1980); Michael E. Porter, "Beyond Comparative Advantage," Working Paper, Harvard Graduate School of Business Administration, August 1985.

6. For a description of this research, see Michael E. Porter, ed., *Competition in Global Industries* (Boston, MA: Harvard Business School Press, forthcoming).

7. The distinction between multidomestic and global competition and some of its strategic implications were described in T. Hout, Michael E. Porter, and E. Rudden, "How Global Companies Win Out," *Harvard Business Review* (September/ October 1982), pp. 98-108.

8. Howard V. Perlmutter, "The Tortuous Evolution of the Multinational Corporation," *Columbia Journal of World Business* (January/February 1969), pp. 9-18. Perlmutter's concept of ethnocentric, polycentric, and geocentric multinationals takes the *firm* not the industry as the unit of analysis and is decoupled from industry structure. It focuses on management attitudes, the nationality of executives, and other aspects of organization. Perlmutter presents ethnocentric, polycentric, and geocentric as stages of an organization's development as a multinational, with geocentric as stages of an organization's development as a multinational, with geocentric as the goal. A later paper (Yoram Wind, Susan P. Douglas, and Howard V. Perlmutter, "Guidelines for Developing International Marketing Strategies," *Journal of Marketing*, Vol. 37 (April 1973: 14-23) tempers this conclusion based on the fact that some companies may not have the required sophistication in marketing to attempt a geocentric strategy. Products embedded in the lifestyle or culture of a country are also identified as less susceptible to geocentrism. The Perlmutter et al. view does not link management orientation to industry

structure and strategy. International strategy should grow out of the net competitive advantage in a global industry of different types of worldwide coordination. In some industries, a country-centered strategy, roughly analogous to Perlmutter's poly-centric idea, may be the best strategy irrespective of company size and international experience. Conversely, a global strategy may be imperative given the competitive advantage that accrues from it. Industry and strategy should define the organization approach, not vice versa.

9. Michael E. Porter, *Competitive Advantage: Creating and Sustaining Superior Performance* (New York, NY: The Free Press, 1985).

10. Buzzell (Robert D. Buzzell, "Can You Standardize Multinational Marketing," *Harvard Business Review* [November/December 1980], pp. 102–113); Pryor (Millard H. Pryor, "Planning in a World-Wide Business," *Harvard Business Review*, Vol. 23 [January/February 1965]); and Wind, Douglas, and Perlmutter (op. cit.) point out that national differences are in most cases more critical with respect to marketing than with production and finance. This generalization reflects the fact that marketing activities are often inherently country-based. However, this generalization is not reliable because in many industries, production and other activities are widely dispersed.

11. A number of authors have framed the globalization of industries in terms of the balance between imperatives for global integration and imperatives for national responsiveness, a useful distinction. See, C.K. Prahalad, "The Stategic Process in a Multinational Corporation," unpublished DBA dissertation, Harvard Graduate School of Business Administration, 1975; Yves Doz, "National Policies and Multi-national Management," an unpublished DBA dissertation, Harvard Graduate School of Business Administration, 1976; and Christopher A. Bartlett, "Multinational Structural Evolution: The Changing Decision Environment in the International Division," unpublished DBA dissertation, Harvard Graduate School of Business Administration, 1979. I link the distinction here to where and how a firm performs the activities in the value chain internationally.

12. See, for example, Oliver Williamson, *Markets and Hierarchies* (New York, NY: The Free Press, 1975). For an international application, see Mark C. Casson, "Transaction Costs and the Theory of the Multinational Enterprise," in Alan Rugman, ed., *New Theories of the Multinational Enterprise* (London: Croom Helm, 1982); David J. Teece, "Transaction Cost Economics and the Multinational Enterprise: An Assessment," *Journal of Economic Behavior and Organization* (forthcoming, 1986).

13. The difficulties in coordinating are internationally parallel to those in coordinating across business units competing in different industries with the diversified firm. See Michael E. Porter, *Competitive Advantage: Creating and Sustaining Superior Performance* (New York, NY: The Free Press, 1985), Chapter 11.

14. Empirical research has found a strong correlation between R&D and advertising intensity and the extent of foreign direct investment (for a survey, see Caves, 1982, op. cit.). Both these factors have a place in our model of the determinants of globalization, but for quite different reasons. R&D intensity suggests scale advantages for the global competitor in developing products or processes that are manufactured abroad either due to low production scale economies or government pressures, or which require investments in service infrastructure. Advertising intensity, however, is much closer to the classic transfer of marketing knowledge to foreign subsidiaries. High advertising industries are also frequently those where local tastes differ and manufacturing scale economies are modest, both reasons to disperse many activities.

15. For an interesting description of the industry, see the paper by Michael Yoshino in Porter, ed., op. cit., (forthcoming).

16. It has been recognized that comparative advantage in different stages in a vertically integrated industry such as aluminum can reside in different countries. Bauxite mining will take place in resource-rich countries, for example, while smelting will take place in countries with low electrical power cost. See R.E. Caves and Ronald W. Jones, op. cit. The argument here extends this thinking *within* the value chain of any stage and suggests that the optimal location for performing individual activities may vary as well.

17. The firm need not necessarily be owned by investors in the country, but the country is its home base for competing in a particular country.

18. See Porter, *Competitive Advantage*, op. cit.

19. See S. Linder, *An Essay on Trade and Transformation* (New York, NY: John Wiley, 1961); Vernon, op. cit., (1966); W. Gruber, D. Mehta, and R. Vernon, "R&D Factor in International Trade and International Investment of United States Industries," *Journal of Political Economics*, 76/1 (1967):20–37.

20. Where it does recognize scale economies, trade theory views them narrowly as arising from production in one country.

21. See Alfred Chandler in Porter, ed., op. cit., (forthcoming) for a penetrating history of the origins of the large industrial firm and its expansion abroad, which is consistent with the discussion here.

22. Ibid.

23. For data on auto assembly, see "Note on the World Auto Industry in Transition," Harvard Business School Case Services (#9–382–122).

24. For a supporting view, see Theodore Levitt, "The Globalization of Markets," *Harvard Business Review* (May/June 1983), pp. 92–102.

25. The implications of the shift from multidomestic to global competition were the theme of a series of papers on each functional area of the firm prepared for the Harvard Business School of Colloquium on Competition in Global Industries. See Porter, ed., op. cit., (forthcoming).

26. For a discussion, see Hout, Porter, and Rudden, op. cit. For a recent treatment, see Gary Hamel and C.K. Prahalad, "Do You Really Have a Global Strategy," *Harvard Business Review* (July/August 1985), pp. 139–148.

27. David J. Teece, "Firm Boundaries, Technological Innovation, and Strategic Planning," in L.G. Thomas, ed., *Economics of Strategic Planning* (Lexington, MA: Lexington Books, 1985).

28. For a treatment of coalitions from this perspective, see Porter, Fuller, and Rawlinson, in Porter, ed., op. cit., (forthcoming).

29. Hladik's recent study of international joint ventures provides supporting evidence. See K. Hladik, "International Joint Ventures: An Empirical Investigation into the Characteristics of Recent U.S.-Foreign Joint Venture Partnerships," unpublished Doctoral dissertation, Business Economics Program, Harvard University, 1984.

30. For the seminal work on contractual failures, see Williamson, op. cit.

31. For a thorough and sophisticated treatment, see Christopher A. Bartlett's paper in Porter, ed., op. cit., (forthcoming).

32. For a good discussion of the mechanisms for facilitating international coordination in operations and technology development, see M.T. Flaherty in Porter, ed., op. cit., (forthcoming). Flaherty stresses the importance of information systems and the many dimensions that valuable coordination can take.

33. For a discussion, see Michael E. Porter and Victor Millar, "How Information Gives You Competitive Advantage," *Harvard Business Review* (July/August 1985), pp. 149–160.

34. Prewar international sales enjoyed by Japanese firms were handled largely through trading companies. See Chandler, op. cit.

7

Global Strategy: An Organizing Framework*

Sumantra Ghoshal

*Source: *Strategic Management Journal*, 8 (1987), pp. 425–440.

Global strategy has recently emerged as a popular concept among managers of multinational corporations as well as among researchers and students in the field of international management. This paper presents a conceptual framework encompassing a range of different issues relevant to global strategies. The framework provides a basis for organizing existing literature on the topic and for creating a map of the field. Such a map can be useful for teaching and also for guiding future research in this area. The article, however, is primarily directed at managers of multinational corporations, and is aimed at providing them with a basis for relating and synthesizing the different perspectives and prescriptions that are currently available for global strategic management.

Over the past few years the concept of global strategy has taken the world of multinational corporations (MNCs) by storm. Scores of articles in the *Harvard Business Review, Fortune, The Economist* and other popular journals have urged multinationals to 'go global' in their strategies. The topic has clearly captured the attention of MNC managers. Conferences on global strategy, whether organized by the Conference Board in New York, *The Financial Times* in London, or Nomura Securities in Tokyo, have invariably attracted enthusiastic corporate support and sizeable audiences. Even in the relatively slow-moving world of academe the issue of globalization of industries and companies has emerged as a new bandwagon, as manifest in the large number of papers on the topic presented at recent meetings of the Academy of Management, the Academy of International Business and the Strategic Management Society. 'Manage globally' appears to be the latest battlecry in the world of international business.

Multiple Perspectives, Many Prescriptions

This enthusiasm notwithstanding, there is a great deal of conceptual ambiguity about what a 'global' strategy really means. As pointed out by Hamel and Prahalad (1985), the distinction among a global industry, a global firm, and a global strategy is somewhat blurred in the literature. According to Hout, Porter and Rudden (1982), a global strategy is appropriate for global industries which are defined as those in which a firm's competitive position in one national market is significantly affected by its competitive position in other national markets. Such interactions between a firm's positions in different markets may arise from scale benefits or from the potential of synergies or sharing of costs and resources across markets. However, as argued by Bartlett (1985), Kogut (1984) and many others, those scale and synergy benefits may often be created by strategic actions of individual firms and may not be 'given' in any *a priori* sense. For some industries, such as aeroframes or aeroengines, the economies of scale may be large enough to make the need for global integration of activities obvious. However, in a large number of cases industries may not be born global but may have globalness thrust upon them by the entrepreneurship of a company such as Yoshida Kagyo KK (YKK) or Procter and Gamble. In such cases the global industry–global strategy link may be more useful for ex-post explanation of outcomes than for ex-ante predictions or strategizing.

Further, the concept of a global strategy is not as new as some of the recent authors on the topic have assumed it to be. It was stated quite explicitly about 20 years ago by Perlmutter (1969) when he distinguished between the geocentric, polycentric, and ethnocentric approaches to multinational management. The starting point for Perlmutter's categorization scheme was the world-view of a firm, which was seen as the driving force behind its management processes and the way it structured its world-wide activities (see Robinson, 1978 and Rutenberg, 1982 for detailed reviews and expositions). In much of the current literature, in contrast, the focus has been narrowed and the concept of global strategy has been linked almost exclusively with how the firm structures the flow of tasks within its world-wide value-adding system. The more integrated and rationalized the flow of tasks appears to be, the more global the firm's strategy is assumed to be (e.g. Leontiades, 1984). On the one hand, this focus has led to improved understanding of the fact that different tasks offer different degrees of advantages from global integration and national differentiation and that, optimally, a firm must configure its value chain to obtain the best possible advantages from both (Porter, 1984). But, on the other hand, it has also led to certain dysfunctional simplifications. The complexities of managing large, world-wide organizations have been obscured by creating polar alternatives between centralization and decentralization, or between global and multidomestic strategies (e.g. Hout *et al.*, 1982). Complex management tasks have been seen as composites of simple global and local components. By emphasizing the importance of rationalizing the flow of components and final products within a multinational system, the importance of internal flows of people, technology, information, and values has been de-emphasized.

Differences among authors writing on the topic of global strategy are not limited to concepts and perspectives. Their prescriptions on how to manage globally have also been very different, and often contradictory.

1. Levitt (1983) has argued that effective global strategy is not a bag of many tricks but the successful practice of just one: product standardization. According to him, the core of a global strategy lies in developing a standardized product to be produced and sold the same way throughout the world.
2. According to Hout, *et al.* (1982), on the other hand, effective global strategy requires the approach not of a hedgehog, who knows only one trick, but that of a fox, who knows many. Exploiting economies of scale through global volume, taking pre-emptive positions through quick and large investments, and managing interdependently to achieve synergies across different activities are, according to these authors, some of the more important moves that a winning global strategist must muster.
3. Hamel and Prahalad's (1985) prescription for a global strategy contradicts that of Levitt (1983) even more sharply. Instead of a single standardized product, they recommend a broad product portfolio, with many product varieties, so that investments on technologies and distribution channels can be shared. Cross-subsidization across products and markets, and the development of a strong world-wide distribution system, are the two moves that find the pride of place in these authors' views on how to succeed in the game of global chess.
4. If Hout, *et al.*'s (1982) global strategist is the heavyweight champion who knocks out opponents with scale and pre-emptive investments, Kogut's (1985b) global strategist is the nimble-footed athlete who wins through flexibility and arbitrage. He creates options so as to turn the uncertainties of an increasingly volatile global economy to his own advantage. Multiple sourcing, production shifting to benefit from changing factor costs and exchange rates, and arbitrage to exploit imperfections in financial and information markets are, according to Kogut, some of the hallmarks of a superior global strategy.

These are only a few of the many prescriptions available to MNC managers about how to build a global strategy for their firms. All these suggestions have been derived from rich and insightful analyses of real-life situations. They are all reasonable and intuitively appealing, but their managerial implications are not easy to reconcile.

The Need for an Organizing Framework

The difficulty for both practitioners and researchers in dealing with the small but rich literature on global strategies is that there is no organizing framework within which the different perspectives and prescriptions can be assimilated. An unfortunate fact of corporate life is that any particular strategic action is rarely an unmixed blessing. Corporate objectives are multidimensional, and often mutually contradictory. Contrary to received wisdom, it is also usually difficult to prioritize them. Actions to achieve a particular objective often impede another equally important objective. Each of these prescriptions is aimed at achieving certain objectives of a global strategy. An overall framework can be particularly useful in identifying the trade-offs between those objectives and therefore in understanding not only the benefits but also the potential costs associated with the different strategic alternatives.

The objective of this paper is to suggest such an organizing framework which may help managers and academics in formulating the various issues that arise in global strategic management. The underlying premise is that simple categorization schemes such as the distinction between global and multidomestic strategies are not very helpful in understanding the complexities of corporate-level strategy in large multinational corporations. Instead, what may be more useful is to understand what the key strategic objectives of an MNC are, and the tools that it possesses for achieving them. An integrated analysis of the different means and the different ends can help both managers and researchers in formulating, describing, classifying and analyzing the content of global strategies. Besides, such a framework can relate academic research, that is often partial, to the totality of real life that managers must deal with.

The Framework: Mapping Means and Ends

The proposed framework is shown in Table 1. While the specific construct may be new, the conceptual foundation on which it is built is derived from a synthesis of existing literature.

The basic argument is simple. The goals of a multinational—as indeed of any organization—can be classified into three broad categories. The firm must achieve efficiency in its current activities; it must manage the risks that it assumes in carrying out those activities; and it must develop internal learning capabilities so as to be able to innovate and adapt to future changes. Competitive advantage is developed by taking strategic actions that optimize the firm's achievement of these different and, at times, conflicting goals.

A multinational has three sets of tools for developing such competitive

Table 1 Global strategy: an organizing framework

	Sources of competitive advantage		
Strategic objectives	*National differences*	*Scale economies*	*Scope economies*
Achieving efficiency in current operations	Benefiting from differences in factor costs— wages and cost of capital	Expanding and exploiting potential scale economies in each activity	Sharing of investments and costs across products, markets and businesses
Managing risks	Managing different kinds of risks arising from market or policy-induced changes in comparative advantages of different countries	Balancing scale with strategic and operational flexibility	Portfolio diversification of risks and creation of options and side-bets
Innovation learning and adaptation	Learning from societal differences in organizational and managerial processes and systems	Benefiting from experience—cost reduction and innovation	Shared learning across organizational components in different products, markets or businesses

advantage. It can exploit the differences in input and output markets among the many countries in which it operates. It can benefit from scale economies in its different activities. It can also exploit synergies or economies of scope that may be available because of the diversity of its activities and organization.

The strategic task of managing globally is to use all three sources of competitive advantage to optimize efficiency, risk and learning simultaneously in a world-wide business. The key to a successful global strategy is to manage the interactions between these different goals and means. That, in essence, is the organizing framework. Viewing the tasks of global strategy this way can be helpful to both managers and academics in a number of ways. For example, it can help managers in generating a comprehensive checklist of factors and issues that must be considered in reviewing different strategic alternatives. Such a checklist can serve as a basis for mapping the overall strategies of their own companies and those of their competitors so as to understand the comparative strengths and vulnerabilities of both. Table 1 shows some illustrative examples of factors that must be considered while carrying out such comprehensive strategic audits.

Another practical utility of the framework is that it can highlight the contradictions between the different goals and between the different means, and thereby make salient the strategic dilemmas that may otherwise get resolved through omission.

In the next two sections the framework is explained more fully by describing the two dimensions of its construct, viz. the strategic objectives of the firm and the sources of competitive advantage available to a multinational corporation. Subsequent sections show how selected articles contribute to the literature and fit within the overall framework. The paper concludes with a brief discussion of the trade-offs that are implicit in some of the more recent prescriptions on global strategic management.

The Goals: Strategic Objectives

Achieving Efficiency

A general premise in the literature on strategic management is that the concept of strategy is relevant only when the actions of one firm can affect the actions or performance of another. Firms competing in imperfect markets earn different 'efficiency rents' from the use of their resources (Caves, 1980). The objective of strategy, given this perspective, is to enhance such efficiency rents.

Viewing a firm broadly as an input–output system, the overall efficiency of the firm can be defined as the ratio of the value of its outputs to the costs of all its inputs. It is by maximizing this ratio that the firm obtains the surplus resources required to secure its own future. Thus it differentiates its products to enhance the exchange value of its outputs, and seeks low cost factors to minimize the cost of its inputs. It also tries to enhance the efficiency of its throughput processes by achieving higher scale economies or by finding more efficient production processes.

The field of strategic management is curently dominated by this

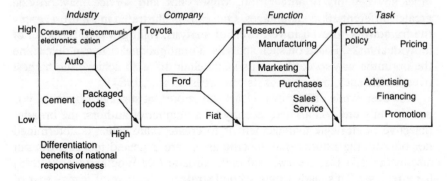

Figure 1 The integration–responsiveness framework (reproduced from Bartlett, 1985)

efficiency perspective. The generic strategies of Porter (1980), different versions of the portfolio model, as well as overall strategic management frameworks such as those proposed by Hofer and Schendel (1978) and Hax and Majluf (1984) are all based on the underlying notion of maximizing efficiency rents of the different resources available to the firm.

In the field of global strategy this efficiency perspective has been reflected in the widespread use of the integration—responsiveness framework originally proposed by Prahalad (1975) and subsequently developed and applied by a number of authors including Doz, Bartltt and Prahalad (1981) and Porter (1984). In essence, the framework is a conceptual lens for visualizing the cost advantages of global integration of certain tasks *vis-à-vis* the differentiation benefits of responding to national differences in tastes, industry structures, distribution systems, and government regulations. As suggested by Bartlett (1985), the same framework can be used to understand differences in the benefits of integration and responsiveness at the aggregate level of industries, at the level of individual companies within an industry, or even at the level of different functions within a company (see Figure 1, reproduced from Bartlett, 1985). Thus the consumer electronics industry may be characterized by low differentiation benefits and high integration advantages, while the position of the packaged foods industry may be quite the opposite. In the telecommunications switching industry, in contrast, both local and global forces may be strong, while in the automobile industry both may be of moderate and comparable importance.

Within an industry (say, automobile), the strategy of one firm (such as Toyota) may be based on exploiting the advantages of global integration through centralized production and decision-making, while that of another (such as Fiat) may aim at exploiting the benefits of national differentiation by creating integrated and autonomous subsidiaries which can exploit strong links with local stakeholders to defend themselves against more efficient global competitors. Within a firm, research may offer greater efficiency benefits of integration, while sales and service may provide greater differentiation advantages. One can, as illustrated in Figure 1, apply the framework to even lower levels of analysis, right down to the level of individual tasks. Based on such analysis, a multinational firm can determine the optimum way to configure its value chain so as to achieve the highest overall efficiency in the use of its resources (Porter, 1984).

However, while efficiency is clearly an important strategic objective, it is not the only one. As argued recently by a number of authors, the broader objective of strategic management is to create value which is determined not only by the returns that specific assets are expected to generate, but also by the risks that are assumed in the process (see Woo and Cool (1985) for a review). This leads to the second strategic objective of firms—that of managing risks.[1]

Managing Risks

A multinational corporation faces many different kinds of risks, some of which are endemic to all firms and some others are unique to organizations operating across national boundaries. For analytical simplicity these different kinds of risks may be collapsed into four broad categories.

First, an MNC faces certain *macroeconomic risks* which are completely outside its control. These include cataclysmic events such as wars and natural calamities, and also equilibrium-seeking or even random movements in wage rates, interest rates, exchange rates, commodity prices, and so on.

Second, the MNC faces what is usually referred to in the literature as political risks but may be more appropriately called *policy risks* to emphasize that they arise from policy actions of national governments and not from either long-term equilibrium-seeking forces of global markets, nor from short-term random fluctuations in economic variables arising out of stickiness or unpredictability of market mechanisms. The net effect of such policy actions may often be indistinguishable from the effect of macroeconomic forces; for example, both may lead to changes in the exchange rate of a particular currency. But from a management perspective the two must be distinguished, since the former is uncontrollable but the latter is at least partially controllable.

Third, a firm also faces certain *competitive risks* arising from the unertainties of competitors' responses to its own strategies (including the strategy of doing nothing and trying to maintain the status quo). While all companies face such risks to varying extents (since both monopolies and perfect competition are rare), their implications are particularly complex in the context of global strategies since the responses of competitors may take place in many different forms and in many different markets. Further, technological risk can also be considered as a part of competitive risk since a new technology can adversely affect a firm only when it is adopted by a competitor, and not otherwise.[2]

Finally, a firm also faces what may be called *resource risks*. This is the risk that the adopted strategy will require resources that the firm does not have, cannot acquire, or cannot spare. A key scarce resource for most firms is managerial talent. But resource risks can also arise from lack of appropriate technology, or even capital (if managers, for reasons of control, do not want to use capital markets, or if the market is less efficient than finance theorists would have us believe).

One important issue with regard to risks is that they change over time. Vernon (1977) has highlighted this issue in the context of policy risks, but the same is true of the others. Consider resource risks as an example. Often the strategy of a multinational will assume that appropriate resources will be acquired as the strategy unfolds. Yet the initial conditions on which the plans for on-going resource acquisition and development have been based may change over time. Nissan, for instance, based its aggressive internationalization strategy on the expectation of developing technological, financial, and managerial resources out of its home base. Changing competitive positions among local car manufacturers in Japan have affected these resource development plans of the company, and its internationalizing strategy has been threatened significantly. A more careful analysis of alternative competitive scenarios, and of their effects on the resource allocation plans of the company, may have led Nissan to either a slower pace of internationalization, or to a more aggressive process of resource acquisition at an earlier stage of implementing its strategy.

The strategic task, with regard to management of risks, is to consider these different kinds of risks *jointly* in the context of particular strategic decisions. However, not all forms of risk are strategic since some risks can be easily diversified, shifted, or shared through routine market transactions. It is only those risks which cannot be diversified through a readily available external market that are of concern at the strategic level.

As an example, consider the case of currency risks. These can be classified as contractual, semi-contractual and operating risks (Lessard and Lightstone, 1983). Contractual risks arise when a firm enters into a contract for which costs and revenues are expected to be generated in different currencies: for example a Japanese firm entering into a contract for supplying an item to be made in Japan to an American customer at a price fixed in dollars. Semi-contractual risks are assumed when a firm offers an option denominated in foreign currencies, such as a British company quoting a firm rate in guilders. Operating risks, on the other hand, refer to exchange rate-related changes in the firm's competitiveness arising out of long-term commitments of revenues or costs in different currencies. For example, to compete with a Korean firm, an American firm may set up production facilities in Singapore for supplying its customers in the United States and Europe. A gradual strengthening of the Singapore dollar, in comparison with the Korean won, can erode the overall competitiveness of the Singapore plant.

Both contractual and semi-contractual currency risks can be easily shifted or diversified, at relatively low cost, through various hedging mechanisms. If a firm does not so hedge these risks, it is essentially operating as a currency speculator and the risks must be associated with the speculation business and not to its product-market operations. Operating risks, on the other hand, cannot be hedged so easily,[3] and must be considered at the strategic rather than the operational level.

Analysis of strategic risks will have significant implications for a firm's decisions regarding the structures and locations of its cost and revenue streams. It will lead to more explicit analysis of the effects of environmental uncertainties on the configuration of its value chain. There may be a shift from ownership to rental of resources; from fixed to variable costs. Output and activity distributions may be broadened to achieve the benefits of diversification. Incrementalism may be given greater emphasis in its strategy in comparison to pre-emptive resource commitments and long-term planning. Overall strategies may be formulated in more general and flexible terms, so as to be robust to different environmental scenarios. In addition, side-bets may be laid to cover contingencies and to create strategic options which may or may not be exercised in the future (see Kogut, 1985b; Aaker and Mascarenhas, 1984; and Mascarenhas, 1982).

Innovation, Learning and Adaptation

Most existing theories of the multinational corporation view it as an instrument to extract additional rents from capabilities internalized by the firm (see Calvet, 1981, for a review). A firm goes abroad to make more profits by exploiting its technology, or brand name, or management capabilities in different countries around the world. It is assumed that the key competencies of the multinational always reside at the center.

While the search for additional profits or the desire to protect existing revenues may explain why multinationals come to exist, they may not provide an equally complete explanation of why some of them continue to grow and flourish. An alternative view may well be that a key asset of the multinational is the diversity of environments in which it operates. This diversity exposes it to multiple stimuli, allows it to develop diverse capabilities, and provides it with a broader learning opportunity than is available to a purely domestic firm. The enhanced organizational learning that results from the diversity internalized by the multinational may be a key explanator of its ongoing success, while its initial stock of knowledge may well be the strength that allows it to create such organizational diversity in the first place (Bartlett and Ghoshal, 1985).

Internal diversity may lead to strategic advantages for a firm in many different ways. In an unpredictable environment it may not be possible, ex ante, to predict the competencies that will be required in the future. Diversity of internal capabilities, following the logic of population ecologists (e.g. Hannan and Freeman, 1977; Aldrich, 1979), will enhance the probability of the firm's survival by enhancing the chances that it will be in possession of the capabilities required to cope with an uncertain future state. Similarly, diversity of resources and competencies may also enhance the firm's ability to create joint innovations, and to exploit them in multiple locations. One example of such benefits of diversity was recently described in the *Wall Street Journal* (April 29, 1985):

P&G [Procter and Gamble Co.] recently introduced its new Liquid Tide, but the product has a distinctly international heritage. A new ingredient that helps suspend dirt in wash water came from the company's research center near P&G's Cincinnati headquarters. But the formula for Liquid Tide's surfactants, or cleaning agents, was developed by P&G technicians in Japan. The ingredients that fight mineral salts present in hard water came from P&G's scientists in Brussels.

As discussed in the same *WSJ* article, P&G's research center in Brussels has developed a special capability in water softening technology due, in part, to the fact that water in Europe contains more than twice the level of mineral content compared to wash water available in the United States. Similarly, surfactant technology is particularly advanced in Japan because Japanese consumers wash their clothes in colder waters compared to consumers in the US or Europe, and this makes greater demands on the cleaning ability of the surfactants. The advantage of P&G as a multi-national is that it is exposed to these different operating environments and has learned, in each environment, the skills and knowledge that coping with that environment specially requires. Liquid Tide is an example of the strategic advantages that accrue from such diverse learning.

The mere existence of diversity, however, does not enhance learning. It only creates the potential for learning. To exploit this potential, the organization must consider learning as an explicit objective, and must create mechanisms and systems for such learning to take place. In the absence of explicit intention and appropriate mechanisms, the learning potential may be lost. In some companies, where all organizational resources are centralized and where the national subsidiaries are seen as mere delivery pipelines to supply the organization's value-added to different countries, diverse learning may not take place either because the subsidiaries may not possess appropriate sensing, analyzing, and responding capabilities to learn from their local environments, or because the centralized decision processes may be insensitive to knowledge accumulated outside the corporate head-quarters. Other companies, in which the subsidiaries may enjoy very high levels of local resources and autonomy, may similarly fail to exploit global learning benefits because of their inability to transfer and synthesize knowledge and expertise developed in different organizational components. Local loyalties, turf protection, and the 'not invented here' (NIH) syndrome—the three handmaidens of decentralization—may restrict internal flow of information across national boundaries which is essential for global learning to occur. In other words, both centralization and decentralization may impede learning.

The Means: Sources of Competitive Advantage

Most recent articles on global strategy have been aimed at identifying generic strategies (such as global cost leadership, focus or niche) and advocating particular strategic moves (such as cross-subsidy or pre-emptive investments). Underlying these concepts, however, are three fundamental tools for building global competitive advantage: exploiting differences in input and output markets in different countries, exploiting economies of scale, and exploiting economies of scope (Porter, 1985).

National Differences

The comparative advantage of locations in terms of differences in factor costs is perhaps the most discussed, and also the best understood, source of competitive advantage in international business.

Different nations have difference factor endowments, and in the absence of efficient markets this leads to inter-country differences in factor costs. Different activities of the firm, such as R&D, production, marketing, etc., have different factor intensities. A firm can therefore gain cost advantages by configuring its value-chain so that each activity is located in the country which has the least cost for the factor that the activity uses most intensely. This is the core concept of comparative advantage-based competitive advantage—a concept for which highly developed analytical tools are available from the discipline of international economics. Kogut (1985a) provides an excellent managerial overview of this concept.

National differences may also exist in output markets. Customer tastes and preferences may be different in different countries, as may be distribution systems, government regulations applicable to the concerned product-markets, or the effectiveness of different promotion strategies and other marketing techniques. A firm can augment the exchange value of its output by tailoring its offerings to fit the unique requirements in each national market. This, in essence, is the strategy of national differentiation, and it lies at the core of what has come to be referred to as the multi-domestic approach in multinational management (Hout *et al.*, 1982).

From a strategic perspective, however, this static and purely economic view of national differences may not be adequate. What may be more useful is to take a dynamic view of comparative advantage and to broaden the concept to include both societal and economic factors.

In the traditional economics view, comparative advantages of countries are determined by their relative factor endowments and they do not change. However, in reality one lesson of the past four decades is that comparative advantages change and a prime objective of the industrial policies of many nations is to effect such changes. Thus, for any nation, the availability and cost of capital change, as do the availability of technical manpower and the wages of skilled and unskilled labor. Such changes take place, in the long run, to accommodate different levels of economic and social performance of nations, and in the short run they occur in response to specific policies and regulations of governments.

This dynamic aspect of comparative advantages adds considerable complexity to the strategic considerations of the firm. There is a first-order effect of such changes—such as possible increases in wage rates, interest rates or currency exchange rates for particular countries that can affect future viability of a strategy that has been based on the current levels of these economic variables. There can also be a more intriguing second-order effect. If an activity is located in an economically inefficient environment, and if the firm is able to achieve a higher level of efficiency in its own operations compared to the rest of the local economy, its competitive advantage may actually increase as the local economy slips lower and lower. This is because the macroeconomic variables such as wage or exchange rates may change to reflect the overall performance of the economy relative to the rest of the world and, to the extent that the firm's performance is better than this national aggregate, it may benefit from these macro-level changes (Kiechel, 1981).

Consistent with the discipline that gave birth to the concept, the usual view of comparative advantage is limited to factors that an economist admits into the production function, such as the costs of labor and capital. However, from a managerial perspective it may be more appropriate to take a broader view of societal comparative advantages to include 'all the relative advantages conferred on a society by the quality, quantity and configuration of its material, human and institutional resources, including "soft" resources such as inter-organizational linkages, the nature of its educational system, and organizational and managerial know-how' (Westney, 1985: 4). As argued by Westney, these 'soft' societal factors, if absorbed in the overall organizational system, can provide benefits as real to a multinational as those provided by such economic factors as cheap labor or low-cost capital.

While the concept of comparative advantage is quite clear, available evidence on its actual effect on the overall competitiveness of firms is weak and conflicting. For example, it has often been claimed that one source of competitive advantage for Japanese firms is the lower cost of capital in Japan (Hatsopoulos, 1983). However, more systematic studies have shown that there is practically no difference in the risk-adjusted cost of capital in the United States and Japan, and that capital cost advantages of Japanese firms, if any, arise from complex interactions between government subsidies and corporate ownership structures (Flaherty and Itami, 1984). Similarly, relatively low wage rates in Japan have been suggested by some authors as the primary reason for the success of Japanese companies in the US market (Itami, 1978). However, recently, companies such as Honda and Nissan have commissioned plants in the USA and have been able to retain practically the same levels of cost advantages over US manufacturers as they had for their production in Japan (Allen, 1985). Overall, there is increasing evidence that while comparative advantages of countries can provide competitive advantages to firms, the realization of such benefits is not automatic but depends on complex organizational factors and processes.

Scale Economies

Scale economies, again, is a fairly well established concept, and its implications for competitive advantage are quite well understood. Micro-economic theory provides a strong theoretical and empirical basis for evaluating the effect of scale on cost reduction, and the use of scale as a competitive tool is common in practice. Its primary implication for strategy is that a firm must expand the volume of its output so as to achieve available scale benefits. Otherwise a competitor who can achieve such volume can build cost advantages, and this can lead to a vicious cycle in which the low-volume firm can progressively lose its competitive viability.

While scale, by itself, is a static concept, there may be dynamic benefits of scale through what has been variously described as the experience or learning effect. The higher volume that helps a firm to exploit scale benefits also allows it to accumulate learning, and this leads to progressive cost reduction as the firm moves down its learning curve.

The concept of the value-added chain recently popularized by Porter (1985) adds considerable richness to the analysis of scale as a source of competitive advantage. This conceptual apparatus allows a disaggregated analysis of scale benefits in different value-creating activities of the firm. The efficient scale may vary widely by activity—being higher for component production, say, than for assembly. In contrast to a unitary view of scale, this disaggregated view permits the firm to configure different elements of its value chain to attain optimum scale economies in each.

Traditionally, scale has been seen as an unmixed blessing—something that always helps and never hurts. Recently, however, many researchers have argued otherwise (e.g. Evans, 1982). It has been suggested that scale efficiencies are obtained through increased specialization and through creation of dedicated assets and systems. The same processes cause inflexibilities and limit the firm's ability to cope with change. As environmental turbulence has increased, so has the need for strategic and operational flexibility (Mascarenhas, 1982). At the extreme, this line of argument has led to predictions of a re-emergence of the craft form of production to replace the scale-dominated assembly form (Piore and Sabel, 1984). A more typical argument has been to emphasize the need to balance scale and flexibility, through the use of modern technologies such as CAD/CAM and flexible manufacturing systems (Gold, 1982).

Scope Economies

Relatively speaking, the concept of scope economies is both new and not very well understood. It is based on the notion that certain economies arise from the fact that the cost of the joint production of two or more products can be less than the cost of producing them separately. Such cost reductions can take place due to many reasons—for example resources such as information or technologies, once acquired for use in producing one item,

Table 2 Scope economies in product and market diversification

	Sources of scope economies	
	Product diversification	*Market diversification*
Shared physical assets	Factory automation with flexibility to produce multiple products	Global brand name
	(Ford)	(Coca-Cola)
Shared external relations	Using common distribution channel for multiple products	Servicing multi-national customers world-wide
	(Matsushita)	(Citibank)
Shared learning	Sharing R&D in computer and communications businesses	Pooling knowledge developed in different markets
	(NEC)	(Procter and Gamble)

may be available costlessly for production of other items (Baumol, Panzer and Willig, 1982).

The strategic importance of scope economies arise from a diversified firm's ability to share investments and costs across the same or different value chains that competitors, not possessing such internal and external diversity, cannot. Such sharing can take place across segments, products, or markets (Porter, 1985) and may involve joint use of different kinds of assets (see Table 2).

A diversified firm may share physical assets such as production equipment, cash, or brand names across different businesses and markets. Flexible manufacturing sytems using robots, which can be used for production of different items, is one example of how a firm can exploit such scope benefits. Cross-subsidization of markets and exploitation of a global brand name are other examples of sharing a tangible asset across different components of a firm's product and market portfolios.

A second important source of scope economies is shared external relations: with customers, suppliers, distributors, governments, and other institutions. A multinational bank like Citibank can provide relatively more effective service to a multinational customer than can a bank that operates in a single country (see Terpstra, 1982). Similarly, as argued by Hamel and Prahalad (1985), companies such as Matsushita have benefited considerably from their ability to market a diverse range of products through the same distribution channel. In another variation, Japanese trading companies have expanded into new businesses to meet different requirements of their existing customers.

Table 3 Selected references for further reading

Strategic objectives	Sources of competitive advantage		
	National differences	*Scale economies*	*Scope economies*
Achieving efficiency in current operations	Kogut (1985a); Itami (1978); Okimoto, Sugano and Weinstein (1984)	Hout, Porter and Rudden (1982); Levitt (1983); Doz (1978); Leontiades (1984); Gluck (1983)	Hamel and Prahalad (1985); Hout, Porter and Rudden (1982); Porter (1985); Ohmae (1985)
Managing risks	Kiechel (1981); Kobrin (1982); Poynter (1985); Lessard and Lightstone (1983); Srinivasula (1981); Herring (1983)	Evans (1982); Piore and Sabel (1984); Gold (1982); Aaker and Mascarenhas (1984)	Kogut (1985b); Lorange, Scott Morton and Ghoshal (1986)
Innovation, learning and adaptation	Westney (1985); Terpstra (1977); Ronstadt and Krammer (1982)	BCG (1982); Rapp (1973)	Bartlett and Ghoshal (1985)

Finally, shared knowledge is the third important component of scope economies. The fundamental thrust of NEC's global strategy is 'C&C'— computers and communication. The company firmly believes that its even strengths in the two technologies and resulting capabilities of merging them in-house to create new products gives it a competitive edge over global giants such as IBM and AT&T, who have technological strength in only one of these two areas. Another example of the scope advantages of shared learning is the case of Liquid Tide described earlier in this paper.

Even scope economies, however, may not be costless. Different segments, products or markets of a diversified company face different environmental demands. To succeed, a firm needs to differentiate its management systems and processes so that each of its activities can develop *external consistency* with the requirements of its own environment. The search for scope economies, on the other hand, is a search for *internal consistencies* within the firm and across its different activities. The effort to create such synergies may invariably result in some compromise with the objective of external consistency in each activity.

Further, the search for internal synergies also enhances the complexities in a firm's management processes. In the extreme, such complexities can overwhelm the organization, as it did in the case of EMI, the UK-based music, electronics, and leisure products company which attempted to manage its new CT scanner business within the framework of its existing organizational structure and processes (see EMI and the CT scanner, ICCH case 9–383–194). Certain parts of a company's portfolio of businesses or markets may be inherently very different from some others, and it may be best not to look for economies of scope across them. For example, in the soft drinks industry, bottling and distribution are intensely local in scope, while the tasks of creating and maintaining a brand image, or that of designing efficient bottling plants, may offer significant benefits from global integration. Carrying out both these sets of functions in-house would clearly lead to internalizing enormous differences within the company with regard to the organizing, coordinating, and controlling tasks. Instead of trying to cope with these complexities, Coca-Cola has externalized those functions which are purely local in scope (in all but some key strategic markets). In a variation of the same theme, IBM has 'externalized' the PC business by setting up an almost stand-alone organization, instead of trying to exploit scope benefits by integrating this business within the structure of its existing organization (for a more detailed discussion on multinational scope economies and on the conflicts between internal and external consistencies, see Lorange, Scott Morton and Ghoshal, 1986).

Prescriptions in Perspective

Existing literature on global strategy offers analytical insights and helpful prescriptions for almost all the different issues indicated in Table 1. Table 3 shows a selective list of relevant publications, categorized on the basis of issues that, according to this author's interpretations, the pieces primarily focus on.[4]

Pigeon-holing academic contributions into different parts of a conceptual framework tends to be unfair to their authors. In highlighting what the authors focus on, such categorization often amounts to an implicit criticism for what they did not write. Besides, most publications cover a broader range of issues and ideas than can be reflected in any such categorization scheme. Table 3 suffers from all these deficiencies. At the same time, however, it suggests how the proposed framework can be helpful in integrating the literature and in relating the individual pieces to each other.

From Parts to the Whole

For managers, the advantage of such synthesis is that it allows them to combine a set of insightful but often partial analyses to address the totality of a multidimensional and complex phenomenon. Consider, for example, a topic that has been the staple for academics interested in international management: explaining and drawing normative conclusions from the global successes of many Japanese companies. Based on detailed comparisons across a set of matched pairs of US and Japanese firms, Itami concludes that the relative successes of the Japanese firms can be wholly explained as due to the advantages of lower wage rates and higher labor productivity. In the context of a specific industry, on the other hand, Toder (1978) shows that manufacturing scale is the single most important source of the Japanese competitive advantage. In the small car business, for example, the minimum efficient scale requires an annual production level of about 400,000 units. In the late 1970s no US auto manufacturer produced even 200,000 units of any subcompact configuration vehicle, while Toyota produced around 500,000 Corollas and Nissan produced between 300,000 and 400,000 B210s per year. Toder estimates that US manufacturers suffered a cost disadvantage of between 9 and 17 percent on account of inefficient scale alone. Add to it the effects of wage rate differentials and exchange rate movements, and Japanese success in the US auto market may not require any further explanation. Yet process-orientated scholars such as Hamel and Prahalad suggest a much more complex explanation of the Japanese tidal wave. They see it as arising out of a dynamic process of strategic evolution that exploits scope economies as a crucial weapon in the final stages. All these authors provide compelling arguments to support their own explanations, but do not consider or refute each other's hypotheses.

This multiplicity of explanations only shows the complexity of global strategic management. However, though different, these explanations and prescriptions are not always mutually exclusive. The manager's task is to find how these insights can be combined to build a multidimensional and flexible strategy that is robust to the different assumptions and explanations.

The Strategic Trade-offs

This, however, is not always possible because there are certain inherent contradictions between the different strategic objectives and between the different sources of competitive advantage. Consider, for instance, the popular distinction between a global and a multidomestic strategy described by Hout *et al.* (1982). A global strategy requires that the firm should carefully separate different value elements, and should locate each activity at the most efficient level of scale in the location where the activity can be carried out at the cheapest cost. Each activity should then be integrated and managed interdependently so as to exploit available scope economies. In essence, it is a strategy to maximize efficiency of current operations.

Such a strategy may, however, increase both endogenous and exogenous risks for the firm. Global scale of certain activities such as R&D and manufacturing may result in the firm's costs being concentrated in a few countries, while its revenues accrue globally, from sales in many different countries. This increases the operating exposure of the firm to the vicissitudes of exchange rate movements because of the mismatch between the currencies in which revenues are obtained and those in which costs are incurred. Similarly, the search for efficiency in a global business may lead to greater amounts of intra-company, but inter-country, flows of goods, capital, information and other resources. These flows are visible, salient and tend to attract policy interventions from different host governments. Organizationally, such an integrated system requires a high degree of coordination, which enhances the risks of management failures. These are lessons that many Japanese companies have learned well recently.

Similarly, consideration of the learning objective will again contradict some of the proclaimed benefits of a global strategy. The implementation of a global strategy tends to enhance the forces of centralization and to shift organizational power from the subsidiaries to the headquarters. This may result in demotivation of subsidary managers and may erode one key asset of the MNC—the potential for learning from its many environments. The experiences of Caterpillar is a case in point. An exemplary practitioner of global strategy, Cat has recently spilled a lot of red ink on its balance sheet and has lost ground steadily to its archrival, Komatsu. Many factors contributed to Caterpillar's woes, not the least of which was the inability of its centralized management processes to benefit from the experiences of its foreign subsidiaries.

On the flipside of the coin, strategies aimed at optimizing risk or learning may compromise current efficiency. Poynter (1985) has recommended 'upgrade', i.e. increasing commitment of technology and resources in subsidiaries, as a way to overcome risk of policy interventions by host governments. Kogut (1985b), Mascarenhas (1982) and many others have suggested creating strategic and operational flexibility as a mechanism for coping with macroenvironmental risks. Bartlett and Ghoshal (1985) have proposed the differentiated network model of multinational organizations as a way to operationalize the benefits of global learning. All these recommendations carry certain efficiency penalties, which the authors have ignored.

Similar trade-offs exist between the different sources of competitive advantages. Trying to make the most of factor cost economies may prevent scale efficiency, and may impede benefiting from synergies across products or functions. Trying to benefit from scope through product diversification may affect scale, and so on. In effect these contradictions between the different strategic objectives, and between the different means for achieving them, lead to trade-offs between each cell in the framework and practically all others.

These trade-offs imply that to formulate and implement a global strategy, MNC managers must consider all the issues suggested in Table 1, and must evaluate the implications of different strategic alternatives on each of these issues. Under a particular set of circumstances a particular strategic objective may dominate and a particular source of competitive advantage may play a more important role than the others (Fayerweather, 1981). The complexity of global strategic management arises from the need to understand those situational contingencies, and to adopt a strategy after evaluating the trade-offs it implies. Existing prescriptions can sensitize MNC managers to the different factors they must consider, but cannot provide ready-made and standardized solutions for them to adopt.

Conclusion

This paper has proposed a framework that can help MNC managers in reviewing and analyzing the strategies of their firms. It is not a blueprint for formulating strategies; it is a road map for reviewing them. Irrespective of whether strategies are analytically formulated or organizationally formed (Mintzberg, 1978), every firm has a realized strategy. To the extent that the realized strategy may differ from the intended one, managers need to review what the strategies of their firms really are. The paper suggests a scheme for such a review which can be an effective instrument for exercising strategic control.

Three arguments underlie the construct of the framework. First, in the global strategy literature, a kind of industry determinism has come to prevail not unlike the technological determinism that dominated management literature in the 1960s. The structures of industries may often have important influences on the appropriateness of corporate strategy, but they are only one of many such influences. Besides, corporate strategy may influence industry structure just as much as be influenced by it.

Second, simple schemes for categorizing strategies of firms under different labels tend to hide more than they reveal. A map for more detailed comparison of the content of strategies can be more helpful to managers in understanding and improving the competitive positions of their companies.

Third, the issues of risk and learning have not been given adequate importance in the strategy literature in general, and in the area of global strategies in particular. Both these are important strategic objectives and must be explicitly considered while evaluating or reviewing the strategic positions of companies.

The proposed framework is not a replacement of existing analytical tools but an enhancement that incorporates these beliefs. It does not present any new concepts or solutions, but only a synthesis of existing ideas and techniques. The benefit of such synthesis is that it can help managers in integrating an array of strategic moves into an overall strategic thrust by revealing the consistencies and contradictions among those moves.

For academics this brief view of the existing literature on global strategy will clearly reveal the need for more empirically grounded and systematic research to test and validate the hypotheses which currently appear in the literature as prescriptions and research conclusions. For partial analyses to lead to valid conclusions, excluded variables must be controlled for, and rival hypotheses must be considered and eliminated. The existing body of descriptive and normative research is rich enough to allow future researchers to adopt a more rigorous and systematic approach to enhance the reliability and validity of their findings and suggestions. The proposed framework, it is hoped, may be of value to some researchers in thinking about appropriate research issues and designs for furthering the field of global strategic management.

Acknowledgements

The ideas presented in this paper emerged in the course of discussions with many friends and colleagues. Don Lessard, Eleanor Westney, Bruce Kogut, Chris Bartlett and Nitin Nohria were particularly helpful. I also benefited greatly from the comments and suggestions of the two anonymous referees from the *Strategic Management Journal.*

Notes

1. In the interest of simplicity the distinction between risk and uncertainty is ignored, as is the distinction between systematic and unsystematic risks.
2. This assumes that the firm has defined its business correctly and has identified as competitors all the firms whose offerings are aimed at meeting the same set of market needs that the firm meets.
3. Some market mechanisms such as long-term currency swaps are now available which can allow at least partial hedging of operating risks.
4. From an academic point of view, strategy of the multinational corporation is a specialized and highly applied field of study. It is built on the broader field of business policy and strategy which, in turn, rests on the foundation of a number of academic disciplines such as economics, organization theory, finance theory, operations research, etc. A number of publications in those underlying disciplines, and a significant body of research carried out in the field of strategy, in general, provide interesting insights on the different issues highlighted in Table 1. However, given the objective of suggesting a limited list of further readings that *managers* may find useful, such publications have not been included in Table 3. Further, even for the more applied and perspective literature on global strategy, the list is only illustrative and not exhaustive.

References

Aaker, D. A. and B. Mascarenhas. 'The need for strategic flexibility', *Journal of Business Strategy*, 5(2), Fall 1984, pp. 74–82.

Aldrich, H. E. *Organizations and Environments*, Prentice-Hall, Englewood Cliffs, NJ, 1979.

Allen, M. K. 'Japanese companies in the United States: the success of Nissan and Honda'. Unpublished manuscript, Sloan School of Management, MIT, November 1985.

Bartlett, C. A. 'Global competition and MNC managers', ICCH Note No. 0–385–287, Harvard Business School, Boston, 1985.

Bartlett, C. A. and S. Ghoshal. 'The new global organization: differentiated roles and dispersed responsibilities', Working Paper No. 9–786–013, Harvard Business School, Boston, October 1985.

Baumol, W. J., J. C. Panzer and R. D. Willig. *Contestable Markets and the Theory of Industry Structure*, Harcourt, Brace, Jovanovich, New York, 1982.

Boston Consulting Group, *Perspectives on Experience*, BCG, Boston, MA, 1982.

Calvet, A. L. 'A synthesis of foreign direct investment theories and theories of the multinational firm', *Journal of International Business Studies*, Spring–Summer 1981, pp. 43–60.

Caves, R. E. 'Industrial organization, corporate strategy and structure', *Journal of Economic Literature*, XVIII, March 1980, pp. 64–92.

Doz, Y. L. 'Managing manufacturing rationalization within multinational companies', *Columbia Journal of World Business*, Fall 1978, pp. 82–94.

Doz, Y. L., C. A. Bartlett and C. K. Prahalad. 'Global competitive pressures and host country demands: managing tensions in MNC's', *California Management Review*, Spring 1981, pp. 63–74.

Evans, J. S. *Strategic Flexibility in Business*, Report No. 678, SRI International, December 1982.

Fayerweather, J. 'Four winning strategies for the international corporation', *Journal of Business Strategy*, Fall 1981, pp. 25–36.

Flaherty, M. T. and H. Itami. 'Finance', in Okimoto, D.I., T. Sugano and F. B. Weinstein (Eds), *Competitive Edge*, Stanford University Press, Stanford, CA, 1984.

Gluck, F. 'Global competition in the 1980's', *Journal of Business Strategy*, Spring 1983, pp. 22–27.

Gold, B. 'Robotics, programmable automation, and international competitiveness', *IEEE Transactions on Engineering Management*, November 1982.

Hamel, G. and C. K. Prahalad. 'Do you really have a global strategy?', *Harvard Business Review*, July–August 1985, pp. 139–148.

Hannan, M. T. and J. Freeman. 'The population ecology of organizations', *American Journal of Sociology*, **82**, 1977, pp. 929–964.

Hatsopoulos, G. N. 'High cost of capital: handicap of American industry', Report Sponsored by the American Business Conference and Thermo-Electron Corporation, April 1983.

Hax, A. C. and N. S. Majluf. *Strategic Management: An Integrative Perspective*, Prentice-Hall, Englewood Cliffs, NJ, 1984.

Herring, R. J. (ed.), *Managing International Risk*, Cambridge University Press, Cambridge, 1983.

Hofer, C. W. and D. Schendel, *Strategy Formulation: Analytical Concepts*, West Publishing Co., St. Paul, MN, 1978.

Hout, T., M. E. Porter and E. Rudden. 'How global companies win out', *Harvard Business Review*, September–October 1982, pp. 98–108.

Itami, H. 'Japanese–U.S. comparison of managerial productivity', *Japanese Economic Studies*, Fall 1978.

Kiechel, W. 'Playing the global game', *Fortune*, November 16, 1981, pp. 111–126.

Kobrin, S. J. *Managing Political Risk Assessment*, University of California Press, Los Angeles, CA, 1982.

Kogut, B. 'Normative observations on the international value-added chain and strategic groups', *Journal of International Business Studies*, Fall 1984, pp. 151–167.

Kogut, B. 'Designing global strategies: comparative and competitive value added chains', *Sloan Management Review*, **26**(4), Summer 1985a, pp. 15–28.

Kogut, B. 'Designing global strategies: profiting from operational flexibility', *Sloan Management Review*, Fall 1985b, pp. 27–38.

Leontiades, J. 'Market share and corporate strategy in international industries', *Journal of Business Strategy*, **5**(1), Summer 1984, pp. 30–37.

Lessard, D. and J. Lightstone. 'The impact of exchange rates on operating profits: new business and financial responses', mimeo, Lightstone-Lessard Associates, 1983.

Levitt, T. 'The globalization of markets', *Harvard Business Review*, May–June 1983, pp. 92–102.

Lorange, P., M. S. Scott Morton and S. Ghoshal. *Strategic Control*, West Publishing Co., St Paul, MN, 1986.

Mascarenhas, B. 'Coping with uncertainty in international business', *Journal of International Business Studies*, Fall 1982, pp. 87–98.

Mintzberg, H. 'Patterns in strategic formation', *Management Science*, **24**, 1978, pp. 934–948.

Ohmae, K. *Triad Power: The Coming Shape of Global Competition*, Free Press, New York, 1985.

Okimoto, D. I., T. Sugano and F. B. Weinstein (eds). *Competitive Edge*, Stanford University Press, Stanford, CA, 1984.

Perlmutter, H. V. 'The tortuous evolution of the multinational corporation', *Columbia Journal of World Business*, January–February 1969, pp. 9–18.

Piore, M. J. and C. Sabel. *The Second Industrial Divide: Possibilities and Prospects*, Basic Books, New York, 1984.

Porter, M. E. *Competitive Strategy*, Basic Books, New York, 1980.

Porter, M. E. 'Competition in global industries: a conceptual framework', paper presented to the Colloquium on Competition in Global Industries, Harvard Business School, 1984.

Porter, M. E. *Competitive Advantage*, Free Press, New York, 1985.

Poynter, T. A. *International Enterprises and Government Intervention*, Croom Helm, London, 1985.

Prahalad, C. K. 'The strategic process in a multinational corporation'. Unpublished doctoral dissertation, Graduate School of Business Administration, Harvard University, 1975.

Rapp, W. V. 'Strategy formulation and international competition', *Columbia Journal of World Business*, Summer 1983, pp. 92–112.

Robinson, R. D. *International Business Management: A Guide to Decision Making*, Dryden Press, Illinois, 1978.

Ronstadt, R. and R. J. Krammer. 'Getting the most out of innovations abroad', *Harvard Business Review*, March–April 1982, pp. 94–99.

Rutenberg, D. P. *Multinational Management*, Little, Brown, Boston, MA, 1982.

Srinivasula, S. 'Strategic response to foreign exchange risks', *Columbia Journal of World Business*, Spring 1981, pp. 13–23.

Terpstra, V. 'International product policy: the role of foreign R&D', *Columbia Journal of World Business*, Winter 1977, pp. 24–32.

Terpstra, V. *International Dimensions of Marketing*, Kent, Boston, MA, 1982.

Toder, E. J. *Trade Policy and the U.S. Automobile Industry*, Praeger Special Studies, New York, 1978.

Vernon, R. *Storm Over the Multinationals*, Harvard University Press, Cambridge, MA, 1977.

The Wall Street Journal, April 29, 1985, p. 1.

Westney, D. E. 'International dimensions of information and communications technology'. Unpublished manuscript, Sloan School of Management, MIT, 1985.

Woo, C. Y. and K. O. Cool. 'The impact of strategic management of systematic risk', Mimeo, Krannert Graduate School of Management, Purdue University, 1985.

8

Getting Back to Strategy*

Kenichi Ohmae[†]

*Source: *Harvard Business Review*, 66 (1988), pp. 149–156.

"Competitiveness" is the word most commonly uttered these days in economic policy circles in Washington and most European capitals. The restoration of competitive vitality is a widely shared political slogan. Across the Atlantic, the sudden nearness of 1992 and the coming unification of the Common Market focus attention on European industries' ability to compete against global rivals. On both continents, senior managers, who started to wrestle with these issues long before politicians got hold of them, search actively for successful models to follows, for examples of how best to play the new competitive game. With few exceptions, the models they have found and the examples they are studying are Japanese.

To many Western managers, the Japanese competitive achievement provides hard evidence that a successful strategy's hallmark is the creation of sustainable competitive advantage by beating the competition. If it takes world-class manufacturing to win, runs the lesson, you have to beat competitors with your factories. If it takes rapid product development, you have to beat them with your labs. If it takes mastery of distribution channels, you have to beat them with your logistics systems. No matter what it takes, the goal of strategy is to beat the competition.

After a painful decade of losing ground to the Japanese, managers in the United States and Europe have learned this lesson very well indeed. As a guide to action, it is clear and compelling. As a metric of performance, it is unambiguous. It is also wrong.

Of course, winning the manufacturing or product development or logistics battle is no bad thing. But it is not really what strategy is – or should be – about. Because when the focus of attention is on ways to beat the competition, it is inevitable that strategy gets defined primarily in terms of the competition. For instance, if the competition has recently brought out an electronic kitchen gadget that slices, dices, and brews coffee, you had better get one just like it into your product line – and get it there soon. If the competition has cut production costs, you had better get out your scalpel. If they have just started to run national ads, you had better call your agency at once. When you go toe-to-toe with competitors, you cannot let them build up any kind of advantage. You must match their every move. Or so the argument goes.

Of course it is important to take the competition into account, but in making strategy that should not come first. It cannot come first. First comes painstaking attention to the needs of customers. First comes close analysis of a company's real degrees of freedom in responding to those needs. First comes the willingness to rethink, fundamentally, what products are and what they do, as well as how best to organize the business system that designs, builds, and markets them. Competitive realities are what you test possible strategies against; you define them in terms of customers. Tit-for-tat responses to what competitors do may be appropriate, but they are largely reactive. They come second, after your real strategy. Before you test yourself against competition, strategy takes shape in the determination to create value for customers.

It also takes shape in the determination to *avoid* competition whenever and wherever possible. As the great Sun Tzu observed 500 years before Christ, the smartest strategy in war is the one that allows you to achieve your objectives without having to fight. In just three years, for example, Nintendo's "family computer" sold 12 million units in Japan alone, during which time it had virtually no competition at all. In fact, it created a vast network of companies working to help it succeed. Ricoh supplied the critical Zylog chips; software houses produced special games to play on it like Dragon Quest I, II, and III. Everyone was making too much money to think of creating competition.

The visible clashing between companies in the marketplace – what managers frequently think of as strategy – is but a small fragment of the strategic whole. Like an iceberg, most of strategy is submerged, hidden out of sight. The visible part can foam and froth with head-to-head competition. But most of it is intentionally invisible – beneath the surface where value gets created, where competition gets avoided. Sometimes, of course, the foam and froth of direct competition cannot be avoided. The product is right, the company's direction is right, the perception of value is right, and managers have to buckle down and fight it out with competitors. But in my experience, managers too often and too willingly launch themselves into old-fashioned competitive battles. It's familiar ground. They know what to do, how to fight. They have a much harder time seeing when an effective customer-oriented strategy could avoid the battle altogether.

The Big Squeeze

During the late 1960s and early 1970s, most Japanese companies focused their attention on reducing costs through programs like quality circles, value engineering, and zero defects. As these companies went global, however, they began to concentrate instead on differentiating themselves from their competitors. This heavy investment in competitive differentiation has now gone too far; it has already passed the point of diminishing returns – too many models, too many gadgets, too many bells and whistles.

Today, as a result, devising effective customer-oriented strategies has a special urgency for these companies. A number of the largest and most successful face a common problem – the danger of being trapped below low-cost producers in the NIEs (newly industrialized economies) and high-end producers in Europe. While this threat concerns managers in all the major industrial economies, in Japan, where the danger is most immediate and pressing, it has quickly led companies to rethink their familiar strategic goals. As a consequence, they are rediscovering the primary importance of focusing on customers – in other words, the importance of getting back to what strategy is really about.

In Japan today, the handwriting is on the wall for many industries: the strategic positioning that has served them so well in the past is no longer tenable. On one side, there are German companies making top-of-the-line products like Mercedes or BMW in automobiles, commanding such high prices that even elevated cost levels do not greatly hurt profitability. On the other are low-price, high-volume producers like Korea's Hyundai, Samsung, and Lucky Goldstar. These companies can make products for less than half what it costs the Japanese. The Japanese are being caught in the middle: they are able neither to command the immense margins of the Germans nor to undercut the rock-bottom wages of the Koreans. The result is a painful squeeze.

If you are the leader of a Japanese company, what can you do? I see three possibilities. First, because Korean productivity is still quite low, you can challenge them directly on costs. Yes, their wages are often as little as one-seventh to one-tenth of yours. But if you aggressively take labor content out of your products, you can close or even reverse the cost gap. In practice, this means pushing hard – and at considerable expense – toward full automation, unmanned operations, and totally flexible manufacturing systems.

Examples prove that it can be done. NSK (Nikon Seiko), which makes bearings, has virtually removed its work force through an extensive use of computer-integrated manufacturing linked directly with the marketplace. Mazak Machinery has taken almost all the labor content out of key components in its products. Fujitsu Fanuc has so streamlined itself that it has publicly announced that it can break even with as little as 20% capacity utilization and can compete successfully with a currency as strong as 70 yen to the dollar.

This productivity-through-automation route is one way to go. In fact, for commodity products such as bearings it may be the only way. Once you start down this path, however, you have to follow it right to the end. No turning back. No stopping. Because Korean wages are so low that nothing less than a total commitment to eliminating labor content will suffice. And China, with wage rates just one-fifth of those in the newly industrialized economies, is not far behind Korea and Taiwan in such light industries as textiles, footwear, and watchbands. Although the currencies of the newly industrialized economies are now moving up relative to the dollar, the difference in wage rates is still great enough to require the fiercest kind of across-the-board determination to get rid of labor content.

A second way out of the squeeze is for you to move upmarket where the Germans are. In theory this might be appealing; in practice it has proven very hard for the Japanese to do. Their corporate cultures simply do not permit it. Just look, for example, at what happened with precision elec- tronic products like compact disk players. As soon as the CD reached the market, customers went crazy with demand. Everybody wanted one. It was a perfect opportunity to move upscale with a "Mercedes" compact disk player. What did the Japanese do? Corporate culture and instinct took over, and they cut prices down to about one-fifth of what U.S. and European companies were going to ask for their CDs. Philips, of course, was trying to drive them down. The Western companies wanted to make money; the Japanese instinct was to build share at any cost.

This is foolishness – or worse. Of course, it is perfectly clear why the Japanese respond this way. They are continuing to practice the approach that served them well in the past when they were playing the low-cost market entry game that the Koreans are playing now. It's the game that they know how to play. But now there's a new game, and the Japanese companies have new positions. The actions that made sense for a low-cost player are way off course for a company trying to play at the high end of the market.

There is another reason for this kind of self-defeating behavior. Sony is really more worried about Matsushita than about Philips, and Matsushita is more worried about Sanyo. This furious internal competition fuels the Japanese impulse to slash prices whenever possible. That's also why it's so difficult for Japanese companies to follow the German route. To do it, they have to buck their own history. It means going their own way, and guarding against the instinct to backpedal, to do what their domestic competitors are doing.

Hard as it is, a number of companies *are* going their own way quite successfully. Some, like Seiko in its dogfight with Casio and Hong Kong- based watchmakers, had been badly burned in the low-price game and are now moving to restore profits at the high end of the market. Others, like Honda, Toyota, and Nissan in the automobile industry, are launching more expensive car lines and creating second dealer channels in the United States through which to compete directly for the upscale "German" segment. Still others, like Nakamichi in tape recorders, have always tried to operate at the high end and have never given in on price. Such companies are, however, very rare. Instinct runs deep. Japanese producers tend to compete on price even when they do not have to.

For most companies, following the Korean or German approach is neither an appealing nor a sustainable option. This is not only true in Japan but also in all the advanced industrial economies, if for different reasons. What sets Japanese companies apart is the consideration that they may have less room to maneuver than others, given their historical experience and present situation. For all these companies, there is a pressing need for a middle strategic course, a way to flourish without being forced to go head-to-head with competitors in either a low-cost or an upmarket game. Such a course exists – indeed, it leads managers back to the heart of what strategy is about: creating value for customers.

Five-Finger Exercise

Imagine for a moment that you are head of Yamaha, a company that makes pianos. What are your strategic choices? After strenuous and persistent efforts to become the leading producer of high-quality pianos, you have succeeded in capturing 40% of the global piano market. Unfortunately, just when you finally became the market leader, overall demand for pianos started to decline by 10% every year. As head of Yamaha, what do you do?

A piano is a piano. In most respects, the instrument has not changed much since Mozart. Around the world, in living rooms and dens and concert halls and rehearsal halls, there are some 40 million pianos. For the most part they simply sit. Market growth is stagnant, in polite terms. In business terms, the industry is already in decline; and Korean producers are now coming on-line with their usual low-cost offerings. Competing just to hold share is not an attractive prospect. Making better pianos will not help much; the market has only a limited ability to absorb additional volume. What do you do? What can you do?

According to some analysts, the right move would be to divest the business, labeling it a dog that no longer belongs in the corporate portfolio. But Yamaha reacted differently. Rather than selling the business, Yamaha thought long and hard about how to create value for customers. It took that kind of effort – the answers were far from obvious.

What Yamaha's managers did was look – they took a hard look at the customer and the product. What they saw was that most of these 40 million pianos sit around idle and neglected – and out of tune – most of the time. Not many people play them anymore – and one thing learning to play the piano takes is lots of time. What sits in the homes of these busy people is a large piece of furniture that collects dust. Instead of music, it may even produce guilt. Certainly it is not a functioning musical instrument. No matter how good you are at strategy, you won't be able to sell that many new pianos – no matter how good they are – in such an environment. If you want to create value for customers, you're going to have to find ways to add value to the millions of pianos already out there.

So what do you do? What Yamaha did was to remember the old player piano – a pleasant idea with a not very pleasant sound. Yamaha worked hard to develop a sophisticated, advanced combination of digital and optical technology that can distinguish among 92 different degrees of strength and speed of key touch from pianissimo to fortissimo. Because the technology is digital, it can record and reproduce each keystroke with great accuracy, using the same kind of 3½" disks that work on a personal computer. That means you can now record live performances by the pianists of your choice – or buy such recordings on a computerlike diskette – and then, in effect, invite the artists into your home to play the same compositions on your piano. Yamaha's strategy used technology to create new value for piano customers.

Think about it. For about $2,500 you can retrofit your idle, untuned, dust-collecting piece of oversized furniture so that great artists can play it for you in the privacy of your own home. You can invite your friends over and entertain them as well – and showcase the latest in home entertainment technology. If you are a flutist, you can invite someone over to accompany you on the piano and record her performance. Then, even when she is not there, you can practice the piece with full piano accompaniment.

Furthermore, if you have a personal computer at home in Cambridge and you know a good pianist living in California, you can have her record your favorite sonata and send it over the phone; you simply download it onto your computer, plug the diskette into your retrofitted piano, and enjoy her performance. Or you can join a club that will send you the concert that a Horowitz played last night at Carnegie Hall to listen to at home on your own piano. There are all kinds of possibilities.

In terms of the piano market, this new technology creates the prospect of a $2,500 sale to retrofit each of 40 million pianos – not bad for a declining industry. In fact, the potential is even greater because there are also the software recordings to market.

Yamaha started marketing this technology last April, and sales in Japan have been explosive. This was a stagnant industry, remember, an industry which had suffered an annual 10% sales decline in each of the past five years. Now it's alive again – but in a different way. Yamaha did not pursue all the usual routes: it didn't buckle down to prune costs, proliferate models, slice overhead, and all the other usual approaches. It looked with fresh eyes for chances to create value for customers. And it found them.

It also found something else: it learned that the process of discovering value-creating opportunities is itself contagious. It spreads. For instance, now that customers have pianos that play the way Horowitz played last night at Carnegie Hall, they want their instrument tuned to professional standards. That means a tuner visits every six months and generates substantial additional revenue. (And it is substantial. Globally, the market for tuning is roughly $1.6 billion annually, a huge economic opportunity long ignored by piano manufacturers and distributors.) Yamaha can also give factory workers who might otherwise lose their jobs a chance to be tuners.

As the piano regains popularity, a growing number of people will again want to learn how to play the instrument themselves. And that means tutorials, piano schools, videocassettes, and a variety of other revenue-producing opportunities. Overall, the potential growth in the piano industry, hardware and software, is much bigger than anyone previously recognized. Creating value for the customer was the key that unlocked it.

But what about people's reluctance today to spend the time to learn piano the old-fashioned way? We are a society that prizes convenience, and as the many years of declining piano sales illustrate, learning to play a musical instrument is anything but convenient. Listening to music, as opposed to making music, is more popular than ever. Look at all the people going to school or to the office with earphones on; music is everywhere. It's not interest in music that's going down; it's the interest in spending years of disciplined effort to master an instrument. If you asked people if they would like to be able to play an instrument like the piano, they'd say yes. But most feel as if they've already missed the opportunity to learn. They're too old now; they don't have the time to take years of lessons.

With the new digital and sound-chip technologies, they don't have to. Nor do they have to be child prodigies. For $1,500 they can buy a Klavinova, a digital electrical piano, that allows them to do all kinds of wonderful things. They can program it to play and then croon along. They can program it to play the left hand part and join in with a single finger. They can listen to a tutorial cassette that directs which keys to push. They can store instructions in the computer's memory so that they don't have to play all the notes and chords simultaneously. Because the digital technology makes participation easy and accessible, "playing" the instrument becomes fun. Technology removes the learning barrier. No wonder this digital segment is now much bigger than the traditional analog segment of the market.

Most piano manufacturers, however, are sticking with traditional acoustic technologies and leaving their futures to fate. Faced with declining demand, they fight even harder against an ever more aggressive set of competitors for their share of a shrinking pie. Or they rely on government to block imports. Yamaha has not abandoned acoustic instruments; it is now the world leader in nearly all categories of acoustic and "techno" musical instruments. What it did, however, was to study its music-loving customers and to build a strategy based on delivering value linked to those customers' inherent interest in music. It left nothing to fate. It got back to strategy.

Cleaning Up

This is how you chart out a middle course between the Koreans and the Germans. This is how you revitalize an industry. More to the point, this is how you create a value-adding strategy: not by setting out to beat the competition but by setting out to understand how best to provide value for customers.

Kao is a Japanese toiletry company that spends 4% of its revenues on fundamental R&D, studying skin, hair, blood, circulation – things like that. (This 4% may, at first, sound low, but it excludes personnel cost. This matters because as many as 2,800 of the company's 6,700 or so employees are engaged in R&D.) Recently it developed a new product that duplicates the effect of a Japanese hot spring. A hot spring has a high mineral content under extreme pressure. Even the right chemicals thrown into a hot bath will not automatically give you the same effect. Babu, Kao's new bath additive, actually produces the same kind of improvement in circulation that a hot spring provides. It looks like a jumbo-sized Alka-Seltzer tablet. When you throw one Babu into a bath, it starts to fizz with carbon dioxide bubbles as minerals dissolve in the hot water.

Kao's strategy was to offer consumers something completely different from traditional bath gel. Because of its effects on overall health and good circulation, Babu competes on a different ground. In fact, it wiped out the old Japanese bath gel and additives industry in a single year. It's the only product of its kind that now sells in Japan. There is no competition because potential competitors cannot make anything like it. Kao is playing a different game.

For the new breed of Japanese companies, like Yamaha and Kao, strategy does not mean beating the competition. It means working hard to understand a customer's inherent needs and then rethinking what a category of product is all about. The goal is to develop the right product to serve those needs – not just a better version of competitors' products. In fact, Kao pays far less attention to other toiletry companies than it does to improving skin condition, circulation, or caring for hair. It now understands hair so well that its newest hair tonic product, called Success, falls somewhere between cosmetics and medicine. In that arena, there is no competition.

Brewing Wisdom

Getting back to strategy means getting back to a deep understanding of what a product is about. Some time back, for example, a Japanese home appliance company was trying to develop a coffee percolator. Should it be a General Electric-type percolator, executives wondered? Should it be the same drip-type that Philips makes? Larger? Smaller? I urged them to ask a different kind of question: Why do people drink coffee? What are they looking for when they do? If your objective is to serve the customer better, then shouldn't you understand why that customer drinks coffee in the first place? Then you know what kind of percolator to make.

The answer came back: good taste, I then asked the company's engineers what they were doing to help the consumer enjoy good taste in a cup of coffee. They said they were trying to design a good percolator. I asked them what influences the taste of a cup of coffee. No one knew. That became the next question we had to answer. It turns out that lots of things can affect taste – the beans, the temperature, the water. We did our homework and discovered all the things that affect taste. For the engineers, each factor represented a strategic degree of freedom in designing a percolator – that is, a factor about which something can be done. With beans, for instance, you can have different degrees of quality or freshness. You can grind them in various ways. You can produce different grain sizes. You can distribute the grains differently when pouring hot water over them.

Of all the factors, water quality we learned, made the greatest difference. The percolator in design at the time, however, didn't take water quality into account at all. Everyone had simply assumed that customers would use tap water. We discovered next that the grain distribution and the time between grinding the beans and pouring in the water were crucial. As a result, we began to think about the product and its necessary features in a new way. It *had* to have a built-in dechlorinating function. It *had* to have a built-in grinder. All the customer should have to do is pour in water and beans; the machine should handle the rest. That's the way to assure great taste in a cup of coffee.

To start you have to ask the right questions and set the right kinds of strategic goals. If your only concern is that General Electric has just brought out a percolator that brews coffee in ten minutes, you will get your engineers to design one that brews it in seven minutes. And if you stick with that logic, market research will tell you that instant coffee is the way to go. If the General Electric machine consumes only a little electricity, you will focus on using even less.

Conventional marketing approaches won't solve the problem. You can get any results you want from the consumer averages. If you ask people whether they want their coffee in ten minutes or seven, they will say seven, of course. But it's still the wrong question. And you end up back where you started, trying to beat the competition at its own game. If your primary focus is on the competition, you will never step back and ask what the customer's inherent needs are or what the product really is about. Personally, I would much rather talk with three housewives for two hours each on their feelings about, say, washing machines than conduct a 1,000-person survey on the same topic. I get much better insight and perspective on what they are really looking for.

Taking Pictures

Back in the mid-1970s, single-lens reflex (SLR) cameras started to become popular, and lens-shutter cameras declined rapidly in popularity. To most people, the lens-shutter model looked cheap and nonprofessional and it took inferior quality pictures. These opinions were so strong that one camera company with which I was working had almost decided to pull out of the lens-shutter business entirely. Everyone knew that the trend was toward SLR and that only a better version of SLR could beat the competition.

I didn't know. So I asked a few simple questions: Why do people take pictures in the first place? What are they really looking for when they take pictures? The answer was simple. They were not looking for a good camera. They were looking for good pictures. Cameras – SLR or lens-shutter – and film were not the end products that consumers wanted. What they wanted were good pictures.

Why was it so hard to take good pictures with a lens-shutter camera? This time, no one knew. So we went to a film lab and collected a sample of some 18,000 pictures. Next we identified the 7% or so that were not very good; then we tried to analyze why each of these picture-taking failures had occurred. We found some obvious causes – even some categories of causes. Some failures were the result of poor distance adjustment. The company's design engineers addressed that problem in two different ways: they added a plastic lens designed to keep everything in focus beyond three feet (a kind of permanent focus), and they automated the focus process.

Another common problem with the bad pictures was not enough light. That way, the poor fellow who left his flash attachment on a closet shelf could still be equipped to take a good picture. Still another problem was the marriage of film and camera. Here the engineers added some grooves on the side of the film cartridges so that the camera could tell how sensitive the film is to light and could adjust. Double exposure was another common problem. The camera got a self-winder.

In all, we came up with some 200 ideas for improving the lens-shutter camera. The result – virtually a whole new approach to the product – helped revitalize the business. Today, in fact, the lens-shutter market is bigger than that for SLRs. And we got there because we did a very simple thing: we asked what the customer's inherent needs were and then re-thought what a camera had to be in order to meet them. There was no point slugging it out with competitors. There was no reason to leave the business. We just got back to strategy – based on customers.

Making Dinner

There is no mystery to this process, no black box to which only a few gurus have access. The questions that have to be asked are straightforward, and the place to start is clear. A while ago, some people came to met with a set of excellent ideas for designing kitchen appliances for Japanese homes. They knew cooking, and their appliances were quite good. After some study, however, I told them not to go ahead.

What I did was to go and visit several hundred houses and apartments and take pictures of the kitchens. The answer became clear: there was no room. There were even things already stacked on top of the refrigerators. The counters were already full. There was no room for new appliances, no matter how appealing their attributes.

Thinking about these products, and understanding the customer's needs, however, did produce a different idea: build this new equipment into something that is already in the kitchen. That way there is no new demand for space. What that led to, for example, was the notion of building a microwave oven into a regular oven. Everyone looked at the pictures of 200 kitchens and said, no space. The alternative was, rethink the product.

Aching Heads, Bad Logic

Looking closely at a customer's needs, thinking deeply about a product – these are no exotic pieces of strategic apparatus. They are, as they have always been, the basics of sound management. They have just been neglected or ignored. But why? Why have so many managers allowed themselves to drift so far away from what strategy is really about?

Think for a moment about aching heads. Is my headache the same as yours? My cold? My shoulder pain? My stomach discomfort? Of course not. Yet when a pharmaceutical company asked for help to improve its process for coming up with new products, what it wanted was help in getting into its development pipeline new remedies for standard problems like headache or stomach pain. It had assembled a list of therapeutic categories and was eager to match them up with appropriate R&D efforts.

No one had taken the time, however, to think about how people with various discomforts actually feel. So we asked 50 employees in the company to fill out a questionnaire – throughout a full year – about how they felt physically at all times of the day every day of the year. Then we pulled together a list of the symptoms described, sat down with the company's scientists, and asked them, item by item: Do you know why people feel this way? Do you have a drug for this kind of symptom? It turned out that there were no drugs for about 80% of the symptoms, these physical awarenesses of discomfort. For many of them, some combination of existing drugs worked just fine. For others, no one had ever thought to seek a particular remedy. The scientists were ignoring tons of profit.

Without understanding customers' needs – the specific types of discomfort they were feeling – the company found it all too easy to say, "Headache? Fine, here's a medicine, an aspirin, for headache. Case closed. Nothing more to do there. Now we just have to beat the competition in aspirin." It was easy not to take the next step and ask, "What does the headache feel like? Where does it come from? What is the underlying cause? How can we treat the cause, not just the symptom?" Many of these symptoms, for example, are psychological and culture-specific. Just look at television commercials. In the United States, the most common complaint is headache; in the United Kingdom, backache; in Japan, stomachache. In the United States, people say that they have a splitting headache; in Japan it is an ulcer. How can we truly understand what these people are feeling and why?

The reflex, of course, is to provide a headache pill for a headache – that is, to assume that the solution is simply the reverse of the diagnosis. That is bad medicine and worse logic. It is the kind of logic that reinforces the impulse to direct strategy toward beating the competition, toward cutting costs when making traditional musical instruments or adding a different ingredient to the line of traditional soaps. It is the kind of logic that denies the need for a detailed understanding of intrinsic customer needs. It leads to forklift trucks that pile up boxes just fine but do not allow the operators to see directly in front of them. It leads to dishwashers that remove everything but the scorched eggs and rice that customers most want to get rid of. It leads to pianos standing idle and gathering dust.

Getting back to strategy means fighting that reflex, not giving in to it. It means resisting the easy answers in the search for better ways to deliver value to customers. It means asking the simple-sounding questions about what products are about. It means, in short, taking seriously the strategic part of management.

Note

† *Kenichi Ohmae* is the author of *The Mind of the Strategist: The Art of Japanese Business* (McGraw-Hill, 1982), *Triad Power: The Coming Shape of Global Competition* (Free Press, 1985), and *Beyond National Borders* (Dow Jones-Irwin, 1987).

9

The Hypermodern MNC–A Heterarchy?*

Gunnar Hedlund

*Source: *Human Resource Management*, 25 (1986), pp. 9–35.

Commenting upon an early b7-b6 (or, in an alternative notation, PQKn2-Kn3 as black), Aron Nimzowitsch advertised his move as one of "hypermodern daring." The exaggeration contained in the expression served two purposes. It helped selling Nimzowitsch's pathbreaking books on chess strategy. It focused attention on the novelty of his ideas and thus inspired attempts to refute his conclusions.

The present paper is restricted to the second goal. The term "hypermodern MNC" is meant to convey the suspicion that some crucial aspects of developments of and in multinational corporations (MNCs) cannot be grasped by notions in the merely "modern" schools of thought. Even more than in the case of the grandmaster's rallying calls for the "hypermodern school," "my system," etc., the departure from supposedly conventional views is bound to be exaggerated. However, some polarization of issues is desirable in order to arrive at greater conceptual clarity. In addition, it seems that concepts and theories older than present variations on the theme of "global strategy," and sometimes not used by protagonists of the said theme, can usefully be applied.

The other word in the title—heterarchy—is no less problematical. It was used in a recent study by the Stanford Research Institute to describe a shift of perspective in a wide range of sciences. (See also Ogilvy, 1977.) A key idea is that of reality being organized non-hierarchically. A special case is holographic coding where entire systems are represented and, as it were, "known" at each component of the system. (As in a hologram, each part contains information sufficient to reproduce the whole original image, albeit somewhat blurred.)

The concept of heterarchy does not seem to have been used much, if at all, in discussing MNCs. Nor has it inspired more than passing allusions in organization studies in general. Sjöstrand (1985) uses the concept in contrast to hierarchy, but he does not give any definition, nor does the notion figure much in his discussion. The holographic paradigm is encountered more frequently (Mitroff, 1983; El Sawy, 1985). The discussion in Faucheux and Laurent (1980) about integrating others' roles and vantage point, and about "internalizing the environment" in decision-making in a more indirect way touches on many of the issues brought up below concerning heterarchy. So do contributions on self-referential systems, such as Varela (1975). Also Laurent (1978) discusses the concept of hierarchy.

As the previous discussion indicates, there are no strict definitions to hold on to. As always, consultation of the Oxford English Dictionary gives food for thought. The only direct reference to "heterarchy" gives the meaning "the rule of an alien." This is exactly what heterarchy in the present use of the term is not. The use, as well as SRI's and Ogilvy's, builds on putting "homo," rather than "auto," as the opposite of "hetero." It is not easy to arrive at a simple definition, for example by contradistinction in relation to "hierarchy." The apparent superiority of this latter term as to clarity of meaning derives mostly from the dulling effects of old habits. We have become so accustomed to the concept of hierarchy that we forget exactly what it is that we want to conceive of with it. For example, the etymological meaning of "ruling through the sacred" or "rule of the episcopate" is rather alien to transaction cost analyses of markets and "hierarchies." Certainly it would not make much sense to define heterarchy as non-hierarchy, meaning ruling through the profane. The abstruseness of novelty in "heterarchy" thus partly derives from the abstruseness of convention in "hierarchy." Many authors hail hierarchy as the dominant or even only stable form of organization of human as well as other systems. Space limitations do not permit a thorough discussion of this strain of thought. One contribution will, however, be briefly mentioned. Koestler (1978, p. 290) puts the argument for hierarchy very strongly:

> All complex structures and processes of a relatively stable character display hierarchic organization, and this applies regardless whether we are considering inanimate systems, living organisms, social organizations, or patterns of behaviour.

Koestler himself mentions the suspicion that the hierarchic model's universal applicability may originate in the model being logically empty, or merely a reflection of the way in which a perceiver approaches an object or situation. He rejects these possibilities but does not discuss them at length. The pervasiveness of hierarchical thinking models is treated by Ogilvy (1977) and Bouvier (1984), who support the view that hierarchy to a large extent is in the eye of the beholder. Some other comments should also be made in relation to Koestler's arguments.

A key idea with Koestler is the existence of parts which are self-regulating, relatively autonomous, and which exhibit properties not deducible from lower units. At the same time, they are parts of larger wholes. Koestler calls these units "holons." This is not inconsistent with the hierarchy notion. However, he also discusses more complex networks, where "vertical" and "horizontal" connections intertwine. We are warned, however, not to forget the primacy of the vertical, hierarchical, dimension (ibid., p. 289):

It is as if the sight of the foliage of the entwined branches in a forest made us forget that the branches originate in separate trees. The trees are vertical structures. The meeting points of branches from neighbouring trees form horizontal networks at several levels. Without the trees there could be no entwining, and no network. Without the networks, each tree would be isolated, and there would be no integration of functions. Arborization and reticulation seem to be complementary principles in the architecture of organisms. In symbolic universes of discourse arborization is reflected in the 'vertical' denotation (definition) of concepts, reticulation in their 'horizontal' connotations in associative networks.

The last paragraph indicates a tendency to define whatever cannot be captured in a hierarchical order as only a looser kind of "association." Another example is the discussion of "abstract" and "spotlight" memory. The latter—very vivid, almost photographic images resembling total recall of past situations—seems not to fit the hypothesis of hierarchic storing of information. Koestler (ibid., p. 48 ff, 296–297) "solves" this problem by assuming that there is something he calls "emotional relevance," which leads to lack of schematization in hierarchies. He also regards spotlight memory as more "primitive" (ibid., p. 53), and possibly phylogenetically older than abstractive memory.

Koestler even regards the supposedly older principles of storing and managing information in the human brain as harmful. He suggests to initiate (ibid., p. 103):

Not an amputation, but a process of harmonization which assigns each level of the mind, from visceral impulses to abstract thought, its appropriate place in the hierarchy. This implies reinforcing the new brain's power of veto against that type of emotive behavior—and that type only—which cannot be reconciled with reason, such as the 'blind' passions of the group-mind.

The "process of harmonization" cannot be achieved by education: "It can be done only by 'tempering' with human nature itself to correct its endemic schizopsychological disposition" (p. 104). He expects "the laboratories to succeed in producing an immunizing substance conferring mental stability" (p. 105).

To the present author, this line of reasoning seems like trying to expurge and, if possible, eradicate thought patterns which do not fit a hierarchical model. The tree metaphor also hides an important aspect of much social organization. Any given unit may be a member of *several* systems, which each may be conceived of as a hierarchy. In a tree, every branch obviously primarily "belongs" to one tree. However, is it equally clear to what "arborizing structure" a U.S. citizen, born by Jewish parents, working for a French company in Spain belongs? Koestler quotes Hyden (1961), who suggests that the same neuron may be a member of several functional "clubs," as support for the distinction between arborizing and reticulating structures. However, it seems that this could rather be taken as an example of non-hierarchy. (Below, a heterarchy will be endowed with the attributes of having many centers of different kinds. This seems to fit the neuronal clubs better.)

Also on the empirical level, some of Koestler's examples of hierarchic organization may be questioned. Later research on memory, and on the entire functioning of the brain, does not appear to fit the hierarchic model (McCulloch, 1965; Pribram, 1971). Organizations, in their actual functioning, are far less hierarchic than their organization charts would imply. Action systems do not always work as a hierarchy of strategies transformed into action programs and simple final acts (Allison, 1971; Mintzberg, 1978).

The "holon property" of Koestler is fully consistent with the heterarchy model outlined below. The supposed inevitability of hierarchy, however, seems to be a Procrustean bed in describing life in real organizations. Therefore, rather than continuing the conceptual discussion, I will try to sketch some developments in MNCs, illustrating the need for a concept covering these developments. Thereafter, a tentative delimitation of the concept of a heterarchical MNC will be provided.

A pioneer in reviewing the development of different kinds of MNCs was Howard V. Perlmutter (1965). His original scheme of an evolution of, or at least a distinction between, ethnocentric, polycentric, and geocentric MNCs has hardly been improved upon. Therefore, this is a natural starting point to discuss tendencies of change in the nature of multinational business.

Ethnocentrism

Almost all now existing firms have started on a national basis and only gradually developed international ties. Foreign business was initially only marginal, more so for companies from large nations than for those with small "home markets." Internationalization was often based on monopolistic advantages which could be exploited by internalizing transactions within the firm. (See Hymer, 1976; and Dunning, 1977 for early and representative statements of theories of foreign direct investment based on "firm-specific advantages.") These advantages, in terms of, for example, proprietary technology were exploited in a slow, gradual process, by moving concentrically to markets further away from the home country, and by investing in increasingly committing forms. From sales outlets in the neighboring country, the firm cautiously moved towards manufacturing plants on alien continents. (Vernon, 1966; Stopford and Wells, 1972; and Johanson & Vahlne, 1977 are good examples of gradual learning theories of foreign direct investment.)

Ethnocentric companies are managed by home country people, and with time there is a lot of rotation between HQ and subsidiaries. The control style will vary in accordance with practice in the parent company and parent country. For example, Swedish firms transferred a reliance on normative control (Etzioni, 1961) to their international operations. U.S. companies used relatively more of calculative and coercive control, with less autonomy for the subsidiaries (Hedlund, 1980, 1984; Hedlund and Aman, 1983).

The role of a foreign subsidiary in such a company is operational rather than strategic. Strategies are derived from the prospects of extending the geographical scope of firm-specific advantages and formulated at the center. The subsidiaries implement, but there is also an entrepreneurial element to early stages of internationalization, which is lost as the firm gets used to going to foreign lands.

The environment of the MNC—as far as aspects of internationalization are concerned—could be characterized as Type 1 (placid random) or Type 2 (placid clustered) in the Emery and Trist (1965) classification. That is, opportunities and problems are either randomly distributed (Type 1) or clustered (Type 2), but competitive relations are not primary as in Type 3, nor is drastic environmental turbulence the main issue (Type 4). The absence of strategy in a Type 1 situation is particularly apparent in the subsidiary. The best strategy is to do as well as possible on a purely local and perhaps also short-term basis.

Interdependencies between the center and the subsidiaries in the enterprise are primarily sequential (Thompson, 1967). Products, knowhow, and money for investment are sent from the center to the periphery. There is a vertical division of labor, so that activities up-stream the value-added chain are conducted at the center and down-stream operations at the periphery. (This, of course, does not hold for raw materials-based MNCs.) The novelty and uncertainty of foreign operations favor hierarchy rather than market or federation solutions (Williamson, 1975; Daems, 1980). That is, subsidiaries are controlled rather tightly, either through orders or shared outlooks; for example, by transferring people between units in the firm (Edström & Galbraith, 1977).

Polycentrism

As time goes by, foreign business may become dominant rather than marginal, the subsidiaries get more activities and become more self-sufficient, management becomes more host-country oriented and consisting of host-country nationals. The MNC becomes an assemblage of semi-independent units. There is less rotation of personnel, and in a way, the polycentric MNC is less trans- or international than the ethocentric version. Indeed, the term *multinational* fits better for the polycentric firm than for the other archetypes.

The competitive strengths move from proprietary technology to access to distribution channels, brand name, international experience, and finance. Economies of scale and scope become important. New investments are sought worldwide, almost as in a portfolio placement strategy. As long as the firm stays in the original line of business, the size of the host market will be an important criterion for the decision on where to invest. The ethnocentric stage of confinement to near and familiar abodes loses in significance. (See Vernon, 1979; and Hedlund and Kverneland, 1984 for a discussion and some empirical support. Some of the results reported have to do with changes in the environment of MNCs, allowing "instant polycentrism," rather than with firm-specific developments.)

Subsidiaries are operationally independent and increasingly forced to take strategic decisions with respect to their operations in their market ("Disturbed reactive" local environment for the subsidiary). HQ control moves towards calculative, based on financial results rather than on influencing the substance of decisions. The extreme is reached when the parent company acts only as a holding company, buying and selling assets internationally, with no view to anything but the financial outcomes of its dispositions.

Interdependence between subsidiaries and center is *pooled.* Financial resources and some specialist competence are kept at the center, whereas product and technology flows are less pronounced. Activities are duplicated internationally, so that manufacturing, for example, is undertaken in most subsidiaries.

The tendency in terms of control mode is to move toward looser coupling between units and from the hierarchy (in this case also somewhat in the etymological sense) of ethnocentrism to market solutions. Transfer pricing based on market prices rather than internal costs, freedom to choose external suppliers, rewards and punishment in monetary terms, and elaborate bonus payment systems accompany greater turnover rates of personnel and organizational units being sold off and bought. Internationalization is more and more conducted through acquisitions rather than green-field ventures. The tendency to market solutions could be interpreted in terms of increased routinization of international transactions, with consequent reduction of uncertainty. Also, the idiosyncracy of assets (technology, people, etc.) is not as pronounced as in the initial stages. According to Williamson (1975), this should lead to markets rather than hierarchies.

Geocentrism

Perlmutter's (1965) original classification defines the various "centrisms" primarily according to the attitudes of management. Above, such aspects have been linked to strategic situations, stages in the "life cycle of internationalization," types of interdependence between parts of the firm, types of environment facing the company, etc. It becomes even more necessary to discuss these other aspects when describing a geocentric firm. One reason for this is that "geocentric strategies" may be accompanied by ethnocentric attitudes. Indeed, the shift from poly- to geocentric strategic focus is often perceived by host country management as a shift back to HQ and home country attitudes.

Writers on "global strategy" mostly mention interdependence between units in the firm as a distinguishing characteristic. (See, for example, Porter, 1980 and 1984.) The actions of a subsidiary in country A influence prospects for the subsidiary in country B, perhaps because they face the same competitor, who has to divide his resources between the two markets. Thus, competition is not confined within each national market, but system-wide. The MNC exploits systems advantages, subsidiaries, and country-specific advantages being considered the parts of the system. Thus, at the extreme, subsidiaries specialize and operate globally in limited fields. The MNC in this way *internalizes the exploitation of (country) comparative advantages.* This is very important from the point of view of theories of international trade and investment. Ricardo never thought that the same agent would produce both wine and cloth. Assumptions that the MNC is a reflection of firm-specific advantage à la Hymer must confront a very peculiar type of advantage, that is *multinationality in itself.* To say that the MNC exists because it exploits the advantages of being an MNC is tautological, so the convenient theoretical starting point in monopolistic advantages dissolves when applied to the geocentric firm. As Vernon (1979) himself has noted, the product life cycle theory of international trade and investment becomes less useful as the international spread of companies is extended.

Global competition, where a firm faces the same rivals on most markets, means that gradual internationalization strategies pose problems. Hedlund and Kverneland (1984) and Lundgren and Hedlund (1983) show how market entry by Swedish firms into Japan and South-East Asia respectively is faster and more committing than theories of gradualism would lead one to expect. Firms do not follow a neat sequence from agent over sales subsidiary and some local manufacturing to large-scale local production. Instead, the pattern is one of jumping steps in the chain and building up positions very rapidly. International strategy is increasingly driven by considerations of rivals', and sometimes actual or potential cooperators', behavior, rather than by the exploitation of FSAs (firm-specific advantages) as in the ethnocentric firm, or by the attractiveness of markets one by one as in the polycentric firm. Oligopolistic reaction, in terms of *imitating* competitors' moves (Knickerbocker, 1973) as well as *avoiding* competitors and building up *mutual hostage positions*, becomes common.

Perlmutter saw the use of third country nationals (TCNs) in management as a sign of geocentricity. Other aspects concerning the management process are reliance on global profitability goals and increased rotation of personnel. Probably a shift back to less calculative and more normative and coercive control is required in order for global strategies to work. The subsidiaries have to implement strategies formulated according to a global logic, they have to be able to act quickly in response to competitive conditions, they must be encouraged to look at a wider picture. Most writings on global strategy give the subsidiaries a less independent role than that implied in a polycentric MNC. A recentralization of authority to HQ often follows, and is recommended to follow, a globalization of competition. (See, for example, Channon and Jalland, 1979; Hedlund and Aman, 1983.) Often, global divisions structured around products, technologies, or customer types are created to coordinate activities in specific competitive niches. The business environment can be characterized as a global disturbed reactive one in the terms of Emery and Trist (1965).

Interdependence between parts of the firm moves from the polycentric pooling of resources at the center to sequential and *reciprocal*. Products, know-how, money, and people flow in increasingly complex patterns, and not as in the ethnocentric firm from one core to the periphery. (See also Bartlett, 1984 and his discussion of the "integrated network model" of an MNC. His other concepts of "centralized hub" and "decentralized federation" can be compared with ethnocentrism and polycentrism, respectively.) Particularly reciprocal interdependence is expected to lead to internalization in a hierarchy (cf Thompson, 1967), so the trend towards markets in the polycentric MNC is reversed. Also reversed is the tendency to duplicate activities in various subsidiaries.

The discussion so far is summarized in Table 1. Obviously, it ignores many complexities and gives a very simple picture of the range of possibilities. For example, there certainly exist geocentric MNCs which build

Table 1

	Ethnocentrism	Polycentrism	Geocentrism
Importance of foreign business	Marginal	Substantial/dominant	Dominant
Basis for international strategy	Exploit firm-specific advantages	Market size, scale and scope economies, finance	Competition, multinationality as such
Expansion mode	Gradual, concentric, green-field	Market-driven, acquisitions, cash-constrained	Quick, direct, competition-driven
Organization structure	Mother/daughter international division	Mother/daughter, international division, holding company	Global divisions or matrix organization
Type of interdependence	Sequential center-subsidiary	Pooled center-subsidiary	System of sequential and reciprocal
Governance mode	Hierarchy	Market	Hierarchy, "hierarchy"
Specialization in value-added chain	Specialization up-downstream HQ-subsidiaries	Duplication	Specialization up-downstream, between subsidiaries
Control style	HQ-derived, coercive, normative	Calculative	Normative, coercive
MNC Internationalization environment	Placid-random Type I	Placid-clustered Type II	Disturbed-reactive, turbulent Type III→IV
Subsidiary environment	Type I, II	Type I, II, III	Type III→IV
Autonomy of subsidiary	Low–Medium	High	Low–Medium
Strategic role of subsidiary	Implement local strategy	Formulate + implement local strategy	Implement + adapt to global strategy
Recruitment and rotation	Home-country managers, much rotation	Local managers, little rotation	Mixed, TCNs, much rotation

primarily upon sequential interdependencies between center and periphery. A clear example would be mining companies in highly concentrated industries. Nevertheless, one can better understand the character of most geocentricity and globality of competition if several strains of—in this context—often forgotten theoretical heritage are applied:

- Thompson's (1967) classification of various types of interdependence, and his hypotheses of mechanisms of integration related to those types.
- Transaction cost theorists' (Coase, 1937; Williamson, 1975) notions of alternative governance modes and the determinants of effective solutions to the governance problem.
- Classification of mechanisms of social integration such as Etzioni's (1961).
- Typologies of organizational environments (Emery and Trist, 1965) and hypotheses about behavioral implications of those environments.

Three entries in Table 1 have not been adequately foreshadowed in the discussion above. Organization structure has been added, using the results of Stopford and Wells (1972), Franko (1976) and others linking strategy to the structure of the international organization. "Hierarchy" as one governance mode in geocentric firms will be explained in the next section. I believe that pure hierarchy will be detrimental to many global strategies, and that there nevertheless is a strong possibility that this is what will happen in many firms. Emery and Trist's type 4 environment—the turbulent one—has been introduced as a likely development for both the entire geocentric MNC and its subsidiaries. This will also be discussed in the next section.

Strains on the Geocentric MNC

A radical view concerning geocentrism and globality is that we are witnessing the disappearance of the international dimension of business. For commercial and practical purposes, the nations do not exist, and the relevant business arena becomes something like a big unified "home market." Business action as well as concepts to describe firms and the situations they face will be similar to the base of a company working in one national market.

However, there are a number of difficulties facing the MNC, which wants to act as if the world was one big market and competitive arena, to be adapted to in a scaled-up version of "ordinary", national strategy.

- In spite of proclaimed increased homogenization of demand (Vernon, 1979), there are still strong differences between nations and regions. Protectionism is furthermore on the increase rather than the other way around. The loyalty of many employees is still primarily with their home country. (See Doz, 1979, and Doz and Prahalad, 1980).

- The need for cooperation, in joint ventures or in other forms, characteristic of many branches of industry, makes unilateral strategy making problematical.
- Cultural differences in management style makes one at least question the viability of uniform, worldwide control systems and other management practices.
- Economizing by sharing resources between different lines of business, with different customers and competitors, mitigates against totally subduing the local country dimension in organization and strategy.
- Size itself may be a severe problem in coordinating operations globally in the same way as one would coordinate national business. The complexity and variability of environmental circumstances compound the size of problems. Response times may be too long to keep up with changes in markets. The cognitive limitations of integrating information are very real. Particularly at the strategic level, advances in information technology may not be sufficient, although no doubt be of value.
- The supply of managers able to carry out ambitious global strategies already is a bottleneck today for most firms. If strategy making is recentralized to the HQ "brain," it will become even more difficult to fill positions, since this requires more transfer of personnel.
- With the development of specialization between subsidiaries, these will become so large and important that it will be detrimental to assign narrow strategic roles to them. For example, a research center in India serving the whole network of an MNC would probably, with time, develop ideas and products which do not fit the prevailing strategies of the group, but which could well be a basis for a new line of business. It would be wasteful not to entertain a capacity to utilize the creativity and entrepreneurship of people at all nodes of the network. Besides, those people would probably resign if they did not get such opportunities.
- Finally, centrally guided global strategies for given products aimed at beating given competitors, looking at the world as one market, may lead to neglect of opportunities to exploit existing differences between nations. If the global thrust is combined with a reemphasis on HQ and home-country guidance, the company may return to ethnocentrism, only being able to exploit ideas originating at home. Advantage seeking and advantage development will not be main concerns, but only the exploitation of existing advantages. In the long run, such a firm may become sterile. The results in Davidson & Haspeslagh (1982) indicate that the global product division as an organizational solution may indeed entail such risks.

Most of the points illustrate the danger of seeing geocentricity just as the scaling up of the national corporation, thereby getting rid of the international dimension of business and reestablishing central strategic direction from a center, which is at the apex of one, big global hierarchy. Even if this characterization of global strategy is a caricature and may seem to be set up as a straw-man, I believe that both academic discussion and—but less so—practice in large MNCs are affected by outlooks, philosophies, strategies, and management practices similar to the ones described.

Perlmutter's original conception of geocentricity was not as restricted as the "mononational" version sketched above. He sketched a situation where subsidiaries were "parts of a whole whose focus is on worldwide objectives as well as local objectives, each part making its unique contribution with its unique competence." These lines do not clearly denote the attributes of geocentricity, but their connotative meaning is very rich. I believe one can usually single out some of those connotations and specify a special case of geocentricity, an option which is still not fully developed in actuality but towards which many companies probably will, and should, move. This is the hypermodern MNC, and one of its distinguishing marks is its heterarchical nature.

The Heterarchical MNC

The heterarchical MNC differs from the standard geocentric one both in terms of strategy and in terms of structure. Strategically, the main dividing line is between exploiting competitive advantages derived from a home country base on the one hand, and actively seeking advantages originating in the global spread of the firm on the other. In its most extreme form, this would mean that one could not assign the company to any particular industry. Any opportunity which activates the potential inherent in broad geographical coverage would be a candidate for inclusion in the company's repertoire of products and services. Obviously, no MNC would like to go to this extreme. Specialization benefits apply also to information search, and in many contexts existing barriers to entry into a global industry would be prohibitively restrictive.

However, the concept of exploiting the advantage of multinationality as such also applies within a rather limited field of business. Information on competition, technological trends, developments in related fields, aspects of national environments, etc. lead to opportunities not easily identified by purely local firms, or by polycentric MNCs, or even by ethnocentrically tainted global MNCs. The difference between the latter and the heterarchy is most pronounced when it comes to the *structure* of the enterprise and the processes of managing it. Indeed, it may be that the idea of structure determining strategy (see Hall and Saias, 1980) is a fundamental one for the

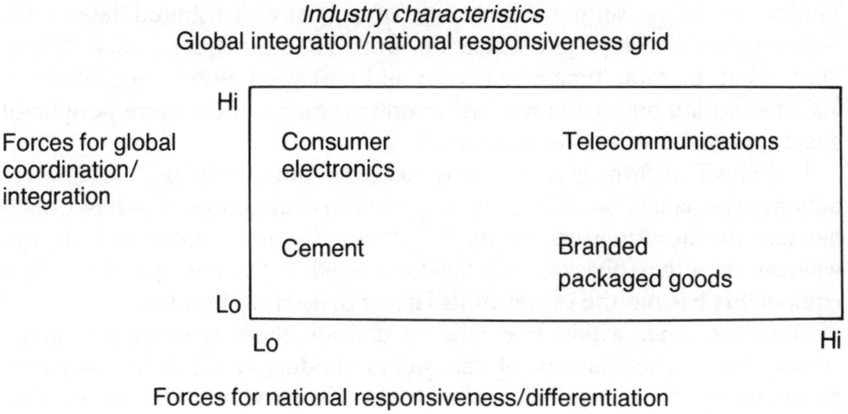

Industry characteristics
Global integration/national responsiveness grid

Hi

Forces for global
coordination/
integration

	Consumer electronics	Telecommunications
	Cement	Branded packaged goods

Lo

Lo   Hi

Forces for national responsiveness/differentiation

Figure 1 (Source: Bartlett, 1984).

heterarchical MNC. Rather than identifying properties of the industry in which it competes and then adapting its structure to the demands thus established, the hypermodern MNC first defines its structural properties and then looks for strategic options following from these properties. In actual life, of course, every candidate for heterarchy will have come from a history in a given set of industries, regions, etc. The MNCs most likely to face the indeterminacy of strategically relatively open vistas are probably those described by Bartlett (1984) as "transnational." Such firms are active in industries where it is important both to achieve global integration and local differentiation, for example, adaptation to host government demands (see Figure 1).

Thus, strategic imperatives of dual focus force some MNCs to adopt structural solutions and management practices in consonance with these task demands. These adaptations then constitute an opportunity for sometimes much wider and diverse strategic options, or at least more intensive utilizations of the global spread of the company. In order to achieve this, further development of structural traits are desirable. Their archetypical expressions will be enumerated below.

1. First, the heterarchical MNC has *many centers.* One could speak of a polyarchical rather than monarchical MNC, were it not for the lack of integration implied in the former term. The main idea is that the foundations of competitive advantage no longer reside in any one country, but in many. New ideas and products may come up in many different countries and later be exploited on a global scale. A geographically diffused pattern of expertise is built up, corresponding to unique abilities in each node of the network. These abilities may be a reflection of dissimilarities between countries as in "demand theories" of international trade (Burenstam-

Linder, 1961) or simply expressions of spatially distributed talents for technological development within the firm. At the extreme, each "subsidiary" is at the same time a center for and perhaps a global coordinator of activities within one field (such as for one product), and a more peripheral agent for local distribution in another.

In diversified firms it is obviously easier to find examples of such international specialization. For example, the Swedish company Atlas Copco has had the headquarters for its Air Power division located in Belgium, whereas the other divisions are headquartered in Sweden. Esselte (office equipment) has put the center of its largest division in London.

However, even within one product division there is scope for multi-centeredness. The dangers of the global product division undiluted by geographical considerations have been discussed by Davidson and Haspeslagh (1982). Relations are restricted to those between one center and units in the periphery. Relations within the supposed periphery are not exploited, and information overload on the center and lack of motivation in subsidiaries create grave problems. Hedlund (1980) documents the strategic alienation of subsidiary managers in Swedish MNCs, and gives some suggestions of how to involve the subsidiaries more in strategy formulation. In this case, the mother—daughter structure, rather than global product divisions, is the organizational background. This seems to support the views of Bartlett (1981, 1984) that the importance of the formal organization structure is easily exaggerated. Simmonds (1985), reviewing the literature and discussing various ways to "achieve the geocentric ideal," concludes that other management systems, such as the planning, accounting, and reporting systems, are important obstacles.

2. A key idea in the conception of a heterarchical MNC is that *subsidiary managers are also given a strategic role, not only for their "own" company, but for the MNC as a whole.* The notions of "headquarters," "center," "home country," and "corporate level" dissolve and are not synonymous. Corporate level strategy has to be implemented and formulated in a geographically scattered network.

3. Heterarchy implies *different kinds of centers.* There is not only a set of global divisions and subdivisions, or only a set of geographical divisions further split up in national and regional subunits. A heterarchy consists of a mix of organizing prinicples. There may be an R&D center in Holland with global responsibilities for coordinating product development, product division headquarters in Germany responsible for the main product, a marketing center for Asia in Singapore, and a center for dealing with global purchases in London. The multidimensionality of organizing principles (functions, products, geography, customer type, etc.) reflects the need to coordinate activities along each and all of those dimensions. In a heter-

The distribution of information in every part of a hologram is possible because of laser technology. One could say that the corporate ethos is the analogue of the laser light. By sharing certain conceptions about the firm, and certain ways of acting in relation to other members of the firm, it becomes possible to rapidly share information, interpret the meaning of events in and outside the organization in similar ways, and see opportunities for local action in the interest of the global good. The laser beam effect of corporate culture is the unifying element of a heterarchical organization. It is crucial to support the formation of such a culture, since the risks of anarchy are otherwise very great.

Pessimism regarding the efficiency and integrity of non-hierarchical and unified control is less warranted on empirical than on "theoretical" grounds. Ogilvy (1977) discusses how ambitions to organize societies and polities hierarchically are influenced by and influence modes of thought and even the structure of the personality. The fact that a phenomenon may be hard to grasp and explain in terms familiar to the grasper does not mean, however, that the phenomenon does not exist. Ogilvy quotes McCulloch (1965) on heterarchical patterns of preference in neural networks.

Circularities in preference instead of indicating inconsistencies, actually demonstrate consistency of a higher order than had been dreamed of in our philosophy. An organism possessed of this nervous system—six neurons—is sufficiently endowed to be unpredictable from any theory founded on a scale of values. It has a heterarchy of values, and is thus internectively too rich to submit to a summum bonum. (McCulloch, 1965, p. 43)

Yet, although we cannot explain how we are able to walk, for example, we still do. It is worth quoting McCullogh again, for some clues about the properties of heterarchies and possible analogies (no more but also no less) with a discussion on organization and control in human institutions. (Emphases added by the present author.)

The details of its (the brain) neurons and their specific connections need not concern us here. In general, you may think of it as a computer *to any part* of which come signals from many parts of the body and from other parts of the brain and spinal cord. It is *only one cell deep* on the path from input to output, but it can set the filters on all of its inputs and can control the behavior of the programmed activity, the half-centers, and the reflexes. It gets a *substitute for depth by its intrinsic fore-and-aft connections.* Its business, given its *knowledge of the state* of the whole organism and the world impingent upon it, is to decide whether the rule is one requiring fighting, fleeing, eating, sleeping, etc. It must do it with millisecond component action and conduction velocities of usually less than 100 meters per second, and *do it in real time*, in a third of a second. That it has worked so well throughout evolution, without itself evolving, points to its structure as the natural solution of the organization of appropriate behavior. We know much experimentally of the behavior of the components, but still have no theory worthy of the name to explain its circuit actions. (McCulloch, 1965, p. 397.)

7. The foregoing discussion on the heterarchical nature of the nervous system leads to another, perhaps hair-raising, analogy. The metaphor underlying much thought on corporate strategy is one of the firm consisting of a brain and a body. The strategy makers in the center are the brain, and the implementors in the periphery are the body. Thinking and acting take place at different locations. Books like *The brain of the firm* (Beer, 1972) testify to the forcefulness of the metaphor. However, the dangers of separating thinking and acting too much in an organization have been well illustrated by the decline and often fall of formal long-range planning departments in companies. One way of describing the heterarchical MNC is to say that thinking is not only restricted to one exclusive center, but goes on in the whole enterprise. Thus, an appropriate metaphor for discussing a heterarchical firm would be a *"firm as a brain"* model rather than a "brain of the firm" model.

A weakness of the metaphor is that it may lead one to see the firm as only a cognitive entry. However, the core of the idea is that not only does thinking take place also in the periphery, but it *goes together with and directly informs action.*

8. *Coalitions with other companies and also other types of actors* are frequent in the heterarchical MNC. Exploiting global reach will often mean to serve as a catalyst, bringing together elements with synergistic potential, perhaps firms from different continents previously not known to one another. It may be of interest to note that Emery and Trist (1965) saw as two primary ways of coping with turbulence:

(I) The creation of common values, binding people and organizations together and enabling them to respond quickly to environmental change. This corresponds to the emergence of corporate culture as a binding element discussed above.
(II) Cooperation between heterogenous elements rather than competition between homogenous elements (as in "Type 3") as the primary occupation of top leaders.

The latter point includes things such as joint ventures and cooperation between firms and governments. A heterarchical MNC will share and pool its power with other actors in order to benefit maximally from its global capabilities. This does not mean that it will do so in all fields of business. Again, it is the *multitude* of governance forms and degrees of internalization which characterizes a heterarchy.

9. Finally, and returning to the strategic ambitions rather than the structural properties of heterarchy, this type of MNC would be fit to attack the most difficult global problems of today. This may seem naive and even ridiculous to managers busy surviving producing and selling a narrow line of products or services. However, assuming a type of company that sees the exploitation of globality as such as its main source of strength, it does not seem that far-fetched to consider *radical problem-orientation* as guiding strategy formulation. (Rather than starting from existing physical or human resources, or from competitive positions in narrow fields of business.)

Human Resource Management in a Heterarchical MNC

No full discussion of human resource management in the context of a heterarchy will be attempted here. Instead, a few important points will be brought up, without pretense of exhaustive treatment.

1. Concerning *organization structure,* many models will be simultaneously used in a heterarchical MNC. The flexibility and multidimensionality of the structure defy easy categorization. Change of the formal organization will not give rise to heterarchy. Subtler changes in management processes are required. However, the formal organization may stop a movement towards heterarchy.

One consequence of breaking down (up?) a large hierarchy is that it is *no longer possible to promote people mainly by giving them jobs "higher up."* Movement between centers will be more common, and movement from periphery towards center in the same unit will be less common. Also, the need to build up the "nervous system" of the heterarchy is of importance here, as is the need to use personal competence wherever it pays off best.

2. The core of a heterarchical enterprise will consist of *people with a long experience in it.* A firm invests considerably in the employee, and vice versa. The latter is a part of the communication system of the firm, and the history of the human system in the company may be its most strategic resource. This is often said and may sound like a platitude. However, it is less so in an organization which builds its strategy on advantage seeking and using its global coverage, rather than on advantage exploitation on the basis of known and stable assets.

This communication network is not easily imitable by other firms. Much less so can a small part of it be used by others. In a limited sense, the employee is of value to competitors as a source of information, since he has a lot of it, also of a strategic nature. After having interrogated and "emptied" the unfaithful soul, however, it is of little use. Thus, from the point of view of the employee, the idiosyncrasy of his relation with the firm is very great. This is also true the other way around, since it takes a long time to find and train a replacement. However, the "hologram quality" makes the firm *more* robust than in a hierarchy. Many employees will share the same information and be able to support or replace each other. This does not mean that the firm can easily fire the employee, since such behavior would undermine the mutual trust necessary to encourage investment in the long-term future of the MNC. Idiosyncratic assets should lead to internalization, according to Williamson (1975), so one can expect *more encompassing and long-term contracts* with employees. Another possibility is participation in the ownership of the company.

One can exaggerate the need for permanence, however. There is considerable flux in the activities of the heterarchical MNC, and this requires flexibility also concerning personnel. Joint ventures and other forms of cooperation, sometimes on a project basis, by definition mean that the new members continuously enter and leave the system. Perhaps one can speak of a *dual career system*, just as one speaks of dual labor markets in some countries. There will be a limited but still numerous core of almost life-time employees, and a much larger number of people with more fleeting association with the firm. In the debate on the Japanese labor system, it is often pointed out that the core enjoying life-time employment and other marvels of the Japanese employment system is rather small. What has surprised most analysts is that the duality of the labor market has not disappeared with modernization. Perhaps the solution with an integrated core surrounded by quasi-integrated satellites (which themselves might constitute cores in other systems) is a good combination of stability and flexibility?

The core provides the memory and the information infrastructure necessary to grasp opportunities on a global scale. The looser links to the outside help against rigidification of response by establishing channels for the communication of new ideas. In this context, the *balance between young and old members* of the organization is probably critical. (See the discussion by Lorenz, 1971, on the balance between processes of acquiring, retaining, and dismantling cultural knowledge, and the importance of age in this respect.) Company demography needs to be planned more systematically than when the firm is a system of roles which can be easily communicated and learnt. Not allowing steady recruitment of "new blood," or dismantling of knowledge by early retirement, are traps in this area. However, much more research is needed on company demography before any strong statements can be made.

3. In order for internalization of norms to take place, *a lot of rotation of personnel* and international travel and postings are necessary. The tendency to man purportedly global firms with home country managers—and more so than in polycentric firms—will not work in a heterarchical MNC. Advances in information technology may help the formation of the nervous system of the firm, but this will not be enough for building strong internal cultures.

The problems on the practical level of international transfers of people are well known. The solutions are less well known, apart from obvious hints such as paying well, giving spouses jobs, and being aware of re-entry problems. Perhaps recruitment of candidates for the core should be very selective, with a strong emphasis on willingness to travel and change function in the company. Sending people abroad very early is probably a good idea, possibly even before they have formed families. (Would the best be to have the new employee swear to chastity and keep unmarried, like in the very successful international operations of some ecclesiastical organizations such as the Jesuit Order?)

4. A much *broader range of people in the firm must develop capacity for strategic thinking and action.* This implies open communication of strategies and plans, decentralization of strategic tasks, using task forces on strategic issues actively, and providing early opportunities for development of "top management capabilities" also for "subsidiary" employees. (The words "subsidiary" and even "manager" sound a bit funny in the context of a heterarchical MNC. There is less obvious subordination, and the clear distinction between managing and operational functions is less relevant than in a clear hierarchy. Heterarchy may mean the beginning of the decline of the professional manager as a species within the organizational zoo.)

Control systems which measure performance along many dimensions (products, regions, short and long term, etc.) are necessary. This is also almost a platitude, but in actual practice many companies who claim they do this really do not. Even if the systems are there, they are not used for more than very limited purposes. (Hedlund and Zander, 1985, report on the economic control systems of Swedish MNCs. See also Business International, 1982.)

5. *Reward and punishment systems are critical.* Carriers of bad news must not be killed. Kobrin (1984) shows how MNCs neglect to use the expertise of host country managers for the assessment of political risk. The long term must not be sacrificed. Perhaps a bonus should be given on the basis of profitability in the unit where the employee served five years ago? Particularly at very high levels, an effective career strategy is to turn "star" and "question mark" jobs into "cash cow" jobs, and leave just before they start

looking like "dogs." Top managers are rather adept at taking credit for other people's work and avoiding criticism for their own, and temporal extension of the review period may counter the tendency to misuse such talents.

Similarly, the global aspects may be supported by rewarding people for global rather than local profits, or whatever the objective is. The difficulty lies in matching responsibility with authority. Probably, a heterarchical MNC has to refrain from mechanical compensation formulae to a large extent. It is not possible to construct perfect equations for the distribution of bonuses, for example, particularly when circumstances change often and drastically. Paying employees partly on the basis of the performance of the entire firm is one possibility. SAB-Nife, a small Swedish MNC, has a large bonus element in its system for paying subsidiary managers. Half of the bonus is based on the performance of the entire company (90 percent of sales are abroad), and half depends on the results of the individual subsidiary.

Shareholding by employees may be a very potent instrument to stimulate action in the interest of the total company, and to encourage normative integration. Would it not be better to have the employees in, say, the Indian subsidiary own shares in the parent company than the Indian government forcing the subsidiary to joint ventures with local partners, some more sleeping than others? Not that the former would stop the latter, but in the long run this would constitute an important change in the identity of the MNC.

Global mentality may be required far "down" in the organization. Starting up new and closing down old activities is helped by understanding of the reasons for change. Technological developments are turning many workers into technicians, and to technicians needing to know a lot about customers. Global competition is changing the rules of the game for all employees. Some examples of action in Swedish firms in the direction indicated is given by:

- Volvo's gigantic program for improving substantially the technical know-how at all levels in the company.
- SAS' focus on foreign competition in mobilizing for turn-around, and the very public nature of its corporate strategy.
- SKF Steel's program to import steel technology from Japan and teach its employees about competitive facts (and, of course, technical matters) by sending workers on assignments with the Japanese licensor. (An informal race on productivity ensued, and the Swedes caught up with their teachers in Japan.)

6. It is hard to tell what the *personality type best suited to heterarchy* is. Ogilvy (1977) argues that a sort of "polytheistic" personality, and acceptance of such Protean prospects, go together with more decentralized

organizations and societies. Speculating on this, one could argue that people from polytheistic or atheistic cultures would be most comfortable in such situations. Old Greeks, Vikings, Hindus, and Japanese would do well. Christians (particularly protestants), Moslems, Jews, communists, and people affected by "scientism" would do worse. The representatives of western culture included in the former list are all dead, so many firms would do well to look around a bit for new managers.

Such speculation aside, it seems clear that a heterarchical MNC would require many employees with the following qualities:

- Aptitude for *searching for and combining elements* in new ways. Probably good knowledge in several fields of science and technology is one precondition for this.
- Skill in *communicating ideas* and rapidly *turning them into action.*
- Very good *command of several lanaguages* and knowledge of and sympathy for several cultures. (Steiner, 1975, argues that bilingualism is *qualitatively* different from monolingualism, in that it gives a "stereo quality" to perception and interpretation. See also Maruyama, 1978.)
- *Honesty and personal integrity.* These old fashioned ideals are critical for heterarchy not to turn into chaos.
- *Willingness to take risks and to experiment.* Advantage seeking is much more risky than advantage exploitation. The organization must support such learning from failures. The heterarchical MNC would mean an attempt to innovate from the basis of a large firm, working across national boundaries at very early stages in the innovation process. As in all entrepreneurial activity, a high failure rate is to be expected. Therefore, in practice, every company needs *also* a part which makes money in more stable and predictable ways. The theoretical alternative of a perfect external capital market can be ignored for the moment, because of agency cost considerations (Jensen and Meckling, 1976). It would be very difficult for anonymous shareholders, as well as for lenders, to assess ex ante, monitor constantly, and even evaluate ex post, the activities of a genuinely and entirely heterarchical MNC. This also means that the financial strength of a well-run, fairly large traditional MNC makes it the *only* realistic candidate for heterarchy on an international level. Neither small firms on their own or together through market relationships nor governments, for various reasons but in both cases having to do with agency cost problems, are likely to succeed.
- *"Faith" in the company* and its activities. Enthusiasm for the company need not go to the etymological limits of the word, but genuine appreciation of the company and its culture is valuable. Perhaps this means that the widely admired sceptical thinking type of person is of less interest than the person able to form strong attachments?

7. *Management development activities* (in the more restricted sense) *should be seen as a primary instrument to build a corporate culture,* formulate and disseminate strategies, and establish links in the communication system of the firm. Its role for acquiring skills and for learning facts and methods is perhaps only subsidiary.

Conclusion

The heterarchical MNC is a so far loosely defined concept. It covers a particular brand of geocentric company, which differs significantly from a version that is likely to develop more rapidly in the immediate future. The importance in bringing up and further outlining the demands of and possibilities inherent in heterarchy lies in the risk of the purely global company regressing into a sized-up model of the large national firm. An ethnocentric backlash is a clear possibility, but mostly unnecessarily so. Therefore, firms should actively explore the dangers of recentralization, even if and when such moves are desirable, and find ways of compensating for those dangers. Only the broad outlines of response can be drawn without much experimentation and accumulation of experience. The MNC is a crucial arena for such institutional innovation, since it is uniquely powered to address some of the most urgent problems of a global scale.

Where should one look for signs of heterarchy? In terms of industries, probable fields are those characterized by the use of many different technologies, high but not maximum global homogeneity of demand, fast rate of technical and market change, non-trivial scale economies (but not necessarily in manufacturing), and absence of strong local barriers to entry. This means that information technology and biotechnology come to mind, which should make the reader (and writer) suspicious, since this seems too obvious (and boring). However, also the automobile industry, building and construction, and many services fit many, but not all, of the criteria.

In terms of geographical and corporate origins, heterarchical MNCs are more likely to evolve from less than gigantic firms, and from contexts with a history of rather autonomous and entrepreneurial subsidiaries. This may give European firms an advantage over U.S. ones. In a larger picture, MNCs from newly modernizing nations may stand an even better chance. Chandler and Daems (1980) show how institutional inertia and established forms of corporate organization in Europe delayed the formation of the large, managerially run firm as compared to in the USA. Olsen (1982) has discussed how the same mechanisms may make whole nations rise and fall. The heterarchical prospect may seem too remote, or even silly, to people in successful hierarchies likely to enjoy still some time of harvesting the fruits of investments in a powerful organization for the maximum utilization of existing physical assets and know-how. It may seem less remote for people who have little alternative but to directly exploit the amazing global fluidity of capital, technology, and people to develop *new* products, markets, and competences.

References

Allison, G. T. *Essence of decision: Explaining the Cuban missile crisis.* Little Brown, 1971.

Bartlett, C. A. "Multinational Structural Change: Evolution Versus Reorganization." in L. Otterbeck, (Ed.), *The Management of Headquarters-Subsidiary Relationships in Multinational Companies,* Gower Publishing Company Limited, 1981.

Bartlett, C. A. "Organization and Control of Global Enterprises: Influences, Characteristics and Guidelines." Boston: Harvard Business School, 1984.

Beer, S. *The brain of the firm.* Allen Lane, 1972.

Bouvier, P. L. "Subjectivity and the concept of hierarchy: the dominant paradigm and the prevailing work system." In *Proceedings from the International Conference of Society for General Systems Research,* New York, June 1984.

Burenstam-Linder, S. *Essays on Trade and Transportation.* New York: Wiley, 1961.

Business International Corporation, *Assessing foreign subsidiary performance.* (By Czechowics, I. J., Choi, F. D. S., and Bashivi, V. B.), 1982.

Chandler, A. D. Jr., and Daems, H. (Eds.), *Managerial Hierarchies.* Cambridge, MA and London, England: Harvard University Press, 1980.

Channon, D. F., and Jalland, M. *Multinational Planning.* London: Basingstoke, 1979.

Coase, R. H. "The Nature of the Firm." *Economica N.S.,* 1937, **4**, 386–405.

Daems, H. "The rise of the modern industrial enterprise: A new perspective." In A. D. Chandler and H. Daems (Eds.), *Managerial Hierarchies.* Cambridge, MA and London: Harvard University Press, 1980.

Davidson, W. H., and Haspeslagh, P. "Shaping a Global Product Organization", *Harvard Business Review,* July–August, 1982.

Doz, Y. L. *Government Control and Multinational Strategic Management: Power Systems and Telecommunications Equipment.* Praeger, 1979.

Doz, Y. L., and Prahalad, C. K. "How MNCs Cope with Host Government Intervention." *Harvard Business Review,* March–April 1980.

Dunning, J. H. "Trade, location of economic activity and the multinational enterprise. A search for an eclectic approach." In B. Ohlin, P. O. Hesselbom, and P. J. Wiskman, (Eds.), *The international allocation of economic activity.* London: Macmillan, 1977.

Edström, A., and Galbraith, J. R. "Transfers of Managers as a Coordination and Control Strategy in Multinational Organizations." *Administrative Science Quarterly,* June 1977, 248–263.

El Sawy, O. A. "From separation to holographic enfolding." Paper presented to TIMS meeting, Boston, May 1985.

Emery, F. E., and Trist, E. L. "The Causal Texture of Organization Environments." *Human Relations,* 1965 **18**, pp. 21–32.

Etzioni, A. *A Comparative Analysis of Complex Organizations.* New York: Free Press 1961.

Faucheux, C., and Laurent, A. "Significance of the epistemological revolution for a management science." In *Proceedings from the workshop on the epistemology of management,* EIASM, 1980.

232   *United Nations Library on Transnational Corporations*

Franko, L. G. *The European Multinationals.* Greenwich, CT: Greylock Press, 1976.

Hall, D., and Saias, M. "Strategy Follows Structure." *Strategic Management Journal,* 1980 1(2).

Hedlund, G. "The Role of Foreign Subsidiaries in Strategic Decision-Making in Swedish Multinational Corporations." *Strategic Management Journal,* 1980 **9**, 23–26.

Hedlund, G. "Organization In-Between: The Evolution of the Mother–Daughter Structure of Managing Foreign Subsidiaries in Swedish MNCs." *Journal of International Business Studies,* Fall, 1984.

Hedlund, G., and Kverneland, Å. *Investing in Japan—the experience of Swedish firms.* Stockholm: Institute of International Business, Stockholm School of Economics, 1984.

Hedlund, G., and Åman, P. *Managing Relationships with Foreign Subsidiaries— Organization and Control in Swedish MNCs.* Stockholm: Sveriges Mekanförbund, 1983.

Hedlund, G., and Zander, U. *Formulation of Goals and Follow-up of Performance for Foreign Subsidiaries in Swedish MNCs.* Working Paper 85/4, Institute of International Business, Stockholm School of Economics, 1985.

Hyden, H. "Control of the Mind." In Farber, S. M., and Wilson, R. H. L., (Eds.), *Control of the Mind.* New York, 1961.

Hymer, S. *The International Operations of National Firms: A Study of Direct Foreign Investment.* M.I.T. Press. (Originally published as doctoral dissertation in 1960.) 1976.

Jaeger, A. M., and Baliga, B. R. "Control Systems and Strategic Adaptation: Lessons from the Japanese Experience." *Strategic Management Journal,* 1985, **6**(2).

Jensen, M. C., and Meckling, W. H. "Theory of the firm: managerial behavior, agency costs and ownership structure." *Journal of Financial Economics,* October 1976, 305–360.

Johanson, J., and Vahlne, J-E. "The Internationalization Process of the Firm—A Model of Knowledge Development and Increasing Foreign Market Commitment." *Journal of Management Studies,* 1977, **12**(3).

Knickerbocker, F. T. *Oligopolistic Reaction and Multinational Enterprise.* Boston: Harvard Business School, 1973.

Kobrin, S. J. *Managing political risk assessment.* University of California Press, 1984.

Koestler, A. *Janus—a summing up.* New York: Random House, 1978.

Laurent, A. "Managerial subordinacy." *Academy of Management Review,* 1978, 220–230.

Lorenz, K. "Knowledge, belief and freedom." In P. H. Weiss, (Ed.), *Hierarchically organized systems in theory and practice.* Hafner Publishing Company, 1971.

Lundgren, S., and Hedlund, G. *Svenska företag i Sydostasien.* Stockholm: Institute of International Business, Stockholm School of Economics, 1983.

Maruyama, M. "The epistemological revolution." *Futures,* June 1978, 240–242.

McCulloch, W. *Embodiments of mind.* Cambridge, MA, 1965.

Mintzberg, H. "Patterns in Strategy Formation." *Management Science,* 1978, 934–948.

Mitroff, I. *Why Our Old Pictures of the World Don't Work Anymore.* Research Paper, University of Southern California, 1983.

Ogilvy, J. *Multidimensional man.* Oxford University Press, 1977.

Ohlin, B., Hesselbom, P. O., and Wiskman, P. J. (Eds.) *The international allocation of economic activity.* London: Macmillan, 1977.

Olsen, M. *The rise and decline of nations.* New Haven and London: Yale University Press, 1982.

Perlmutter, H. V. "L'enterprise internationale—trois conceptions." *Revue Economique et Sociale,* 1965, **23**.

Porter, M. E. *Competitive Strategy.* New York: Free Press, 1980.

Porter, M. E. *Competition in global industries—a conceptual framework.* Boston: Harvard Business School, 1984.

Pribram, K. *Languages of the brain.* Englewood Cliffs, NJ: Prentice-Hall, 1971.

Simmonds, K. "Global Strategy: Achieving the Geocentric Ideal." *International Marketing Review,* Spring 1985.

Sjöstrand, S-E, *Samhällsorganisation.* Stockholm: Doxa, 1985.

Steiner, G. *After Babel.* Oxford University Press, 1975.

Stopford, J. M., and Wells, L. T. *Managing the Multinational Enterprise.* New York: Basic Books, 1972.

Thompson, J. D. *Organizations in Action.* New York: McGraw-Hill, 1967.

Varela, F., "A Calculus for Self-Reference." *Int. J. Gen. Systems, 1975,* **2**, 5–24.

Vernon, R. "International investment and International Trade in the Product Cycle." *Quarterly Journal of Economics,* May 1966.

Vernon, R. "The Product Cycle Hypothesis in a New International Environment." *Oxford Bulletin of Economics and Statistics,* 1979, **41**.

Williamson, O. E. *Markets and Hierarchies: Analysis and Antitrust Implications.* New York: Free Press, 1975.

PART THREE: Strategy Implementation: Organization

10

The Multinational Business Enterprise: What Kind of International Organization?*†

Louis T. Wells, Jr.

*Source: R. Keshane and J. Nye, eds., *Transnational Relations and World Politics* (Cambridge, Mass., Harvard University Press, 1972), pp. 97–114.

Introduction

The recent growth in the size and number of private business enterprises that operate in many countries has generated a great deal of speculation as to whether a form of international organization has been created which is able to frustrate the policies of the traditional nation-state. The enterprise with subsidiaries scattered around the globe clearly has the potential to evade the influence of many governmental policies. The firm can circumvent a tight monetary policy in one country by having an affiliate borrow in another country and transfer the funds across national borders. If direct transfers of capital from abroad are restricted, transfer prices, royalty payments, or open accounts between affiliates can be adjusted to bring in the needed financial resources. If taxes are high in one jurisdiction, profits that would be subject to tax can be shifted to another tax jurisdiction through manipulation of affiliate transactions. National labor unions and comparatively harsh labor legislation can be frustrated by moving production to facilities in another country when strikes or high costs threaten a particular market. A governmental program aimed at increasing technical and managerial training to provide a larger domestic supply of skilled personnel may only generate technicians or managers for the multinational enterprise to shift out of the country, back to its head office or to other countries. Technology developed in one country—often through governmental support and often related to defense needs of governments—can be leaked quickly to other countries through the communication network of the multinational enterprise. If the multinational enterprise exercises many of these options, it is an entity that must be understood in any analysis of international relations.

There has also been speculation that multinational enterprise based in the United States is simply an extension of American culture and political interests abroad. The proponents of this view blame the multinational enterprise for carrying American products to countries where they are not in the best interests of the nationals. They note that almost all the top corporate executives of the enterprises are American.[1] The United States government is thought by some critics to use foreign subsidiaries of American companies to carry out its policy aims—whether those aims are to discourage trade with Communist countries, to provide cheap sources of raw materials, or, according to some, to increase the dependence of less developed countries on the United States.

Whether the multinational enterprise actually uses this potential to frustrate the policies of various governments depends a great deal on how the enterprise is organized. One could picture an enterprise with a head office that manipulates subsidiaries in dozens of countries to fulfill objectives that transcend the objectives of any single part of the enterprise located in any one state, or one could envisage the existence of a loosely knit group of companies in different countries, all having a financial relationship and drawing to a certain extent on a common technology and trade name but for the majority of decisions acting like national companies of the host countries. The implications for international relationships are very different for the two models. If decisionmaking is highly centralized, governments are likely to feel increasingly threatened; they might respond by lashing out at the multinational enterprise, or they might try to reach agreements with other governments in order to control the new entity that is escaping the jurisdiction of individual governments. On the other hand, the loosely knit system may pose much less of a threat to the existing order. Each subsidiary unit is likely to respond to the incentives and threats of the country in which it is located in order to maximize its life and profits. Initial feelings of frustration on the part of the government may be tempered as it discovers that it can exercise control over the local subsidiary. But the implicit assumption of most governmental officials is that the multinational enterprise is best described by the model of centralized decisionmaking. The analyst would feel somewhat secure if he could classify the multinational enterprise at one end or the other of such a scale. But as so often is the case, the real world is complex.

Most complicated organizations have elements of centralization and decentralization mixed together. The multinational business enterprise is no exception. What makes a brief description of the multinational enterprise difficult in a short essay is not the complexity of a single firm—the organization of the Roman Catholic church is perhaps more complex—but the wide range of forms in which the multinational enterprise appears. In addition, the organization of most multinational enterprises goes through a series of changes as the firm develops. Although the term "multinational enterprise" is not well defined, there are at least 200 or 300 firms whose operations are sufficiently global that most observers would call them multinational. Even though the variety of organizational forms within these 200 or 300 firms is great, there is sufficient pattern in the development of the enterprises that useful analytic frameworks are appearing. Some parts of one of these frameworks are presented in this essay.[2]

Growth of Multinational Enterprises

The rapid growth of firms that could be called multinational is generally recognized. The existence of important firms operating in many countries has been with us for quite a while. By 1900 a number of American companies had major investments abroad (Otis Elevator Company and Singer Company, for example). By the first decade of this century books that dealt with American investment began to appear in Europe. Titles from this period, such as *The American Invaders*, have a familiar ring today.[3]

The growth of United States foreign investment accelerated dramatically during the 1950s, as illustrated in the first tabulation. By 1966 there were 187 firms that qualified as "multinational," using as the definition of a multinational enterprise an American firm that was large enough to be included in *Fortune*'s 1966 list of the 500 largest corporations and that had manufacturing activities in six or more foreign countries. It is this list of firms that provided the basis for the study of the multinational enterprise from which many of the findings in this essay are drawn.[4]

Year	1929	1946	1950	1957	1960	1964	1966
Amount (in billions of US $)	7.5	7.2	11.8	25.2	32.8	44.4	54.6

The second tabulation, showing the growth of manufacturing subsidiaries of 187 multinational enterprises outside the United States and Canada, indicates the spread of the subsidiaries of these firms. Since Canadian subsidiaries have generally been handled as domestic operations by the managers of these firms, they have been excluded in this tabulation.

Year	1901	1913	1919	1924	1929	1939	1945	1955	1960	1967
Number of subsidiaries	41	86	119	187	330	547	615	1,003	1,789	3,203

These 187 enterprises probably accounted for more than 80 percent of United States foreign investment. The average reported worldwide sales of these enterprises was $927 million in 1964; the typical firm had 22 percent of its sales outside the United States. It is clear that the potential for these enterprises to transfer resources across national boundaries is very large.

Of course, not all multinational enterprises have their origins in the United States. Well known are such European firms as the Royal Dutch Shell group and Unilever. There are at least 49 large European firms for which foreign assets, earnings, employees, or sales account for 25 percent of the total for the firm.[5] But the United States represents the largest single home base of such enterprises and the source of the largest multinational firms.

Spread of Manufacturing Enterprises

The corporate policies that led to the spread of American investment in manufacturing abroad have been far from the planned exploitation of foreign markets that has been described by some authors. The early investments of most firms in manufacturing abroad were defensive actions to keep the enterprises from losing markets that they had gained almost by accident. Only later did global strategies and centralization of policymaking occur. The amount of this centralization has differed dramatically from firm to firm.

The innovation of new products that has occurred in response to high income and high labor costs in the United States provides a natural base for exports.[6] As the demand for these new products increases abroad, orders often simply appear on the doorstep of American firms. The export business grows. But as enterprises in other countries learn how to make the products and as their markets become large enough to support a plant, this export market is threatened. Even though the export business has grown in a rather unplanned way, it has become important to some individuals within the firm. A number of managers whose main responsibility is providing foreign markets are eager to defend the importance of retaining these sales. The phenomenon will be familiar to students of other kinds of bureaucracies in which vested interests are important determinants of policy. The threat of losing exports to a foreign manufacturer often leads managers to decide that the American enterprise should build its own plant abroad to maintain its market. The enterprise slowly becomes multinational without having a conscious plan for doing so.

Autonomous Subsidiaries

These early subsidiaries that are set up abroad to manufacture locally what was previously exported are typically rather autonomous entities. They are often managed by fairly loyal company men who are sent out in much the same spirit that Roman governors were sent out to the colonies.[7] Little direct control is exercised by the parent company over its subsidiaries.

Since the operations are not critical to the strategy of the enterprise, the enterprise can tolerate a wide range of behavior in the periphery. The parent can have some confidence that major policy decisions will be made by managers of the subsidiaries in ways that would be consistent with the company policies with which they have been indoctrinated. For detailed decisions the local manager is essentially a free man.

One of the most important influences on the decisions of the local manager is his desire to retain autonomy.[8] As long as he maintains profitable operations and can avoid turning to the rest of the system for funds, he can at least delay the exercise of control from above. If he needs cash, he is likely to borrow locally rather than turn to the parent company. If the government is restricting credit, he is likely to behave as a local firm does and wait until he can borrow locally instead of using the ability of the enterprise to borrow elsewhere. Since a record of profits is important in retaining autonomy, the manager is likely to fight for transfer prices that show profits in the subsidiary even though they might not minimize the total taxes of the whole multinational enterprise. Similarly, he is likely to be aggressive in trying to supply export markets; he will try to utilize his excess capacity even though long-run costs may be lower elsewhere in the enterprise.

The enterprise can live for a while with a structure that requires subsidiaries to report only to the president of the system. However, as the importance of overseas manufacturing increases, an international division is usually established to which the subsidiary managers report. The international division serves both to concentrate the abilities of the few international managers on the most important problems and to provide a training ground to develop more general managers with international experience. Initially, the international division does not interfere greatly with the autonomy of successful subsidiaries.

Some evidence of the independence of subsidiaries when the country manager reports only to a remote vice-president of the international division is provided by data on the use of joint ventures by multinational enterprises. Local partners can be tolerated only when the subsidiary has a great deal of freedom to maximize its own interests. Since a partner shares only in local profits, policies dictated from above that could shift profits elsewhere in the system for the good of the multinational enterprise lead to such conflicts that local partners can no longer be tolerated. Of the 187 multinational enterprises examined those that had a structure which required the local manager to report only to a remote vice-president with no intervening structure had local partners in 43 percent of their manufacturing operations in countries in which joint ventures were not required by the government. For the other firms the number was only 21 percent.

This is hardly the exploitative kind of enterprise pictured in some of the attacks on multinational business. Consistent system objectives generally reach far-flung subsidiaries only indirectly and in a modified form. Subsidiaries behave much like local firms with a few annoying exceptions, for example, the tendency of new managers to ignore local customs until the penalties of behaving as if they were at home are made painfully clear.

However, when the international division is established, a process is begun that *can* lead to a great deal of control over the local subsidiary. But not every firm moves toward centralization. The most certain result is an almost irreversible commitment on the part of the enterprise to international business. The careers of several highly placed managers in the firm are based on the success of overseas operations. They are likely to deal with weak performance in a subsidiary even if a little more control is exercised over the successful units in the periphery.

The continued growth of foreign business appears to lead almost inevitably to the end of the international division.[9] The division was established originally to maximize the use of a scarce resource in the firm, management with international know-how, and to provide a training opportunity to increase the quantity of this resource. As the international division succeeds, it provides its own destruction. As it becomes large, other parts of the organization fear its power and want its profits included in their operations. Sufficient international skills have been developed so that the division's activities can be split and assigned, with international personnel, to other parts of the organization.

Area versus Product Commitment

The choice of organizational structure is one of the most frustrating issues for the manager of a large enterprise. The selection that is made is critical in determining the response of the local subsidiary to local governmental policies. Typically, the businessman is committed to some very basic concepts of organizational structure. These include the principles that there should be an unambiguous chain of command, with each man having one clear boss, and that responsibility for the performance of subordinate units should be assigned to an individual. If the nature of decisions is complex, an ideal organization based on these principles is simply very difficult to develop. The manager who must decide what way to divide the assignments of the international division when it is disbanded is faced with difficult trade-offs. He must decide questions such as whether his West German appliance plant manager should report to a European headquarters that covers a number of product lines in the area or to an appliance division in the United States that is responsible for appliance manufacture all over the world. If the manager assigns responsibility on the basis of geographical area, he may ease coordination within Europe for a number of product lines. Marketing policies most appropriate for the region and rationalization of production facilities can best be entrusted to an area manager. But there is a cost entailed in this route. The most advanced know-how for the product line is likely to be in the product division in the United States. If the product-division manager sees no profits allocated to his unit for using scarce knowledgeable men to transfer know-how to the West German subsidiary, he is likely to be stingy with assistance. On the other hand, if the responsibility is vested in the product division, geographical area coordination is likely to be minimized. It will be difficult to establish common marketing policies in Europe for the appliance and other lines of the enterprise. Duplicate distribution channels are likely to be built, and advertising programs are likely to overlap and conflict. The number of plants may proliferate beyond what "rational" planning would dictate.

The manager faces a dilemma. He hesitates to give up his principles of unity of command and clear responsibility which would be sacrificed if he were to try to live with both forms of organization. The subsidiary manager would have to report to two kinds of bosses, and each would have only very limited responsibility assigned to him.

The choice, as one might guess, is far from random. Firms that have few products usually go the area route. Such firms most commonly sacrifice little on the technological transfer side because they tend to be firms that do little new product development. Area coordination becomes the critical element of strategy. Marketing and production techniques can become relatively standardized. Area-wide planning to transfer successful marketing strategies, to coordinate marketing programs, and to lower costs through production rationalization are critical parts of the international strategy of those firms. On the other hand, firms with many products usually assign responsibility for overseas operations to product divisions. New product developments are transferred more easily, but area coordination is difficult.

The choice is one that has important implications for the behavior of local subsidiaries of a multinational enterprise. Transnational actors that emerge under the area choice are very different from those that develop from the product route.

The Area Organization

The choice of an area organization is the most interesting to those who are looking for transnational actors that exercise many of the options that are open to multinational enterprises. The decision to organize subsidiaries on a geographical basis leads to the removal of a great deal of autonomy from the individual subsidiary to a higher level in the firm. The multinational enterprise that is organized on an area basis is the firm that is most likely to shift funds from subsidiary to subsidiary to avoid controls that an individual government tries to impose. Its production rationalization generates large amounts of trade between subsidiaries and allows it to manipulate transfer prices to shift significant amounts of profits from one jurisdiction to another. If there is a bête noire of the host government's desire for control, it is the area-organized multinational enterprise. It is probably also more independent of the home government's incentives or controls over capital exports than are other multinational enterprises. Although it is an organization that is most difficult for a host government to control, this kind of firm can also bring advantages that other multinational enterprises cannot. It is likely to locate its production facilities in patterns much more like those that the theory of comparative advantage would suggest. Longer runs of different parts might be made in two countries with trade of parts for local assembly. The result will probably be more efficient use of resources in both countries. But increased international efficiency comes at a cost of sovereignty to the nation-state.

The removal of decisionmaking power from the local subsidiary is easily traced. It begins when area structures appear within the international division. The next step is a reorganization of the enterprise into divisions with geographical responsibilities. There may be, for example, a division responsible for the Western Hemisphere, one for Europe, one for the Middle and Far East, and one for the rest of the world. Answers to questionnaires which I distributed to managers of multinational enterprises indicate that area-organized firms are the ones that are standardizing marketing and production policies for large geographical areas. Not surprisingly, joint ventures begin to disappear and few more are entered when the enterprise starts to organize along area lines. A recent study of joint ventures has indicated that the change to an area organization is typically accompanied by a "peaking" of instability of joint-venture arrangements, through buying out the local partner's interests or selling off the parent's equity within three years of the change of organization structure.[10] The change to an area organization is also accompanied by a reduction in the number of entries into new joint ventures. Firms that had an area organization within the international division or which were organized at the division level by geographical areas in 1966 had joint ventures in only 16 percent of their manufacturing operations in countries in which they had relative freedom to choose their ownership structure. The equivalent figure for other firms was a significantly different 36 percent.

The area-organized multinational enterprise is the one most likely to have subsidiaries that do not respond like local firms to governmental incentives. The enterprise has the ability to see the advantage of and to implement policies that maximize the interests of the system, even if they come at a cost of profits to an individual subsidiary. These firms may bring advantages to the host country, but they are frustratingly difficult to control. Their ability to ignore the interest of a single subsidiary often extends to policies that do not maximize the interest of an operation in the country in which they originated. When cheaper sources are found abroad for a product, the system is likely to transfer production to a cheaper country and to import the product back into the United States. Transfer pricing for foreign assembly might well be set up to reduce United States taxes and duties. These firms are truly transnational actors.

The Product Organization

Much less centralized in its structure is the multinational enterprise that chooses the product form of organization. An enterprise that decides to partition its organization by product line rather than by geographical area seems to be unable and unwilling to remove a great deal of autonomy from the individual subsidiary. Evidence of this autonomy is provided by the retention of joint ventures and the continued entry into new ones by this form of organization. The study of joint-venture instability referred to earlier found that changes to worldwide product divisions were not accompanied by significant purchases of the interests of local partners or sales of the parent company's equity in joint ventures.[11] The firms that were organized by product division in 1966 had local partners in 30 percent of their foreign manufacturing operations in that year.

The decision to assign responsibilities by product line is typically taken by enterprises that have a wide range of products. The firm finds more need for close coordination within product groups than it does by geographical area.

Product diversity is strongly associated with a policy of developing new products. The local subsidiary is much more likely to move on to new models of a product than it is to fight a war of cost reduction by production rationalization and maximum use of area-wide marketing policies. Area standardization is not critical to the enterprise's strategy. Many more decisions are likely to be left to the local manager who will try to maximize the interests of the subsidiary. This subsidiary will behave much more like a local firm in responding to governmental policies than will the subsidiary of an area system. The product division enterprise is a transnational actor but perhaps a much less frustrating one for the host government than is the area-structured firm.

Other Organizations

Obviously, this brief presentation has oversimplified the types of multinational enterprises that manufacture abroad. Some firms choose organizations that are mixtures of these forms. In these enterprises some of the products may be handled on an area basis, others by worldwide product divisions. But the analytic framework applies equally well to these enterprises.

More important to those interested in understanding decisionmaking processes in the multinational enterprise is the emergence of a new form of organization in recent years—the grid structure. A few managers have been willing to drop the heretofore sacred principles of unity of command and clear assignment of responsibility. These managers have not been willing to choose between area and product divisions but have the subsidiary report to both kinds of bosses. The frustrations of those working in such an organization will be familiar to academic readers who have been lost in the maze of a university organization in which responsibilities for disciplines (economics, political science, etc.) cross with responsibilities for programs (undergraduate, graduate, professional schools). Not surprisingly, the grid form is being tried in enterprises that have a great deal of product and area diversity.

The grid form of business organization has not existed long enough to provide a very clear indication of the degree of autonomy it grants the local subsidiary. The enterprising subsidiary manager, like the enterprising professor, can perhaps survive with a great deal of autonomy. Very limited data (on three firms) indicates that grid enterprises stay away from local partners in overseas manufacturing operations. This may be a clue to a tendency to remove autonomy from the local subsidiary in the grid structure. In fact, this may be the case par excellence of the need to rely on indoctrination of subsidiary managers into the company philosophy for management control. However, local partners are hard to indoctrinate with corporate myths.

If the grid form of organization is successful in avoiding the dilemma faced in product versus area choice, it will, no doubt, grow in importance. We will have to await new data in order to form a firm basis for deciding the nature of this transnational actor.

The Extractive Enterprise

The history of foreign investment by American enterprise for raw material extraction is rather different from the story of the manufacturing enterprise.[12] While the history of the manufacturing enterprise is one of continued centralization for some firms and only partial centralization for others, the history of the extractive enterprise in international business typically begins with centralization and currently includes some efforts at decentralizing the structures in certain parts of the organization.

Involvement by American firms with overseas sources of raw materials has been planned by the headquarters management from the earliest years much more carefully than were the initial investments in manufacturing abroad. Cheap sources of raw materials from other countries for American manufacturing and marketing operations could not be left to a partially loyal, rather autonomous manager who was far from the central office. Shipments had to occur on schedule to meet the needs of the United States plants; quality had to be right. With the need to control schedules and quality closely came a communication network that enabled most important decisions that affected the foreign operations to be made in the United States headquarters. Rubber plantations maintained by Firestone Tire and Rubber Company in Liberia, for example, had direct radio connection to Akron which enabled quick control of these important operations long before rapid airplane connections were available. If the extractive operations of multinational enterprises behaved as a local firm did, it was only a coincidence. The host government quickly felt the frustration of trying to induce the local manager to respond to its wishes; the local manager, however, typically did not have the authority to do so. Transfer prices, volume of shipments, choice of carriers, etc., were almost always decided in the United States. As the local tax authorities soon discovered, the important financial records were also kept in head offices. Here was a transnational actor that fit many of the characterizations of the centralized decisionmaker. Management of extractive operations has changed only little to this day except in the very important cases in which direct local governmental participation in management, through holdings of equity or rights acquired in the concession agreement, has driven a wedge into the absolute power of the headquarters.

Joint ventures with local partners for extractive operations have come only through insistence by the host government and only when its bargaining power was great.[13] The partner has usually been a state agency. The resistance of the enterprise to any threat to its centralized control has been broken only when technology or marketing control has slipped out of the hands of the oligopolists.

In activities other than their purely extractive operations, extractive-oriented firms have developed looser organizations. As the enterprises discover the potential of foreign markets for their raw materials, they set up manufacturing and distribution operations in other countries to provide outlets for the output of mines, wells, and plantations. Most of these facilities were initially in advanced countries, but markets in less developed countries are increasing in importance. Many extractive firms have been able to take a large portion of their profits through oligopolistic pricing of the raw material (copper, for example) or of processed intermediates (aluminum, for example). The point at which profits can be taken depends on the location of the oligopolistic control. In the downstream stage when oligopolistic control is not possible, a great deal of autonomy can be given to anyone who can dispose of the output of the controlled states. The incremental costs of additional output from the upstream stages are usually low; what the multinational enterprise needs are users that are tied to it as a unique or major source of supplies. Joint ventures have been frequent at the downstream stages. Between 1960 and 1967 petroleum firms that were examined entered joint ventures with local partners in 53 percent of their manufacturing operations. Mining firms included local partners in 71 percent of their manufacturing activities. These facilities often reported through a completely different part of the organization from that which controlled the extractive operations.

Only when different activities of the extractive multinational enterprises are segregated can one understand their role as transnational actors. Extractive operations have remained tightly controlled from the center; the overseas manufacturing and distribution operations of the same firms have typically been given much more autonomy.

Centralization by Function

Centralization and decentralization are terribly crude concepts. Rarely are decisions in different functional areas of business uniformly centralized or decentralized in a particular organization. The evidence is clear, however, that certain decisions are more likely to be centralized than others in a multinational enterprise. Unfortunately, too little is known about decision-making processes in the various functional areas of the enterprise. A study currently in progress promises to shed some light on how financial decisions are made.[14] Tentative results seem to indicate a complex pattern with firms moving from considerable autonomy in the subsidiary, through a great deal of centralization with attempts to maximize profits from financial transactions, to a system based on rules of thumb as the enterprise matures and as foreign operations account for a larger portion of earnings.[15] When foreign operations are small, the gains from having a specialized staff to solve complicated financial problems appear to be outweighed by the costs of the staff. As the problems become more important, the staff begins to pay for itself. However, when the problems reach a certain complexity, optimization becomes too difficult, and rules of thumb are substituted for ad hoc analysis. A study of consumer durables has shed some light on decisions in the marketing area.[16] The study indicates that marketing decisions for one industry are more likely to be centralized when foreign operations as a whole account for a large part of a firm's business and when an individual subsidiary is itself relatively large. This study also found a great deal of variation in the degree of centralization by the type of marketing decision that was examined. For example, product design decisions were much more centralized than decisions on prices and advertising. Standardization of decisions on price was found for products that were easily transported from one market to another. Transportability presumably increased the possibility that outsiders would perform arbitrage in response to price differences. Advertising tended to be more standardized when the media flowed across boundaries.

Studies of financial and marketing decisions indicate that in order to identify the locus of decisionmaking in a multinational enterprise the kind of decision in question must be specified. The crude concept of centralization versus decentralization does, however, provide some help in predicting the amenability of a given multinational enterprise to its use as a tool of governmental policy or the response of the enterprise to governmental incentives and penalties. Some broad generalizations can be made on the basis of the organizational structures described thus far.

Influence of Governments

Host Government

The official in the host government that faces a multinational enterprise which grants a great deal of autonomy to its subsidiary can feel somewhat confident that many policies which affect local companies will elicit somewhat similar responses out of the local subsidiary of the foreign firm. Incentives for exports are likely to induce the local manager to consider export markets. Credit restrictions are likely to pinch the foreign subsidiary. New taxes are less likely to generate shifts in transfer prices that negate the effects of high tax rates. Within limits the host government can control the subsidiary. These limits are approached only when the subsidiary's actions are sufficiently injurious to the multinational enterprise that the parent company responds by restricting the freedom of a local manager. If the enterprise is not organized to do this easily, the host government may be able to exercise a great deal of control over the subsidiary.

However, the centralized organization presents a different picture for the host government. The subsidiary manager is not very responsive to local incentives and penalties. Decisions such as who supplies what market are made at a higher level. The higher level will not ignore local governmental policies, but the outcome of the calculations that result from a governmental policy change may be different from what it would be if the subsidiary were free to maximize its own interest. Export market allocation might, for example, be based on long-run average cost curves when the subsidiary would be responsive to profits on incremental costs. In addition, means are readily at hand to evade direct governmental controls. Accounts payable to other affiliates might be allowed to lag, for example, to accumulate funds when credit is tightened.

The host government does not, of course, bargain with an enterprise; it negotiates with an individual who has personal goals that may be different from the goals of the enterprise. The negotiator who is sent from the headquarters to arrange an agreement with the host government may be motivated by a desire to return with as many concessions as other firms have received. In his eagerness to show his bargaining skills to his supervisors, the negotiator may obtain concessions that have little value to the enterprise.[17] Many cases could be described in which the company representative bargained determinedly for relief from local taxes even though the savings would be almost exactly offset by the higher United States taxes that result from the loss of foreign tax credits.

On the other hand, the multinational enterprise also does not bargain with a monolithic structure. The various agencies of the host government may have different interests. Not unusual is the case of a United States subsidiary of a foreign enterprise that was under pressure from United States customs officials to increase the transfer price of goods imported from foreign affiliates to raise the duty and, at the same time, under pressure from the Internal Revenue Service to lower the transfer price so that the resulting higher reported profits would mean more United States income taxes.[18]

The interests of pressure groups in the host country are likely also to be varied. Businessmen who supply a foreign investor with inputs are likely to align themselves with the multinational enterprise; those that view him as a competitor are likely to seek other allies against the foreigner.

Home Government

Little hard evidence is available to estimate the ability of the home government to influence its firms when they operate in foreign countries. One or two policies of the United States government are frequently cited as examples of the use of the multinational enterprise to extend national power. Yet, the fact that so few examples are presented as illustrations of attempts at control by home governments suggests that their role may have been very limited.

The extraterritorial application of the United States Trading with the Enemy Act is the most commonly cited example. Rarely mentioned is the recent attempt of the American government to limit United States investment in Namibia as long as the Republic of South Africa refuses to honor United Nations directives. In addition, there are a few defensive threats posed in support of American investment abroad such as those contained in the Hickenlooper amendment.[19] But these are hardly in the nature of aggressive use of multinational enterprises for the ends of the home country's government.

The argument is often presented that aid flows are conditioned on open reception of American foreign investment. However, the fact that large amounts of aid have continued to move to countries that are tough on American investors (for example, India, Pakistan, and Peru) indicates that this is at most a minor factor in determining the recipients of American assistance. This is not to deny that a local Agency for International Development (AID) (or United States embassy) official sometimes gets carried away by the arguments of potential American investors or by an ideological commitment to free enterprise. Nonetheless, his support of the multinational firm can be quickly eroded when word reaches Washington that he is upsetting the local government.[20]

It is too simple to say that the home government never attempts to use the multinational enterprise to further its policies, but it is probably fair to say that the historical use of this vehicle for foreign policy by the United States government has been very limited.

Too little empirical work has been done on the ways in which the policies of the United States government and multinational business influence each other; even less is known about the relationship between multinational enterprises that originate in other countries and their relationships to their home governments. One can only guess that these relationships will vary considerably and in systematic ways. In countries where communication, trust, and coordination between government and business have historically been close, one would expect the cooperation to continue for some time when its business firms go abroad. It is not surprising to find occasional confusion on the part of host-government officials in less developed countries when they are negotiating terms of entry for Japanese business, for example. Some say that they are not always sure when they are talking to a businessman or when the businessman is an official of the Japanese government. One might expect similar coordination between French firms and the French government where historically the relationship has been close. But the separation and mistrust that have characterized business-government relations in Anglo-Saxon countries will probably continue for some time to characterize their relationship when the firms go abroad.

An alliance of a multinational enterprise with the government of the country in which it originated can be short-lived. As foreign business begins to supply a large portion of its income, it may become less and less eager to follow policies that coincide with the desires of the home government. Tightened credit in the home country may send the multinational enterprise to the Euro-currency markets. Balance-of-payments problems at home may lead the multinational enterprise that fears devaluation or controls on capital exports to aggravate the problems by withholding remissions of profits from overseas. Increasing costs of local labor may be countered by moving production overseas more rapidly than would have taken place in the absence of a multinational firm with the ability to transfer technological and marketing know-how across international boundaries.

Especially for non-American enterprises threats by the home government may become less frightening. As foreign business grows, the portion subject to pressure by the country of origin may come to represent only a relatively insignificant source of profits to the firm.

Conclusion

Multinational business enterprises are clearly important transnational actors. They move large amounts of resources across international boundaries. Some of them have organizations that centralize decisionmaking processes so that these resources can be used to fulfill objectives that may be at variance with those of a particular country in which a subsidiary is located. These firms have at their disposal many tools for frustrating governmental policies, but the policies that they frustrate may be those of the host government or those of the home government.

Some multinational enterprises may seem to form alliances with governments. Yet, as they grow and begin to take a more global view, these alliances may prove to be no more lasting than those of nation-states. Common interests may dominate the alliances initially, but the interests may diverge as the home market becomes just one more piece in the multinational system. Threats of the home government may be taken less seriously as the threatened part of the business becomes relatively small.

The organizational structures of multinational enterprises are not very different from those that characterize other international organizations. Their ability to coordinate policies of units in the periphery can be analyzed in ways that are similar to the analysis of other organizations. The kinds of management problems faced by the multinational enterprise are similar to those of governments. A highly centralized system is limited in its ability to span diversity. If it expands too much, it has tendencies to grow baronies in the periphery that begin to maximize local interests rather than those of the center. Elements within the organization build alliances which keep the enterprise from behaving according to some centralized set of goals.

The fact that some of these organizations are operating in a coordinated fashion or that they even seem to have the potential for doing so makes them appear to governments as a challenge to their control. The result is a feeling of frustration on the part of governmental officials that results in occasional lashing out at foreign investment. In many cases these attacks may appear to an economist to hurt the national interest. However, the set of objectives that determines governmental actions is no less complex than that of the multinational enterprise. The desire of the government to retain control leads to attacks on enterprises that appear to challenge its sovereignty.

The multinational enterprise is important because of its ability to move resources across international boundaries. It is also important, in some instances, as a transnational actor that makes decisions without regard to the direct interests of its operations in any single country. It is equally important because of the responses that it engenders from governments of nation-states that react to its potential for weakening their control. There is, however, a great deal of danger in treating multinational enterprises as homogeneous entities. Enterprises differ greatly in their organizational structures, and these structures, moreover, change over time. For many purposes a better understanding of the role of the multinational business enterprise in international affairs can be obtained by turning to the concepts of the organization specialist and the frameworks of political analysis than by relying solely on the models of the economist.

Notes

† This essay is part of a larger study of the multinational enterprises; and the nation-state financed by the Ford Foundation and by the Division of Research of the business school.

1. Kenneth Simmonds, "Multinational? Well, Not Quite," *Columbia Journal of World Business*, Fall 1966 (Vol. 1, No. 4), p. 118. Simmonds concluded that one-fifth of the total employment of the fifteen largest United States industrial corporations was foreign, but only 1.6 percent of their top corporate managers entered the United States after age 25 or remained outside the United States.

2. The material in this essay draws heavily on work done by John Stopford, Lawrence Fouraker, and Lawrence Franko. The results of a study of the organization of the multinational enterprise, authored by John Stopford and Louis T. Wells, Jr., will soon be published by Basic Books, Publishers. See also Lawrence E. Fouraker and J. M. Stopford, "Organizational Structure and Multinational Strategy," *Administrative Science Quarterly*, June 1968 (Vol. 13, No. 1), pp. 47–64; Stopford, "Growth and Organizational Change in the Multinational Firm" (D.B.A. diss., Graduate School of Business Administration, Harvard University, 1968); and Lawrence G. Franko, "Strategy Choice and Multinational Corporate Tolerance for Joint Ventures with Foreign Partners" (D.B.A. diss., Graduate School of Business Administration, Harvard University, 1969).

3. F. A. MacKenzie, *The American Invaders* (London: Grant Richards, 1902).

4. This sample was common to several studies conducted under the general direction of Raymond Vernon in connection with the project, "The Multinational Enterprise and the Nation-State," financed by the Ford Foundation. Data for the first tabulation is drawn from the United States Department of Commerce *Survey of Current Business*.

5. Sidney E. Rolfe, *The International Corporation* (Paris: International Chamber of Commerce, 1969).

6. See Louis T. Wells, Jr., "Test of a Product Cycle Model of International Trade: U.S. Exports of Consumer Durables," *Quarterly Journal of Economics*, February 1969 (Vol. 83, No. 1), pp. 152–162; and Robert B. Stobaugh, Jr., "Where in the World Should We Put That Plant?" *Harvard Business Review*, January–February 1969 (Vol. 47, No. 1), pp. 129–136.

7. See Antony Jay, *Management and Machiavelli: An Inquiry into the Politics of Corporate Life* (New York: Holt, Rinehart & Winston, 1967), for a fascinating and instructive attempt to apply some of the concepts of political analysis to the management of a large business enterprise. This particular analogy is drawn from Jay.

8. See Robert B. Stobaugh, Jr., "Financing Foreign Subsidiaries of U.S. Multinational Enterprises," *Journal of International Business Studies*, Spring 1970 (Vol. 1), pp. 43–64.

9. See Fouraker and Stopford, *Administrative Science Quarterly*, Vol. 13, No. 1.

10. Franko, "Strategy Choice and Multinational Corporate Tolerance for Joint Ventures with Foreign Partners."

11. Ibid.

12. See Raymond Vernon, "Foreign Enterprise and Developing Nations in the Raw Material Industries," *American Economic Review*, May 1970 (Vol. 60, No. 2), pp. 122–126.

13. See Louis T. Wells, Jr., *The Evolution of Concession Agreements* (Economic Development Reports, No. 117) (Cambridge, Mass: Harvard Development Advisory Service, 1969). Joint ventures with other multinational firms have, of course, been common. There was little chance for conflicts of interest; both parties were interested in quality and regularity of supply. There was no chance that the partner would sell to the firms that were outside the oligopoly.

14. Sidney M. Robbins and Robert B. Stobaugh, Jr., under the auspices of the study, "The Multinational Enterprise and the Nation-State," directed by Raymond Vernon.

15. See Stobaugh, *Journal of International Business Studies*, Vol. 1.

16. Richard Aylmer, "Marketing Decisions in the Multinational Firm" (D.B.A. diss., Graduate School of Business Administration, Harvard University, 1968); and Robert Buzzell, "Can You Standardize Multinational Marketing?" *Harvard Business Review*, November–December 1968 (Vol. 46, No. 6), pp. 102–113.

17. See Raymond Vernon, "Indonesia's Policies toward Foreign Direct Investment," Djakarta, September 15, 1969 (Mimeographed.)

18. United States Congress, Joint Economic Committee, *A Foreign Economic Policy for the 1970's, Hearings*, statement by Robert B. Stobaugh, Jr., before the Subcommittee on Foreign Economic Policy, 91st Cong., 2nd sess., July 29, 1970, pp. 874–887.

19. First Hickenlooper amendment to the *Foreign Assistance Act of 1961, United States Code*, Vol. 22, section 2370(e).

20. This is consistent with my experience of having a United States ambassador instruct United States government employees not to cooperate with me when I was advising an African government in negotiations with a United States investor. The instructions of the local ambassador were quickly reversed when complaints reached Washington.

11

MNCs: Get Off the Reorganization Merry-Go-Round*

Christopher A. Bartlett

*Source: *Harvard Business Review*, 26 (1983), pp. 138–146.

For many companies, international expansion has been the major strategic thrust of the postwar era. Yet even successful, well-established organizations face difficult problems in managing global operations. Heady years of overseas expansion have been followed by a persistent organizational hangover, unresponsive to traditional remedies.

In the 1960s, the answer to the international challenge seemed clear: managers simply needed to identify key strategic goals and restructure the corporation around them. But after two decades of experimentation, an "ideal international structure" remains elusive. Many companies still reorganize in the hope of finding it – but with only isolated cases of success.

With so many companies searching for this structural solution, why have results been so poor? Could it be that managers, obsessed with structure, were focusing on the wrong variable? A study I have made of ten diverse and successful MNCs indicates that companies that persistently reorganize may be misdirecting their efforts. The companies I studied have *not* continually reorganized their operations. Each has retained for years a simple structure built around an international division – a form of organization that many management theorists regard as embryonic, appropriate only for companies in the earliest stages of worldwide growth.

These companies see the international challenge as one of building and maintaining a complex decision-making process rather than of finding the right formal structure. The critical task is to develop new management perspectives, attitudes, and processes that reflect and respond to the complex demands companies with international strategies face. Such a process might sound too time consuming, too subtle, or too difficult to imitate. But companies that want to better meet the challenge can use as a guide the patterns established by these successful companies.

Broken Promise

To understand why these companies have succeeded, we first should look at the reasons others have failed. As companies began to feel the strain of controlling fast-growing foreign operations, managements intuitively looked for structural solutions. This generation of top managers was on the front line when the wave of postwar product diversification led to the widespread shift from functional to multidivisional organization structures. They saw, first-hand, the powerful linkage between strategy and structure. The conventional wisdom was that if the divisional organization structure had helped managers implement the corporate strategy of diversification, surely an equivalent structure would facilitate their new international strategic thrust.

Managers had other reasons to reorganize. For one, changing the formal structure was recognized as a powerful tool through which management could redefine responsibilities and relationships. Top managers could make clear choices, have immediate impact, and send strong signals of change to all hierarchical levels. Furthermore, companies were encouraged to pursue such international reorganization because it seemed many others were doing likewise. In fact, the pattern of reorganization became so familiar that management theorists had documented and classified it.

Frustration came when managers discovered that no one structure provided a long-term solution. To many executives, it seemed they had no sooner developed a new set of systems, relationships, and decision-making processes than the international operations again needed to be reorganized. For example:

Westinghouse disbanded its separate international division in 1971 when the 125 domestic product division managers were given worldwide responsibilities. By early 1979, however, concern about the lack of coordination among divisions and the insensitivity to certain nations had mounted. A task force recommended a global matrix, and by mid-year the new structure was in place. It was the third reorganization of international operations in one decade.

Like the executives at Westinghouse, many managers turned to a global matrix because they were frustrated by the one-dimensional biases built into a global-product or area-based structure. It was supposed to allow a company to respond to national and regional differences while simultaneously maintaining coordination and integration of worldwide business. But the record of companies that adopted this structure is disappointing. The promised land of the global matrix quickly turned into an organizational quagmire, forcing a large number of companies to retreat from it. Some of these cases were widely publicized, such as that of Dow Chemical:

Dow, which served as the textbook case study of the global matrix, eventually returned to a more conventional structure in which the emphasis is on geographically based managers. Citibank became the new case illustration in one important book on matrix organization.[1] Yet within a few years, Citibank was reportedly retreating from its global matrix structure.

The same problems with the global matrix kept coming up: tension and uncertainty built into dual reporting channels sometimes escalated to open conflict, complex issues were forced into a rigid two-dimensional decision framework, and minor issues became the subject of committee debates. More important, the design of matrix organization implied that managers with conflicting views or overlapping responsibilities communicate problems and confront and resolve differences. Yet barriers of distance, language, and culture impeded this vital process.

Managing the Process

The ten companies that escaped the organizational merry-go-round had a number of things in common, but the most fundamental was their adaptability to complex demands without restructuring. Underlying the approach to global operations of managers of these companies was the way they thought about the strategic demands and the appropriate organizational response.

Two major forces exerted opposite pressures on international strategies during the 1970s. First, as global competitors emerged in many industries, skirmishes for single-country markets gave way to battles for worldwide market position and global-scale efficiencies. Second, host-country governments raised their demands, and competition for market access tilted the bargaining power more in the governments' favor. MNCs had to increase local equity participation, transfer technology, build local manufacturing and research facilities, and meet export quotas.

With one set of pressures suggesting global integration and the other demanding local responsiveness, it is easy to see why executives of many companies thought in either-or terms and argued whether to centralize or decentralize control and whether to let the product or the geographic managers dominate corporate structure.

While managers in the ten companies remained sensitive to those conflicting demands, they resisted the temptation to view their tasks in such simple either-or terms. The managers understood that such clear-cut answers would not work since *both* forces are present to some degree in all businesses. Moreover, thinking of strategy in "global" or "local" terms ignored the complexity, diversity, and changeability of the demands facing them.

For example, a growing threat of Japanese competitors forced Timken, the leading bearings manufacturer, to become more globally competitive in the 1970s. Unlike the Japanese, Timken chose not to compete solely as the low-cost producer of standard bearings. Rather, the company opted to reinforce its position as the technological leader in the industry. While this strategy required the strengthening and integrating of a worldwide research function, Timken's management thought such global integration was unnecessary in manufacturing. It trimmed and standardized product lines to gain efficiencies, but plants still specialized on a regional – not a worldwide – basis. Moreover, because customer service and response time were at the core of Timken's strategy, sales forces and engineering services retained their strict local focus.

Savvy managers realize that it is often difficult to know how to focus responsibility even within a single function. For example, Corning Glass Works's TV tube marketing strategy required global decision making for pricing and local decision making for service and delivery.

The Challenge of Subtlety

It is not surprising that with this subtle perception of the nature of strategy, the managers in the ten corporations set objectives, adopted a focus, and used tools that were different from those in most other MNCs. They realized that if the pressures in the international operating environment were intrinsically complex, diverse, and changeable, they had to create an internal management environment that could respond to these external demands and opportunities.

With this perception, managers viewed the organizational challenge not as one of finding and installing the right structure but as one of building an appropriate management process. As a result, they focused attention on the individual decision and the way it was reached rather than on the overall corporate structure. Questions changed from "Do we need worldwide product divisions or an area structure?" to "How can the company take the regional product group's perspective more into account in capacity expansion decisions?"

Finally, they looked for management tools with a finer edge than the blunt instrument of formal structural reorganization. Managers in other companies seemed so captivated by architectural problems that they forgot that the boxes they sketched on the back of an envelope represented not just positions but also people: the lines they casually erased and redrew stood not only for lines of authority but also for personal relationships. It was not unusual then to announce major reorganization very suddenly and install the structure in a few weeks or months. The result was often traumatic readjustment, followed by a long recovery. At Westinghouse, for example, the decision to reorganize into a global matrix structure was made by a senior management task force after a 90-day study of the problems and was put in place over the following 90 days.

Managers in the companies studied used tools that influenced individuals' behavior and attitudes or group norms and values in a more discrete and flexible manner.

A Multidimensional Decision Process

The experience of the companies studied suggests that development of the diverse and flexible organizational processes follows three closely related stages. First, because an organization must take into account the richness of the environment it faces rather than view the world through a single, dominant management perspective, the companies developed international groups that allowed the organization to sense, analyze, and respond to a full range of strategic opportunities and demands.

In most companies, a necessarily formal organizational structure limits interaction between such diverse interests. Therefore, during the second stage, the company builds additional channels of communication and forums for decision making to allow greater flexibility.

Finally, in the third stage the company develops norms and values within the organization to support shared decisions and corporate perspectives. Value is placed on corporate goals and collaborative effort rather than on parochial interests and adversary relationships.

Developing Multiple Management Perspectives

In this environment of changeable demands and pressures, managers must sense and analyze complex strategic issues from all perspectives. Top management's job is to eliminate the one-dimensional bias built into most organizations.

The traditional bias in companies with international divisions, for example, allowed country and regional managers to dominate decision making from their line positions, with product and functional staff groups relegated to support and advisory roles. As a result, the companies underestimated or even ignored strategic opportunities that might have been realized by global coordination and integration of operations.

Similarly, organization by product divisions fostered decisions favoring worldwide standardization and integration. The power of headquarters' product managers over their geographic and functional counterparts was usually reinforced within the structure in formal as well as informal ways. For instance, the companies constructed information systems around products that allowed headquarters-based product management to collect and analyze data more easily than their functional or geographic counterparts. Furthermore, the strongest managers were appointed to product management positions, which reinforced their influence over the decision process.

Top management can begin to gradually eliminate these biases in the decision process by:

1. Upgrading personnel. Assigning capable people to the right positions not only allows skills to be brought to bear in important areas but also sends strong signals that top management is serious about its objectives and priorities. For example, top managers of the hospital supply company Baxter Travenol decided to counterbalance the strength of country managers in the international division with a strong global business perspective. First, they replaced existing product managers with MBAs who, while lacking the product expertise of their predecessors (ex-sales representatives), brought a more analytical and strategic perspective to the role. While this interim step upgraded the role, it was only with the appointment of more experienced managers from the domestic product divisions and foreign subsidiaries that the company achieved a strong global business perspective in its international strategy decisions.

2. Broadening responsibilities. Aggressive, ambitious, and able managers will naturally resist transfer to positions viewed as less powerful and having fewer responsibilities and lower status. So companies must redefine the role of the positions at the same time they upgrade the personnel. In the example of Baxter Travenol, when top management appointed MBAs to product manager positions, it enlarged the role from primarily a support responsibility to one that focused on monitoring and analyzing global product performance. When experienced product and country managers superseded the MBAs, the company allowed them to get involved in the budgeting and strategic planning processes, making recommendations about the management of their lines of business worldwide.

Such progression of roles is fairly typical when a company is trying to develop groups previously underrepresented in the decision process. The company first broadens advisory and support roles to encompass responsibility for monitoring and control. Exposure to the information necessary to undertake these new tasks then helps develop the ability to make analyses and recommendations of key issues, and finally to implement strategy.

3. Changing managerial systems. The biggest impediment to these changes is often the existing line management group; as happened at Baxter Travenol, country subsidiary managers may greatly resent the increased "interference" of product and functional staff. So top management needs to back up the desired changes.

If the newly upgraded managers are to succeed, they need information tailored to their responsibilities. Management systems usually parallel the formal organization structure and give line managers a tremendous information advantage. Top executives must be sure managers representing other perspectives also have the information needed to support their proposals and arguments.

Originally, Corning consolidated data only by geographic entity. When the company decided to upgrade the role of product and functional managers, however, it found that consolidating data along these dimensions was both difficult and expensive. Inconsistent product-line definitions, different expense allocation practices, and numerous tangled cases of double counting were impediments to system restructuring. By the time management sorted out these problems (with the help of a consultant and a couple of high-powered software packages), the new systems had cost well over $1 million.

Through these three steps, the company elevates previously underrepresented management groups. The organization recognizes the need to monitor the environment from their perspective, acknowledges their competence to analyze the strategic implications of key issues, and accepts the legitimacy of representing such views in the decision process. Happily, many old distinctions between line and staff blur, and organization clichés about the locus of power become less relevant. As the president of Bristol-Myers's international division told me: "The traditional distinctions between line and staff roles are increasingly unclear here.... But by motivating managers and giving them latitude rather than writing restrictive job descriptions, we believe we can achieve much more."

Creating Supplementary Information Channels

It is not enough for a company simply to develop an organization that can sense and analyze issues from various perspectives. Managers representing diverse points of view need access to the decision-making processes.

As I mentioned earlier, in most companies formal communication channels parallel formal organization structures. The focus is one-dimensional, and the decision-making process, hierarchical and formal. The structure reinforces the power of dominant line managers while limiting the influence of managers representing other perspectives.

Top management must create forums for decision making that take many perspectives into account and are flexible. While the formal reporting lines and management systems provide one way to channel communications, management can use an equally strong set of informal channels.

Influencing Informality

Informal relationships among people, of course, naturally develop in any organization, and to date, many corporate executives have regarded them as an uncontrollable by-product of the formal organization. Increasingly, however, they recognize that they can, and indeed should, influence the organization's informal systems if the environment is to allow people representing diverse and frequently conflicting interests to influence decisions. In any MNC, managers are separated by barriers of distance, time, and culture; the extent to which top management works to overcome these barriers, the way in which it builds bridges, and the groups among which it develops contacts and relationships all have an important influence on the organization's informal network and processes.

A variety of tools is available. By bringing certain individuals together to work on common problems, for example, or by assigning a specific manager to a position that requires frequent contact with colleagues, management can influence the development of social relationships. Such personal bonds break down the defensiveness and misunderstanding that often build when line managers feel their power is threatened.

Senior management of Eli Lilly's international division was conscious of this dynamic. As a normal part of career development, it transferred managers from line to staff positions, from one product line to another, and from headquarters to country subsidiaries. Although the original idea was to develop a broad perspective, an equally important benefit has been the development of an informal network of friends and contacts throughout the organization. In the words of one manager, "Those who moved about had far better information sources than computer reports, and more important, they developed the influence that comes with being known, understood, and respected."

Baxter Travenol's top management used frequent, well-planned meetings to help develop informal relationships. The company had long held annual general managers' meetings in which country and regional line managers listened to formal presentations of the year's financial results, of the latest corporate plans, and of one or two new products. Recognizing that staff-line relationships were becoming very strained, the division president changed the traditional meeting into a senior management conference to which product managers and functional managers were also invited. He replaced most formal presentations with discussions, during which senior managers jointly identified and tried to resolve strategic and organizational issues.[2] The team formed bonds that endured far beyond the meetings.

Avoiding Strategic Anarchy

Of course a company cannot resolve complex issues by simply allowing different interests to clash in a trading-room-floor atmosphere. The formal hierarchy will still constrain and limit the influence of nonline managers as key issues are actually decided. There are, however, ways to ensure the representation of appropriate interests and at the same time allow headquarters to retain control.

Most managers are familiar with such things as task forces, interdepartmental teams, and special committees. These devices are often used ad hoc, after the formal decision process has failed, for example, or in response to a crisis. But managers can also use them in a more routine manner to pull certain issues out of the mainstream and to tailor the analysis and decision making.

Bristol-Myers's international organization, for instance, feared that the company was dissipating scarce research resources. Each project typically had the backing of a country subsidiary manager who claimed that the project was absolutely essential to his or her national strategy. By creating a "pharmaceutical council" comprised of senior geographic line managers and division-level business development staff managers, the division president forced these managers to make compromises and to combine these separate proposals into a single cohesive program. By appointing the business development director as the council's chairman, he increased this manager's influence and leverage and ensured that the deliberations would have a global perspective.

In Warner Lambert, country managers had for years influenced decisions on manufacturing capacity toward constructing local plants. Believing that such decisions compromised efficiency, the division president set up a task force of geographic and functional managers to conduct an 18-month review of global capacity needs. Recognizing the sensitivity of country managers to any loss of autonomy, he appointed regional managers to represent the line organization. The task force's manufacturing, finance, and marketing managers convinced regional managers of the need for greater coordination of manufacturing operations and rationalization of facilities to gain scale economies. With regional managers behind the idea, country managers were forced to recognize the program's considerable savings.

One note of caution: the purpose of such temporary task groups is to supplement rather than replace the mainstream decision process. The company must consider carefully which decisions cannot be resolved by the regular managerial process. It should clearly define and limit the number of issues taken "off-line" and keep them out of the mainstream only as long as necessary.

Building a Supportive Culture

There is no guarantee that decisions will reflect the mix of interests and views represented in the process. Simply putting people together does not mean they will interact positively and productively. It is necessary to build an organizational culture that supports multidimensional, flexible decision making.[3]

In many companies, a culture that stresses internal competition has proven the major barrier to the development of a flexible decision process. In one of the companies studied, a well-known motto was that "only your final result counts." The company's formal structure and reward systems reinforced the value.

When internal competition is overemphasized, managers with different perspectives easily become entrenched adversaries and the decision-making process deteriorates, as protecting territory and even subversion become the norms. In fact, many companies discovered that upgrading nonline management groups and supplementing the hierarchical decision process triggered such adverse reactions.

To make the organization flexible, top management of the companies studied made certain that managers understood how their particular points of view fit with corporate strategies; it reinforced this understanding with a culture supportive of cooperation and compromise. The organizational norms and values creating such an environment obviously could not be established by management fiat. Rather, they were carefully developed through a variety of small actions and decisions.

Articulate Goals & Values

Elementary and simplistic as it may seem, one of the most powerful tools for top management is the precise formulation and communication of specific strategic objectives and behavioral norms. In a surprising number of companies, however, middle managers have only the vaguest notion of overall corporate objectives and of the boundaries of acceptable behavior.

Eli Lilly places great importance on mutual trust, openness, and honesty in all interpersonal dealings. In an orientation brochure for new employees, the late Mr. Eli Lilly, grandson of the founder, was quoted as saying: "Values are, quite simply, the core of both men and institutions.... By combining our thoughts and by helping one another, we are able to merge the parts [of this organization] into a rational, workable management system." It is clear that adversary relationships and parochial behavior do not fit in the culture he envisioned.

At Baxter Travenol, senior management conferences provided an ideal communication forum for the international division president. In addition to articulating overall objectives and priorities, he acknowledged the conflicts implicit in particular important issues and encouraged managers to discuss how they might subjugate individual interests to the overall strategy. The participation of managers ensured not only their understanding of the issues but also their involvement in, and commitment to, corporate goals.

Modify Reward Systems

It is clear that a company cannot ask managers to compromise parochial interests for a broader good if it continues to evaluate and reward them on the basis of indicators tied tightly to a small area of responsibility. Successful international companies in the sample made sure managers understood they did not compromise career opportunities or expose themselves to other organizational risks by adopting a cooperative and flexible attitude. Many companies altered management evaluation criteria and modified formal reward systems.

As the decision-making processes became increasingly complex at Corning Glass Works, top managers changed the criteria for promotion. One top manager said to me: "In addition to the analytic and entrepreneurial capabilities we have always required, managers must now have strong interpersonal skills to succeed in key positions. To contribute to our decision-making process, they must be good communicators, negotiators, and team players. We had to move aside some individuals who simply could not work in the new environment."

Eli Lilly's formal evaluation and reward systems are tied even more directly to the need for cooperation and flexibility. Rather than being evaluated only by a direct superior, each manager's performance is also appraised by others with whom he or she deals. This multiple review process not only encourages cooperative behavior but also serves as a control to identify those who are unwilling or unable to develop positive work relationships.

Provide Role Models

Top managers know that their words and actions are models that strongly influence values and behavioral norms in the organization. Yet few top managers routinely use these powerful tools. With a little thought and planning, they can send signals that encourage behavior conducive to achieving the organization's goals.

After one restructuring failed, Corning's president and vice chairman recognized that the role model they were providing as top management was one of the fundamental problems. They were simply not communicating and cooperating on efforts to integrate the international and domestic operations, and this lessened the willingness of domestic division managers to share information and cooperate with their overseas counterparts. Later, as these top managers made a strong effort to work closely on issues and to let the organization see their joint commitment to decisions, they saw their cooperative behavior reflected throughout the organization.

The Key is Flexibility

Clearly, the approach outlined is vastly different from one in which a company installs a new structure to "force the product managers to interact with geographic specialists." Building a multidimensional and flexible decision process means the company will sense and respond to the complex, diverse, and changeable demands most MNCs face.

Several benefits flow from this approach. First, matching decision processes with the task keeps managers' attention focused on the business issues. By contrast, in an organization going through a major restructuring, management's attention tends to be riveted on changes in formal roles and responsibilities, as people debate the implications of the new structure and jockey for position and turf.

Second, by working to achieve a gradual organizational evolution rather than a more rapid structural change, a company can avoid much of the trauma associated with reorganization. Changes in roles and relationships are best achieved incrementally.

Finally, by thinking in terms of changing behavior rather than changing structural design, managers free themselves from the limitations of representing organizations diagrammatically. They are not restricted by the number of dimensions that can be represented on a chart; they are not tempted to view the organization symmetrically; and they are not limited by the innately static nature of an organization diagram.

Notes

1. See Stanley M. Davis and Paul R. Lawrence, *Matrix* (Reading, Mass.: Addison-Wesley, 1977), Citibank CEO. Walter Wriston acknowledged in his foreword to his book the difficulty of managing in a global matrix.

2. For a description of the process used, see my article, written with David W. DeLong, "Operating Cases to Help Solve Corporate Problems," *Harvard Business Review,* March–April 1982, p. 68.

3. This was the objective of the Westinghouse reorganization study, according to the report in "Westinghouse Takes Aim at the World," *Fortune,* January 14, 1980, p. 52.

12

Strategy and Structure of U.S. Multinationals: An Exploratory Study*

John D. Daniels, Robert A. Pitts and Marietta J. Tretter

*Source: *Academy of Management Journal* 27 (1984), pp. 292–307.

This study explores factors influencing international organization structure in 93 large U.S. multinational companies having substantial foreign activity. Organization structure is determined by the way a "typical" foreign operating unit reports up through each firm's corporate hierarchy. Company parameters examined as potential influences of organization structure are diversity, foreign activity, strategic emphasis, integration among facilities in different countries, and the establishment and ownership pattern of foreign facilities. The overall purpose of the study is to develop a theoretical framework that explains the reasons for selecting a particular organizational design.

Background

There are three reasons for believing that organizational characteristics might influence multinational structure. First, several prior authors have argued such a relationship. For example, Chandler showed that diversity influenced organization design (1966), and he hypothesized that foreign involvement would do so too (1975). A major study by Stopford and Wells (1972) also found these two variables to be strong predictors of multi-national structure. More than a decade has transpired since the completion of these studies, however. Furthermore, the intervening period has been marked by considerable disillusionment with structures widely heralded earlier (Vernon, 1980) and by much publicity about structures that were virtually unknown then (Davis, 1976; Davis & Lawrence, 1978; Galbraith, 1971). It therefore seemed useful and timely to undertake a new investigation—especially one that would include a larger number of variables than those examined in earlier studies.

The second reason for expecting a relationship between organizational characteristics and multinational structures is the recent findings of those investigating change within U.S. multinationals (Beer & Davis, 1976; Cascino, 1979; Dance, 1969; Goggin, 1974; McKern, 1971; Menzies, 1980; Prahalad, 1976). These case studies of individual companies show that changes in organizational parameters such as size, diversity, foreign activity, and personnel deployment patterns often lead to shifts in multinational structure. The present authors were reluctant to make hypotheses based on these studies because in most of them neither the names of firms nor precise organizational parameters were revealed. One proposition, however, was adopted. Both the case studies and Stopford and Wells (1972) indicated that a growing dependence on foreign operations led to organizational change. This was especially true of highly diverse firms. It therefore was expected that the present study would show different structures at different levels of foreign sales and diversity.

A third reason for thinking that multinational structure might relate to other organizational characteristics is the evidence that firms often establish practices that have been adopted by leaders in their industries. For example, Westinghouse's decision in 1971 to replace its international division with a worldwide product structure is reported to have been importantly influenced by GE's adoption of the latter structure several years earlier (Daniels, Ogram, & Radebaugh, 1982). Knickerbocker (1973) provides further evidence for this leader-follower phenomenon. He found that after one firm in an industry makes an investment abroad, competitors typically follow fairly quickly by investing in the same locale.

Method

The method used involved selecting and measuring operating variables that might influence multinational structure, classifying multinational structures, and choosing firms for investigating the relationship between these two kinds of variables.

Operating Characteristics

Most of the data on firm operating characteristics used in the study were obtained from published sources, the primary source being Standard and Poor's Compustat II tapes. For gaps in the tape data, supplementary information was obtained from Securities and Exchange Commission 10K reports. The *Forbes* industrial classification ("Where to Find the Company," 1981) was used to categorize firms by industry.

Product diversity was selected as a possible predictor of organization structure because of the previously cited research by Chandler (1966) and Stopford and Wells (1972), which indicated that high diversity leads to the utilization of worldwide product structures. The proxy selected for this measure was the number of two digit Standard Industrial Classification (SIC) code industries in which a firm participated.

Individual case studies and Stopford and Wells (1972) noted that increasing foreign involvement often leads to organization change. Therefore, foreign involvement was selected as one of the independent variables, and it was measured as the ratio of foreign to total corporate sales.

Stopford and Wells (1972) found that heavy reliance on R&D leads to early abandonment of an international division. It seemed plausible that multinational structures therefore might be influenced not only by this, but by other strategic variables as well. R&D and two other strategic variables—marketing and capital intensity—therefore were selected for examination. The proxies used to measure these variables were, respectively, research and development expenditures as a percent of sales, advertising expenditures as a percent of sales, and number of employees divided by asset value.

Because organization structure is a control mechanism, it was decided to examine some international practices that might present control problems. Three such practices were selected for examination—use of shared ownership when investing abroad, acquisition rather than start-up of new foreign ventures, and integration of foreign operations across national boundaries. Information on these practices was not available from published sources. Questions on these matters therefore were included in the questionnaire sent out to sample companies. Specifically, respondents were asked to identify a typical foreign operating facility and then report (1) whether it had been originally acquired or was started up internally, (2) the parent's percentage ownership of the facility, and (3) the degree of production integration between the facility and facilities in other countries.

To investigate possible leader-follower influences on organization structure, *Forbes* 1981 industrial classification ("Where to Find the Company," 1981) was used to classify respondent firms by industry. It lists 49 industries, 32 of which are primarily manufacturing. Respondents in the study participated in 24 of these 32 industries. Five or more of the respondents were uniquely classified (*Forbes* classifies some firms in more than one industry) in six of these 24 industries: energy, 9; chemicals, 7; auto supplies, 6; drugs, 6; branded food, 5; and conglomerates, 6. These 39 uniquely classified firms thus formed a subset for examination.

Multinational Structures

Several studies have classified companies' organization structures according to their placement of international operations (Alpander, 1978; Egelhoff, 1980; Franko, 1973; Lovell, 1966; Stopford & Wells, 1972). Although these studies have differed in many respects, they agree on two points. The first is that it is useful to classify firms according to a few pure structural types through which foreign operations report. Basically, five classifications have been used throughout the present study: worldwide functional, worldwide product, international division, area, and matrix structures.

In a worldwide functional structure, top-level line executives have worldwide responsibility for separate functions, for example, for manufacturing, sales, engineering. In a worldwide product organization, top-level line executives are responsible for one or more worldwide business(es). In an international division form of organization, two kinds of line executives report to the chief operating officer. All but one of these are managers of domestic activities, whereas the remaining executive is in charge of all the company's foreign business. Executives reporting to the chief operating officer in an area organization are responsible for all company businesses within specific geographic regions of the world. The defining characteristic of a matrix organization is the simultaneous reporting by middle level line executives to two or more bosses who do not themselves have exclusive line authority.

The second point of agreement in the prior studies is that, although structural types may be fairly easily defined, classifying companies according to them is difficult. Structures, to some extent, may be mixed because of growth and personnel dynamics. There may be uncertainty about who has the authority over certain decisions, especially if dual relationships exist with line and staff personnel. Managers may continue to use old labels even though the organization has changed; or a structural type may be referred to before it is completely in place. Some discretion therefore is inevitable when classifying firms, regardless of whether the researcher or company respondents do the classifying.

The authors felt that it was more important to minimize company-to-company differences in interpretation than to get types of structures by people with first-hand knowledge of the operations. Therefore, structures were classified by the authors. The information used was obtained by asking respondents in sample companies to trace the flow of financial consolidation from a "typical" foreign production facility to successively higher levels, up to the level of the chief operating officer. If more than one path existed for the same foreign facility, respondents were asked to trace each. Respondents described the breadth of product, function, and geographic responsibility at each successive level so that the expanding breadth of responsibilities could be characterized as one moved upward in the organization. The use of financial consolidation as an indicator of organization structure was based largely on studies showing this to parallel the primary line of superior-subordinate relationships. Personal reward systems and resource allocations largely follow these same lines (Reece & Cool, 1978). This information was requested from the chief financial officer in each firm because he was believed to be knowledgeable about the overall consolidation process. These individuals were asked to trace the reporting relationship for a "typical" Canadian and a "typical" non-Canadian foreign manufacturing or processing operation. It was recognized that respondents had to exercise discretionary judgment to decide what is typical. Firms then were categorized on the basis of these data, and the resulting classifications were checked against organization charts that respondents also were asked to supply. If there were no official organization charts, respondents sketched what one might currently look like. Finally, telephone interviews were used to fill gaps and to clear up inconsistencies.

Managerial responsibility was classified as to type and geographic domain. The former was designated either functional (e.g., just for manufacturing) or product (e.g., manufacturing and sales). Three geographic classifications were established: global (the entire world), international (the globe excluding the United States or the United States and Canada), and regional (an international subregion that may or may not include the United States). A firm's overall organization structure was determined by the responsibility of the executive immediately below the level of the chief operating officer to whom the "typical" foreign facility ultimately reported. Thus, a company was classified as functional or product, depending on the kind of responsibility of this individual. Each of these categories then was subdivided further according to the geographic responsibility of this individual—that is, global, international division, or area. If responsibility was traced to more than a single individual, the firm was classified as matrix.

Sample Selection

Four criteria guided the selection of firms for study. First, only large companies (i.e., those included on the *Fortune* 500 list) were examined. Large firms were judged to be particularly interesting because typically they have become multinational before others and because they control an even greater share of U.S. foreign than of U.S. domestic investment (Daniels et al., 1982). Large firms therefore were likely to have significant foreign operations and to be leaders rather than followers in selecting organization structures to handle foreign activities.

A second selection criterion involved firm nationality. Most studies that have attempted to relate operating variables to multinational structure have dealt in whole or in large part with non-U.S. firms (Egelhoff, 1980; Franko, 1973; Gordon, 1970; Schollhammer, 1971). It was decided to focus exclusively on U.S. multinationals because they typically derive a far larger percentage of their sales and profits from their domestic market than do foreign multinationals. The problem of balancing business, functional, and geographic perspectives (Bartlett, 1979; Davis, 1976; Prahalad, 1976) therefore is likely to be different for them than for their foreign counterparts. It thus seemed desirable not to mix the two kinds of company in the same study.

A third selection criterion involved importance of foreign activity. The desire was to study only firms for which international organization design is a significant issue, and this is unlikely if foreign involvement is very low. The Financial Accounting Standards Board now requires, under ruling 14, that U.S. firms provide segmented information on foreign operations when the latter are "significant"—that is, when they account for 10 or more percent of a firm's total activity. The study was limited to firms that met this minimum significance criterion.

A final selection criterion involved location of foreign facilities. Excluded from the sample were firms whose foreign facilities were limited exclusively to Canada. This exclusion was made because the Canadian operations of U.S. multinationals are often substantially integrated with their U.S. operations. One study noted, for example, that 60 percent of U.S. multinationals using an international division incorporate their Canadian facilities within their U.S. domestic divisions (Lovell, 1966).

The procedure for selecting firms that would meet these requirements was the following. First all firms in the 1978 *Fortune* 500 that segmented their foreign operations were identified. There were 256 such firms. Because there was no certain way of determining how many of the 256 had operations in countries other than Canada, questionnaires were sent to all of them, and 97 firms completed the questionnaire. Of the 97, 3 were discarded because the firms had foreign operations only in Canada. A fourth was later discarded because accurate financial data were not available on the firm from public sources. The final sample, therefore, consisted of 93 companies, or 36 percent of the firms surveyed and 37 percent of those that might have operations outside of Canada.

Of the 93 usable responses, the authors were comfortable in classifying 92 according to one of the five organization types defined earlier. The remaining one was so heterogeneous in its lines of reporting that it was simply called "mixed." These 92 were classified as follows: worldwide functional ($n = 10$, $\% = 11$), worldwide product ($n = 33$, $\% = 36$), international division ($n = 37$, $\% = 40$), area ($n = 11$, $\% = 12$), and matrix ($n = 1$, $\% = 1$). Because of only one matrix response, the analysis of the data excludes that firm.

Findings

Because this was an exploratory study, a number of things were tried in order to find relationships between independent variables and organization structure. Structural group means were compared by *t* tests for all variables and multiple cells by chi square. Firms were placed in rank order for each variable to see if there was concentration in any value area (e.g., from highest dependence on foreign sales to lowest, to see where area structures versus worldwide product structures were concentrated). Scatter diagrams were made for each pair of variables to see if the combination of any two variables resulted in groupings. The results given are limited to those for which a logical theoretical basis for the relationship discovered could be provided.

Worldwide Functional

Table 1 shows that companies handling their foreign operations through a worldwide functional structure could be classified as having low or medium product diversity. This is as one might expect, based on Chandler's earlier work (1966). It seems safe, therefore, to say that highly diversified firms are not likely to handle their foreign operations through a worldwide functional structure. It cannot be said as comfortably, however, that low diversified firms are apt to handle their foreign operations through a worldwide functional structure. Although chi square analysis showed a significant difference at $p < .01$ between functional and product usage by diversity groups, a substantial portion of firms with low diversity (77 percent) are not using a worldwide functional structure.

Why do some firms with low product diversity use a functional structure but most do not? It was thought that the explanation might lie in relative dependence on foreign operations. Chandler (1975) hypothesized that functional structures would give way as dependence on foreign operations increased. This, however, was not the case. Table 2 shows clearly that the firms with functional structures were not concentrated among those with lower dependence on foreign operations. In fact, their ratio of foreign to total sales was highly varied, ranging from 3.7 percent to 77.6 percent.

Table 1 Organization structure by product diversity[a]

	Diversity		
	Low	*Medium*	*High*
Worldwide functional	$n = 6$	$n = 4$	$n = 0$
of diversity group	23%	9%	0%
of organization type	60%	40%	0%
Worldwide product	$n = 5$	$n = 14$	$n = 14$
of diversity group	19%	33%	64%
of organization type	15%	42.5%	42.5%
International division	$n = 10$	$n = 20$	$n = 7$
of diversity group	39%	46%	32%
of organization type	27%	54%	19%
Area	$n = 5$	$n = 5$	$n = 1$
of diversity group	19%	12%	4%
of organization type	45.5%	45.5%	9%

[a]Low diversity = 0–6 two digit SICs; medium diversity = 7–13 two digit SICs; high diversity = 14–30 two digit SICs.

Table 2 Organizational structure by dependence on foreign sales[a]

	Foreign sales		
	Low	*Medium*	*High*
Worldwide functional	*n* = 1	*n* = 6	*n* = 3
of sales group	6%	14%	10%
of organization type	10%	60%	30%
Worldwide product	*n* = 11	*n* = 15	*n* = 7
of sales group	65%	34%	23%
of organization type	33%	46%	21%
International division	*n* = 4	*n* = 21	*n* = 12
of sales group	23%	48%	40%
of organization type	11%	57%	32%
Area	*n* = 1	*n* = 2	*n* = 8
of sales group	6%	4%	27%
of organization type	9%	18%	73%

[a]When foreign sales as percent of total sales was less than .13, classification was low; when between .13 and .3, classification was medium; and when .3 and above, classification was high.

On looking elsewhere for an explanation, it was discovered that the 10 functional firms were all raw material extractors—8 of them involving energy and distinguished by high capital intensity. Of these 10, 8 appeared among the 10 most highly capital intensive firms in the sample (i.e., employees to assets ratio of less than .01). Raw material extractor firms deal largely with very homogeneous raw materials that do not have to be altered substantially from one country to another. Their key strategic need therefore is coordination among functions (e.g., exploration, productions, and sales), not new product introduction or marketing. This need is reflected by their relatively high integration score, shown in Table 3. Very likely to avoid complications that might impede functional coordination, these firms generally have not used shared ownership or acquisitions when establishing foreign facilities (see Table 3).

Worldwide Product

Shared common characteristics did not as easily set apart firms with worldwide product structures as they did those using worldwide functional structures. The worldwide product group included firms with a wide range of product diversity, dependence on foreign sales, and strategic variables employed. Some tendencies were found, however. For instance, a high portion of the firms with a worldwide product structure (85 percent) were classified as having medium or high product diversity.

Some firms with low diversity nevertheless had a worldwide product structure, and some with high diversity did not. Why? Consider first the

Table 3 Organization structure by control problem

	Ownership		Acquisition Method[a]		International Production Integration	
	100%	Shared	Start-up	Buy-in	High	Low
Worldwide function						
n	10	0	9	0	4	6
%	100	0	100	0	40	60
Worldwide product						
n	29	4	17	15	9	24
%	88	12	53	47	27	73
International division						
n	28	5	22	13	15	20
%	85	15	63	37	43	57
Area						
n	9	2	8	3	4	7
%	82	18	73	27	36	64

[a]In some cases the MNC participating in this study acquired a U.S. firm that already had foreign operations of its own. If the acquired U.S. firm, itself, had established the typical foreign facility, the acquisition method was classified as start-up.

former. Table 4 shows them to be significantly less involved internationally than firms using international division or area structures. This finding suggests that at a low level of foreign investment, foreign operations may be best handled by domestic product divisions. However, as foreign sales increase, there is a need to combine foreign operations by forming either an international or an area division structure. This shift may come about for several reasons: to prevent duplication of specialized international activities; to create a new division of about the same size as the existing ones; or to focus on an area that has demonstrated recent growth.

At high diversity levels, dependence on foreign operations did not significantly differentiate organization structures, although the authors had expected that it would—that is, that product divisions would be adopted as foreign involvement and product diversity increased simultaneously. Contrary to expectations, however, the international division firms in this category actually had higher foreign sales on average than did those with worldwide product structures.

The variable that best predicted whether a high diversity firm would use a worldwide product rather than an international division structure was the method of entering new businesses. All six sample firms that *Forbes* classified as conglomerates—firms that diversify primarily by acquisition—fell in the high diversity category, and all six used worldwide product structures. This preference of acquisitive diversifiers for worldwide product structures may stem from their special need to provide divisions a high level of

Table 4 Strategic variables mean values (standard deviations)

Strategic variable	Diversity level	Worldwide product		International division		Area	
				Organizational structure			
Foreign sales/corporate sales	High	.27	(.154)	.32	(.159)	.18	(.000)
	Medium	.20	(.114)	.29	(.156)	.40	(.154)
	Low	.18[i.a.]	(.051)	.29[g]	(.138)	.39[gg]	(.188)
R&D expenditures/ corporate sales	High	.017	(.013)	.045	(.007)	.010	(.000)
	Medium	.023	(.020)	.024	(.024)	.020	(.010)
	Low	.015	(.009)	.014	(.011)	.025	(.020)
Advertising expenditures/ corporate sales	High	.016	(.006)	.019	(.011)	(NA)	(.000)
	Medium	.017[ii]	(.027)	.020[gg]	(.012)	.018	(.013)
	Low	.059	(.000)	.025[aa]	(.030)	.100[ii]	(.078)
Total employees/ corporate assets	High	.031[ii]	(.010)	.019[gg]	(.004)	.021	(.000)
	Medium	.027	(.010)	.024	(.008)	.018	(.008)
	Low	.021	(.011)	.022	(.012)	.028	(.023)

[g]Significantly different ($p < .1$) from worldwide product firms at same diversity level.
[i]Significantly different ($p < .1$) from international division firms at same diversity level.
[a]Significantly different ($p < .1$) from area firms at same diversity level.
[gg]Significantly different ($p < .05$) from worldwide product firms at same diversity level.
[ii]Significantly different ($p < .05$) from international division firms at same diversity level.
[aa]Significantly different ($p < .05$) from area firms at same diversity level.

operating autonomy (Berg, 1973; Pitts, 1977a, 1977b).

The outstanding characteristic of the seven high diversity firms using international divisions was their high level of R&D expenditure, which averaged 4.5 percent of sales, compared to only 1.7 percent of sales for the high diversity firms using worldwide product structures. Why the technologically-oriented firms chose international divisions rather than worldwide product structures is discussed in the next section.

International Division

The international division structure conceivably can operate alongside a domestic structure that is organized by either function or product; however, of the 37 international division firms examined, 36 organized domestic activities along product lines. The international division, therefore, is largely a special structure adopted by companies that depend domestically on product divisions.

Why do some firms with product divisions choose to separate their foreign operations into a separate international division? The evidence suggests that dependence on foreign operations exerts an important influence. Consider the data in Table 4. Regardless of level of diversity, firms using international divisions have higher dependence on foreign sales than do those using worldwide product structures. Further support for the same tendency comes from data on specific industries. Two industry groups, energy firms and conglomerates, have been discussed, with the conclusion that their special characteristics determine the types of structures that they use. Of the remaining four industries that were examined separately, three (auto suppliers, branded foods, and chemicals) follow the pattern of going from worldwide product to international division as foreign sales grow as a percentage of total sales. In every case for these industries, firms with an international division have higher dependence on foreign sales than do those companies in the same industries with worldwide product structures.

Traditional theory argues a reverse tendency for high diversity firms— that is, replacement of international division structures by worldwide product designs as foreign involvement increases. Those making this claim argue that domestic divisions possess the product expertise needed by foreign units, yet are reluctant to transfer it when the latter reside in an international division (Chandler, 1975; Fouraker & Stopford, 1968; Stopford & Wells, 1972). The solution, claim these authors, is a reorganization that does away with the international division and places foreign responsibility for products within worldwide product divisions.

The present findings conflict directly with this conclusion. As shown in Table 4, foreign involvement was higher for international division than for worldwide product firms even in the high diversity subgroup. The reason why high diversity multinationals do not shun international divisions, as traditional theory proposes, perhaps is to be found in several recent investigations that show that, except for conglomerates, such firms do not turn over resources entirely or even mainly to product divisions, but rather centralize them to a considerable extent at the corporate level. Such centralization has been shown for R&D (Berg, 1973; Pitts, 1977a), personnel (Galbraith & Edstrom, 1976; Pitts, 1977b), marketing (Aylmer, 1970), and finance (Stobaugh, 1970). In firms in which such centralization has taken place, foreign units need not rely on domestic divisions for needed resources. They can obtain them directly from the corporate level in much the same way that domestic product divisions do. An additional explanation for the present finding may be found in Bartlett's (1979) research. He concluded that an international division promotes foreign expansion more effectively than does a worldwide product structure because it places a spokesman for geographic interest at the same level as spokesmen for product and functional interests.

The traditional view thus would appear to apply only to conglomerates. They do not typically centralize key resources, and their foreign units must rely much more heavily on domestic product divisions for help. Under such conditions, a worldwide product structure, which provides the latter direct incentive to help the former, is needed to ensure effective exploitation of foreign potential.

Area

Whereas area organizations are widely used by European firms (Franko, 1975), few U.S. firms (12 percent) employing this structure were found in the present study. Its limited use by U.S. firms may be attributed to the usual dominance of the U.S. market. Only one third of the respondents had foreign sales comprising as much as 30 percent of total sales; consequently, an area division comprising U.S. operations usually would be much larger than the two or more foreign area divisions. It is not surprising, therefore, that companies using area structures were found almost entirely among the firms with high foreign sales (Table 2).

Evidence also was found that firms may move from international divisions to area structures as foreign sales increase. In those same three industries (auto supplies, branded foods, and chemicals) in which there appeared to be a move from worldwide product to international division as foreign sales increased, there was a move to area structures at an even higher foreign sales level. Of the 18 firms examined in these industries, only 1 firm was an exception to this pattern.

But then why do many firms with a high dependence on foreign sales utilize other structures? The answer here seems to lie in the diversity factor. Table 1 shows that the area structure is concentrated among companies with low and medium diversity. It already has been speculated that acquisitive diversifiers are not good candidates for any structure except the worldwide product one. The tendency of internal diversifiers to choose international divisions also has been discussed. But why do the latter not switch to an area structure as foreign sales grow?

The answer may lie in their need to exploit new products in different foreign markets quickly but sequentially (Stobaugh, 1969). It seems logical that the sequencing of countries for exploiting new products will be more coherent when only one division makes such decisions than when several area divisions compete to get a new product before the others. This notion is consistent with Davidson's (1980) finding that the international division is the fastest structure for transferring new products abroad. Once again this finding is counter to what was expected at the start of our study.

At a low level of diversity, it was found that companies with area structures have a significantly higher advertising intensity than do firms with international divisions. Although this difference does not show up at higher diversity levels, it does lead to the intriguing possibility that the area structure is preferable when marketing is the major competitive advantage. Spillover of advertising from one country to another, for example, may necessitate regional control.

Implications and Conclusions

Based on a substantial literature, it was expected that companies with a given organization structure generally would have some characteristics different from those of firms with other structures. Rather than testing a theory as to which characteristics relate to which structure, a theoretical framework, based on the findings, was developed. A number of studies were used to guide in the selection of variables, and some preliminary expectations based on those studies were set up. Nevertheless, the method of inquiry was essentially exploratory.

Even as an exploratory study, some inherent limitations are recognized. First, the study is based on a group of firms that may not be representative. All the firms are large; and the only ones included are those that completed the questionnaire, could be classified according to one of five organizational types, and for which substantial operating data are available from public sources. Second, respondents, in describing foreign operations, had to use personal discretion to determine what is a typical foreign operation. The researchers, in turn, had to use further discretion in order to classify their responses. The methodology forced placement of each firm into a single organizational category. Such "pure" structures are rare. In future research it may prove useful to score each firm on the degree to which it utilizes various multinational structures. Third, the analysis of company characteristics is not exhaustive. Some important variables may have been overlooked. For some variables, the cell sizes were too small to test conclusively. For others proxies had to be used as indicators of characteristics of interest. Finally, the perspective is limited. Examination was made of a cross-section of firms at a given time, and inferences were made as to how structures evolve; historical analysis might have yielded different results.

Despite these weaknesses and limitations, the findings shed preliminary light on important factors influencing the choice of organization structure of U.S. firms that have significant foreign operations. Furthermore, there are logical explanations for the way these factors exert such influence; thus, there are theoretical underpinnings for further development. If future research supports the framework that these findings suggest, then students and practitioners may better understand how and why multinational firms adopt specific organization structures. Figure 1 summarizes what is hypothesized from the findings.

As long as foreign sales are low as a portion of total sales, most companies handle foreign operations merely as an appendage to existing product or functional divisions. Although firms with worldwide product and worldwide functional structures together comprised 47 percent of the total sample, they made up 71 percent of the firms whose foreign sales were no more than 13 percent of their total sales.

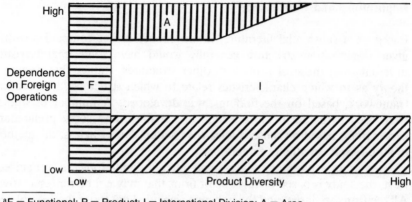

^aF = Functional; P = Product; I = International Division; A = Area.

Figure 1 Structural evolution of nonconglomerate U.S. multinational firms^a

Whether firms at a low foreign sales level adopt a functional or a product structure depends primarily on their level of product diversity. All the firms with a functional structure are classified as low or medium diversifiers, whereas 85 percent of firms with a worldwide product structure are medium or high diversifiers.

Increasing dependence on foreign sales seems to be the major impetus for change from a worldwide product to an international division structure. Most worldwide product firms (79 percent) had low or medium levels of foreign sales, whereas most international division firms (89 percent) fell in the medium and high foreign sales categories. The separation of international activities takes place in order to create a spokesman for geographic expansion at the same organizational level as spokesmen for product and functional interests. An international division head is able to handle high product diversity, contrary to traditional theory, because many functional responsibilities are put under corporate as opposed to divisional control.

Once an international division grows to be larger than domestic product divisions, there is a tendency to split it into two or more areas to provide better balance among divisions in terms of size. This tendency is less pronounced among firms that become diverse through internal development of new products, however. They tend to maintain international divisions, despite high levels of foreign sales, to ensure effective sequencing of new product introduction abroad.

Conglomerates are a case apart. Like their nonconglomerate counterparts, they typically adopt a worldwide product structure early in their diversification. However, because of their reluctance to disturb divisional autonomy, they generally do not discard it in favor of international division and area structures as their foreign sales and/or diversity increase. Instead, they tend to retain a worldwide product structure even after achieving very high values with respect to these two parameters.

It is hoped that future researchers will find this framework useful for developing and testing additional hypotheses about the effects of operating characteristics on international organization design. Although directional support has been found for the relationships discussed here, more conclusive data are necessary in order to support or reject the tentative findings.

References

Alpander, G. G. Multinational corporations: Homebase-affiliate relations. *California Management Review*, 1978, 20(3), 47–56.

Aylmer, R. J. Who makes marketing decisions in the multinational firm? *Journal of Marketing*, 1970, 34(4), 17–29.

Bartlett, C. A. *Multinational structural evolution: The changing decision environment in international divisions*. Doctoral dissertation, Harvard Business School, 1979.

Beer, M., & Davis, S. Creating a global organization: Failures along the way. *Columbia Journal of World Business*, 1976, 11(2), 72–84.

Berg, N. A. Corporate role in diversified companies. In B. Taylor & N. MacMillan (Eds.), *Business policy: Teaching and research*. New York: Wiley, 1973, 298–347.

Cascino, E. How one company "adapted" matrix management in a crisis. *Management Review*, 1979, 68(11), 57–61.

Chandler, A. D., Jr. *Strategy and structure*. Garden City, N.Y.: Anchor, 1966.

Chandler, A. D. The multi-unit enterprise: A historical and international comparative analysis and summary. In H. F. Williamson (Ed.), *Evolution of international management structures*. Newark, Del.: University of Delaware Press, 1975, 225–254.

Dance, W. D. An evolving structure for multinational operations. *Columbia Journal of World Business*, 1969, 4(6), 25–30.

Daniels, J. D., Ogram, E. W., Jr., & Radebaugh, L. H. *International business environments and operations*. 3rd ed. Reading, Mass.: Addison-Wesley, 1982.

Davidson, W. H. *Experience effects in international investment and technology transfer*. Ann Arbor, Mich.: UMI Research Press, 1980.

Davis, S. Trends in the organization of multi-national corporations. *Columbia Journal of World Business*, 1976, 11(2), 59–71.

Davis, S., & Lawrence, P. R. Problems of matrix organizations. *Harvard Business Review*, 1978, 56(3), 131–142.

Egelhoff, W. G. Matrix strategies and structures in multinational corporations. Paper presented at the Academy of International Business Annual Meeting, New Orleans, 1980.

Fouraker, L. E. & Stopford, J. M. Organizational structure and multinational strategy. *Administrative Science Quarterly*, 1968, 13, 47–64.

Franko, L. G. Who manages multinational enterprises? *Columbia Journal of World Business*, 1973, 8(2), 30–42.

Franko, L. G. Organization change in European multinational enterprise. Unpublished manuscript, Center for Education in International Management, Geneva, Switzerland. Cited in H. F. Williamson (Ed.), *Evolution of international management structures*. Newark, Del.: University of Delaware Press, 1975, 237.

Galbraith, J. R. Matrix organization designs—How to combine functional and project forms. *Business Horizons*, 1971, 14(1), 29–40.

Galbraith, J., & Edstrom, A. International transfer of managers: Some important policy considerations. *Columbia Journal of World Business*, 1976, 11(2), 100–112.

Goggin, W. C. How the multi-dimensional structure works at Dow Corning. *Harvard Business Review*, 1974, 55(1), 54–65.

Gordon, P. J. Organizational strategies: The case of foreign operations by non-U.S. companies. *Journal of Comparative Administration*, 1970, 2(1), 81–108.

Knickerbocker, F. *Oligopolistic reaction and multinational enterprise*. Cambridge, Mass.: Harvard University, Graduate School of Business, Division of Research, 1973.

Lovell, E. B. *The changing role of the international executive*. New York: National Industrial Conference Board, 1966.

McKern, R. B. The Dow Chemical Company: Organizing multinationally. Intercollegiate Case Clearing House, 9–371–419, 1971.

Menzies, H. D. Westinghouse takes aim at the world. *Fortune*, January 14, 1980, pp. 48–53.

Pitts, R. A. Strategies and structures for diversification. *Academy of Management Journal*, 1977a, 20, 197–208.

Pitts, R. A. Unshackle your "comers." *Harvard Business Review*, 1977b, 55(3), 127–136.

Prahalad, C. K. Strategic choices in diversified MNC's. *Harvard Business Review*, 1976, 54(4), 67–78.

Reece, J. S., & Cool, W. R. Measuring investment center performance. *Harvard Business Review*, 1978, 56(3), 28–46.

Schollhammer, H. Organization structures of multinational corporations. *Academy of Management Journal*, 1971, 14, 345–363.

Stobaugh, R., Jr., Where in the world should we put that plant? *Harvard Business Review*, 1969, 47(1), 132–134.

Stobaugh, R., Jr., Financing foreign subsidiaries of U.S. controlled multinational enterprises. *Journal of International Business Studies*, 1970, 1(1), 43–64.

Stopford, J. M., & Wells, L. T., Jr., *Managing the multinational enterprise*. New York: Basic Books, 1972.

Vernon, R. Gone are the cash cows of yesterday. *Harvard Business Review*, 1980, 58(6), 150–155.

Where to find the company. *Forbes*, January 5, 1981, pp. 50–66.

13

Strategy and Structure in Multinational Corporations: A Revision of the Stopford and Wells Model*

William G. Egelhoff

*Source: *Strategic Management Journal*, 9 (1988), pp. 1–14.

The Stopford and Wells study of strategy and structure in multinational corporations produced a now familiar model relating certain types of structure to certain elements of a firm's international strategy. This paper re-examines the important relationships expressed by the model, using data from a recent study of 34 large U.S. and European multinationals. While some of the relationships are supported, others are not. A new element of strategy, the relative size of foreign manufacturing, is introduced, and found to be an important predictor of structure. Based on the findings, a revised model for relating strategy and structure in MNCs is proposed.

Introduction

As the international strategies of firms evolve, and become more complex, it is increasingly difficult to know which types of organizational structure facilitate implementing them. While models linking strategy and structure exist, there is a pressing need for further development. The first empirical work which sought to relate structure to the strategy of an organization was Chandler's (1962) study of 70 large U.S. corporations. It tended to show that as a company's product/market strategy changed it was important that the organization's structure also change to support implementation of the new strategy. Additional studies by Pavan (1972), Channon (1973), Rumelt (1974), and Dyas and Thanheiser (1976) further demonstrated that certain strategies need to be supported by certain structures. A number of empirical studies have also attempted to describe the relationship between strategy and structure for multinational corporations (MNCs) (Brooke and Remmers, 1970; Daniels, Pitts and Tretter, 1984, 1985; Fouraker and Stopford, 1968; Franko, 1976; Stopford and Wells, 1972). Of these, the Stopford and Wells study was the largest and most comprehensive, and it also developed the most explicit theory linking strategy and structure in MNCs.

The Stopford and Wells Models of International Strategy and Structure

In their book on strategy implementation, Galbraith and Nathanson (1978) credit Stopford and Wells with having extended the earlier strategy–structure models of Chandler (1962) and Scott (1971) to include international strategy and structure. Figure 1 shows the critical variables and relationships of the Stopford and Wells Model, which was empirically derived from data collected on 187 large U.S. MNCs.

Below the international division boundary in Figure 1, foreign product diversity and foreign sales are both relatively low. MNCs employing this strategy tended to support it with an international division structure. As foreign product diversity increased, companies in the sample tended to use product division structures. Similarly, companies pursuing strategies leading to a relatively high percentage of foreign sales tended to use area division structures. When a company's strategy contained both high foreign product diversity and a high percentage of foreign sales, Stopford and Wells hypothesized that MNCs will tend to employ matrix or mixed structures, but the question mark (placed there by Galbraith and Nathanson) indicates there was only weak support for this in Stopford and Wells' data. Although the Stopford and Wells study took place in U.S. MNCs, subsequent research by Franko (1976) in European MNCs tended to confirm the relationships shown in Figure 1.

Recent Concerns About International Strategy and Structure

While recent research has raised some questions about the validity of the international division boundary of the Stopford and Wells Model (Bartlett, 1979, 1983; Daniels *et al.*, 1984; Davidson, 1980; Davidson and Haspeslagh, 1982), the other relationships have essentially gone unchallenged and remain intact. In fact, with the exception of a study by Daniels *et al.* (1985), the upper and right-hand sides of the model (those portions associated with relatively high levels of foreign sales and/or foreign product diversity) have remained largely untested since the original research by Stopford and Wells and Franko. These portions of the model (and especially the portion represented as a question mark) are of growing significancce, however, since the strategies of more and more MNCs are moving in this direction.

In fact, recent literature has raised a number of specific questions about strategy–structure relationships in the more strategically complex portions of the model. First, Galbraith and Nathanson (1978) ask what international strategy fits the matrix structure, since both they and Davis and Lawrence

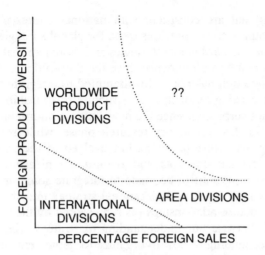

Figure 1 The Stopford and Wells Model showing the relationship between strategy and structure in multinational corporations (Reprinted by permission from *Strategy Formulation: The Role of Structure and Process*, by Galbraith and Nathanson. Copyright © 1978 by West Publishing Company. All rights reserved.)

(1977) noted a probable trend toward matrix structures in MNCs. Stopford and Wells suggested that matrix (and mixed) structures might be appropriate for firms in the upper right-hand corner of the model (where both foreign sales and foreign product diversity are high), but their data provided only weak support for this relationship. Since the widespread move to matrix structures expected by Davis and Lawrence has not occurred, despite the fact that many MNC strategies today contain relatively high levels of foreign sales and foreign product diversity, the question about what international strategy fits a matrix structure would still seem to be an open one.

A second issue with strategy–structure implications seems to be raised by Hout, Porter and Rudden (1982). They believe that the increasing growth in global interdependency can best be exploited by global strategies, where the appropriate unit of analysis for strategic planning and management is the global market for a product instead of multiple domestic markets. They point out that global strategies require new, more centralized forms of structure, that can integrate managerial decision-making across many domestic markets that were previously dealt with in a decentralized manner.

A third issue that seems to be influencing international strategy is increasing host government pressure for more national responsiveness in the strategies of MNCs (Doz, 1980; Doz and Prahalad, 1980). This pressure is generally reflected in calls for more local manufacture and R&D, a balance between exports and imports, and sometimes products and technologies that are consistent with national interests. This trend obviously runs counter to the previous trend for global strategies.

These new trends toward global strategies and more national responsiveness have largely come to prominence since the Stopford and Wells study, and subsequent research has not really attempted to integrate these developments into the existing set of strategy–structure relationships for MNCs. This is perhaps not surprising, since the new issues in international strategy seem to be still in the exploratory research phase, while research done under the strategy–structure paradigm has evolved to the point where it requires clearly defined concepts and operational measures. Yet it is important that attempts start to be made to integrate some understanding of the new issues and trends in international strategy into the established set of strategy–structure relationships (as represented by the Stopford and Wells Model). Otherwise our understanding of strategy will increasingly outstrip our understanding of how to organize to implement such strategy. In contrast to the decade-long lags between changes in strategy and changes in structure observed by Chandler's study (1962), it is increasingly important for MNC managements to understand strategy–structure relationships and anticipate changes in order to minimize periods of misfit.

The purpose of the present study is to reexamine the key strategy–structure relationships of the Stopford and Wells study and to introduce a new element of international strategy—foreign manufacturing—which Stopford and Wells and other researchers have not considered. The new element is especially important because it seems to capture some of the more recent changes and trends that are altering and complicating the international strategies of MNCs.

Structures for Conducting International Business

This section describes the five types of structure that appeared in the Stopford and Wells study, and are presently used to manage international operations: international divisions, worldwide product divisions, area divisions, matrix structures, and mixed structures. With an international division structure, all foreign subsidiaries report to an international division that is separate from the domestic operations. Communications between the international division and the company's domestic operations are usually poor (Brooke and Remmers, 1970), but there is generally considerable flexibility for foreign subsidiaries to develop strategies that vary according to local conditions. Thus an international division structure facilitates implementing strategies that are responsive to local or national concerns, while it hinders carrying out global product/market strategies.

A worldwide product division structure extends the responsibilities of the domestic product divisions to cover their product lines on a worldwide basis. It tends to centralize and integrate strategic decision-making for a product line, since a single subunit (the product division) had global responsibility for the performance of a product line. This structure is especially suited for realizing global specialization and economies of scale in R&D, manufacturing, and even marketing. At the same time this structure will be less sensitive to local political and economic conditions, since it emphasizes optimizing strategic performance on a global basis.

An area division structure divides the world into geographical areas, each with its own HQ. Each HQ is responsible for all the company's products and business within its geographical area. Consequently this structure tends to coordinate around, and optimize, performance within a geographical area. Coordination between areas is usually poor (Williams, 1967). To the extent that political and economic conditions within an area are more similar than they are between areas, this structure should lead to strategies that are more responsive to local conditions than those of a worldwide product division structure, but less so than those of an international division structure.

A matrix structure is an overlaying of two of the structures already discussed. Foreign operations report in along two different channels to two different kinds of HQs. For example, in a product division × area division matrix structure, a plastics business in Germany would report in to both the worldwide plastics division HQ (the product channel) and the European area HQ (the geographical area channel). Such a structure can simultaneously develop and implement strategy along two different dimensions. The product division hierarchies will each tend to optimize their product line's performance by coordinating R&D, manufacturing, and perhaps certain aspects of marketing on a global basis. The area division hierarchies, on the other hand, will be largely concerned with exports into and out of a region, achieving economies of scale and market share within a region, and conforming to local government, union, and societal conditions within the region. This added flexibility to simultaneously develop and implement strategy along two different dimensions is not without cost (Davis and Lawrence, 1977; Goggin, 1974). Dual hierarchies involve more managers and staffs, and since the goals and strategic concerns of the two often concern the same resources, considerable managerial effort has to be put into constructive conflict resolution.

Mixed structures involve some foreign operations reporting in to one kind of HQ and other foreign operations reporting in to a different kind of HQ. For example, in a product division and area division mixed structure, the German plastics operations may report in to the worldwide plastics division HQ, while the German cosmetics operations report in to the European HQ. Mixed structures are appropriate when one product line requires a global strategy while another needs to be largely responsive to regional or national conditions.

Hypotheses to be Tested

The Stopford and Wells Model can be represented by the following three hypotheses, which the present study will empirically test:

> *Hypothesis 1: Companies with worldwide product division structures will tend to have higher levels of foreign product diversity than companies with international division or area division structures.*
>
> *Hypothesis 2: Companies with area division structures will tend to have a greater percentage of foreign sales than companies with international division or product division structures.*
>
> *Hypothesis 3: Companies with matrix and mixed structures will tend to have relatively high levels of both foreign product diversity and foreign sales.*

Not included in these hypotheses is the influence of a new element of strategy on structure, which was included in the present study after preliminary interviews with MNC executives revealed that they thought it significantly affected the parent–foreign subsidiary relationship. This element was what a number of executives saw as a growing shift from exports (from the parent country) to foreign manufacture and the trans-shipment of products within regions. Pressures for more local manufacture and fewer exports from the parent have been discussed by others (Doz and Prahalad, 1980). While there appear to be various reasons for this increase in foreign manufacturing (e.g. host government pressures for local manufacturing, the emergence of tariff-free trading areas such as the Common Market, lower manufacturing costs), they were not *per se* the subject of this study. Instead, it was the influence that this factor seemed to have on the structuring of the parent–subsidiary relationship that argued for its inclusion in the study.

Not only does foreign manufacturing reduce the operating interdependency between the parent's domestic operations and a foreign subsidiary, it seems to frequently increase interdependency among subsidiaries within a region. Since many foreign markets are too small to justify world-class production facilities, there has been a tendency to concentrate production of a product at one point in a region and then trans-ship such products between countries within a region. This kind of regional interdependency appeared to be most strong in Europe (where it is obviously facilitated by the Common Market), but was also apparent in the Far East and to a lesser extent in parts of Latin America. Managers indicated that growth in foreign manufacturing and regional interdependency required regional plans, staffs, and sometimes regional headquarters.

Methods

Sample

The sample contained 24 U.S. and 26 European headquartered MNCs and was spread across the following industry groups: auto/truck, electrical/ telecommunications equipment, industrial equipment, chemicals, pharmaceuticals, consumer-packaged goods, and tires. From the *Fortune Directories of the 500 Largest U.S. Industrial Corporations* and the *500 Largest Industrial Corporations Outside the U.S.*, the 50 largest companies in these industries (including three not in these industries) were selected. Companies with less than 15 percent foreign sales, or with only minimal foreign manufacturing, were excluded for not being sufficiently multinational. Several companies were also excluded because it was common knowledge they were experiencing major international operating problems. Thus the sample should be representative of the population of large, successful MNCs. This approach is generally similar to that used in the Stopford and Wells study, which also confined itself to firms in the *Fortune 500*.

Data for the present study were collected through structured interviews conducted at each company's headquarters and from published company documents. Type of structure was first discovered during the interviews. Thirty-four companies had one of the structures covered by the Stopford and Wells Model (see Table 1). Of the remaining 16 MNCs, five had a worldwide functional division structure, one a direct reporting structure, one a structure based on size of foreign subsidiary, and nine some form of matrix or mixed structure that was not based on area divisions and product divisions. Since the purpose of this paper is to deal with those structures represented in the Stopford and Wells Model, only the 34 MNCs with similar structures are used in the subsequent analyses.

Table 1 shows considerable relationship between nationality and the type of structure used by a company. MNCs with an international division or area division structure tend to be U.S. companies, while those with worldwide product division structures tend to be European. As a result of differences in goals and environments, European MNCs may consistently possess different international strategies than U.S. MNCs, and, as a consequence, they may frequently require different structures than U.S. companies. Chandler (1962), Stopford and Wells (1972), and other strategy–structure researchers have argued that all organizations must achieve a satisfactory fit or congruence between their strategies and structures if they are to be successful. The present study takes the view that the nature of this fit between strategy and structure should not differ with the nationality of the parent company, even though strategies and their elements (such as the percentage of foreign sales) will clearly vary with nationality.

Studies of U.K. companies (Channon, 1973); French and German companies (Dyas and Thanheiser, 1976); and Italian companies (Pavan, 1972) have tended to find the same relationships between specific elements of strategy (e.g. product diversity) and structure as Chandler and Stopford and Wells found in U.S. companies. Egelhoff (1982) has advanced a conceptual argument for the invariance of critical strategy–structure relationships across cultures. He argues that the information-processing capacities of a structure are essentially the same whether the structure is populated with Germans or Americans, and, consequently, the capacity of a structure to cope with or fit a given strategy can be generalized across nationalities.

Measures

The classification of organizational structure was done by either obtaining, or in some cases constructing with the help of organizational members, organization charts for each company. At least $1/2$ hour was spent with organization members directly discussing the structure and how it worked. The total interview time spent in each company varied from 5 to 8 hours, and a great deal of additional data, not used in the present study, was also collected. The collection of this additional data generally provided an opportunity to validate the initial classification of structure.

Foreign product diversity was measured by the number of broad product lines a company offered for sale in two designated foreign countries. In all but a few cases, one was the company's largest European subsidiary and the other was Brazil. Since both tended to be large, actively developed markets for most companies in the sample, the product offerings in these two markets were considered representative of the company's total foreign product offering. Correlation between these two measures was high ($R = 0.87$), and the highest of these two measures was used to represent the company's foreign product diversity.

The number of broad product lines in a subsidiary was measured during interviews with knowledgeable company executives. In order to be considered a separate broad product line, products had to have either a different manufacturing technology (i.e. cannot be made with the same manufacturing facility) or different customers and end uses, or both. For example in a pharmaceutical company, pharmaceuticals, veterinary supplies and cosmetics are considered separate broad product lines. This approach led to eight categories of foreign product diversity, where the final category was 'eight or more' broad product lines (four companies fell into this final category).

The concept of product diversity as an important contingency variable for organizational structure was first defined and operationalized by Chandler (1962). Although he did not develop a quantitative measure of product diversity, he identified its impact on organizational structure in

Table 1 Structure and nationality of companies

	U.S.	Europe	Total
International divisions	6	1	7
Area divisions	8	2	10
Product divisions	2	10	12
PD × AD matrix		2	2
PD & AD mixed	2	1	3
	18	16	34

Note: PD × AD = Product divisions × Area divisions matrix structures:
PD & AD = Product divisions & Area divisions mixed structures

terms of the different kinds of technical knowledge and customer charac-teristics with which the organization had to cope. The present study's attempt to measure product diversity in terms of technological and market differences is consistent with Chandler's original notion about why product diversity creates pressures for new organizational structures.

The Stopford and Wells study used a different operational measure of foreign product diversity. It measured the number of two-digit SIC codes which were represented by a company's foreign manufacturing. Using this method, Stopford and Wells identified three levels of foreign product diversity, ranging from none (all products in one SIC code) to high (pro-ducts in three or more SIC codes). Generally, it appears the SIC codes reflect technology and market differences, although the linkage has not been made as explicit as with the broad product line measure used in the present study.

The percentage of foreign sales was measured by the percentage of a company's sales occurring outside of the parent country. In instances where a U.S. company's Canadian operations were organizationally treated as a part of U.S. operations and management for the two was integrated, Canadian sales were considered to be domestic rather than foreign. The Stopford and Wells study treated all Canadian sales as domestic sales for U.S. firms.

Some have also wondered whether the European countries should not be treated as a part of the domestic market for European MNCs. This is a debatable issue, but at the present time we think European managers tend not to view Europe as a single national market. While European MNCs often treat neighboring countries as markets they understand very well and can depend upon, both strategically and organizationally they tend to respect and distinguish between the national differences more than U.S. or Canadian firms generally do with the North American market. Among the sample companies, the only exception was the way some German MNCs tended to treat the Austrian market.

Table 2 Correlation among the contingency variables ($N = 28$–33)

		1	2
1	Foreign product diversity		
2	Percentage foreign sales	0.49*	
3	Percentage foreign manufacturing	−0.16	−0.25

* $p < 0.01$

The size or percentage of foreign manufacturing was operationalized as the percentage of foreign sales accounted for by foreign manufacturing rather than exports from the parent country. This was measured by dividing the value of foreign manufacturing (adjusted by the gross profit margin to make it equivalent to sales volume rather than cost of goods sold) by foreign sales. In a few instances where this information was not available, it was calculated by using foreign manufacturing assets to estimate the percentage of total company manufacturing occurring outside of the parent country, which was then divided by the percentage of foreign sales. This concept has not been previously measured and, of course, was not included in the Stopford and Wells Model.

It is important to notice how the concept of a firm's strategy has been operationally measured in the study. Mintzberg has defined strategy as 'consistent patterns in streams of organizational decisions' (1979: 25). If various decisions made in a firm have led it to diversify into many different product areas (as measured by the number of broad product groups or SIC codes in its product line), we say it is pursuing a diversified product strategy. Similarly, if decisions in a firm have led it to develop many foreign manufacturing facilities (as measured by the percentage of foreign manufacturing), we say it pursues a strategy of sourcing foreign sales from local

Table 3 Mean values of elements of strategy by type of structure

	Mean values of elements of strategy				
	International divisions	*Area divisions*	*Product divisions*	*PD × AD matrix*	*PD & AD mixed*
Foreign product diversity	1.7	3.4	5.8[a]	6.0	4.3
Percentage foreign sales	34[b]	47	61	92	52
Percentage foreign manufacturing	76	91[c]	61	86	82

[a]Different from area divisions at $p < 0.01$ and international divisions at $p < 0.001$.
[b]Different from area divisions at $p < 0.05$ and product divisions at $p < 0.01$.
[c]Different from product divisions at $p < 0.001$.

manufacturing rather than from parent country exports. Thus we tend to operationally measure a strategy with its trail of outcomes, because it is too difficult to directly measure the 'streams of organizational decisions' in order to discern the 'patterns', which actually comprise the strategy. Other research studies that have attempted to quantitatively measure strategy have also tended to measure outcomes rather than decisions (Daniels *et al.*, 1984; Franko, 1976; Stopford and Wells, 1972).

Table 2 shows the correlation among the three contingency variables. As might be expected in relatively mature, successful MNCs, there is a significant positive correlation between foreign product diversity and the percentage of foreign sales, but they are still sufficiently independent elements of a company's strategy to be considered separately.

Results

Several types of analyses were performed on the data. First, one-way ANOVA was used to directly test the first two hypotheses developed from the Stopford and Wells Model. The third hypothesis had to be examined visually, since there are not enough firms with matrix and mixed structures in the sample to support statistical analysis. Finally, a multivariate discriminant analysis was used to simultaneously examine the relationship between structure and all three of the contingency variables (elements of strategy).

Testing the Stopford and Wells Hypotheses

Table 3 shows the mean levels of the three elements of strategy by type of structure. One-way ANOVA contrasts were used to determine the significance of the differences between international division, area division, and product division structures. Since there are only two firms with matrix structures and three with mixed structures in the sample, significance of difference involving these types of structure could not be measured. Hypothesis 1 stated that MNCs with worldwide product division structures will tend to have more foreign product diversity than firms with either an international division or area division structure. The sample data clearly support this hypothesis.

Hypothesis 2 stated that MNCs with area division structures will tend to have a greater percentage of foreign sales than firms with either international division or product division structures. This hypothesis is only partially supported by the data. Companies with area division structures do have a significantly greater percentage of foreign sales than companies with international division structures, but less than companies with worldwide product division structures. The Stopford and Wells study found that companies with area division structures tended to have a greater percentage of foreign sales than companies with product division structures. This was reflected in the model, which further implied that if companies possess both high product diversity and a high percentage of foreign sales, they should tend to have matrix or mixed structures. In the present study, however, the group of MNCs operating with worldwide product division structures tend to possess both high foreign product diversity and a high percentage of foreign sales.

Hypothesis 3 stated that MNCs with matrix and mixed structures will tend to have relatively high levels of both foreign product diversity and foreign sales. While this cannot be tested with any statistical measure, we can examine whether the few matrix and mixed structures in the sample tend to support or contradict this hypothesis. Clearly the two MNCs with matrix structures tend to support it. Their mean foreign product diversity is 6 (ranging from 5 to 7) and their mean percentage of foreign sales is 92 (ranging from 88 to 96).

The three MNCs with mixed product and area division structures provide a somewhat different picture. Their mean foreign product diversity is 4.3 (ranging from 2 to 7). Their mean percentage of foreign sales is 52 (ranging from 36 to 71). The high variance would seem to indicate that it is impossible to generalize about the levels of foreign product diversity and foreign sales that are or should be associated with mixed structures. Actually, mixed structures are some weighted average of product division and area division structures (i.e. some percentage of an MNCs foreign operations are organized under worldwide product divisions and the remaining percentage is organized under area divisions). Since the weighting will vary from company to company, there is no conceptual basis for specifying a unique set of contingency conditions for mixed structures.

Thus the results support some parts of the Stopford and Wells Model, but raise questions about other parts of the model. Hypothesis 1 is fully supported, while hypotheses 2 and 3 are partially supported. Where the present study primarily differs from the Stopford and Wells study is in how to distinguish between the strategic domains of MNCs with product division structures and those with area division structures. Stopford and Wells concluded that high levels of foreign product diversity lead to product division structures while high levels of foreign sales lead to area division structures. The present study finds that both structures tend to be associated with relatively high percentages of foreign sales, and that only foreign product diversity distinguishes in a significant way between the strategic domains of the two.

Stopford and Wells also suggested that strategies involving high levels of both foreign product diversity and foreign sales could best be addressed with matrix and mixed structures. The present study finds that this particular strategic domain seems to be occupied by MNCs with product division and matrix structures. The present findings also suggest that mixed structure companies can vary widely in their strategic domains (as measured by

Table 4 Multiple discriminant analysis of the three elements of strategy on type of structure

Dependent variable: Type of structure

Independent variable	Discriminant function			F-value
	1	2	3	
Foreign product diversity	0.72	0.08	0.70	8.76***
Percentage foreign sales	0.59	0.38	−0.71	7.18**
Percentage foreign manufacturing	−0.35	0.93	0.14	3.76*
Canonical correlation	0.84	0.50	0.27	
Wilks lambda	0.21***	0.69†	0.93	

$†p = 0.11$; $*p < 0.05$; $**p < 0.01$; $***p < 0.001$
Note: All values under the three discriminant functions are standardized discriminant coefficients.

foreign product diversity and foreign sales) and that they should be excluded from the kind of contingency model Stopford and Wells have attempted to construct.

The Influence of Size of Foreign Manufacturing

Table 3 shows how the third element of strategy, percentage of foreign manufacturing, varies across the five structures in the sample. MNCs with area division structures tend to be associated with significantly higher levels of foreign manufacturing than MNCs with worldwide product division structures. As previously discussed, strategies which provide for a high level of foreign manufacturing create high interdependencies between foreign subsidiaries within a region and reduce interdependency between foreign subsidiaries and the parent's domestic operations. The area division structure fits this kind of interdependency. It provides a high level of co-ordination and information processing between subsidiaries within a region. A lower percentage of foreign manufacturing and more exports means there is less opportunity for economies of scale through regional coordination and integration. Following this strategy implies less inter-dependency among subsidiaries within a region, and more interdependency between a subsidiary and the parent. The worldwide product division struc-ture provides the kind of coordination and information processing which fits this kind of interdependency. Thus, foreign manufacturing, the third element of strategy, seems to provide a meaningful way of distinguishing between the strategic domains of MNCs with area division structures and those with worldwide product division structures.

Table 5 Predicted type of structure from coefficients of discriminant functions

Actual group membership	Predicted group membership			
	International divisions	*Area divisions*	*Product divisions*	*PD × AD matrix*
International divisions	6	1	0	0
Area divisions	2	7	1	0
Product divisions	1	1	8	2
PD × AD matrix	0	0	0	2

Note: Structures of MNCs correctly classified = 74 percent.

A Multivariate Analysis

In order to examine the fit between structure and the three elements of strategy simultaneously, a multiple discriminant analysis was run using the four types of structure as the groups and the three elements of strategy as the independent variable. Mixed structures were excluded from the analysis, since their high variance along the dimensions of strategy makes them indistinguishable as a separate group or category. The results of the discriminant analysis appear in Table 4. The standardized discriminant coefficients indicate the relative contributions of the independent variables to the discriminant function. Both foreign product diversity and the percentage of foreign sales load heavily on the first function. The second discriminant function can largely be associated with the percentage of foreign manufacturing. It is statistically significant at the $p = 0.11$ level. The third discriminant function is neither meaningful nor statistically significant.

Table 5 shows how successful the discriminant model is in predicting the structure of each company, given knowledge of the three elements of strategy. The discriminant model could predict the actual structure of a company in 74 percent of the cases, which is significantly better than the chance probability of predicting only 31 percent of the cases correctly.

Table 6 shows the centroids of each of the four groups (types of structure) measured along the three discriminant functions. The first discriminant function, which most heavily reflects foreign product diversity, clearly separates product division and product division × area division matrix structures from international division and area division structures. This can be viewed as another test of hypothesis 1. The second discriminant function, which largely reflects the percentage of foreign manufacturing, separates area division and product division × area division matrix structures from international division and product division structures. While the second discriminant function is only significant at the $p = 0.11$ level, it is consistent with the previous significant finding in Table 3, that level of

Table 6 Centroids of the four structural groups measured along the discriminant functions

Group	Discriminant function		
	1	*2*	*3*
International divisions	−1.90	−0.55	−0.13
Area divisions	−0.63	0.68	0.13
Product divisions	1.47	−0.29	0.09
PD × AD matrix	1.82	0.79	−1.16

foreign manufacturing (and not level of foreign sales, as hypothesized by Stopford and Wells) best distinguishes between the strategic domains of area division and worldwide product division structures. It is also clear from the analysis of centroids that the strategic domain of the product division × area division matrix structure resembles that of the product division structure when it comes to foreign product diversity (discriminant function 1), and resembles that of the area division structure when it comes to percentage of foreign manufacturing (discriminant function 2). Thus the multivariate discriminant analysis tends to support and extend the conclusions which were drawn from the earlier bivariate analysis.

Discussion and Revision of the Stopford and Wells Model

The sample data of the present study have supported some of the hypotheses underlying the Stopford and Wells Model, but failed to support others. Stopford and Wells observed that the strategic domain of international division companies can be characterized by relatively low levels of foreign product diversity and foreign sales. This is confirmed by the present study.

Product Divisions Versus Area Divisions

Stopford and Wells further hypothesized that the strategic domains of area division and product division MNCs differed by level of foreign product diversity and level of foreign sales, since these differences occurred in their sample. The present study confirms the hypothesized difference in foreign product diversity, but fails to find a significant difference in terms of percentage of foreign sales. Both area division and product division structures seem to fit strategies that involve relatively high percentages of foreign sales (the mean being 47 percent for area structures and 61 percent for product division structures). This is a highly significant deviation from the Stopford and Wells findings and Model.

The reason why MNCs in the present study with product division structures possess such a high percentage of foreign sales undoubtedly lies in the fact that the majority are European-headquartered, while those in the Stopford and Wells study were all U.S.-headquartered. It is difficult for European companies to become large, prominent MNCs without having a high percentage of foreign sales, due to the limited size of most home country markets. While this explains the relatively higher percentage of foreign sales in European MNCs, it does not explain why these companies operate with worldwide product division structures instead of matrixing or mixing product divisions with area divisions as the Stopford and Wells Model would predict. It would appear that Stopford and Wells have found part of the answer, but not all of it. Clearly, worldwide product division structures can and do support international strategies containing high percentages of foreign sales.

The reason this was not apparent in the Stopford and Wells study is because it was confined to U.S. MNCs and did not measure the percentage of foreign manufacturing (a third important element for defining the strategic domain of MNCs). The MNCs with area division structures in both the Stopford and Wells study and the present study tend to have high percentages of foreign sales. The present study, however, found that while this strategic condition is necessary, it is not sufficient to specify an area division structure. Large European MNCs with worldwide product divisions also tend to have a high percentage of foreign sales. It is possible that the Stopford and Wells companies with area division structures also had a high percentage of foreign manufacturing—and that it was this strategic condition along with a high percentage of foreign sales that led to the selection of an area division structure. It is also possible that the Stopford and Wells companies with product division structures possessed relatively lower levels of foreign manufacturing, insufficient to require the kind of coordination and information processing necessary to realize area synergies and economies of scale. Thus, the empirical findings of both the Stopford and Wells study and the present study might be consistent and reconcilable, if all of the data were available.

When MNCs support foreign sales with exports from the parent, the primary interdependency is between a foreign subsidiary and the parent's domestic operations. The worldwide product division structure provides the kind of information processing and integration required to coordinate this kind of interdependency. When the strategy is to support foreign sales with extensive foreign manufacturing, important interdependencies usually develop between foreign subsidiaries within a region or area, as the company now attempts to realize area economies of scale to replace the economies of scale which were formerly provided by centralizing production of the product in the parent. The area division structure provides the kind of information processing and integration required to coordinate this kind of interdependency.

Matrix Structures

A second major area where the present study differs from the Stopford and Wells Model deals with matrix structures. Here the difference is not so much contradiction as extension of the model. Both the Stopford and Wells study and the present study observed very few product division × area division matrix structure companies (three and two respectively). This part of the model must therefore rely more on the logic underlying it, and the consistency of the limited empirical data with that logic, than upon any significant empirical testing. Davis and Lawrence (1977) have argued that matrix structures tend to fit situations requiring a dual focus (e.g. equal pressures to organize around products and areas) and high information processing within the organization. The present study found that product division × area division matrix structures tend to occur when there is both high foreign product diversity and a high percentage of foreign manufacturing. These two elements of strategy require a dual focus and different kinds of information processing. They require the kind of information processing and integration that can only be provided by the simultaneous existence of product divisions and area divisions.

The product division × area division matrix companies in the sample also tend to have a high percentage of foreign sales, as hypothesized by Stopford and Wells. Unlike the Stopford and Wells Model, however, the present study found a high percentage of foreign sales and high foreign product diversity to be necessary but not sufficient conditions for a product division × area division matrix structure. A high percentage of foreign manufacturing is also required. It is, again, quite possible that the three Stopford and Wells matrix companies had a high percentage of foreign manufacturing, but this was not measured. Thus the present study extends the Stopford and Wells Model to include a third precondition for product division × area division matrix structures.

A Revised Model

Based on the above findings, Figure 2 shows a revised model linking strategy and structure in MNCs. International strategies which involve a relatively low percentage of foreign sales and low foreign product diversity tend to fit international division structures. Such strategies and structures facilitate responsiveness to national interests. Both the Stopford and Wells and the present study supported this relationship.

Strategies involving high foreign product diversity and a low percentage of foreign sales probably tend to be transitional strategies for successful companies, as they attempt to increase their percentage of foreign sales by introducing more product lines. The Stopford and Wells study found these strategies to be associated with worldwide product division structures. The present study, which observed only the largest MNCs, found no companies in this strategic domain and, therefore, could not test this relationship.

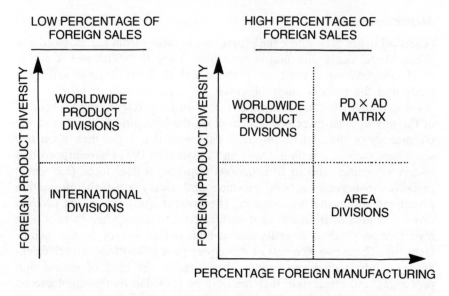

Figure 2 Revised model showing the relationship between strategy and structure in multinational corporations

When international strategies involve relatively high percentages of foreign sales, supporting structures tend to be those which provide higher levels of coordination and information processing between a foreign subsidiary and other sectors of the company. It is in this area that the revised model based on the present study alters and extends the Stopford and Wells Model. Worldwide product division structures provide a high level of coordination and information processing between a company's foreign operations and its domestic product operations. This tends to fit strategies involving high foreign product diversity and substantial exports from the parent to the foreign subsidiaries. This is a global strategy that requires a global structure with less potential for national or even regional responsiveness.

When the strategy involves manufacturing a high percentage of the goods needed to support foreign sales abroad, foreign subsidiaries become relatively more interdependent with each other, and interdependency between the foreign and domestic operations of the company decreases for operational matters. The revised model shows that area division structures provide the type of coordination and information processing needed to handle the interdependency associated with this strategy. Such strategies and structures are not global, but regional, and therefore more responsive to regional and national interests than global product strategies and structures.

When the international strategy involves both high levels of foreign product diversity and foreign manufacturing, foreign subsidiaries will tend to be highly dependent on the parent for product and technical knowledge, and highly interdependent with neighboring subsidiaries in the area for operating synergies and economies of scale. This requires the dual co-ordination and information processing provided by worldwide product divisions and area divisions. The model shows that matrix structures containing both product divisions and area divisions fit such strategies.

Managerial Implications

There are a number of managerial implications which follow from this revision of the Stopford and Wells Model. The first is that MNCs do not have to abandon worldwide product division structures when the size of foreign operations becomes large, as Stopford and Wells suggest. There are numerous successful European MNCs with worldwide product division structures. A second implication is that MNCs should not adopt an area division structure if they still rely largely on exports from the parent country to supply foreign operations. Most large U.S. MNCs have developed large foreign manufacturing operations to support their foreign sales, but many European MNCs still rely heavily on exports from the parent country. If these European MNCs move to supply more of their foreign sales with foreign manufacturing, one would expect that ultimately they will also change their structures to either area division or product division × area division matrix structures, to restore good fit between strategy and structure.

Research Implications

The primary implication for researchers of strategy and structure in MNCs is the importance of foreign manufacturing as an element of international strategy. This variable appears to significantly modify the impact of the size of foreign operations on structure, and in the present study was the most important discriminator between area division and product division structures. It is possible that foreign manufacturing is operationally measuring some of the difference between global product strategies and more regionally and nationally responsive strategies. Doz (1980), Doz and Prahalad (1980), and Hamel and Prahalad (1983) have generally defined the forces favoring such responsiveness in terms of political and cultural factors. While this is undoubtedly true, the potential for area synergies and economies of scale, as reflected in the size of foreign manufacturing, probably combines with political and cultural factors to encourage regional strategies and structures.

By revising and extending the original Stopford and Wells Model, the present study has sought to advance our understanding of critical relationships between strategy and structure in MNCs. The revised model is unfortunately more complex than the original model. It uses a three-dimensional instead of a two-dimensional framework to partition the strategic domains of MNCs. Yet this complexity seems warranted, since it allows the model to identify and take into account increasingly important trends toward globalism and regionalism in international strategies.

Both the recent Daniels *et al.* (1985) study and the present study reveal a strong need for additional research on the more strategically complex portions of the strategy–structure relationship. The present study has suggested that foreign manufacturing is an important aspect of the recent trends toward global strategies and more national and regional responsiveness. Other contingency variables need to be identified and operationalized that will tap other dimensions of these trends. Examples would include the role of international versus domestic R&D in a firm's strategy, and the need to globally transfer technology within and between firms. As mentioned earlier, exploratory research seems to be uncovering increasingly complex forms of international strategy, and extending the strategy–structure paradigm and model to address it is a major challenge facing those who seek to better understand the multinational corporation.

Our bias is to study strategy–structure fit in multinational samples of MNCs. As was the case in the present study, this tends to widen both the range of available international strategies and the number of structural alternatives employed. Both of these encourage the development of more comprehensive strategy–structure models. As international competition has become increasingly multinational (i.e. involving MNCs from different countries) there is an accompanying need to understand both strategy and strategy–structure relationships from a more comprehensive or multinational perspective.

References

Bartlett, C. A. 'Multinational structural evolution: the changing decision evironment in international divisions', Doctoral dissertation, Harvard Business School, Boston, MA, 1979.

Bartlett, C. A. 'MNCs: get off the reorganization merry-go-round', *Harvard Business Review*, **61**(2), 1983, pp. 138–146.

Brooke, M. Z. and H. L. Remmers. *The Strategy of Multinational Enterprise.* American Elsevier, New York, 1970.

Chandler, A. D. *Strategy and Structure: Chapters in the History of Industrial Enterprise.* MIT Press, Cambridge, MA, 1962.

Channon, D. F. *The Strategy and Structure of British Enterprise*, Division of Research, Graduate School of Business Administration, Harvard University, Boston, MA, 1973.

Daniels, J. D., R. A. Pitts and M. J. Tretter. 'Strategy and structure of U.S. multinationals: An exploratory study', *Academy of Management Journal*, **27**(2), 1984, pp. 292–307.

Daniels, J. D., R. A. Pitts and M. J. Tretter. 'Organizing for dual strategies of product diversity and international expansion', *Strategic Management Journal*, 6, 1985, pp. 223–237.

Davidson, W. H. *Experience Effects in International Investment and Technology Transfer.* UMI Research Press, Ann Arbor, MI, 1980.

Davidson, W. H. and P. Haspeslagh. 'Shaping a global product organization', *Harvard Business Review*, **60**(4), 1982, pp. 125–132.

Davis, S. M. and P. R. Lawrence. *Matrix*, Addison-Wesley, Reading, MA, 1977.

Doz, Y. L. 'Strategic management in multinational companies', *Sloan Management Review*, Winter 1980, pp. 27–46.

Doz, Y. L. and C. K. Prahalad. 'How MNCs cope with host government intervention', *Harvard Business Review*, March–April 1980, pp. 149–157.

Dyas, G. P. and H. T. Thanheiser. *The Emerging European Enterprise: Strategy and Structure in French and German Industry.* Macmillan, London, 1976.

Egelhoff, W. G. 'Strategy and structure in multinational corporations: An information-processing approach', *Administrative Science Quarterly*, **27**, 1982, pp. 435–458.

Fouraker, L. E. and J. M. Stopford. 'Organizational structure and multinational strategy', *Administrative Science Quarterly*, **13**, 1968, pp. 47–64.

Franko, L. G. *The European Multinationals: A Renewed Challenge to American and British Big Business*, Greylock Publishing, Stamford, CT, 1976.

Galbraith, J. R. and D. A. Nathanson. *Strategy Implementation: The Role of Structure and Process*, West Publishing, St Paul, MN, 1978.

Goggin, W. C. 'How the multidimensional structure works at Dow Corning', *Harvard Business Review*, January–February 1974, pp. 54–65.

Hamel, G. and C. K. Prahalad. 'Managing strategic responsibility in the MNC', *Strategic Management Journal*, **4**, 1983, pp. 341–351.

Hout, T., M. E. Porter and E. Rudden. 'How global companies win out', *Harvard Business Review*, September–October 1982, pp. 98–108.

Mintzberg, H. *The Structuring of Organizations: A Synthesis of the Research.* Prentice-Hall, Englewood Cliffs, NJ, 1979.

Pavan, F. D. J. 'The strategy and structure of Italian enterprise', Doctoral dissertation, Harvard Business School, Boston, MA, 1972.

Rumelt, R. P. *Strategy, Structure, and Economic Performance.* Division of Research, Graduation School of Business Administration, Harvard University, Boston, MA, 1974.

Scott, B. R. Stages of corporate development, 9-371-294, BP, 988, Intercollegiate Case Clearinghouse, Harvard Business School, Boston, MA, 1971.

Stopford, J. M. and L. T. Wells, Jr. *Managing the Multinational Enterprise*, Basic Books, New York, 1972.

Williams, C. R. 'Regional management overseas', *Harvard Business Review*, **45**, 1967, pp. 87–91.

PART FOUR: Strategy Implementation: Strategic Control and Ownership

14

Bringing the Environment Back In: The Social Context of Business Strategy*

Jeffrey Pfeffer

*Source: *The Competitive Challenge: Strategies for Industrial Innovation and Revival* (Cambridge, Mass., Ballinger, 1987), pp. 119–135.

The academic field of business strategy or strategic management has developed in a fashion consistent with many of the other branches of U.S. social science that are focused on understanding organizations, particularly business organizations. The disciplines of economics, political science, organization theory, psychology, and even sociology, for the most part, have been characterized by two perspectives that are at once both taken for granted and problematic for furthering our analysis of organizations: (1) an analytical approach that Baysinger and Mobley (1983) characterize as methodological individualism, in which the individual is the unit of analysis, or if larger social aggregates are being studied, they are analyzed as if they were individual actors; and (2) a focus on rational action as the explanation or prediction of action taken by these individual social units. As Granovetter (1985) has noted, there has already been extensive critique of the logic of rational action and, moreover, the assumptions of rational models of choice are powerful both in generating predictions of behavior and in serving as parsimonious explanations of empirical observations.

This chapter critiques the approach to analyzing action that is based on methodological individualism. First, it briefly reviews the existing approaches to strategic management, indicating how all such currently popular approaches fail to pay attention to the relational, social nature of organizational life. Then it reviews evidence indicating the importance of interorganizational power and consequently why interorganizational power should be a (if not *the*) focus of strategic management and strategic action. Next, it considers what we know about the development and explanation of variation in interorganizational power. Finally, the chapter concludes by demonstrating how this perspective, rooted more firmly in the realities of the social nature of organizational and interorganizational life, both broadens and alters the conception of strategy and the types of studies of strategic management one might undertake.

The Existing Strategy Literature

Without reviewing the strategy literature in great detail, let me note that the literature is often, and I believe, usefully categorized as follows. In the first instance, there is a distinction between the content aspects of strategy, what the firm should do in terms of what markets to be in and how to approach those markets, and the process aspects of strategy, most often encapsulated in the idea of issues of implementation. Within the content domain, there is often a distinction made between corporate strategy, which focuses on what markets or businesses the firm should be in, and business-level strategy, which "focuses on competition within particular product/market segments" (Astley 1984: 528). Thus, corporate strategy directs attention to what environments to operate in, and business-level strategy focuses on how to compete effectively within those environments—for example, through pursuing strategies based on economies of scale and low-cost production or, alternatively, product differentiation and service.

It is fair to state that both corporate and business-level strategy research has, to this point, been characterized by a fundamentally internal focus with the single organization as the unit of analysis. Although it is clearly true that no strategic research or practice fails to take into account the nature and characteristics of the environment facing the firm, such as the number of competitors, market shares, the dimensions of competition, and so forth, it is also the case that in most research and practice in the domain of strategy, these external constraints are taken as given, as characteristics of the environment to which the firm must adapt in order to be successful. Thus, as Astley (1984: 526) has noted, "organizations are viewed, basically, as solitary units confronted by faceless environments." It is in this sense that we can speak of an internal focus of strategy and strategy research. Astley and Fombrun (1983: 576) have noted that "Strategic action therefore is characterized in terms of a predominantly internal focus, and concern with matching organizational capacities to environmental demands." The focus is internal in that action is directed internally, in lowering production costs, in integrating to absorb sources of supply and lower transaction and production costs, in altering product positioning and product development and introduction strategies. Although each of these actions affects the environment, the actions are taken within the organization's boundaries and are, in this sense, internal.

That the organization is viewed as an isolated unit is, perhaps, more obvious. Strategy research is written from the point of view of the focal organization. Even analyses that presumably focus on population or industry-level conditions—such as population ecology (Hannan and Freeman 1977) in organization theory and competitive industry analysis in economics (Porter 1980)—really do not implicate the structure of relationships among organizations or the embedded, situational character of relationships among units in their analyses. In both instances, environments are characterized in terms of niches, resource pools, and the dynamics of competition but in terms of an undifferentiated mass of faceless competitors who are at once both not proximately tied nor, at times, even presumed to be responsive to the actions of the focal organization. Thus, industry conditions, or niche conditions, become environmental attributes or dimensions to be included in the analysis as factors to which the focal organization is presumed to adapt internally or, in the case of ecology, as dimensions along which the organization will be selected depending on its fit.

The process approaches to strategy, dealing with issues of implementation and strategy formulation (Hrebiniak and Joyce 1984; Mumford and Pettigrew 1975), are even more focused both internally and on the organization as the unit of analysis. The issues confronted include ones such as whether or not strategy—in the sense of rational, conscious, foresightful planning—is possible under the pressures of day-to-day activities and internal political jostling (Bower 1970) if strategies are developed, how can they be communicated in such a way as to be implemented in the myriad decisions made not only at corporate headquarters but in the business units themselves; and how the planning process itself can be best organized and conducted, including the accessing of relevant expertise and involvement of line managers.

These approaches to understanding both the content and process of strategy have been useful but are clearly incomplete. Their incompleteness is difficult to comprehend because of the pervasiveness of the emphasis on methodological individualism in both social science and social thought. Their incompleteness comes from the fact that in a way analogous to individuals within organizations, organizations themselves exist as part of networks and systems of other organizations. Relations among organizations are embedded, to use Granovetter's 1985 term, and they are embedded in the sense that they have a history (almost invariably neglected in all the formulations present in the literature) and a structure, also always neglected. Just as organizations are structured, systems of organizations are structured, and there exist institutional elements of these structures that need to be attended to in doing either research or practice in the area of strategy. But before getting to this point more explicitly, perhaps we can motivate the argument even more by considering the evidence on the relationship between power and profits.

Interorganizational Power and Profits

In both economics and sociology, there has been continuing interest in the effect of power on profits, although as is noted below, other dependent measures beside profit might be more appropriate. In the case of industrial organization in economics, the studies have examined the effect of market power, first measured by things such as the concentration ratio and then by more refined measures of market structure such as the Herfindahl index, on outcomes such as the price-cost margin, profitability, and the excess of the firm's market to book value (see Weiss 1963; Collins and Preston 1968).

In sociology and organization theory, this work is exemplified by Burt's (1980) analysis of the relationship between structural autonomy and profit. Burt (1980: 895–96, 899) argued that there were two aspects to autonomy:

> one aspect of autonomy concerns the relations among actors jointly occupying a status in a system.... The actors ... will be able to escape the constraints of supply and demand imposed by actors in other positions and, accordingly, will be "autonomous" within their system, to the extent that among persons, or corporate actors, occupying the position there exists an oligopoly ... or, in the extreme of centralization, a monopoly.

> a second aspect of autonomy concerns the manner in which actors jointly occupying a status are related to actors occupying other statuses in their system.... Actors ... will be able to balance demands from other actors, and accordingly, will be "autonomous" within their system, to the extent that the pattern of relations ... ensures high competition among those actors who interact with the occupants of position ... a measure of autonomy via group-affiliation must consider two things: the extent to which actors occupying a status have diversified relations with other statuses, and the extent to which they have relations only with statuses that are too poorly organized to make collective demands.

In other words, power in a network comes from having centralized control or coordination over those similarly situated in the network and from dealing in a more diversified way with the rest of the network and particularly with other groups that are not organized or centralized.

Burt (1980) found that his measure of structural autonomy was related to profit margins at the industrial sector level of aggregation. Of course, as various economists (such as Caves 1970) have noted, firms may choose to take some of the benefits that accrue from positions of power in things other than profit, such as reduced variation in performance or, in other words, more certainty and stability. One useful extension of Burt's work would be to replicate his results using other dependent measures besides the one he used, including variation in profits as well as measures of performance and risk more directly tied to security prices. Indeed, given an appropriate sample in which there was mortality observed over the time period of the study, one would predict that Burt's measure of structural autonomy would be related to survival prospects, with more autonomous organizations being more likely to survive.

Two elaborations on the Burt study are important. First, from the point of view of strategic management, Burt's methodology enables one to, given the availability of the necessary data, find positions in transaction networks in which there will be more autonomy and hence greater likelihood of earning a higher return. Thus, Burt's network formulation can guide the choice of market environments for the firm to be in. Second, and possibly more important, note how Burt's framework, or any other that would explicitly incorporate network thinking, differs from other formulations. For instance, in the Freeman and Hannan (1983) study of restaurants, a given restaurant's likelihood of survival was predicted by its form (specialism or generalism) interacting with the conditions of the environment in terms of grain and variability. No consideration is built into the analysis of the restaurant's patterns of relations with suppliers, customers, or competitors in the area. Yet no study of the retail industry is really complete without such factors being included. In the grocery industry, for example, wholesalers often furnish the capital for retail stores (independents) to modernize, and relationships with wholesalers affect the availability and cost of credit as well as the goods actually sold. In the motel and, I suspect, the restaurant industry, network relations are developed with client organizations such as corporations (in the case of motels) and corporations and organizations (in the case of restaurants) to ensure to the extent possible a steady base of business. One of the most important determinants of the profitability of motels in the Palo Alto area is whether or not the motel has developed a stable client relation with some set of local businesses. Although the motels may look alike, or may have similar characteristics in terms of their form, their network positions and consequently their financial success differ vastly. It is exactly this distinction that demarcates, in my view, approaches to analyzing strategy that are fundamentally individualistic in their orientation to those that are more explicitly relational and structural.

If profits and possibly survival and stability are related to the position of interorganizational power, then it makes sense to argue that at least one important objective of strategic management should be to enhance the firm's interorganizational power. And accepting that premise moves us even further into considering the relational aspects of organizational life.

Determinants of Interorganizational Power

A number of theoretical perspectives address the issue of the determinants of interorganizational power. One, the structural autonomy approach of

Burt (1980, 1982, 1983), has already been mentioned. According to Burt, power accrues to those actors that occupy positions with other actors that are centralized or coordinated and deal with a diversity of other sectors that are themselves uncentralized and unable to engage in coordinated action. This perspective suggests that actions taken that (1) diversify the firm's dependencies, (2) direct transactions to less organized or centralized sectors, or (3) facilitate coordination within the firm's own sector, should enhance power and consequently those outcomes that follow from power. Following this logic, what is critical about diversification is not necessarily product diversification but, rather, diversification that causes the firm to depend on less concentrated and more dispersed sources of supply and customers. Providing products that require essentially the same inputs to similar markets would not constitute an increase in the firm's power. It is particularly critical to diversify away from concentrated sectors. This is consistent with the finding reported by Pfeffer (1972) that firms that tended to transact more with the government tended to engage more in mergers for diversification. Accomplishing the third part of the strategy, coordinating activity within the sector, might be achieved either through horizontal mergers to absorb competitors or through other forms of coordination—such as trade or industry associations, interlocking directorates, or joint ventures—or having coordination imposed by the government as through regulation.

Another perspective on interorganizational power comes from network analysis. Actors that are more centrally located and more interconnected should have more power. Note that this approach leads to a somewhat different set of predictions, as structural centrality is certainly not the same thing as structural autonomy. According to this approach, firms or sectors that are more central in exchange relations should have more power. Mackenzie and Frazier (1966), some years ago, measured structural centrality in the network of transactions associated with a wood products market. Following the argument that centrality is related to power and power to profits and other such outcomes, one could use his methodology to study other markets as well as the consequences of centrality in those markets.

Both structural autonomy and network approaches focus on transactions as they occur. But transactions and the discretion to use the power that emerges from networks of exchange relationships are both under the partial control of other authority such as the government. This institutional structure, as well as power emanating from patterns of resource exchanges, is somewhat better captured by resource dependence theory (Pfeffer and Salancik 1978: 75). This approach specified ten conditions that would affect whether or not a given organization would comply with external demands and, by extension, its degree of autonomy or power:

1. The focal organization is aware of the demands.
2. The focal organization obtains some resources from the social actor making the demands.
3. The resource is a critical or important part of the focal organization's operation.
4. The social actor controls the allocation, access, or use of the resource; alternative sources for the resource are not available to the focal organization.
5. The focal organization does not control the allocation, access, or use of other resources critical to the social actor's operation and survival.
6. The actions or outputs of the focal organization are visible and can be assessed by the social actor to judge whether the actions comply with its demands.
7. The focal organization's satisfaction of the social actor's requests are not in conflict with the satisfaction of demands from other components of the environment with which it is interdependent.
8. The focal organization does not control the determination, formulation, or expression of the social actor's demands.
9. The focal organization is capable of developing actions or outcomes that will satisfy the external demands.
10. The focal organization desires to survive.

Note that interdependence, in the sense of exchange of resources, is the focus of only two of the ten conditions. Other conditions focus on the ability of external agents to enforce demands (that is, for price, quality, or quantity), the nature of external actors' dependencies on organizations operating in the sector, and the visibility of the response of the organization or set of organizations. As noted in their analysis, power that emerges from resource exchanges is often proscribed on the one hand, and other forms of power are derived from governmental and other institutional actions and arrangements.

Some Implications for the Research and Practice of Strategy

The implications of the preceding argument for the study of strategic management can be articulated at several levels of generality. At the most general, it suggests an appreciation of the concept of "collective strategy" (Astley 1984; Astley and Fombrun 1983). Collective strategy involves "collaboration, or joint action by organizations on matters of strategic importance" (Astley 1984: 254). As Astley and Fombrun (1983: 577) have noted, "in a corporate environment characterized by increasing interdependence and ever more intricate networks of linked organizations, individual strategies are overwhelmed by proactive choice at the collective level. ... there is the increasing emergence of structures of collective action, ranging from informal arrangements and discussions to formal devices such as interlocking directorates, joint ventures, and mergers."

Hirsch (1975), almost a decade ago, taught us that in spite of numerous similarities in the characteristics of the product and the fact that both were essentially distributed through intermediaries, there were vast differences in profitability between firms operating in the pharmaceutical and the record industry, and indeed, recent evidence indicates that the pharmaceutical industry in different countries varies tremendously in its profitability. Hirsch's analysis points to the differences in profitability deriving from conditions of the institutional environment faced by the two industries, including restrictions on product entry, pricing, and promotion that are mandated by legislation and regulation. Hirsch's work suggests that understanding strategy in the two industries should begin by considering what the drug companies have done to both attain and maintain a favored competitive position and how they have done so. Many of these actions are cooperative and collaborative; most involve activities well beyond diversification, integration, and product market positioning, which constitutes the focus of more conventional strategic analysis.

Hirsch's analysis and argument also teaches us that there is probably more variation in profits or other measures of performance between industries than within. Ironically, most of the research and thinking on strategy seeks to achieve competitive advantage or compare performance variation across individual units. But this is not where most of the variation or the strategic action is. As Hirsch argued, the critical factor may be the particular sector or institutional environment itself and how and why it came to be structured the way it is. Thus, Burt's analysis of intersector variation in profits may be couched at precisely the right level of analysis, and the idea that strategy be analyzed at the sector or industry level of analysis is similarly useful.

As another example of collaborative strategy, consider the automobile industry. Two conditions stand out in this industry. First, it is likely that the recent robust profits are at least partly the result of import restrictions placed on the Japanese. Such restrictions were obtained through a coalition of automobile companies and autoworker organizations. Second, without exception all of the U.S. manufacturers are involved in joint ventures with either Japanese or European automobile companies. Furthermore, this practice of joint venturing now extends to some segments of the computer industry, to aerospace, to farm equipment, and Hall (1984) has argued that joint responses to industry changes is the coming modal strategic response. If such is the case, issues of coalition formation and negotiating the terms and participation in these interorganizational organizations will become increasingly important activities.

On a somewhat less general level, the focus proposed here implies attending to a range of strategic actions and responses that is considerably broader than that traditionally included in the rubric of either business or corporate strategy. Such activities include not only mergers to reduce both competitive and symbiotic interdependence (vertical integration), but also joint ventures, board of director interlocks, and perhaps most important, political activity of all shapes and varieties. The merger of subject matter occasionally occurring in business schools between the fields of business and society and strategy is more than serendipitous—it is essential given the critical role of political action in the context of corporate and business strategy.

And finally, on the level of specific research hypotheses and directions, numerous areas for study are suggested. If power accrues to those sectors of the economy that are able to coordinate and organize, we need much more systematic study of what Phillips (1960) termed *interfirm organiz-ations.* Pfeffer and Leblebici (1973) suggested that the movement of executives across firms may facilitate interfirm coordination, but they investigated only some of the determinants, not the consequences, of such interfirm movement. Similarly, Pfeffer and Salancik (1978) argued that interlocks among directors of competing or potentially competing organiz-ations facilitated coordination, but, again, the causes, not the conse-quences, of such patterns of relationships were partly assessed. Burt (1983) has investigated whether firms that attempted to coopt constraining sectors were more profitable, finding little effect. However, this may be for two reasons. First, as Burt (1983) noted, most of these interorganizational linkages already followed the pattern of constraints. More important, Burt's analysis tended to focus on coopting relations *across* sectors, rather than on organizing and coordinating activities accompanied by interfirm activities *within* sectors. An expansion of his analysis to incorporate the possibility of intrasector coordination as a predictor of profit and other outcomes would seem to be warranted.

We have already noted that network position might be used to predict survival as well as profits at the firm as well as the industry-sector level of analysis. The more structurally autonomous the position, the higher should survival prospects be. But ecology concerns birth as well as death, and it would be interesting to examine whether there is also more entry in structurally autonomous network positions than in positions in transaction networks that are more constrained. If Burt's analysis is correct and profit is higher under less constraint, and higher profit stimulates entry, then birth as well as death should be at least partly predictable from network charac-teristics.

However, entry into an industry depends on the stability as well as the pattern of network relationships. Consider a firm that is thinking about or actually trying to enter a service supplier segment of the construction industry, such as painting, plumbing, or electrical work. Certainly at times, the apparent monetary rewards look large. Furthermore, there are many general contractors and many suppliers of services, so that the industry would appear to be competitive. With limited capital required to enter many of these lines of work, and with the technology fairly rudimentary and stable, there should be both rapid and successful entry, particularly in times of high demand. I suspect there is not because as Eccles (1981) has noted, in this industry as in many others, apparently independent entities are actually organized and structured as quasi-firms. In this instance, each general contractor does business with one or only a very few subcontractors of each type, and these relationships are stable over time. Thus, this apparently diffuse and amorphous industry is, in fact tightly structured—so tightly structured that entry may be difficult, particularly for firms entering when there is not a corresponding increase in the number of general contractors so that success becomes dependent on actually disrupting existing trading relationships. This analysis and this example suggests that the investigation of network stability would be another important predictor of the likelihood of observing organizational births and the survival chances of already existing organizations and that the demographic (age-related) characteristics of such networks are critical.

If network stability is important, then factors that affect such stability are important foci of investigation. At the intraorganizational level of analysis, the argument has been made that the demography affects integration and cohesion (Wagner, Pfeffer, and O'Reilly 1984). In particular, individuals who enter the organization at the same time have fewer relationships already developed and yet need to develop networks for both task-related and social functions. Consequently, they are likely to develop interactions with each other, and interaction is argued to follow cohort lines. Extension of these arguments to the organizational level of analysis is straightforward. It suggests in the first place that firms that are of about the same age are more likely to trade with each other, ceteris paribus, and that transactions in markets may follow cohort lines where the cohorts are defined by the age of firms or by their date of entry into the market. It also suggests that entry into markets will be easier to the extent that there is more heterogeneity or diversity in the age of market participants. When there are relatively few and distinct cohorts, breaking into existing trading relationships, which are more likely to be more integrated and cohesive, may be more difficult. And, in general, the line of argument suggests that the demography of firms may be an important factor affecting the operation of markets and the structure of competition and entry, with these effects being particularly pronounced to the extent that the transactions are importantly mediated by personal or institutional relationships.

Two other implications for analysis of the content of strategy also emerge fairly directly from this line of argument. One has to do with cross-cultural comparisons and, particularly, with the issue of understanding Japanese business and their comparative success. Although the role of the

Ministry of Trade and Industry in actually organizing Japanese industry is debated, with some thinking there is a Japan, Inc., and others noting the tendency for firms to act independently of MITI's wishes, there is little doubt that Japanese industry is structured in a way that U.S. industry is not (see Clark 1979). There are stable customer-supplier relationships, not only in the automobile industry but in many others, as well as relationships among banks and industrial firms. Indeed, Clark (1979) has argued that Japanese firms are, on the whole, substantially less diversified (and often less integrated) than their U.S. counterparts but achieve many of the effects of diversification and integration through the development of stable and substantial interfirm organizations, bound together not only through commercial or trading relations and the transfer of capital but also frequently through the movement of employees from the central firm or firms to periphery organizations in times of economic slack and or at the time of retirement.

If we move the level of analysis up from industry sectors to nation states, this may help to explain Japanese industry success. For what may be occurring is an organized, fairly centralized sector trading with a diversified set of relatively unorganized sectors, exactly the conditions that should lead to structural autonomy and profit. The Japanese example suggests other cross-industry comparisons both within the United States and within Japan, as well as cross-national comparisons of the organization of industry as a predictor of profit and other outcomes. We clearly need much better information about the consequences of various forms of industry organization and structure, and here I refer to something much more than the level of concentration or the form of competition.

The second implication is that we also need to understand much better how industries do or do not come to be organized and structured. This might be accomplished in part by doing historical studies of industries. For instance, MacAvoy (1965) has written a very interesting book on the development of the Interstate Commerce Commission (ICC). He found that the railroads in the midwest were continually attempting to develop cartels in the mid-1800s to control the price charged for shipping grain to the east coast ports. The problems of cartel maintenance were severe because the industry had very high fixed and low variable costs and essentially sold an undifferentiated service, rail transportation. Thus, there were tremendous inducements for firms to cheat on the established cartel price, thereby generating additional revenues in the short run that exceeded their variable costs of providing the additional cargo carrying service. The history of the industry prior to the ICC was one of the cartel forming, breaking apart, and reforming. Of course, the creation of the ICC provided what the railroads had long needed, an effective sanctioning mechanism, and MacAvoy noted that once the ICC was created, freight rates went up to their highest and most stable level. A history of the railroads' involvement in the agency's creation, and as important, their attempts to influence its operation once created, would be an important contribution to our understanding of how industries organize. Similar studies might be conducted of other governmental economic regulatory agencies such as the Civil Aeronautics Board, utility rate regulating organizations, the Federal Communications Commission, and so forth. In this analysis, we need to go beyond the already numerous studies of the effects of such agencies on price, entry, and profits and to understand better how and why they were created and the specific strategic actions taken by the firms in the industry during this creation process and afterwards.

In addition to such natural histories, it is clear we need a much better understanding of how various interfirm arrangements actually affect centralization and coordination within sectors. As Burt has argued with respect to interlocking directorates, the presence of ties neither demonstrates cooptive intent by itself nor, certainly, cooptive effect. In this regard, the research that emanated from the resource dependence perspective on interfirm movement of executives (Pfeffer and Leblebici 1973), joint ventures (Pfeffer and Nowak 1976), and board of directors interlocks (Pfeffer and Salancik 1978) represented a very partial beginning of this line of inquiry. Demonstrating correlates of interfirm arrangements is not sufficient at all to indicate their effects; moreover, much more dynamic, time-dependent analyses of these processes are required. This area of inquiry remains an important and comparatively unexplored one for understanding how industries do or do not get organized.

There are also some implications of this recognition of the interdependent, relational nature of interorganizational activity to public policy. In particular, much of the current writing on strategy, such as Lawrence and Dyer (1983), Hayes and Wheelwright (1984), and Ouchi (1984) assumes a virtually complete correspondence of interests between private firms and public policy. The Panglossian argument is made that what is good for restoring profit and health to U.S. industries is also inevitably and invariably in the best interests of public policy and the U.S. consumer more generally. Such arguments are plausible only because these authors have either restricted themselves to internally focused responses that increase efficiency (such as manufacturing efficiencies as in Hayes and Wheelwright or organizational efficiencies as in Lawrence and Dyer) or because, as in Ouchi's case, the assumption is made that the inevitable conflicts of interest between organized industries among themselves and with other sectors of the society are best resolved when they are made explicit and worked out between formally organized and recognized contending groups. The first limited focus is clearly at best incomplete if not incorrect, and the second assertion that helping industries to organize themselves will serve the public interest is certainly an empirical question.

Rather, it is clear that profit is achieved in many ways and that its role as a signal of economic efficiency is not quite as good and pure as economic theory suggests. Profit is achieved by restricting imports, by obtaining industry subsidies from the government, by achieving the ability to legally fix price and restrict entry, and by more generally achieving power with respect to one's environment. Profit, measured in any way, is more than just the result of managerial good behavior and efficient production of what the customer wants. It is sometimes that, but sometimes not.

Most of these profit-enhancing actions come through political mechanisms, sometimes through bureaucratic agencies, sometimes through legislation, at various levels of government. There have been useful studies of the tobacco industry (such as Miles 1982; Grefe 1981) that indicate how the surgeon general's report discouraged new entry into the industry, which was also forestalled by heavy production and advertising barriers, thereby protecting cigarette makers' markets even as the manufacturers were able to achieve public actions that encouraged and facilitated cigarette export and forestalled action that delimited opportunities to smoke. The result is that most of even the most diversified cigarette companies' profits still come from the production and sale of cigarettes, not from the soft drinks, beer, or shipping lines and fast foods they diversified into.

This suggests that the role of the state and the production of public policy is inextricably linked to the study of strategy and of organizations, in a way that the current literature does not recognize at all. It might be noted that currently popular theories of public policy formulation retain much of the emphasis on methodological individualism and see governmental agencies as mere arenas in which the preferences and demands of individuals and other social actors become articulated and resolved. March and Olsen (1984) have recently critiqued this view of public institutions as mere settings, arguing for much more explicit attention to institutional factors in political life and the role of state institutions in both shaping as well as reflecting public attitudes and public preferences. Suffice it to say that the relationships of economic organizations to the state, broadly conceived, and a better understanding of the institutional factors of political life are requisite for the further development of a theory or practice of strategic management.

Finally, we can speak to the implications of this perspective for management, but here management is, as I alluded to earlier, well ahead of academic research. One set of implications has to do with the skills required by particularly those managers concerned with the formulation and implementation of strategy and the career paths by which such skills get developed and tested. If the goal of strategic management is the development of interorganizational power, then political skills, broadly defined, become critical. It becomes necessary to have skill at identifying and building coalitions of support, of being able to organize and mobilize sometimes diverse interests, of being able to effectively use political language

(Edelman 1964), and of being sensitive to external, collective factors that affect the organization's well-being. There is some evidence that corporations are already beginning to recognize this through formal job rotation and career development policies that bring high-potential managers to the firms' Washington offices or provide them exposure and experience in trade association or other broader, interorganizational roles. We would hypothesize that such career paths, including hiring executives directly from government service, would be more important and more observed in industries needing to develop more structural autonomy and would furthermore be associated with enhanced performance to the extent such strategies of career development were successfully implemented. No industry perhaps better exemplifies this approach than the oil industry, which has been a model both of joint action and, in the present instance of ensuring that executives on their way to the top achieved government and industry association exposure and experience. There are numerous possibilities for studies of executive career histories and how these have varied both over time, over industries, and even cross-nationally with respect to the incorporation of political or at least collaborative experience in the training and development profile.

Yet another implication is simply on the focus of attention of top management. If success is, at least partly, the consequence of the development and exercise of interorganizational power, and such power comes from the organization of one's own sector and the pattern of transactions and organization of other sectors, this suggests a focus on the task of strategic management that includes but also extends well beyond a fixation with product market entry and abandonment and the latest technique to try to wring more efficiency from the existing technology and workforce. It is indeed possible that in our focus on just-in-time inventory systems and lifetime employment and Type Z organizations (Ouchi 1981) we may have missed the critical, structural elements that contribute to the functioning, both good and not so good, of the Japanese economy. Here, too, the internal focus needs to be broadened for purposes of both academic research and policy analysis.

Finally, the skills of the strategic manager extend beyond those of implementing strategy within the organization to those involved in cross-organizational implementation. It is not by accident that when Peter Ueberroth stepped down as chairman of the U.S. Olympic Committee he had numerous offers from industry as well as from organized baseball. I believe there is growing, even if only implicit, awareness in industry that cross-organizational implementation of strategy, and the development of collaborative relationships across organizations is important and will become increasingly so. This is an area of research and practice that has yet to receive virtually any attention.

It is clear that the alternative conceptualization of business strategy discussed here broadens our view of strategic skills, strategic research issues, and what is involved in strategic management. In particular, the focus is directed outside the organization, to the structural and relational elements of societies and economies, and to the fundamentally political (in the broadest sense) nature of organizational strategy.

Conclusion

The argument made in this chapter is a simple one. As Presthus (1978) and Coleman (1974) have noted, we live in a society of organizations. But, as in most if not all social systems, that society is structured and furthermore is structured at times by institutions and by institutional arrangements such as governments, associations, professional associations, regulatory agencies, legislatures, and so forth (see Meyer and Scott 1983). The fact that relationships are patterned and that these patterns are at once social creations as well as determinants of social processes suggests that research on strategy incorporate this relational, institutional element to an extent it has yet to do. This requires moving away from the focus and emphasis on amorphous, undifferentiated environmental circumstances, broadening attention to incorporate a wider range of strategic actions and responses, and moving concern from internal adjustments and responses to attempts to manage, structure, and in other ways create a negotiated environment or order. It is a call to take relationships, quasi-firms, trade associations, and interfirm organizations of all types and other manifestations of networks, resource dependencies, and relations more seriously. Managers, it would seem, already are ahead of academic research in this regard, though theory is already available that can be used to help guide both research and practice of strategy in some new directions.

References

Astley, W. Graham. 1984. "Toward an Appreciation of Collective Strategy." *Academy of Management Review* 9: 526–35.

Astley, W. Graham, and Charles J. Fombrun. 1983. "Collective Strategy: Social Ecology of Organizational Environments. *Academy of Management Review* 8: 576–87.

Baysinger, B.D., and W.H. Mobley. 1983. "Employee Turnover: Individual and Organizational Analysis." In *Research in Personnel and Human Resources Management, Vol. 1,* edited by K. Rowland and G. Ferris, pp. 269–320. Greenwich, Conn.: JAI Press.

Bower, Joseph L. 1970. *Managing the Resource Allocation Process.* Boston: Harvard Business School.

Burt, Ronald S. 1980. "Autonomy in a Social Topology." *American Journal of Sociology* 85: 892–925.

——, 1982. *Toward a Structural Theory of Action: Network Models of Social Structure, Perception, and Action.* New York: Academic Press.

——, 1983. *Corporate Profits and Cooptation: Networks of Market Constraints and Directorate Ties in the American Economy.* New York: Academic Press.

Caves, Richard E. 1970. "Uncertainty, Market Structure and Performance: Galbraith as Conventional Wisdom." In *Industrial Organization and Economic Development,* edited by J.W. Markham and G.F. Papanek, pp. 283–302. Boston: Houghton Mifflin.

Clark, Rodney. 1979. *The Japanese Company.* New Haven, Conn.: Yale University Press.

Coleman, James S. 1974. *Power and the Structure of Society.* New York: Norton.

Collins, Norman R., and Lee E. Preston. 1968. *Concentration and Price-Cost Margins in Manufacturing Industries.* Berkeley: University of California Press.

Eccles, Robert G. 1981. "The Quasifirm in the Construction Industry." *Journal of Economic Behavior and Organization* 2: 335–57.

Edelman, Murray. 1964. *The Symbolic Uses of Politics.* Urbana, Ill.: University of Illinois Press.

Freeman, John, and Michael T. Hannan. 1983. "Niche Width and the Dynamics of Organizational Populations." *American Journal of Sociology* 88: 1116–45.

Granovetter, Mark. 1985. "Economic Action and Social Structure: A Theory of Embeddedness." *American Journal of Sociology* 91: 481–510.

Grefe, Edward. 1981. *Fighting to Win: Business Political Power.* New York: Harcourt Brace Jovanovich.

Hall, William K. 1984. "Global Competition in Basic Industries: Some Predictions on the Next Round." Presentation at Graduate School of Business, Stanford University, October 17, 1984.

Hannan, Michael T., and John H. Freeman. 1977. "The Population Ecology of Organizations." *American Journal of Sociology* 82: 929–64.

Hayes, Robert H., and Steven C. Wheelwright. 1984. *Restoring Our Competitive Edge: Competing Through Manufacturing.* New York: John Wiley.

Hirsch, Paul M. 1975. "Organizational Effectiveness and the Institutional Environment." *Administrative Science Quarterly* 20: 327–44.

Hrebiniak, Lawrence G., and William F. Joyce. 1984. *Implementing Strategy.* New York: Macmillan.

Lawrence, Paul R., and Davis Dyer. 1983. *Renewing American Industry.* New York: Free Press.

MacAvoy, Paul W. 1965. *The Economic Effects of Regulation.* Cambridge, Mass.: MIT Press.

Mackenzie, Kenneth D., and George D. Frazier. 1966. "Applying a Model of Organization Structure to the Analysis of a Wood Products Market." *Management Science* 12: B-340–52.

March, James G., and Johan P. Olsen. 1984. "The New Institutionalism: Organizational Factors in Political Life." *American Political Science Review* 78: 734–49.

Meyer, John W., and W. Richard Scott. 1983. *Organizational Environments: Ritual and Rationality.* Beverly Hills, Calif.: Sage.

Miles, Robert H. 1982. *Coffin Nails and Corporate Strategies.* Englewood Cliffs, N.J.: Prentice-Hall.

Mumford, Enid, and Andrew Pettigrew. 1975. *Implementing Strategic Decisions.* London: Longman Group.

Ouchi, William. 1981. *Theory Z.* Reading, Mass.: Addison-Wesley.

——, 1984. *The M-Form Society.* Reading, Mass.: Addison-Wesley.

Pfeffer, Jeffrey. 1972. "Merger as a Response to Organizational Interdependence." *Administrative Science Quarterly* 17: 382–94.

Pfeffer, Jeffrey, and Huseyin Leblebici. 1973. "Executive Recruitment and the Development of Interfirm Organizations." *Administrative Science Quarterly*. 18: 449–61.

Pfeffer, Jeffrey, and Phillip Nowak. 1976. "Joint Ventures and Interorganizational Interdependence." *Administrative Science Quarterly*. 21: 398–418.

Pfeffer, Jeffrey, and Gerald R. Salancik. 1978. *The External Control of Organizations: A Resource Dependence Perspective*. New York: Harper & Row.

Phillips, Almarin. 1960. "A Theory of Interfirm Organization." *Quarterly Journal of Economics* 74: 602–13.

Porter, Michael E. 1980. *Competitive Strategy: Techniques for Analyzing Industries and Competitors*. New York: Free Press.

Presthus, Robert. 1978. *The Organizational Society*. New York: St. Martin's Press.

Wagner, W. Gary, Jeffrey Pfeffer, and Charles A. O'Reilly III. 1984. "Organizational Demography and Turnover in Top Management Groups." *Administrative Science Quarterly* 29: 74–92.

Weiss, Leonard W. 1963. "Average Concentration Ratios and Industrial Performance." *Journal of Industrial Economics* 11: 237–54.

15

Joint Ventures with Japan Give Away our Future*

Robert B. Reich and Eric D. Mankin

*Source: *Harvard Business Review*, 29 (1986), pp. 78–86.

Listen to what these four businessmen have to say about U.S.–Japanese joint ventures:

> "They buy energy-intensive components here, like glass, tires, and steel. But when it comes to things that are labor-intensive, that stays in Japan." – Terrence J. Miller, official, Automotive Parts and Accessories Association.

> "People we used to do business with, we can't anymore [because they aren't competitive]. Instead of buying a given part from a supplier down the street in Chicago, I buy it from a supplier down the street in Osaka." – Robert W. Galvin, chairman, Motorola.

> "Cross & Trecker is committed to the business of machine tools, but it is not committed to build in the United States all or any portion of the machine tools that it sells here." – Richard T. Lindgren, president, Cross & Trecker.

> "First you move the industrial part to the Far East. Then the development of the product goes there because each dollar you pay to the overseas supplier is ten cents you're giving them to develop new devices and new concepts to compete against you." – C.J. Van der Klugt, vice chairman, Philips N.V.

Each of these businessmen is commenting on aspects of a trend that is reshaping America's trade relations with Japan and creating a new context for international competition. Very simply, this is the situation: to avert rising U.S. protectionist sentiment, Japanese companies are setting up plants in the United States, either as joint ventures or on their own; to obtain high-quality, low-cost products and components, U.S. companies are making joint venture agreements with Japanese companies. At the same time, U.S. companies are licensing their new inventions to the Japanese. (The *Exhibit* lists recent U.S.–Japanese coalitions in high-technology industries.)

On the surface, the arrangements seem fair and well balanced, indicative of an evolving international economic equilibrium. A closer examination, however, shows these deals for what they really are – part of a continuing, implicit Japanese strategy to keep the higher paying, higher value-added jobs in Japan and to gain the project engineering and production process skills that underlie competitive success.

In contrast, the U.S. strategy appears dangerously shortsighted. In exchange for a few lower skilled, lower paying jobs and easy access to our competitors' high-quality, low-cost products, we are apparently prepared to sacrifice our competitiveness in a host of industries – autos, machine tools, consumer electronics, and semiconductors today, and others in the future.

Before this trend becomes an irrevocable destiny, U.S. business and government leaders need to review the facts carefully and decide if they should follow a different course. Two questions, in particular, frame the issue: What skills and abilities should be the basis for America's future competitive performance? And how does the current strategy of Japanese investments and joint ventures affect those skills and abilities?

The quotes cited earlier and an examination of U.S.–Japanese coalitions across a range of industries suggest disturbing answers to these questions. Through these coalitions, Japanese workers often gain valuable experience in applications engineering, fabrication, and complex manufacturing – which together form the critical stage between basic research and final assembly and marketing. U.S. workers, in contrast, occupy the two perimeters of production: a few get experience in basic research, and many get experience in assembly and marketing.

But the big competitive gains come from learning about manufacturing processes – and the result of the new multinational joint ventures is the transfer of that learning from the United States to Japan. The Japanese investment in U.S. factories gives the Americans experience in component assembly but not component design and production. Time after time, the Japanese reserve for themselves the part of the value-added chain that pays the highest wages and offers the greatest opportunity for controlling the next generation of production and product technology.

In the auto industry, for example, General Motors has formed a joint venture with Toyota, while Chrysler has teamed up with Mitsubishi, and Ford with Mazda. All three deals mean that auto assembly takes place in the United States. But in each case, the U.S. automakers delegated all plant design and product engineering responsibilities to their Japanese partners.

Exhibit A sampling of U.S.–Japanese joint ventures

Bendix-Murata Manufacturing Company	Machine tools
Boeing-Mitsubishi Heavy Industries Boeing-Kawasaki Heavy Industries Boeing-Fuji Heavy Industries	Airplanes
Armco-Mitsubishi Rayon	Lightweight plastic composites
General Motors-Fujitsu Fanuc	Machine tools
General Motors-Toyota	Automobiles
Ford-Mazda	Automobiles
Chrysler-Mitsubishi Motors	Automobiles
Westinghouse-Komatsu Westinghouse-Mitsubishi Electric	Robots and small motors
IBM-Matsushita Electric	Small computers
IBM-Sanyo Seiki	Robots
Allen Bradley-Nippondenso	Programmable controllers and sensors
General Electric-Matsushita	Disc players and air conditioners
Kodak-Canon	Copiers and photographic equipment
Sperry Univac-Nippon Univac	Computers
Houdaille-Okuma	Machine tools
National Semiconductor-Hitachi	Computers
Honeywell-NEC	Computers
Tandy-Kyocera	Computers
Sperry Univac-Mitsubishi	Computers

The only aspect of production shared equally is styling. Under the Chrysler–Mitsubishi agreement, the joint venture will import the engine, transmission, and accelerator from Japan.

Or take the example of the IBM PC, which is assembled in the United States. The total manufacturing cost of the computer is about $860, of which roughly $625 worth, or 73%, of the components are made overseas. Japanese suppliers make the graphics printer, keyboard, power supply, and half the semiconductors. America's largest contribution is in manufacture of the case and assembly of the disk drives and the computer.

This trend spells trouble. If a Japanese company handles a certain complex production process, its U.S. partner has little incentive to give its skilled workers the time and resources required to design and debug new products and processes. Thus as their employers turn to Japanese partners for high value-added products or components, America's engineers risk losing the opportunity to innovate and thereby learn how to improve existing product designs or production processes.

Unless U.S. workers constantly gain experience in improving a plant's efficiency or designing a new product, they inevitably fall behind the competition. This is especially true in high-technology sectors, where new and more efficient products, processes, and technologies quickly render even state-of-the-art products obsolete. For example, as the Japanese moved from supplying cheap parts to selling finished products in the consumer electronics industry, vital U.S. engineering and production skills dried up through disuse. The U.S. work force lost its ability to manufacture competitive consumer electronics products.

The problem snowballs. Once a company's workers fall behind in the development of a rapidly changing technology, the company finds it harder and harder to regain competitiveness without turning to a more experienced partner for technology and production know-how. Westinghouse, for example, closed its color television tube factory in upstate New York ten years ago because it could not compete with Japanese imports. That same plant will soon reopen as a joint venture with Toshiba – but only because Toshiba is supplying the technology. Westinghouse engineers, who had not worked on color television tubes for at least a decade, could not develop the technology alone.

On the other hand, continual emphasis on and investment in the production part of the value-added chain will result in low-cost, high-quality products and a steady stream of innovations in products and processes. If current trends persist, Japanese companies will keep gaining experience and skill in making products. They will continue to develop the capacity to transform raw ideas into world-class goods, both efficiently and effectively.

The implications of this trend for U.S. companies, workers, and the national economy are uniformly bad. The Japanese are gradually taking charge of complex production – the part of the value-added chain that will continue to generate tradable goods in the future and simultaneously raise the overall skill level of the population. The entire nation benefits from a large pool of workers and engineers with skills and experience in complex production.

The United States, however, will own only the two ends of the value-added chain – the front end, where basic research and invention take place, and the back end, where routine assembly, marketing, and sales go on. But neither end will raise our overall skill level or generate a broad base of experience that can be applied across all kinds of goods.

As more and more production moves to Japan, our work force will lose the capacity to make valuable contributions to production processes. An economy that adds little value to the production process can hardly expect to generate high compensation for less valuable functions. If the current trend continues, our national income and standard of living may be jeopardized.

Japan's Investment in America

Japanese investment in the United States has given rise to automobile plants producing Nissans, Hondas, Toyotas and, in the near future, Mazdas and Mitsubishis. Japanese semiconductor and computer manufacturers have helped create a "silicon forest" in Oregon. In the last four months of 1984, Japanese electronics companies established 40 new plants in the United States that produce everything from personal computers to cellular mobile telephones. According to the Japan Economics Institute, there are now 522 factories in the United States in which Japanese investors own a majority stake.

Japanese companies are also building laboratories here. Nippondenso's research center in Detroit will focus on automobile electronics and ceramics, and Nakamichi's in California will develop innovations in computer peripherals. Furthermore, nearly every major Japanese company now funds research at American universities in return for the right of first refusal in licensing any products or technologies that are developed.

Although Japanese companies fund basic research at American universities, the results of that research go back to Japan for commercialization. At the other end of the manufacturing process, Japanese plants in the United States take the results of complicated production done in Japan and assemble the final products. NEC's new computer facility in Massachusetts assembles computers from Japanese central processing units and memory chips. The most sophisticated components and systems of automobiles are apt to be produced in Japan, even if the car is assembled in Michigan, California, or Tennessee.

Heart of the Matter

At the heart of a growing number of U.S.–Japanese joint ventures is the agreement that the Japanese will undertake the complex production processes. These agreements need not automatically turn out this way. In fact, there are many different types of international joint venture, and each type has different implications for production, distribution, and division of profit between the partners.

Consider the recent agreement between AT&T and Philips N.V., under which Philips will distribute AT&T products in Europe. The two companies each contributed resources to the formation of a new jointly owned entity. AT&T's stated goal was to enter the European market; Philips presumably wanted access to AT&T's products. AT&T could have sold Philips an exclusive European license to manufacture and distribute its products; it could have leased Philip's factories or built its own in Europe and used Philips as a distributor; or it could have bought Philips, a move that would have given it the Dutch company's factories and distribution network, as well as all of its proprietary products.

U.S. companies planning joint ventures with Japan usually find that at least one of these options is unavailable: they cannot buy a Japanese company. Still, U.S. companies can enter a wide range of potential joint venture agreements. Most of the high-technology joint ventures that we examined, however, were agreements in which the U.S. partner would sell and distribute the Japanese product; our study of 33 joint ventures between U.S. and Japanese companies in consumer electronics industries showed that roughly 70% took this form.

Under the typical agreement, the U.S. company buys products from its Japanese partner and sells them in the United States under its own brand name, using its own distribution channels. The IBM graphics printer is made by Epson in Japan. The Canon LBP-CX laser printer is manufactured in Japan and sold in the United States by Hewlett-Packard and Corona Data Systems. Even Eastman Kodak is joining the bandwagon: Canon of Japan will make a line of medium-volume copiers for sale under Kodak's name; Matsushita will manufacture Kodak's new video camera and recorder system, called Kodavision.

This type of arrangement is not unique to U.S.–Japanese joint ventures; European high-technology computer, semiconductor, and telecommunications companies are also entering into a disproportionately large number of sales and distribution agreements with the Japanese.

For many U.S. managers, these joint ventures make good business sense. Faced with seemingly unbeatable foreign competition, many U.S. companies have decided that it is more profitable to delegate complex manufacturing to their Japanese partners. Consider Houdaille Industries, a Florida-based manufacturer of computer-controlled machine tools. Beginning in 1982, the company set out to block imports of competing Japanese machine tools. It petitioned Washington for protection, accusing the Japanese of dumping and receiving subsidies from the Japanese government. When that strategy failed, Houdaille tried to persuade the Reagan administration to deny the 10% federal investment tax credit on equipment to U.S. buyers of Japanese machine tools. The administration rejected this proposal as well. Finally, Houdaille announced that it would seek a joint venture with Japan's Okuma Machinery Works.

The Machine Tool Story

Houdaille is not the only machine tool manufacturer to look for Japanese partners. James A.D. Geier, chairman of Cincinnati Milacron, the nation's largest machine tool manufacturer, noted in 1984 that "50% of the products we sold last year did not even exist five years ago. We've gone from being an industry with very little change in products to one with a revolutionary change in products." Many U.S. companies were unprepared for such a transition and as a result can make money only by selling advanced products manufactured in Japan. In 1983, more than 75% of all machining centers sold in the United States were made in Japan (even though many ended up with American nameplates), and domestic production has declined dramatically.

As imports have increased, international joint venture activity in the machine tool industry has accelerated. A recent National Research Council report on machine tools noted that "most of these joint ventures have offered the potential for low-cost, reliable overseas manufacturing for the U.S. partner, and an enhanced marketing network in this country for the foreign one."[1] For example, Bendix sells a small turning machine in the United States for $105,000. It can produce the device in Cleveland for $85,000. The same machine, produced in Japan by Bendix's new partner, Murata Manufacturing, and then shipped to Cleveland, costs the company only $65,000. Such compelling economics underlie Bendix's decision to transfer nearly all its machine tool production to Japan.

Or consider the case of Pratt & Whitney, which earns profits by distributing foreign-made machine tools. In July 1984, its president, Winthrop B. Cody, told the *New York Times*: "I wish we could make some of these machine tools here, but from a business point of view it's just not possible." Even U.S. companies that develop new products look to Japan for manufacturing. Acme-Cleveland's state-of-the-art numerically controlled chucker, jointly developed with Mitsubishi Heavy Industries, will be produced in Japan.

The Semiconductor Story

While not in quite the same straits as machine tool producers, U.S. semiconductor manufacturers also face increasing competition from Japan and thus increasing pressure to enter into coalitions with Japanese companies. Traditionally, the Japanese have entered semiconductor markets as followers, thereby enabling U.S. companies to reap high profits before the product's price drops. Once the Japanese enter, they rapidly gain market share by competing on the basis of a lower price.

Some of the most famous examples of the "Japanese invasion" come from the memory chip wars of 1973–1975 and 1981–1983, when U.S. chip makers ceded a large part of the 16k and then the 64k dynamic memory market to Japanese manufacturers producing at lower cost. In the spring of 1984, Japanese manufacturers controlled about 55% of the U.S. market for 64k RAM chips. Taking a lesson from these battles, some U.S. companies decided to delegate production to the Japanese at the start of a new project: in 1982, Ungermann-Bass made an agreement with Japanese chip maker Fujitsu by which Ungermann-Bass designs very large scale integrated circuits for local area networks. The company then sends the designs to Fujitsu in Japan for manufacturing.

Innovations and new products in the semiconductor industry are a predictable function of experience and engineering know-how: 16k RAM chips precede 64k RAMs; the development of the 16-bit microprocessor follows logically from the existence of its 8-bit forebear. Since technological leadership is linked so closely to production experience, the emergence of pioneering Japanese products will only be a matter of time. In December 1984, for example, Hitachi introduced a 32-bit microprocessor, thus signaling its intention to compete aggressively against U.S. companies in leading-edge semiconductor technologies. While both Motorola and National Semiconductor are producing a 32-bit chip, Hitachi's entry predates Intel's new product announcement. Intel introduced its new 32-bit microprocessor in October of 1985.

Hitachi's push toward state-of-the-art semiconductor production fore-shadows a new round of sales and distribution agreements. Soon executives at Intel or National Semiconductor will realize that Hitachi or another Japanese semiconductor manufacturer can sell advanced semiconductor products at prices that U.S. companies cannot match. These semiconductor companies might go to Washington looking for trade protection. More likely, however, they will try to preserve their profitability by negotiating sales and distribution agreements. National Semiconductor already has trading ties with Hitachi through which it markets Hitachi's computer in the United States.

A comparison of two joint ventures – National Semiconductor–Hitachi and Amdahl–Fujitsu – illustrates the different approaches U.S. and Japanese companies take toward joint ventures. Fujitsu and National Semiconductor both fabricate integrated circuits, while Hitachi and Amdahl manufacture IBM-compatible mainframe computers. Both ventures link a computer and a semiconductor manufacturer.

The agreement between National Semiconductor and Hitachi is similar to sales and distribution agreements in other industries. In an attempt to diversify downstream, National Semiconductor will sell Hitachi's IBM-compatible mainframe computers in the United States. Hitachi, however, will be under no obligation to use any National Semiconductor products in making its computer. National Semiconductor may thus find itself in the position of manufacturing chips for Hitachi's competitors while selling a Japanese-made computer that contains none of its own components.

In contrast, Fujitsu purchased a controlling interest in Amdahl in 1983. As a result, Amdahl will now buy from Fujitsu most of the semiconductors it uses in the manufacture of its mainframe computers. Fujitsu will not, however, sell Amdahl computers in Japan. In both cases, Japanese companies add to their manufacturing experience. Complex production stays in Japan, and the final products are sold in the United States.

The Story Behind the Stories

What lies behind Japan's direct investment in the United States and the coalition-building activities of U.S. and Japanese high-technology companies? What motivates U.S. and Japanese managers?

The Japanese hope to mitigate future U.S. trade barriers by investing in the United States and allying with U.S. companies. In 1981, nontariff import restrictions protected about 20% of U.S. manufactured goods; by 1984, protection covered 35%. To the Japanese, the trend is clear. If the Reagan administration succumbed so readily to protectionism, what can the Japanese expect from future administrations that may be less ideologically committed to free trade? Mazda is investing $450 million in a new auto assembly plant in Flat Rock, Michigan because quotas had prevented Mazda from importing enough cars to meet demand. Despite the recent expiration of voluntary import restraints on Japanese automobiles, Chrysler and Mitsubishi came to an agreement in April 1985 to assemble Mitsubishi automobiles in Illinois. Concern over future trade barriers was a strong motivating factor for Mitsubishi.

From the Japanese perspective, joint ventures with U.S. companies will also help forestall further protectionism. RCA was notably absent from the 1977 dumping case over Japanese color television sets. Because it had licensed technology to Japanese television manufacturers, RCA was benefiting from Japanese imports. In the same way, now that RCA is distributing a PBX system manufactured by Hitachi, it has no interest in pushing for trade barriers in telecommunications equipment.

In both joint ventures and direct investments, U.S. companies and workers become partners in Japanese enterprises. Japanese direct investment puts Americans to work assembling Japanese-made components. Joint ventures and coalitions employ Americans selling Japanese products. If trade barriers limit the flow of products from Japan, American workers will lose their jobs assembling and distributing these goods and U.S. corporations will lose money.

Why do U.S. companies find joint ventures with Japanese companies so attractive? Companies in emerging industries often view a joint venture with a Japanese company as an inexpensive way to enter a potentially lucrative market; managers in mature industries view the joint venture as a low-cost means of maintaining market share. In industries ranging from consumer electronics to machine tools, the Japanese have the advanced products American consumers want. Joint ventures allow U.S. companies to buy a product at a price below the domestic manufacturing cost. The Japanese partner continues to move down its production learning curve by making products destined for U.S. markets. Thanks to these joint ventures and coalitions, the efficiency gap between U.S. and Japanese manufacturing processes will continue to widen.

A Japanese Strategy

The trends of the past 40 years as well as current Japanese actions in the United States suggest the existence of a long-term Japanese strategy. The overriding goal of Japanese managers is to keep complex production in Japan. They intend to develop national competitive strength in advanced production methods. U.S. managers who want to take advantage of Japan's manufacturing strength may do so by selling Japanese products in the United States. They may also set up production facilities in Japan, provided they are run and staffed by Japanese.

Increasingly, American managers are aiding the Japanese in achieving their goals by channeling new inventions to Japan and providing a sales and distribution network for the resulting products. Burroughs and Hewlett-Packard, for example, have just set up buying offices in Japan to procure high-tech components from Japanese manufacturers. Over the next five years, we expect sales and distribution agreements to result in lower profitability and reduced competitiveness for the U.S. companies that enter into them.

The reason is simple: the value provided by the U.S. partner in a sales and distribution agreement is potentially replaceable. The U.S. company gives away a portion of its market franchise by relying on a Japanese company for manufactured products – in essence, it encourages the entry of a new competitor. As shown by the Japanese-dominated consumer electronics industry, these agreements can act like a Trojan horse: the U.S. company provides the Japanese company access to its customers, only to see the Japanese decide to go it alone and set up a distribution network on the basis of a reputation gained with the help of the U.S. partner. Even if the Japanese do not terminate the agreement after establishing a presence in the United States, Japanese manufacturers are in a position to squeeze their U.S. distributors' profit margins precisely because sales and distribution functions are so vulnerable to replacement.

U.S. companies are selling themselves too cheaply; in letting their Japanese partners undertake product manufacturing, they are giving away valuable production experience. Instead, U.S.-based companies could begin to invest in more sophisticated production within the United States. They could seek to develop in our work force the same base of advanced manufacturing experience that Japanese managers are now creating among their workers. Unfortunately, from the standpoint of a typical U.S. company, the guaranteed return on this sort of an investment is often not enough to justify its cost, especially when the alternative of Japanese manufacture is so easy to choose.

Production experience is essentially social. It exists in employees' minds, hands, and work relationships. It cannot be patented, packaged, or sold directly. It is thus a form of property that cannot be claimed by the managers who decide to invest in it and the shareholders they represent. This form of property belongs entirely to a company's work force. It will leave the company whenever the workers do.

An Economic Fable

Imagine the following: the chief executive of a U.S. company decides to invest in production experience. Instead of relying on a Japanese supplier for a complex component, top management decides to produce it in America, inside its own operation. The component costs more to produce here than in Japan – the equivalent of $1,000 more per employee. The higher cost partly reflects the overvalued dollar, but it occurs mainly because the Japanese have already invested in producing this component cheaply and reliably. The chief executive sees the added expense as an investment. Once the workers and engineers gain experience in making the component, they will be better able to make other products. They will learn about the technology and will be able to apply that learning in countless ways to improve the company's other processes and products. As a result, the company will gain $1,500 per worker in present-value terms. Thus the initial $1,000 investment is well worth it.

As might be imagined, the chief executive cannot get anywhere near the $1,500 return envisioned from this investment. As soon as the workers and engineers realize their increased value, they ask for more money. In this fable, they can, of course, ask for $1,499, since they are now worth an extra $1,500.

If the executive refuses to give the workers a raise, they can simply leave the company and work for the competition. Faced with a sizable loss on the investment, our executive vows that from now on the company will buy advanced components from Japan.

This fable is not so farfetched. Studies show that companies retain an average of only 55% of their engineering trainees after two years. In one study, the factor cited most often by departing engineers was "inadequate compensation," followed closely by "uncertain future with the company" and "higher salary offer elsewhere."[2] Thanks to such high job mobility, the engineers responsible for developing a new product or designing a cost-saving manufacturing process at one company in one year may find themselves using their expertise to help another company in another year – perhaps their first employer's chief competitor. Thus, companies that invest in production experience may ultimately produce profits for the competition.

The Japanese system of lifetime employment eliminates this problem. While not all Japanese companies subscribe to such a policy, most of the large companies making advanced products for export do. This system makes it unthinkable for workers to join the competition; they would leave behind friends, homes, social status – in short, much more than a job. In this atmosphere, an investment in production experience comes quite naturally. Benefits resulting from such an investment tend to remain with the company.

Furthermore, because of the abundance of engineers and because engineers stay with their original employers, Japanese managers can give factory workers more engineering support. As Andrew Weiss noted in an HBR article, for high-volume, low-technology products like radios, the ratio of production workers to engineers in Japan is about four to one. In divisions making more sophisticated products, such as very large scale integrated circuits, the Japanese manufacturers observed by Weiss employed more engineers than production workers. Weiss attributes the high levels and rapid increases in Japanese companies' labor productivity to heavy investment in engineering.[3] Most conventionally organized U.S. companies, faced with high turnover, cannot afford to invest so heavily in their engineers.

As a result of these organizational differences, U.S. managers have little incentive to invest in production experience. The Japanese, however, will be able to capture most of the returns from their investments in Japanese workers. U.S. managers are happy to buy components from the Japanese or build new factories in Japan, thus further contributing to the production experience of the Japanese work force. But what is really at stake is not where company headquarters are located for profits remitted, but rather the value added by a nation's work force to an increasingly global process of production and the capacity of that work force to generate new wealth in the future. We are falling behind in this high-tech race, and actions taken by both U.S. and Japanese companies only serve to further weaken the U.S. work force.

Changing Course

The current situation has severe drawbacks for U.S. companies over the next five years. Over the long term, U.S. companies that enter joint ventures with Japan cannot maintain high profitability by providing services, such as assembly and distribution, which add very little value to the product being sold. The resulting interplay, while superficially promising, could really be just an extended dance of death.

Profit Sharing?

As profits dwindle, management might at last look to profit sharing or other forms of employee ownership that reduce turnover rates. The lower the turnover, the more profitable are investments in the work force. Furthermore, profit-sharing programs will enable workers to gain directly from a company's investments in them. To return to our fable, when workers in a company practicing profit sharing demand their raises, our chief executive need only say, "Wait, and you will get higher compensation when our investments start paying off and the company makes more money."

In practice, however, it may be impossible to devise a profit-sharing system that solves the problem. In a large company, for example, employees of different divisions would have to be compensated based on their divisional performance – a difference sure to create resistance to transfer among divisions, which makes it hard to share production experience. Furthermore, a new system of ownership and an immediate change in managerial or worker attitudes do not automatically go together. Consider Hyatt Clark Industries of Clark, New Jersey, a worker-owned company in which management refused to distribute company profits, or the Rath Packing Company of Waterloo, Iowa, a worker-owned company in which the workers went out on strike.

Moreover, corporate objectives are often inconsistent with a goal of profit sharing or employee ownership. Unlike workers, corporations can move overseas. Why make risky investments in workers when safer Japanese alternatives present themselves? If we wait for U.S. corporations to increase their investments in their workers, we may have to wait too long. The plants that these companies will eventually sell to their workers will be obsolete, and America's comparative disadvantage will be too great to overcome.

Public Benefits, Private Costs

In this situation, government has an appropriate role. The difference between the social and private returns on investments in production experience is an example of what economists call an "externality." Other examples of externalities abound: when a company pollutes the air, it is using a public resource – clean air – for which it is not paying. The private company is, in essence, shifting a cost to the public – and thereby boosting its rate of return at public expense. In this case, government's role is to ensure that the company's costs reflect the value of resources used in production. The clean air regulations of the 1970s made managers include the costs of pollution – or pollution cleanup – in their investment decisions.

In the case of production experience, the balance between cost and reward is reversed: society as a whole benefits more than do most companies from investments in workers and engineers. Government should thus create incentives for companies that are doing business in the United States – regardless of where the company is headquartered – to invest in complex production here, using American workers and engineers. Companies should reap an extra public reward for investing in production experience to make up for the diminished short-term private reward of doing so. The government could subsidize investments in production experience through, for example, a human investment tax credit. The object would be for government to accept part of the economic cost of creating an important national economic good: more highly skilled, trained, and experienced workers and engineers.

In addition, government could support private investment in production experience in other, less direct ways. Federal and state governments could sponsor "technology extension services" modeled on the highly successful agricultural forerunner. An extension service could inform smaller businesses about the latest methods in manufacturing technology and undertake pilot programs and demonstrations. By sharing information and conducting classes, an extension service could help smaller manufacturers – the under-pinnings to the industrial base – keep pace with change.

Antitrust laws could be modified to permit American companies to invest jointly in complex production in the United States, thereby spreading the cost of the investment over several companies. The Federal Trade Commission allowed General Motors and Toyota to form a joint venture; would it have also approved a GM-Ford deal?

Our future national wealth depends on our ability to learn and relearn how to make things better. The fruits of our basic research are taking seed abroad and coming back home as finished products needing only distribution or components needing only assembly. America's capacity to produce complex goods may be permanently impaired. As a production-based economy, the United States will be enfeebled. What will also be lost is the wealth – the value added – contributed by the center of the value-added chain. And that is a prospect that should concern executives and government leaders alike.

Notes

1. Committee on the Machine Tool Industry, Manufacturing Studies Board, Commission on Engineering and Technical Systems, National Research Council, *The U.S. Machine Tool Industry and the Defense Industrial Base* (Washington, D.C.: National Academy Press, 1983), p. 44.

2. Eugene Raudsepp, "Reducing Engineer Turnover," *Machine Design,* September 9, 1982, p. 52.

3. Andrew Weiss, "Simple Truths of Japanese Manufacturing," HBR July–August 1984, p. 119.

16

The Characteristics of Joint Ventures in Developed and Developing Countries*

Paul W. Beamish

*Source: *Columbia Journal of World Business*, XX (1985), pp. 13–19.

By analyzing recent empirical evidence, the author shows that certain characteristics of joint venture multinational enterprises differ between developed and developing countries (LDCs), and that joint ventures in LDCs are characterized by a higher instability rate and greater managerial dissatisfaction.

Introduction

In order to manage numerous foreign subsidiaries and affiliates, multi-national enterprise (MNE) executives have sometimes treated the management of their joint ventures, wherever they were located, in a similar fashion. This has frequently resulted in serious performance problems. Why is it that all joint ventures cannot be managed the same way? As a partial explanation, this article argues that because environments differ, the rules of thumb which executives have derived from experiences in certain groups of countries will not be applicable in other locales.

Harrigan's "Dynamic Model of Joint Venture Activity" (1984) suggests in part that the external environment influences both the initial configuration and the stability of a joint venture. In this analysis, the external environment is considered to include such things as industry structure, competitive behavior, technology and government policies.

The purpose of this article is to demonstrate that developed and developing countries represent different external environments; the developing countries (LDCs) are considered a more complex and difficult environment in which to manage joint ventures than developed countries. This article shows that certain characteristics of joint ventures differ between developed and developing countries, and that joint ventures in LDCs are characterized by a higher instability rate and greater managerial dissatisfaction. The characteristics examined include reasons for creating the venture, autonomy, stability, performance, frequency of government partners, and ownership. Particular emphasis is placed on ownership/ control results and their relationship to performance because this has been the focus of most previous research attention.

The evidence to support these observations was based on the author's 66-firm sample of joint ventures in LDCs[1] and results from a dozen other empirical studies of joint ventures from both developed and developing countries. Not included are studies which look at joint ventures between firms from two Third World countries (see Wells, 1983).

Venture-Creation Rationales

In a sample of 34 joint ventures in developed countries, Killing (1983) divided the reasons for creating a venture into three groups: (a) government suasion or legislation, (b) partner's needs for other partner's skills; and (c) partner's needs for the other partner's attributes or assets. Assets include such items as cash or patents, while attributes which make a firm desirable for joint venture purposes are the use or manufacture of certain products.

Table 1 illustrates how joint ventures are created for different reasons in developed and developing countries. Sixty-four percent of the ventures in Killing's (1983) developed country sample were created because each partner needed the other's skills. Only 38% of the joint ventures in Beamish's (1984) LDC sample were created for this reason. The primary skill required by the MNE partner of the local firms was its knowledge of the local economy, politics and culture.

Nineteen percent of the ventures in the developed country sample were created because one partner needed the other's attributes or assets. Only 5% of the LDC sample was created for this reason.

Seventeen percent of the ventures in the developed country sample were created as the result of government suasion or legislation, whereas 57% of joint ventures were created for this reason in LDCs. Janger (1980) obtained a similar result in LDCs, noting that nearly half of the companies in his sample which formed joint ventures did so as a result of government requirements. Gullander (1976) added that the primary reason for many multinational firms, particularly in LDCs, to accept the joint-venture structure would be political. Tomlinson (1970), using a sample of joint ventures in India and Pakistan, also noted that the major reason for using joint venture organization was government pressure, explicit or otherwise.

A common misconception is that countries either do or do not require the use of joint ventures. In LDCs it is seldom so clear: a few LDCs require most companies to form joint ventures, while most LDCs require only a

Table 1 Relationship of stage of development to venture-creation rationales

	Developed country (%)	LDC (%)
Government suasion or legislation	17	57
Skills needed	64	38
Assets or attribute needed	19	5

few companies, usually those in strategic sectors, to form joint ventures. In several firms surveyed, the MNE realized after-the-fact that its earlier perception of being forced to form a joint venture by the local government was false.

Multinationals formed joint ventures in LDCs for a variety of government-related reasons. These range from the MNEs being legislatively required to become a joint venture to the multinational seeking an advantage in attaining government contracts by having local ownership. A frequently occurring scenario was one where non-tariff barriers such as import restrictions were initiated to the extent that the multinational would lose its access to the market if it did not establish a local manufacturing facility.

A number of multinational companies establishing joint ventures in LDCs already had manufacturing facilities (usually wholly-owned subsidiaries) in the host country. Most frequently, the subsidiary was converted to a joint venture after serious problems were encountered in trying to do business in the local market.

Stability

A joint venture instability rate in LDCs of 45–50% was observed by both Beamish (1984) and Reynolds (1979). This is consistently higher than the 30% joint venture instability rate found by Killing (1983) and Franko (1971) in developed countries (see Table 2).

It was possible to compare the stability rates of joint ventures between foreign partners and both local government and local private partners (see Table 3). Whether in mining (see Stuckey, 1983) or manufacturing, those ventures involving government partners had an overall instability rate of 56%–58%. This was much higher than the 43% instability rate of joint ventures between foreign and local private partners. Thus, even when the more unstable government ventures are excluded from the LDC sample, it was still well above the developed-country level.

A possible influence on joint venture stability is the age of the joint venture. The research partially controlled for this by including in the sample only ventures which were in existence for at least three years. Sufficient data was, however, not available to correlate stability further with age.

Table 2 Relationship of stage of development to joint venture instability and a managerial assessment of performance

Sample size	Development level of country	Unstable* (%)	Unsatisfactory performance (%)
1100	Primarily developed (DC)—Franko	30	**
36	Developed (DC)—Killing	30***	36
168	Mixed (DC and LDC)—Janger	**	37
60	Mixed (DC and LDC)—Stuckey	42***	**
66	Developing—Beamish	45***	61
52	Developing—Reynolds	50	**

* Franko defined a joint venture as unstable when the holdings of the MNE crossed the 50% or 95% ownership lines, the interests of the MNE were sold, or the venture was liquidated.
** No data provided.
*** Includes major reorganizations.

Performance

In Beamish's (1984) sample, MNE managers assessed 61% of their joint ventures as unsatisfactory performers. In itself, this statistic is useful because it provides some perspective on just how pervasive performance problems are with joint ventures in developing countries. This is contrasted with the much lower 36% level found in developed countries. These differences are summarized in Table 2.

Most of the joint ventures in the LDC sample that ceased operations did so because they failed. However, it would be technically incorrect to class all ventures that have ceased operations as unsatisfactory performers. For example, in one case the local government partner bought out the foreign partner's share in a venture after six years because it felt locals were capable of running it (which the foreign partner reluctantly agreed was true). Also, some ventures cease operations for reasons unrelated to being a joint venture, or as part of an intentional strategy. These are, however, all exceptions.

Many joint ventures involve more than two partners. However, there was no difference in performance between ventures with two, or more than two, partners.

Twenty of the 66 joint ventures in Beamish's (1984) sample were located in the Caribbean. The performance rates in Caribbean countries and other LDCs were comparable (see Table 4).

Table 3 Stability rates: government vs. private partners

Samples	Government partner			Private partner			Total JVs
	Stable	*Unstable*	*Subtotal*	*Stable*	*Unstable*	*Subtotal*	
Beamish— Manufacturing	5(42%)	7(58%)	12(100%)	31(57%)	23(43%)	54(100%)	66
Stuckey— Aluminum Industry	12(44%)	15(56%)	27(100%)	23(70%)	10(30%)	33(100%)	60
Total	17(44%)	22(56%)	39(100%)	54(62%)	33(38%)	87(100%)	126

Frequency of Government Partners

Few of the studies of joint ventures in developed countries made mention of any significant involvement of government partners. However, where the scale of investment was particularly high, or the business lay in an industrial sector important to the local economy, the use of government partners was higher. For example, in Stuckey's (1983) study of joint ventures in the aluminum industry, the government was involved in 45% of the cases.

In Beamish's (1984) LDC sample, 23 of the 66 ventures involved the foreign private firm having either government partners, public share-holders, or other foreign partners. In addition, in only two of the 23 cases was the foreign partner satisfied with the joint venture's performance; none of the 12 ventures with government partners was deemed satisfactory. Given the higher frequency of joint venture formation between foreign, private and local government firms in LDCs, these performance results are particularly striking. Yet these observations are consistent with those of other joint-venture research. In an LDC-based sample, Raveed and Renforth (1983) found that MNE executives favor forming joint ventures with local, private firms over other forms of foreign equity investment, including both wholly-owned subsidiaries and the other joint venture forms.

Table 4 Venture location—performance relationship

	Satisfactory performance	*Unsatisfactory performance*	*Total*	*% of total unsatisfactory*
JVs in Caribbean countries	7	13	20	65%
JVs in other LDCs	19	27	46	58%
Total	26	40	66	61%

Foreign private firms that had a local private partner were satisfied with performance much more often than with other types of partners (although overall satisfaction was still lower than in samples from developed countries). These performance observations provide support for the view that for MNEs to be successful, they require partners with knowledge of the local economy, politics, and customs.

Ownership

The use of equal ownership was advocated by Killing (1983) in developed country ventures. However, according to one writer on joint ventures in developing countries, "what should be ruled out is a 50–50 shareholding (since) this will invariably lead to a deadlock in corporate decision-making."[2]

In the LDC samples of both Beamish (1984) and Reynolds (1979), in a majority of cases (70%), the foreign firm was in a minority equity position, with only a small proportion (10–20%) of the joint ventures being equally owned. This contrasts sharply with developed country samples, where half had 50–50 ownership. These results are summarized in Table 5.

In an effort to verify the representativeness of the ownership levels found in the developed country sample and the LDC samples, an examination was made of the ownership percentages noted in the Joint Venture Rosters of the management journal, "Mergers and Acquisitions," over the period 1972–77. Of the approximately 1,000 joint ventures described, ownership detail was provided on 200 cases. Of the 153 joint ventures

Table 5 Joint venture ownership in developed and developing countries

		Frequency of equal equity (50–50) ventures	Frequency of majority or minority equity ventures
Developed country samples	Mergers & acquisitions N = 153	43%	57%
	Killing N = 40	50%	50%
Developing country samples	Mergers & acquisitions N = 47	20%	80%
	Beamish N = 66	10%	90%
	Reynolds N = 51	20%	80%

which took place between two firms in developed countries, 43% were equally owned. This is comparable to other developed country samples where 50% were equally owned. In contrast, 80% of the 47 ventures from "Mergers and Acquisitions" (1972–77) that took place between firms in developed and developing countries were majority or minority owned. A similar level was found in the LDC samples.

Also, Berg and Friedman (1978) noted that just over 80% of two-partner, US chemical joint ventures formed from 1924–69 had a 50–50 equity split. This again reinforces the high incidence of equal equity ventures in developed countries, a situation that is in contrast to developing country ventures.

Multinationals have in many cases succeeded in accommodating LDC aspirations for local dominance or equality in the shareholdings of local joint ventures. The MNEs have been able to accommodate the LDC desires by spreading the ownership of each venture over a wider number of parties. As a result, the MNE's share of the equity might still be equal to or greater than that of the largest other shareholder.

In Beamish's (1984) LDC sample, when the MNE owned less than 50% of the equity there was a greater likelihood of satisfactory performance. Also, MNEs which were minority or equal partners performed better than those cases where the MNE was the single, largest shareholder.

The most common reasons cited for a multinational taking a minority equity position were existing regulations and/or local tax advantages. However, the range of reasons cited was wide. One executive explained his decision to take a minority position by noting that "with a high level of corruption in the country, it is better not to be high-profile." A joint venture general manager noted that "those businesses in which the parent company holds less than 50% of the equity appear in the overall financial statements simply as an investment. This means parent company involvement can be much lower." Perhaps the most telling reason given for 50–50 equity arrangements was, as one executive noted, that "then you can't afford to quarrel."

Ownership-Control Relationship

Numerous researchers have correctly pointed out that there is no necessary correlation between ownership and control. While there is no necessary correlation, in practice a correlation has often existed, particularly in developed countries. For example, there were strong links in Killing's (1983) sample of joint ventures between ownership and control in developed countries. Seventy percent of the dominant-management control ventures (those operated like wholly-owned subsidiaries) were majority owned. Conversely, 76% of the shared-management control ventures in Killing's sample were equally owned by the partners. In the developed country sample of joint ventures, when the MNE was the minority partner, its role was often a silent one. This did not hold true in LDCs.

Researchers of joint ventures in developing countries have previously pointed out that local joint venture partners are rarely passive shareholders. In Stopford and Wells' (1972) survey, 88% of MNE respondents indicated that the local partner typically had at least some voice in management. In Schaan's (1983) sample of joint ventures in Mexico, all would be classified as having shared control. In Beamish's (1984) research on joint ventures in LDCs, no correlation could be claimed between ownership and control because the MNE had majority ownership in only 21% of cases.

Control-Performance Relationship

In his study of joint ventures in developed countries, Killing (1983) defined control in terms of the decision-making role of joint venture management, that is, whether it was an active or passive role. Control was measured by administering a questionnaire in which managers were asked to assess the "jointness" of decision-making regarding nine decisions (product pricing, product design, production scheduling, production process, quality standards, replacing a functional manager, budget sales targets, budget cost targets, and budget capital expenditures). To assess the "jointness" of decision-making, six categories of decisions were considered (made by joint venture executives alone, made by joint venture executives with input from local parent, made by joint venture executives with input from foreign parent, made by local parent alone, made by foreign parent alone, and made jointly by parents). Then, depending on the response, ventures were classified as dominant, shared, or independently controlled. The performance of dominant-parent ventures—those in which one parent plays a strong decision-making role and the other partner a minor one—were considered to be higher than shared management ventures. Table 6 correlates joint venture performance with the aggregate measure of control for Killing's sample.

Because two major detriments to joint venture performance—use of functional executives from the passive parent, and a major role played by

Table 6 Performance—aggregate control in Killing's developed country sample

	Dominant control	Shared control
Unsatisfactory performance	3	11
Satisfactory performance	10	9

the board of directors—have been removed in dominant-parent ventures, Killing feels they are easier to manage than shared-management ventures; hence, dominant-parent ventures perform better. He adds that dominant-parent ventures are managed much like wholly-owned subsidiaries: *all* operating and strategic decisions are made by the dominant parent. In dominant-parent ventures, all functional managers will come from, or be selected by, the dominant parent. They and the joint venture general manager will be evaluated on the same basis as plant managers for a wholly-owned subsidiary. In addition, the joint venture will be integrated into the dominant parent's management system. Finally, the board of directors will play a largely ceremonial role.

The third type of venture in this typology (besides dominant and shared) was independent, in which the joint venture management team was highly autonomous—receiving little direction from either parent. All of the joint ventures in the Beamish (1984) sample were managed by people supplied by one of the partners, in contrast to the 16% that were independently managed in Killing's (1983) developed country sample. Not surprisingly, autonomously managed ventures had the highest performance level of all since, to a certain extent, they were independent because of their success.

A second study conducted by Schaan (1983) considered the link between management control and performance. This study examined parent control in terms of mechanisms used to influence *specific* activities or decisions. This differed from Killing's work which focused on the amount of overall control and "who" did the controlling. Schaan's in-depth study of 10 joint ventures in Mexico concluded that parent companies were able to turn joint ventures around by creating a fit between their criteria of joint venture success, the activities or decisions they controlled and the mechanisms they used to exercise control.

A third study that considered the link between management control and performance was Janger's (1980). This American Conference Board report gathered data on the organization of international joint ventures from 168 joint ventures in both developed and developing countries. Using a management control typology roughly comparable to Killing's (1983), the report concluded that the survey and interviews do not identify either dominant or shared ventures as being more successful than the others.

Tomlinson (1970), in his examination of the joint venture process in international business, also looked at the control-performance link. In this study of 71 joint ventures in two developing countries, he examined the argument that a greater level of foreign control should lead to greater profitability. Tomlinson found that "higher levels of return were obtained from joint venture investments by UK firms with a more relaxed attitude toward control. This casts some doubt upon the theory that control is necessary in order to improve the operational effectiveness of a joint venture". Tomlinson feels the MNE should not insist on dominant control

Table 7 Summary of differences of joint venture characteristics

	Developed country	*Developing country*
Major reason for creating venture	Skill required (64%)	Government suasion (57%)
Instability rate	30%	45%
MNE managerial assessment of dissatisfaction with performance	61%	37%
Frequency of association with government partners	Low	Moderate
Most common level of ownership for MNE	Equal	Minority
Ownership-control relationship	Direct (dominant control with majority ownership. Shared control with equal ownership)	Difficult to discern because most MNEs have a minority ownership position
Control-performance relationship in successful JVs	Dominant control	Shared control
Number of autonomously managed ventures	Small (16%)	Negligible (0%)

over the major managerial decisions in the joint venture. He suggests that the sharing of responsibility with local associates will lead to a greater contribution from them and in turn a greater return on investment. Thus the literature seems to indicate a different emphasis—in fact a weakening of the link—between dominant management control and good performance when the focus shifts from the developed countries to the less developed countries.

Data were collected on control in joint ventures in developing countries and compared with observations from samples in developed countries. To increase the comparability of results, the measure of control used by Killing in developed countries was used in a subsample of Beamish's (1984) sample. In the LDC sample, however, consideration was given within the dominant control category as to whether this control was from the foreign or local partner. In the LDC sample, a strong correlation was observed between unsatisfactory performance and dominant foreign control. In only a small minority of cases was unsatisfactory performance associated with local partner involvement in decision making control.

Further reinforcement for the importance of shared decision-making in LDCs was observed when each individual decision was related to control. For example, control was always shared for the generally conceded important decision of capital expenditures, while one of the partners always had dominant control over the less important decision regarding production scheduling.

Conclusion

Table 7 summarizes the eight differences noted in joint venture characteristics between developed and developing countries. Performance problems, whether measured in terms of stability or by managerial assessment, were observed to be higher in LDCs. This held true even when the effect of poor performing business-government ventures in LDCs was taken into consideration.

The major implication of these findings for managers is to suggest that their approach to joint ventures in developed and developing countries should differ. For example, they can now recognize that their typical pattern of involvement with joint ventures (i.e., equal equity, dominant control) is neither common nor likely desirable in LDCs.

By being aware before the original investment that the management of joint ventures may be affected by the different environments, managers can better assess whether they should enter a joint venture in an LDC, as well as improve their understanding as to why their existing joint ventures perform the way they do.

References

Adler, Lee, and James D. Hlavacek, *Joint Ventures for Product Innovation*, New York: Amacom, 1976.

Beamish, Paul, "Joint Venture Performance in Developing Countries," Unpublished Doctoral Dissertation, The University of Western Ontario, 1984.

Berg, Sanford V., and Philip Friedman, "Joint Ventures in American Industry," Parts I, II, III, *Mergers and Acquisitions*, Summer 1978, Fall 1978, Winter 1979.

——, "Corporate Courtship and Successful Joint Ventures," *California Management Review*, Spring 1980, Vol. XXII, No. 3, p. 85–91.

Berlew, F. Kingston, "The Joint Venture—A Way Into Foreign Markets," *Harvard Business Review*, July–August, 1984.

Bivens, K.K., and E.B. Lovell, "Joint Ventures with Foreign Partners," *National Industrial Conference Board*, New York: 1966.

Burton, F.N., and F.H. Saelens, "Partner Choice and Linkage Characteristics of International Joint Ventures in Japan: An Exploratory Analysis of the Inorganic Chemicals Sector," *Management International Review*, Volume 22, 1982, p. 20–29.

Business International, "Joint Venture Checklists: 44–50," *201 Checklists: Decision Making in International Operations*, March 1980, p. 56–62.

Canadian Consulate-General in Brazil, *Joint Business Ventures in Brazil: A Canadian Perspective*, Ottawa: Department of Industry, Trade and Commerce, Government of Canada, April 1981.

Caves, Richard E., *Multinational Enterprise and Economic Analysis*, Cambridge, Mass.: Harvard University Press, 1982.

Cohen, Jerome Alan, "Equity Joint Ventures: 20 Potential Pitfalls that Every Company Should Know About," *The China Business Review*, November–December 1982, p. 23–30.

Coish, H. O., "Joint Ventures and Bilateral Trade Agreements," *Canada Commerce*, January 1981.

Cozzolino, John M., "Joint Venture Risk: How to Determine Your Share," *Mergers and Acquisitions*, Fall 1981.

Dang, Tran, "Ownership, Control and Performance of the Multinational Corporation: A Study of US Wholly-Owned Subsidiaries and Joint Ventures in the Philippines and Taiwan," Unpublished Ph.D. Dissertation, University of California, 1977.

Dilemma & Decision, "Should the CEO Proceed With His Joint Venture Plans?," *International Management*, May 1984.

Encarnation, Dennis J., "The Political Economy of Indian Joint Industrial Ventures Abroad," *International Organization*, Volume 36, Number 1, MIT Press, Winter 1982.

Franko, Lawrence G., "The Art of Choosing an American Joint Venture Partner," *The Multinational Company in Europe*, London: Longman, 1972.

——, "Joint Venture Divorce in the Multinational Company," *Columbia Journal of World Business*, May–June 1971.

——, *Joint Venture Survival in Multinational Corporations*, New York: Praeger Publishers, 1971.

Friedmann, Wolfgang G., and J.P. Beguin, *Joint International Business Ventures in Developing Countries*, New York: Columbia University Press, 1971.

Friedman, Wolfgang G., and George Kalmanoff, *Joint International Business Ventures*, New York: Columbia University Press, 1961.

Friedmann, Wolfgang, and Leo Mates, editors, *Joint Business Ventures of Yugoslav Enterprises and Foreign Firms*, Belgrade: 1968.

Gullander, Staffan, "Joint Ventures and Corporate Strategy," *Columbia Journal of World Business*, Spring 1976.

——, "Joint Ventures in Europe: Determinants of Entry," *International Studies of Management and Organization*, Vol. VI, No. 1–2, Spring–Summer 1976.

Harrigan, Kathryn Rudie, "Joint Ventures and Global Strategies," *Columbia Journal of World Business*, Vol. XIX, No. 2, Summer 1984, pp. 7–16.

Hills, Stephen M., "The Search for Joint Venture Partners," *Academy of Management Proceedings*, 1978.

Hymer, Stephen, "Comment by Stephen Hymer (on "Effects of Policies Encouraging Foreign Joint Ventures in Developing Countries by Wells)," in Ayal, E. (ed.), *Micro Aspects of Development*, New York: Praeger, 1973.

Janger, Allen R., *Organization of International Joint Ventures*, New York: The Conference Board, 1980.

Joint Venture Rosters, *Mergers and Acquisitions*, 1972–76.

Killing, J. Peter, *Strategies for Joint Venture Success*, New York: Praeger, 1983.

——, "How to Make a Global Joint Venture Work", *Harvard Business Review*, May–June 1982.

——, "Technology Acquisition: License Agreement or Joint Venture," *Columbia Journal of World Business*, Fall 1980.

Kobayashi, Noritake, "Some Organizational Problems," *Joint Ventures and Japan*, Tokyo: Sophia University, 1967.

Lecraw, Donald J., "Performance of Transnational Corporations in Less Developed

Countries," *Journal of International Business Studies*, Spring/Summer 1983.

McMillan, C.H., and D.P. St. Charles, *Joint Ventures in Eastern Europe: A Three Country Comparison*, Montreal: C.D. Howe Research Institute, 1974.

Nehemkis, Peter and Alexis Nehemkis, "China's Law on Joint Ventures," *California Management Review*, Summer 1980, Vol. XXII, No. 4, p. 37–46.

Patton, Donald J., and Anh-Dung Do, "Joint Ventures in Yugoslavia," *Management International Review*, 1978.

Peterson, Richard B., and Justin Y. Shimada, "Sources of Management Problems in Japanese–American Joint Ventures," *Academy of Management Review*, October 1978.

Rafii, Farshad, "Joint Ventures and Transfer of Technology to Iran: The Impact of Foreign Control," Unpublished Doctoral Dissertation, Harvard University, 1978.

Raveed, S.R., and W. Renforth, "State Enterprise—Multinational Corporation Joint Ventures: How Well Do They Meet Both Partners' Needs?," *Management International Review*, Vol. 23, No. 1 (1983), pp. 47–57.

Reynolds, John I., "The 'Pinched Shoe' Effect of International Joint Ventures," *Columbia Journal of World Business*, Vol. XIX, No. 2, Summer 1984, pp. 23–29.

——, *Indian–American Joint Ventures: Business Policy Relationships*, Washington, D.C.: University Press of America, 1979.

Riddle, Dorothy I., "Reflections on the Asian Perspective: Joint Ventures with the Japanese," (unpublished mimeo), May 1983.

Robock, S. H., and K. Simmonds, *International Business and Multinational Enterprises*, 3rd Edition, Homewood, Illinois: Irwin, 1983.

Roulac, Stephen E., "Structuring the Joint Venture," *Mergers and Acquisitions*, Spring, 1980.

Schaan, Jean Louis, "Parent Control and Joint Venture Success: The Case of Mexico," Unpublished Doctoral Dissertation, University of Western Ontario, 1983.

Simiar, Farhad, "Major Causes of Joint Venture Failures in the Middle East: The Case of Iran," *Management International Review*, Volume 23, 1983, pp. 58–68.

State Council, "Regulations for the Implementation of the Law of The People's Republic of China on Joint Ventures Using Chinese and Foreign Investment," *Beijing Review*, No. 41, October 10, 1983.

Stevens, J. Hugh, "Joint Ventures in Latin America," *The Business Quarterly*, Winter 1974.

Stuckey, John A., *Vertical Integration and Joint Ventures in the Aluminum Industry*, Cambridge, Mass.: Harvard University Press, 1983.

Sullivan, Jeremiah, and Richard B. Peterson, "Factors Associated with Trust in Japanese–American Joint Ventures," *Management International Review*, Volume 22, 1982, p. 30–40.

Tomlinson, James W. C., *The Joint Venture Process in International Business: India and Pakistan*, Cambridge, Mass.: The MIT Press, 1970.

Tomlinson, J.W.C., and C.S.W. Willie, "Modelling the Joint Venture Process in Latin America: Mexico," *Canadian Journal of Development Studies*, Vol. III, No. 1, 1982.

United Nations, *Manual on the Establishment of Industrial Joint Venture Agreements in Developing Countries*, New York: U.N., 1971.

Walmsley, John, *Joint Ventures in Saudi Arabia*, London: Graham and Trotman Ltd., 1979.

——, *Handbook of International Joint Ventures*, London: Graham and Trotman, 1982.

Wells, Louis T. Jr., "Joint Ventures—Successful Handshake or Painful Headache?," *European Business*, Summer 1973.

——, *Third World Multinationals: The Rise of Foreign Investment from Developing Countries*, Cambridge, Mass.: The MIT Press, 1983.

——, "Effects of Policies Encouraging Foreign Joint Ventures in Developing Countries," in Ayal, E. (ed.), *Micro Aspects of Development*, New York: Praeger, 1973.

Wright, Richard W., and Colin S. Russel, "Joint Ventures in Developing Countries: Realities and Responses," *Columbia Journal of World Business*, Summer 1975.

Wright, Richard W., "Canadian Joint Ventures in Japan," in *International Business: A Canadian Perspective*, edited by K. C. Dhawan, Hamid Etemad, and Richard W. Wright. Don Mills, Ontario: Addison-Wesley, 1981.

Notes

1. Paul W. Beamish, "Joint Venture Performance in Developing Countries," Unpublished Doctoral Dissertation, The University of Western Ontario, 1984.

2. Canadian Consulate General—Brazil, *Joint Business Ventures in Brazil: A Canadian Perspective*, (Ottawa: Department of Industry, Trade and Commerce, Government of Canada, 1981), p. 7.

17

Understanding Alliances: The Role of Task and Organizational Complexity*

J. Peter Killing[†]

*Source: F. Contractor, ed., *Cooperative Strategies in International Business* (Lexington, Lexington Books, D.C. Heath & Co., 1988), pp. 55–67.

Complexity is a key consideration in the design of corporate alliances. Managers of alliances created to undertake complex tasks using complex organizational processes require different skills and a much greater level of commitment than managers of simply organized alliances undertaking relatively simple tasks. It is important that both managers and researchers understand the nature and magnitude of these differences and the fundamental role that both task and organizational complexity play in the design of alliances.

This chapter provides definitions of task and organizational complexity and these definitions are used to plot a number of alliances on a complexity grid. Complex alliances are compared with simpler ones, and implications are drawn for managers trying to reduce the organizational complexity of alliances created to carry out tasks of moderate and high complexity. Among other things, this chapter argues that:

1. Alliances that undertake complex tasks do not always need to be organizationally complex. Task complexity does impact on organizational complexity, but so do a number of other factors.
2. Firms wishing to create an alliance to undertake a complex task should first enter a simpler alliance with their chosen partner, in order that a degree of mutual trust may be established, prior to the formation of the more complex alliance.
3. Relatively weak firms should be wary of entering alliances with strong firms, if those alliances are intended to take on complex tasks.

The ideas in this chapter are based on interviews with managers involved in fifteen alliances (approximately half of which were in the automobile industry) and an extensive review of secondary data pertaining to alliances in the automobile industry. A list of the alliances discussed in the interview sessions is contained in table 1. However, the examples used in this chapter do not all derive from the study.

Table 1 Alliance sample

Company visited	Alliances discussed
A.P.M. Ltd.	A.P.M.–Smorgon (NE)
AT&T-Philips	APT (E)
Ford of Europe	Ford–Fiat (E-NC)
Ford, U.S.A.	Ford–Mazda (ME)
G.E.C.	Six research alliances, all parts
	of the Esprit program (NE)
General Motors	G.M.–Toyota (E)
Saab-Aircraft	Saab–Fairchild (E-T)
Saab-Automobile	Saab–Fiat (NE)
Porsche	Porsche–Audi (NE)
Volvo	Peugot–Renault–Volvo (E)
	Joint Research Committee (NE)

Notes: APM Ltd. is an Australian company. All of the rest are European or American.
(NE) = a nonequity alliance.
(E) = an equity alliance.
(E-NC) = a nonconsummated (never begun) equity alliance.
(ME) = a minority equity alliance.
(E-T) = a terminated equity alliance.
Other alliances are mentioned in the chapter that are not part of this sample.

Three types of alliance were examined. These were traditional joint ventures, nonequity alliances, and minority equity alliances. Traditional joint ventures are created when two or more partners join forces to create a newly incorporated company in which each has an equity position and representation on the board of directors. Nonequity alliances are agreements between partners to cooperate in some way (to jointly carry out a research project, for instance), but they do not involve the creation of a new firm, nor does either partner purchase equity in the other. Minority equity alliances are similar to nonequity alliances in that joint activities are undertaken, but one parent does take an equity position in the other. The Austin Rover–Honda alliance, for example, is a nonequity alliance in which the two firms are working together to develop and produce, but not market, a number of different automobiles. The activities undertaken by the Ford–Mazda alliance are similar, but, because Ford owns 25 percent of Mazda, this is categorized as a minority equity alliance rather than a nonequity alliance.

Alliance Complexity

Although they used different words to do so, virtually all of the twenty or so managers interviewed in this study suggested that the key to successful alliance building is to create an alliance that is simple enough to be manageable. Complexity, they argued, leads to failure. When pressed as to what they meant by complexity, the managers highlighted two aspects: the complexity of the task the alliance was undertaking and the complexity of its organizational arrangements, as shown in figure 1.

Task Complexity

Three factors appear to importantly affect the complexity of the task that an alliance sets out to accomplish. These are the scope of activities the alliance undertakes, the environmental uncertainty surrounding these activities, and the adequacy of the skills within the alliance.

As indicated in figure 2, the scope of an alliance's activities will depend on its objectives, the number of business functions it encompasses, its duration, and the number of products it deals with and markets it serves. Some alliances, such as the 1979 Saab–Lancia alliance to jointly create a new car design, are very narrow in scope. This two-year alliance required engineers from the partners to work together to make basic calculations for the new model, to build prototypes, and to develop and test components. It involved no production and no marketing, and its objective was to reduce costs, rather than directly earn profits. In sharp contrast, Saab's 1980 alliance with Fairchild Industries was created to develop, produce, and market on a world scale a thirty-five-seat commuter aircraft. This venture was to earn profits and had no fixed duration.

The second important factor affecting task complexity is the degree of environmental uncertainty surrounding the activities of the alliance. The Saab-Lancia alliance involved a low degree of environmental uncertainty. Because its output was provided to its parents, the alliance did not have to contend with the potential unpredictability of customers or competitors. In

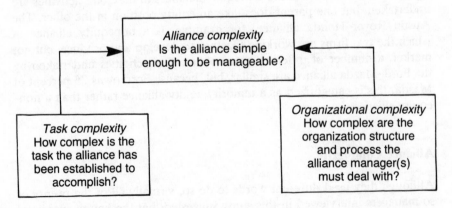

Figure 1 Alliance complexity

fact, it was even possible to specify the tasks to be carried out by each partner and the alliance budget, before the alliance was formally created. The degree of environmental uncertainty in the Saab-Fairchild joint venture was much higher. The purpose of this alliance was to earn a profit in a very competitive market. The attitudes and actions of competitors, customers, and government agencies were important and often difficult to predict. Such uncertainty makes the management of an alliance much more difficult.

Finally, the resources, competence, and familiarity of the partners with the tasks at hand must be considered. What is a complex task for one pair of firms may be much simpler for another pair, because they already have a good knowledge, perhaps, of the products and markets involved. The greater the competences and resources of the partners in relevant areas, the less complex, to them, will be the task that they are undertaking. A summary of the major factors affecting task complexity is presented in table 2.

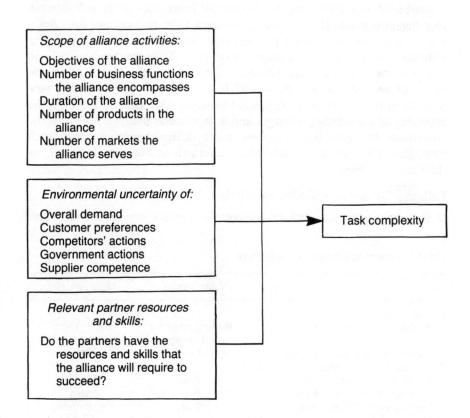

Figure 2 Task complexity, alliance scope, environmental uncertainty, and partner skills

Organizational Complexity

Organizational complexity arises in alliances when personnel from the partner companies interact to make and implement decisions that affect both firms. As indicated in figure 3, the more frequent and less routine in nature are the interactions, the greater will be the organizational complexity.

Causes of Difficulty

The rationale underlying figure 3 is that interactions between personnel from the partner firms are likely to be a source of difficulty because (1) initially, at least, they will not know one another very well, (2) they may hold differing opinions, attitudes, and beliefs, and (3) they may have different objectives for the alliance.

Don't Know Each Other

It can be difficult for managers who do not know each other well to work together effectively. If a marketing manager from one partner provides a market estimate to a production manager from the second partner, for example, the production manager may have difficulty deciding how to interpret the estimate. How reliable a forecaster is the marketer? Is the marketer an optimist or a pessimist? Is he likely to come in with a new forecast in two weeks time? A general manager who has to assess both the estimates of a marketing manager and a production manager's view of the constraints he faces is in an even more difficult position. Until such managers come to know each other, interactions between them can be difficult.

Differing Opinions, Attitudes, and Beliefs

It is quite likely that personnel from the partner companies will have

Table 2 Factors affecting task complexity

	Less complex	More complex
Alliance scope		
Alliance objective	Reduce costs for partner companies	Earn profits
Number of business functions included in alliance	Few	Many
Number of products included	Few	Many
Number of markets to be served	Few	Many
Intended duration of venture	Short	Open-ended
Environmental uncertainty	Low	High
Relevant partner resources and skills	High	Low

Nature of interaction	Nonroutine	moderate complexity	great complexity
	Routine	low complexity	moderate complexity
		Low	High
		Frequency of interaction	

Figure 3 Organizational complexity

differing opinions, attitudes, and beliefs. These differences will stem naturally from the corporate cultures of the firms involved, and they may be accentuated further if the firms are of different nationalities. One group of European managers, for example, was frustrated by the short-term financial outlook of their U.S. partner plus the fact that the Americans placed no value on continuity, changing managers every two years or so, with the result that just as the Europeans were getting to know someone, they had to begin again. Language can also be a problem; more than one alliance partner has chosen an interface manager on the basis of language skills rather than on the basis of whether that person was the best for the job. Possibly even worse off are the firms that appoint interface managers who cannot speak the partner's language.

Differing Objectives

It is no revelation to suggest that the partners in an alliance often have differing objectives. The more joint decision making is called for in such an alliance, the more these differences in activities will be highlighted. Thus, a joint venture, for example, in which the general manager has to refer many decisions to a board, which will contain executives from both partners, will probably be very difficult to manage well. The situation will be even more difficult if the partners have equal influence in the decision-making process.

Factors Affecting Organizational Complexity

Four factors that affect the organizational complexity of an alliance are listed in figure 4 and described briefly. All of these factors are likely to impact on both the nature and the frequency of interaction between personnel from the partner companies.

Number of Partners

The more partners there are in an alliance, the greater is the potential for organizational complexity. This complexity will make itself felt at the board of directors level. The board will consist of members from each partner, all of whom will be expecting, to a greater or lesser extent, to be involved in the decision-making process. An alliance with more than three partners may be quite unmanageable unless each partner has a well-defined role and sphere of influence from the outset, which may include one or more partners agreeing to play a relatively passive role.

Role of Each Partner

The more partners see themselves as having an equal role in managing an alliance, the more organizationally complex the alliance will be. When decision making is shared, there is a need for more (and probably less routine) communication between the partners than would otherwise be the case. For the reasons listed earlier, decision making between partners is likely to be time-consuming and difficult.

Previous research by Killing categorized joint ventures according to the role played by each partner.[1] Descriptions of dominant-parent, split-control, shared-management, and independent joint ventures are given in table 3, as are similar categorizations for nonequity and minority equity alliances.[2] The role played by the partners in an alliance will tend to reflect the quantity and similarity of skills and resources that each brings to the alliance. Generally, the more similar the skills and more equal the contribution, the more likely is a shared–decision-making alliance.[3] The relationship is illustrated in figure 5.

Level of Trust

If the partners in an alliance have previously worked together and established a degree of trust or at least a level of "mutual forbearance,"[4] organizational complexity is likely to be less than it otherwise would be.[5] In some alliances, there is a lot of dysfunctional interaction between the partners because they do not particularly trust one another. Neither is willing to let the other play a dominant role in any area, even though it may

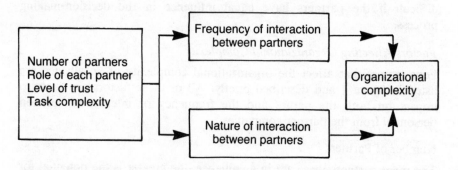

Figure 4 Factors affecting organizational complexity

Table 3 Alliance types and decision-making roles

Traditional joint ventures

Two or more partners join forces to create a new incorporated company in which each has an equity position and representation on the board of directors.

Independent ventures: Joint ventures in which the venture general manager is given a great deal of autonomy to manage as he sees fit.

Dominant parent ventures: Joint ventures in which one parent plays a dominant managerial role.

Split-control ventures: Joint ventures in which each parent plays a separate and distinct role, say, marketing on one hand and technology transfer on the other.

Shared-management ventures: Joint ventures in which both parents play an active managerial role so all significant decisions are shared.

Nonequity alliances

Nonequity alliances are agreements between partners to cooperate in some way, but they do not involve the creation of a new firm, nor does either partner purchase equity in the other.

Trading alliance: An agreement between firms that are actual or potential competitors to buy and/or sell technical information, goods, or services. See text for examples.

Coordinated-activity alliance: An agreement between firms to coordinate activities and perhaps share information to the benefit of all partners. Research alliances in which the total task is divided between the partners, each of whom works separately on the problem, are often of this type.

Shared-activity alliance: An agreement between firms to work directly together to achieve a common objective. An example is the joint research laboratory employing fifty engineers which was established by Bull, ICL, and Siemens in 1984.

Multiple-activity alliance: A nonequity alliance that has many component parts. The Honda-Austin Rover alliance, for example, involves production under license of two cars, the joint design and development of two other cars, and component supply agreements.

Minority equity alliances

Minority equity alliances are similar to nonequity alliances except that one parent has taken a minority equity position in the other.

Passive minority equity alliance: One in which the equity acquisition has been made, but no joint programs have been undertaken.

Single-activity minority equity alliance: One in which one joint activity has been undertaken.

Multiple-activity minority equity alliance: One such as Ford-Mazda, in which a number of joint activities have been undertaken subsequent to Ford's purchase of 25 percent of Mazda.

have little skill or knowledge of its own to add to the managerial process. The greater degree of trust between the partners, the less "unnecessary" interaction there will be between them.

Task Complexity

The simpler the task that an alliance has been created to carry out, the simpler can be its organizational arrangements. Perhaps the simplest of all alliances is the trading alliance in which firms that are otherwise competitors agree to buy or sell goods and/or services to one another. Peugeot's continuing sale of diesel engines to Ford of Europe is a good example. Typically, nonroutine decisions have to be made by both firms at the outset, addressing, on the one hand, "Do we want to sell to a competitor?" and, on the other, "Do we want a competitor's engine in our car?" However, once these nonroutine issues are settled and terms are set, the interface between the firms is typically handled by functional managers (of shipping, purchasing, and so on) doing their normal jobs.

Alliances undertaking tasks that require the combining of skills and resources provided by both parents need more complex organizational arrangements. If a joint venture is being formed, personnel are likely to be provided by each parent, and these people will have links both to the joint venture's general manager and to their original company. If a nonequity alliance is being formed, interfaces will be created between the partners using committees and boards at a number of hierarchical levels. Each of these integrative devices adds to the complexity of the alliance.

Combining Task and Organizational Complexity

The alliances surveyed in this chapter (plus a few other documented in case studies) were plotted according to their task and organizational complexity. A sampling of the results is shown in figure 6. As expected, the relationship between the two types of complexity was not linear—factors other than task

		Dissimilar	Similar
Equality of partner contributions	Equal	split control	shared decision making
	Unequal	dominant partner or split control	one partner probably dominates
		Dissimilar	Similar

Similarity of partner skills

Figure 5 Skills, contributions, and decision-making roles

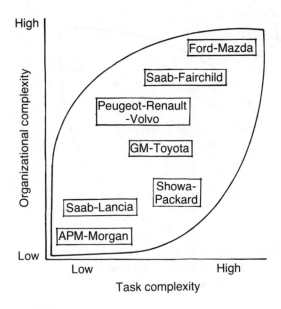

Figure 6 The alliance envelope

complexity do impact on organizational complexity. The Peugeot–Renault–Volvo venture, for example, was off the diagonal largely because of the number of partners involved (three) and the Showa–Packard alliance was located as shown because it was dominated by one partner. There were not, however, any organizationally simple alliances formed to carry out very complex tasks, nor were there any very organizationally complex alliances created to carry out very simple tasks. Thus, there is an "alliance envelope" in which alliances are likely to take place.

The critical issue facing managers is how to create an alliance with no unnecessary organizational complexity, bearing in mind that it has to be capable of accomplishing the task for which it was created. The arguments presented in this chapter suggest that reducing the number of partners, increasing the degree of trust between them, and separating their roles in the alliance are all important. Figure 7 indicates how these variables (with the exception of the number of partners, which is treated as fixed for this illustration) interact. The exhibit should be read as saying that an alliance of task complexity x (which is a split-control alliance with a low degree of trust between the partners) will have organizational complexity y. If the level of trust increases, the organizational complexity will decrease, but only so far.

The dominant-partner band in figure 7 is narrower than the split-control or shared–decision-making bands, reflecting the fact that the degree of trust between the partners in a dominant-partner alliance is likely to be less

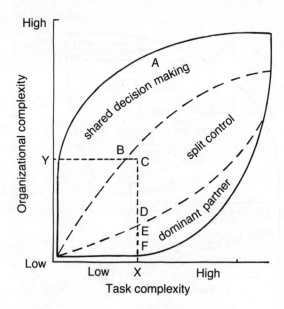

Figure 7 Alliance types

Note: Within each alliance type, low-trust alliances are at the top, high-trust alliances at the bottom. Thus:
Point A is a low-trust, shared–decision-making alliance.
Point B is a high-trust, shared–decision-making alliance.
Point C is a low-trust, split-control alliance.
Point D is a high-trust, split-control alliance.
Point E is a low-trust, dominant-partner alliance.
Point F is a high-trust, dominant-partner alliance.

important than in the other two types. This is because there will be less interaction between the partners in a dominant-partner alliance. Of course, the passive partner has to have sufficient trust to allow the dominant partner to continue to dominate (if, indeed, the passive partner has any choice in the matter once the alliance is formed). But, on a week-to-week basis, the partners in such an alliance will typically have little contact. The managerial implications of figure 7 for managers in alliances of low, moderate, and high task complexity are outlined in the following sections.

Low Task Complexity

Alliances undertaking simple tasks do not usually face a high degree of uncertainty. Whether companies are trading components or jointly developing a new car design which will be separately exploited by the partners, the economics of the alliance are generally quite clear for each firm at the outset. Because the economics and the major activities of the alliance can be specified in advance, there is need for little other than a nominal degree of trust between the partners. In fact, as figure 7 suggests, whether there is a high or low degree of trust between the partners in such an alliance will make little difference–organizational complexity in either case will be low.

Moderate Task Complexity

The organizational complexity of alliances formed to carry out moderately complex tasks can vary from quite low to rather high, depending upon the role played by each partner and the degree of trust between partners. Dominant-partner alliances result in the least organizational complexity, but are not always appropriate, particularly if the skills of both partners are critical to the success of the alliance. If the split-control or shared–decision-making models are used, trust will be very important, because if the partners trust one another, joint decision making and consultation will be restricted to topics and situations in which they are truly important. In fact, if firms are contemplating an alliance to undertake a moderately or highly complex task, they could be well advised to try something simpler first, so a degree of trust can be established prior to the major undertaking.

High Task Complexity

Unless one partner is dominant, these alliances are organizationally complex. They typically comprise a major business undertaking, such as the Saab-Fairchild alliance described earlier, or there are a significant number of component parts to the alliance, as is the case in the Ford–Mazda and Austin Rover–Honda alliances. Because of the complexity of these alliances, their total payoff and the ultimate distribution of the payoff between the partners is much less clear at the outset of the alliance than is the case in simpler alliances. Thus, reassessments, renegotiations, and reorganizations are quite likely. There will be a need for a high degree of mutual forbearance. The danger to a weak company that has entered such an alliance with a strong company is that it may be putting itself at risk in this continuing series of renegotiations. Each new bargaining session may reveal new weaknesses or reemphasize existing ones to the point that the weaker company may find itself in an increasingly poor position in the alliance.[6]

As mentioned earlier, potential partners may be well advised not to jump directly into an alliance of high task complexity. Both the Ford–Mazda and Austin Rover–Honda alliances were built carefully, one piece at a time. Ford and Fiat, on the other hand, tried to create a full-blown complex alliance in 1985 and it did not work. Saab and Fairchild did create a complex alliance in 1980, but, in 1985, Fairchild pulled out, taking a write-off of hundreds of millions of dollars in the process. A complex alliance is a difficult place to begin a relationship.

Conclusions

The purpose of this chapter has been to create a framework for analyzing alliances. It suggests that if managers and researchers explicitly consider both the task and organizational complexity of alliances they are working with, they may gain new insights into their performance problems or opportunities. A high level of complexity in alliances is not a given; complexity is a factor that can and should be managed.

Notes

† This chapter was written with the assistance of Michael Wray and benefitted from the comments of Professors José de la Torré (UCLA), Jim Ellert (IMEDE), Nick Fry and Rod White (University of Western Ontario), and Paul Beamish (Wilfrid Laurier University). Funding was provided by both IMEDE and the University of Western Ontario.

1. J.P. Killing, "How to Make a Global Joint Venture Work," *Harvard Business Review*, volume 60 (3), 120–27, 1982.

2. The notion of a "split-control" alliance, although not using this terminology, was presented in J.A. Cantwell and J.H. Dunning, "The New Forms of International Involvement of British Firms in the Third World," Proceedings of the European International Business Association, 1984.

3. For a discussion of the relationship between ownership and control, see J.P. Killing, *Strategies for Joint Venture Success* (New York: Praeger, 1983); and J.L. Schaan "Parent Control and Joint Venture Success: The Case of Mexico," unpublished doctoral dissertation, University of Western Ontario, 1983.

4. *Mutual forbearance* is a term taken from chapter 2 in this book [*Understanding Alliances*] by P.J. Buckley and M. Casson, "A Theory of Cooperation in International Business," which captures the notion that alliance partners would "deliberately pass up short-term advantages" which they could take at the expense of their partners, in the interests of keeping the alliance alive.

5. The role of trust in alliances is described in more detail by Paul Beamish, "Joint Venture Performance in Developing Countries," unpublished doctoral dissertation. University of Western Ontario, 1984.

6. A similar argument is documented in G. Hamel, Y. Doz, and C.K. Prahalad, "Strategic Partnership: Success or Surrender," prepared for the Rutgers-Wharton Conference on Cooperative Strategies in International Business, held in New Brunswick, N.J., in October 1986.

18

Multinational Corporations: Control Systems and Delegation Issues*

B.R. Baliga and Alfred M. Jaeger†

*Source: *Journal of International Business Studies*, 15 (Fall 1984), pp. 25–40.

Abstract. The paper has 2 major objectives: first, to identify control and delegation issues confronting multinational corporation managers; second, to develop a conceptual model to assist multinational corporation managers in selecting appropriate control systems and determining the extent of delegation to be provided to subsidiary managers. Finally, the paper suggests directions for future research.

Introduction

Students of organizations have been greatly concerned with issues of control and decision making [Mintzberg 1979; Child and Keiser 1978; Khandwalla 1977; Child 1977, 1972; Edström and Galbraith 1977; Beyer and Lodahl 1976; Donaldson 1975; Ouchi and McGuire 1975; Kochen and Deutsch 1973; Galbraith 1973; Hall 1972, 1968; Allison 1971; Perrow 1970; Hage and Aiken 1967; Emery 1969; Crozier 1964; Braybrooke and Lindblom 1963; Simon 1957]. As organizations grow in size they tend to differentiate, that is, the various components of the organization differ on the dimensions of time horizons, goals, interpersonal orientation, and the formality of their structures [Lawrence and Lorsch 1967]. The coordination and integration of the different units emerge as very specific problems that top management has to grapple with [Robbins 1983; Mintzberg 1979; Child 1977; Lorsch 1970]. These problems are all the more acute in the case of multinational corporations (MNCs) that are geographically dispersed and that operate in environments of varying degrees of complexity, heterogeneity, stability, and hostility [Fayerweather 1978]. Various coordinating mechanisms, including direct supervision, mutual adjustment, and standardization of input skills, work processes, and outputs [Mintzberg 1979], are utilized along with control and decision-making systems to integrate the various units. An understanding of these is, therefore, of crucial importance to all managers, particularly the multinational corporation managers for whom these problems are more acute.

This paper will first examine the concept of control and decision making in the context of multinational corporations. Subsequent sections will consider some specific contingencies that affect control and decision making. Finally, a model will be developed to assist multinational corporation managers in selecting systems of control and decision making.

Control and Control Systems

According to Child [1973, p. 117], "Control is essentially concerned with regulating the activities within an organization so that they are in accord with the expectations established in policies, plans, and targets." This definition is consistent with Tannenbaum's definition [1968] which states that the importance of control is to ensure "achievement of the ultimate purposes of the organization." Control, therefore, encompasses any process in which a person (or group of persons, or organization of persons) determines or intentionally affects what another person, group, or organization will do.

At the heart of control is the monitoring process. Ouchi [1977] points out that there are only 2 phenomena which can be monitored and evaluated; behavior and output. If output measures are readily available and valid, then output is monitored and controlled. Mintzberg [1979] labels this "performance control." The focus here is on ends, leaving organizational members flexibility in choosing the means. If output measures are not readily available or their validity is questionable, then another type of control, which Mintzberg labels "action planning," can be employed. Action planning is considerably more restrictive than performance control. It imposes specific decisions and actions at specific points in time. If action planning is carried through to its logical extreme, behavior formalization results wherein the means by which actions and decisions to be carried out are specified. In instances where it is difficult, if not impossible, to specify, monitor, and control behavior or output (foreign missionaries, for example), organizations may have no choice but to indoctrinate their members to the organizational values and mission and hope that their members' acts are consistent with organizational intent. The consequences of member actions in these organizations may not be known for fairly long periods of time, making day-to-day control difficult.

Child [1973, 1972] asserts that organizations can choose between personal control systems or bureaucratic control systems in order to monitor output or behavior. In the MNC context, the personal or direct type of control involves placing a number of trustworthy personnel from headquarters in key positions in the subsidiary to supervise subsidiary functioning. The bureaucratic mode, on the other hand, utilizes extensive sets of rules, regulations, and procedures that clearly limit subsidiary management's role and authority. Edström and Galbraith [1977] claim that a third type of control exists: control by socialization. This is characterized by a significant proportion of expatriates in upper and middle management positions, frequent information exchange between headquarters and subsidiaries, and a de-emphasis of formalization.

It is the contention of this paper that the "personal" type of control and "control by socialization" are specific attributes of what can be termed "cultural control." The focus, therefore, will be on cultural control and bureaucratic control as the 2 dominant control systems that corporate management can utilize to control their subsidiaries. These can be conceptualized as Weberian "ideal types" and in their extreme "pure" form can be regarded as opposite approaches to organizational control. Although such ideal types are never found in the pure form in reality, they are a useful tool for the conceptualization of organizational processes.

Bureaucratic Control

The bureaucratic model is extensively employed in Western organizations. Child [1973] notes that it consists of the utilization of a limited and explicit set of codified rules and regulations which delineate desired performance in terms of output and/or behavior. For an individual to become a functional member of a bureaucratic organization, he must accept the legitimacy of the organization's authority, and he must learn the rules and regulations so that he can indeed follow them. Etzioni [1980] points out that the authority and power exercised in this system is through control over resources, that is, it is of the "remunerative" type, and personal involvement is "calculative" or relatively limited. In Schein's [1980] terms, the individual must only accept the pivotal organizational norms, and these are fairly narrow in scope.

A bureaucratic control system has several implications for the selection, training, and monitoring of organizational members. Persons must be found who have the technical skills required (or are trainable), who will accept the organization's authority, and who can learn the organization's rules and regulations and perform in accordance with them. The selection process is fairly straightforward, as the "zone of indifference" [Barnard 1951] required of individuals is relatively narrow. Training is also relatively straightforward: new members must be taught the rules and regulations which are explicit and written down. In addition, they must learn whatever technical competence is required of their position. Monitoring in a bureaucratic system involves comparing an individual's behavior and output to the standards set forth in the rules and regulations and applying the rewards or sanctions prescribed therein.

Cultural Control

A notable alternative to the bureaucratic model is one that is prevalent in the larger Japanese organizations as well as some Western organizations [Deal and Kennedy 1982]. The Japanese organization has been described in some detail by a number of researchers [for example, Hatvany and Pucik 1981; Pascale and Athos 1981; Clark 1979; Johnson and Ouchi 1974; Rohlen 1974; and Abegglen 1958]. Most noticeable among the Western organizations with an organizational culture are Type Z organizations [Ouchi 1981], and a number of the "excellent" firms described by Peters and Waterman [1983]. Control in all of these organizations is more implicit and informal rather than explicit and formal. The direction that is provided to organizational members is of an aggregate rather than specific nature. Employees are employed for a long period or even for life; they are very loyal to the organization and they behave in accordance with the company "way." Even though explicit formal control mechanisms are present, control is essentially based on a broad organization-wide culture.

Organizational culture has been defined as a "pattern of beliefs and expectations shared by the organization's members" [Schwartz and Davis 1981, p. 32]. It generates over time a system of symbols, language, ideology, rituals, images, and myths that shapes the behavior of individuals and groups in the organization. Keesing [1974] views culture as an individual's "theory of what his fellows know, believe and mean, his theory of the code being followed, the game being played." In a cultural control organization, there exists such an inferred organizational code, an organizational game, which is an important guide to behavior in addition to whatever explicit rules do exist. This view of corporate culture of an adaptive and regulatory mechanism has also been identified in recent reviews of the organization theory literature [Smircich 1983].

OBJECT OF CONTROL	TYPE OF CONTROL	
	Pure bureaucratic/ formalized control	Pure cultural control
Output	Formal performance reports	Shared norms of performance
Behavior	Company manuals	Shared philosophy of management

Figure 1 Comparison of bureaucratic and cultural control mechanisms

A number of organizational practices facilitate the existence of a cultural control system. Most important are long-term employment guarantees, consensual decision making, and nonspecialized career paths. Linton [1936], the anthropologist, has pointed out that stability of membership in a cultural group is necessary for the existence and continuity of a culture. Long-term employment provides such stability. The prospect that a new employee will remain for a long period of time allows the organization to make an investment in the socialization of the individual. [See Hatvany and Pucik 1981 for a further description of this process in large Japanese firms.] The consensual decision-making process forces interaction around organizational issues among organizational members. This interaction is one of the ways in which, through a process of repeated interactions over time, cultural values become systematized and shared. In addition, the fact that career paths in a cultural control organization are less than totally specialized means that persons are rotated through the various functional areas of the organization, thus contributing to a greater organization-wide culture. A less than total commitment to a functional specialty on the part of organizational members reduces competition from outside professional groups for members' loyalty, thus enhancing the potential strength of the corporate culture. As a result, an employee develops the "moral commitment" to the organization which Etzioni [1980] associates with the normative type of power and authority.

The use of a cultural control system has several implications for the selection, training, and monitoring of organizational members. Members of an organization with cultural control must be integrated into the organizational culture in order to be functional members of the organization. Therefore, selection of members is of prime importance. In addition to having the requisite skill necessary for the job, a candidate for organizational membership must be sympathetic to the organizational culture and must be willing to learn and to accept its norms, values, and behavioral prescriptions. Thus, the initial "zone of indifference" required of new members is fairly broad and specific.

Compared to a bureaucratic control system, training and socialization in a cultural control organization are also more important. An organizational member must not only learn a set of explicit, codified rules and regulations, but he must also learn and become a part of a subtle and complex control system which consists of a broad range of "pivotal" values. Thus, training and socialization can be quite intense and extensive. The degree of socialization required is reduced if the broader societal culture is approximately similar to that of the organization.

Monitoring in a pure cultural control system occurs through interpersonal interactions. All members of the culture are familiar with and share its expectations. Performance and compliance with the culture are observed during the course of interpersonal interactions. Feedback is given on a person-to-person basis and can be of a subtle nature. In addition, a culture is a very rich and broad guide to behavior, so that an individual and the persons around him will always have an implicit sense of his perform- ance in the context of that culture. The contrast between bureaucratic control and cultural control is summarized in Figure 1.

The notion of the use of an organizational culture for control of MNC subsidiaries and the processes associated with such control have been examined by Edström and Galbraith [1977]. They studied the transfer of managers between countries in 3 European multinational firms. They concluded that the transfer of managers from subsidiary to subsidiary was a distinct control strategy in one firm. This process created international, interpersonal verbal information networks throughout the firm which were utilized for coordination and control. On a more global level, Stopford and Wells [1972] point out that one way of combatting control problems is the creation of a sense of cooperation and shared values among organization members around the world. They also point out that this requires heavy expenditures for communication, including frequent meetings and retraining sessions.

A final example of studies of organizational culture in a multinational firm is the retrospective look by Peter Kuin [1972] at his experiences as an executive with Unilever. He found that the "magic" which helped Unilever to function multinationally was its distinct corporate culture. This culture was maintainable because of the long tenure of the employees and the fact that almost everyone knew English. He noted a distinct enculturation process which included in-house training programs and the rotation of managers around the world.

Delegation and Control Systems

A parallel issue to that of control is delegation. Although most managers will readily agree that there are very valid reasons for delegation, such as, information overload at the top, need for responsiveness to local con- ditions, and stimulus for motivation down the hierarchy, they are often perplexed by the issue of "how much to delegate?" The issue is particularly complex in the context of multinational corporations. Geographic dispersal, in theory, should encourage headquarters to delegate as much as possible to subsidiary managers because this increases responsiveness to local conditions, results in decisions being made at the level where infor- mation is available, and assists in the development of subsidiary managers. Geographic dispersal, however, also raises fears among top management that subsidiary managers would work toward parochial ends and that head- quarters managers' realization of this would come too late to prevent crises from developing. These fears tend to limit the actual delegation to sub- sidiary management.

Until recently, bureaucratic control, or bureaucratization, was equated with centralization; that is, the authority of lower level managers in the organization to make significant decisions was considered very limited or, in extreme cases, nonexistent. As a result, "bureaucracy" became a pejorative term. Based on data obtained from a study on the structuring of organizations, Child and Mansfield [1972] claimed that it was possible to have decentralization within a bureaucratic framework enabling people lower down in the organization to have power. Crozier [1964], however, has argued otherwise.

A review of other studies by Mintzberg [1979] did not discern any significant relationship between centralization and bureaucratization. He concluded that this finding was not surprising given the lack of conceptual clarity of the variables in these studies. Mintzberg proceeded to explain the conflicting nature of the finding on bureaucratization and centralization by claiming that previous research [Manns 1976; Mansfield 1973; Child 1972; Blau and Schoenherr 1971; Inkson, Pugh, and Hickson 1979; Pugh et al. 1963–64] had failed to discern between 2 types of bureaucracies— machine and professional. Machine bureaucracies operate in relatively simple and stable environments. They are characterized by the existence of a large number of relatively unskilled tasks and decisions that can be programmed easily [Simon 1957] by a cadre of analysts. Coordination is essentially achieved through standardization of work processes and outputs. Professional bureaucracies, on the other hand, operate in relatively complex but stable environments. They are staffed by "professionals" who are highly trained. Coordination is achieved essentially through standardization of skills, and members have relatively wide latitude in decision making; in other words, the organization is relatively decentralized.

Just as bureaucratization was equated with centralization, cultural control systems appear to have been equated with delegation or decentralization. In actuality, the absence of formalization may conceal a high level of centralization that is internally derived (through an extended process of socialization and indoctrination) rather than externally imposed through rules and regulations. In extreme cases, cultural control systems may lead to inappropriate decisions and actions based on trying to be consistent with the corporate culture rather than reacting appropriately to local conditions.

It is important to see that the choice of control systems and extent of delegation provided to subsidiary management can, in fact, be treated independently. There exist certain contingency factors, however, that may tend to reduce this independence. These factors will be considered in the following section.

Contingency Factors in Bureaucratic Control, Cultural Control, and Centralization

The age of the organization, its size (measured in terms of number of employees, asset base, and so on), and the age of the industry in which the organization functions have been found to have a significant influence on the degree of bureaucratization and centralization; the older the organization, the larger its size, and the older the industry in which it operates, the more bureaucratic and centralized the organization tends to be [Khandwalla 1977; Stinchcombe 1959; Kimberly 1976; Blau et al. 1976; Reimann 1973; Pugh et al. 1968]. On the other hand, organizational life-cycle studies indicate that organizations that are young and entrepreneurial tend to be nonbureaucratic [for example, Filley, House, and Kerr 1976; Litterer 1965].

Studies in the relationship between the environment and the organization point to the notion of the appropriate fit between the environment and the organization structure [Khandwalla 1977; Ansoff 1974; Duncan 1972; Galbraith 1973; Thompson 1967; Lawrence and Lorsch 1967; Burns and Stalker 1966]. The environments in these studies have been differentiated along the dimensions of stability, complexity, diversity, and hostility. The general notion appears to be that the more dynamic, complex, diverse, and hostile the environment is, then the more uncertainty it creates for organizational members. Studies suggest that such uncertainty is best coped with in an organization that is characterized by low levels of formalization and centralization [Lawrence and Lorsch 1967; Burns and Stalker 1966].

Multinational corporations are affected by the forementioned factors to varying degrees and in different directions. Many corporations become multinational only after a fairly long period of exclusive domestic activity [Dyas and Thanheiser 1976; Vernon 1966]. As a result, age pushes the multinational corporation toward increased levels of bureaucratization and centralization. One would expect that the multitude of environments and uncertainties which a MNC faces would restrain this growth of bureaucratization and centralization. As Greenwood and Hinings [1976] have observed, however, once organizations start routinizing, bureaucratizing, and centralizing some activities, they extend this tendency to all activities, however inappropriate this may be. This could explain why a number of multinational corporations bureaucratize and centralize their interactions with all their subsidiaries, ranging from those that operate in relatively certain environments to those that operate in very uncertain ones. Extreme cases of such bureaucratization and centralization give rise to the phenomenon of the "headless" subsidiary [Mintzberg 1979], subsidiaries that have essentially no significant decision-making authority.

The quest for power by headquarters' management may also be another critical factor affecting the tendency to bureaucratize and centralize operations in multinational corporate operations. Keeping tabs informally on operations becomes a difficult task in geographically dispersed multinational corporations. Hence, headquarters has to resort to formal methods to keep tabs and exercise power—in other words, bureaucratization and centralization.

Crises confronting subsidiaries appear to be another factor that increases the drift toward bureaucratization and centralization. The general response of many multinational corporation headquarters to poor performance on the part of the subsidiaries is to bureaucratize and centralize. Unfortunately, such bureaucratic centralization assumes that all contingencies are known and that these can be handled through rules and regulations. Although knowledge of a large proportion of the contingencies confronting a small organization operating in a simple and stable environment may, in fact, be known, this is highly unlikely to be the case in most multinational corporations. Furthermore, studies by Aguilar [1967], Jay [1970], and Scharpf [1977] show that such bureaucratization and centralization significantly reduce the quality and timeliness of information required to make critical decisions.

Turning to the factors which contribute to an increased use of cultural control systems in organizations, one notes that research in this area is very sketchy and basically anecdotal [Peters and Waterman 1983; Ouchi 1981; Pascale and Athos 1981; Jaeger 1983]. One conclusion which does emerge from the Japanese experience is that cultural homogeneity and exposure to a cultural ethos are quite important. If the societal culture values selflessness and orientation to the whole rather than independent parts, it is relatively easy for the organization to build, and reinforce, an orientation toward organizational rather than parochial goals. In an American environment, it has been suggested that a cultural control system could be appropriate in those cases where traditional societal sources of affiliation have disappeared, leaving individuals to seek affiliation and identity in the work organization [Ouchi and Jaeger 1978]. Cultural control systems, with their relatively high levels of delegation, appear also to have been fairly successful in jobs that require secrecy (for example, the C.I.A.) or in organizations with geographically remote organizational subunits, such as, those encountered in the U.S. Forest Rangers [Kaufman 1960].

Cultural control systems can only be sustained in those organizations where turnover is relatively low. Low turnover assists in the creation of organizational myths and stories which can be of immense value in indoctrinating new organizational members [Peters and Waterman 1982; Wilkins 1980]. Low turnover also facilitates a continuing process of reinforcing the organizational culture, and breeds trust which may, in turn, lead to increasing levels of delegation. Headquarters is likely to feel more comfortable with a well-trusted, indoctrinated subsidiary manager and to delegate more decisions to him than to someone else. High mobility and turnover, on the other hand, lead to the design of a system wherein the key concern is "how easily can we slot the next person in?" A well-designed set of rules and regulations obviously makes this easier, increasing the tendency to bureaucratize the system which, as noted previously, could increase the tendency to centralize.

Because, as pointed out earlier, large size tends to increase pressures toward adoption of a bureaucratic control system, an apparent prerequisite to using a cultural control system is to have subsidiaries that, within constraints set by technology, are relatively small. Ironically, in many instances, the very prospect of creating and maintaining a cultural control system can drive the organization toward a bureaucratic control system because the explicit costs (such as, greater use of expatriates, and frequent visits between headquarters and subsidiaries) associated with the headquarters-subsidiary relationship in a cultural control system tend to be greater than those of a bureaucratic control system [Wilkins and Ouchi 1983; Jaeger 1982; Kobayashi 1982; Hulburt and Brandt 1976]. Pressures for efficiency, therefore, could push all multinational corporations toward adopting bureaucratic control systems.

The role played by a particular subsidiary in the overall functioning of the multinational corporation generally has a significant influence on the extent of delegation provided to subsidiary management. For instance, top management of a subsidiary that essentially services a very circumscribed host market could probably be accorded a high level of delegation. Furthermore, if the subsidiary contribution to the objectives (sales, profitability, and so on) of the multinational corporation is very limited, then delegation to subsidiary management could be further increased. On the other hand, if a subsidiary is very critical to the overall functioning of the multinational corporation (as a provider of key inputs, absorber of outputs, key contributor to overall corporate objectives, and so on), then delegation would probably be considerably lower. In essence, the extent of delegation, or in Weick's [1976] terms the tightness or looseness of the coupling between headquarters and its subsidiaries, would vary as a function of the interdependence between the headquarters and its subsidiaries.

The degree of interdependence between headquarters and subsidiary would be affected principally by the type of strategy chosen [see Doz 1980] as well as the nature of the firm's technology. Thompson [1967] identifies 3 types of interdependence that exist within organizations: pooled, sequential, and reciprocal. These are represented in Figure 2.

Pooled interdependence exists where organizational members share common resources but are otherwise quite autonomous.

Sequential interdependence exists where the output of one part of the system is fed into another part of the system. For example, if the General Motors (GM) subsidiary in Brazil supplies critical components (such as, engines) to GM, U.S., then these 2 units would be sequentially interdependent. Problems with supply from GM Brazil would have a ripple effect on GM's operations elsewhere, generating a greater need for control and ensuring that decisions taken by GM Brazil are consistent with those in other parts of the system.

Reciprocal interdependence is the most complex form of interdependence. Organizations or organizational units that are reciprocally interdependent feed their work back and forth among themselves. In terms of the above example, GM Brazil and GM U.S. would have a reciprocally interdependent relationship if GM U.S. worked on components provided by GM Brazil and shipped them back to GM Brazil for additional processing. Reciprocal interdependence generates the maximum need for control, coordination, and consistency in decision making. This need clearly would be greater if optimal functioning of the reciprocally interdependent parts of the organization were vital to the achievement of overall organizational goals and objectives. All these factors would move in a direction to strengthen the coupling, that is, reduce delegation to subsidiary management, since inappropriate decisions by subsidiary management can prove particularly costly to the MNC system.

Sequential and reciprocal interdependencies would probably call for some level of action planning. If the interdependencies are very significant, behavior formalization may be required because global output control measures would not be able to handle the interdependencies unless the interdependent systems were decoupled through building up of buffer inventories. Such buffering approaches generally tend to be fairly expensive and, in extreme cases, may produce results in conflict with the very reasons (global rationalization, for example) that generated the interdependencies in the first place.

Choice of Control System and Level of Delegations

In effectively managing its global operations, a multinational corporation has a degree of choice in the type of control relationship it has with each individual overseas subsidiary. Because no organization in the real world is actually a pure "ideal type," all organizations employ a mixture of both cultural and bureaucratic control mechanisms. (Those organizations that are classified as having cultural control have a more pervasive organizational culture and rely more heavily on this culture for control than do their bureaucratic control counterparts.) As an overseas subsidiary is usually quite distant from the headquarters, the interactions between organizational units occur via a relatively limited and definable set of channels. Furthermore, an overseas subsidiary is usually created by the headquarters, giving the headquarters great influence on how it will ultimately be managed. Thus, particularly in the case of the headquarters-subsidiary relationship, the headquarters of a multinational firm can

Figure 2 Types of interdependence within organizations*

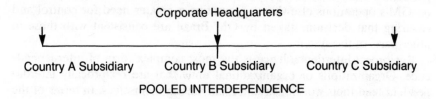

Corporate Headquarters

Country A Subsidiary   Country B Subsidiary   Country C Subsidiary

POOLED INTERDEPENDENCE

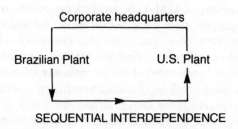

Corporate headquarters

Brazilian Plant   U.S. Plant

SEQUENTIAL INTERDEPENDENCE

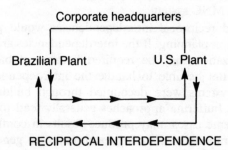

Corporate headquarters

Brazilian Plant   U.S. Plant

RECIPROCAL INTERDEPENDENCE

Key: ——▶ indicates direction of flow of materials.

*Based on Thompson [1967].

exercise a choice in the control system employed and the extent of delegation.

This paper contends that management's choice of control systems and level of delegation should be based on their assessment of the interdependencies (pooled, sequential, reciprocal) generated by their strategies, the environmental uncertainties, and "cultural proximity." "Cultural proximity" is defined as the extent to which the host cultural ethos permits adoption of the home organizational culture. Those that permit easy adoption of the "home" (headquarters) culture would be considered high in cultural proximity. For instance, it would probably be easier for U.S. multinational corporations to transmit an organizational culture to a subsidiary in Australia than to one, say, in Indonesia. Physical proximity is also of value in terms of facilitating cultural proximity (for example, favoring

Mexico over Chile). In addition, availability of communications (such as, telephone, telex, and air link) for frequent contact between home and host can also contribute to cultural proximity (for example, favoring Hong Kong over Shanghai). Cultural proximity becomes an extremely important variable in the selection of control systems, since socialization and indoctrination costs tend to be high.

From an overall perspective, dealing with interdependencies is most crucial. Environmental uncertainty should be then considered and finally cultural proximity. Figure 3 presents the type of control systems and level of delegation that should be provided to subsidiary management under various conditions of interdependence, environmental uncertainty, and cultural proximity.

It should be noted that in 8 of 12 possible situations cultural control is recommended, and in only 3 situations are high levels of delegation recommended. The latter is in recognition of the fact that certain interdependencies require a level of centralization irrespective of the type of control system employed. The systems and levels of delegation described are "ideal"; a degree of variation is expected from these in reality. Nevertheless, the basic thrust should remain as close to the ideal as feasible.

Reciprocal interdependencies are best dealt with through the mechanism of mutual adjustment because the contingencies that can arise are too numerous to plan and formalize for effectively. In this case the cultural control system is the preferred mode, because bureaucratic control systems may generate so many exceptions that headquarters is constantly involved in the fire fighting mode. This implies that even when cultural proximity is low the multinational corporation may have to spend the necessary resources on socialization and indoctrination. The degree of centralization should be higher in those instances where environmental uncertainty is low and ought to be higher as well where cultural proximity is low. What all of this implies is that the costs associated with coping up with reciprocal interdependence may be far greater than the benefits.

Strategies that call for reciprocal interdependence, therefore, should be avoided by multinational corporations except where unavoidable or unless cultural proximity is high.

Many multinationals are confronted with either pooled or sequential interdependence. Under conditions of pooled interdependence, headquarters has the maximum number of degrees of freedom. Sequential interdependence requires more coordination (that is, centralization) between headquarters and subsidiary and is more likely to occur when multinational corporations follow strategies of global rationalization either voluntarily or as a result of demands made by host governments to export a percentage of outputs as a necessary condition for permission to invest.

Regardless of the type of interdependence, under conditions of high environmental uncertainty some degree of delegation should be provided to subsidiary management so that they may be more responsive to their local environment. Conversely, centralization could be extensive under conditions of low uncertainty. Under conditions of low cultural proximity, employment of cultural control systems would probably not be worth the expenditure. Where cultural proximity is high, socialization and indoctrination can be carried out more effectively, and use of cultural control would permit a higher level of delegation.

To the extent that the use of control system and level of delegation are appropriate to the interdependency, environmental uncertainty, and cultural proximity of the given situation, there should be no inherent problems in the headquarters-subsidiary relationship. If a mismatch exists, however, major problems could arise.

First, consider the potential problems associated with bureaucratic control systems. One example would be the situation where a low level of delegation is coupled with a bureaucratic control system in an inappropriate situation. In this situation one would probably find subsidiary managers "faking" reports and "working around" headquarters' mandated rules and regulations in order to wrest a measure of autonomy. Subsidiary managers who do not react in such a manner would probably feel frustrated and leave the firm. A related problem of a high level of bureaucratic control along with centralization is the creation of a "follow the rules and regulations" mind-set in subsidiary executives.

Even if the headquarters-subsidiary relationship is running smoothly, a low level of delegation can cause problems for the subsidiary management. This arises from the position of the subsidiaries (and their managers) in the overall organization. Many subsidiaries and their managers fall in the middle levels of organizational hierarchy, and, thus, are limited in terms of their status and power in the organization. Unfortunately, these very subsidiaries are fairly substantial organizations in their host environment, and their managers are often called upon to make decisions which are strategic in nature. In many instances they are unable to do so without referral to headquarters, and they come to be perceived as mere pawns under direct and total control by headquarters. This perception of a "headless" subsidiary [Mintzberg 1979] reinforces notions of domination by a "foreign" power in many a less-developed country.

A potential advantage to employing bureaucratic control systems in host environments probably stems from its "neutrality." Although formal results and goals must be achieved, the behaviors associated with their attainment can be consistent with local practices. These subsidiaries, in theory, will thus be more able to blend in with the local culture [Jaeger 1982].

A number of concerns are associated also with an organization's use of a cultural control system. An important one is that of costs and the limited ability of the system to handle turnover. As has been pointed out earlier, cultural control systems generally limit the organization size. If a multi-

Figure 3 Control system and level of delegation appropriate to subsidiaries under various conditions

Type of Interdependence	Environmental Uncertainty	Cultural Proximity	Type of Control System	Extent of Delegation
POOLED	H	H	Cultural	Highly decentralized
		L	Bureaucratic	Highly decentralized
	L	H	Cultural	Moderately decentralized
		L	Bureaucratic	Highly decentralized
SEQUENTIAL	H	H	Cultural	Moderately decentralized
		L	Bureaucratic	Moderately decentralized
	L	H	Cultural	Centralized
		L	Bureaucratic	Centralized
RECIPROCAL	H	H	Cultural	Highly decentralized
		L	Cultural	Moderately decentralized
	L	H	Cultural	Centralized
		L	Cultural	Centralized

Key: H — High
L — Low

national were strongly committed to a cultural control system it would probably have to sacrifice some economies of scale, thereby further increasing costs. Furthermore, if demand fluctuates widely, the firm would not be able to adjust its labor force accordingly. Hence, companies that operate in industries that are extremely price-competitive and cost-sensitive or are very cyclical may have a limited ability to utilize cultural control systems.

Another concern could arise from the fact that firms employing cultural control import into a host country a culture that may be distinctly different if cultural proximity is low. Most host governments generally keep an eye on movements of capital and technology but are rarely alert to cultural influences in specific cases. Whether the importation of this culture is positive or negative is difficult to assess generally. If the company culture is in serious conflict with local laws or customs, it might be difficult for the company to change its behavior in order to comply with them, especially if this culture is constantly reinforced by headquarters. Japanese firms have had such problems in imposing their organizational culture in their Asian subsidiaries [Kobayashi 1982].

Although cultural control systems may be of immense value to subsidiaries in reacting to local developments in a manner consistent with headquarters' intent (as a result of the socialization and indoctrination), they may have difficulty responding to a major environmental change, especially if it threatens the culture or calls for a radical change in thinking within the firm. Most change in a cultural control system must, of necessity, be incremental in nature. One cannot change peoples' beliefs overnight nor can one replace people quickly. Radical changes can occur only in extreme cases where the firm's survival is at stake and a "revolutionary" atmosphere can be created.

Overall, however, cultural control systems have many advantages. If, through a process of socialization and indoctrination, the managers do, in fact, develop a "moral commitment" to the organization, they can be accorded wide latitude, enabling them to respond to local conditions quickly and in a manner consistent with overall organizational goals and objectives. Also, if the cultural control system sanctions risk-taking and does not punish it, then managers will attempt innovative approaches to problems. This strengthens the quality of management within the system. Such risk-taking behavior is relatively more difficult to encourage in bureaucratic control systems since rule adherence is prized and too many exceptions cannot be tolerated without violating the sanctity of the rules.

A dilemma facing quite a few multinational corporations is how to keep good subsidiary managers motivated in subsidiaries that demand bureaucratic control systems along with fairly high levels of centralization. Such subsidiaries are ideally suited as initial assignment locations for junior executives. Junior executives can obtain a feel for international operations in a fairly controlled environment. After such exposure they could be transferred to more demanding situations that utilize cultural control and provide higher levels of delegation. In the interim they could be constantly socialized to the organizational culture.

Summary and Conclusions

The foregoing discussion suggests several interesting issues for investigation. For example, do high performance subsidiaries have levels of delegation appropriate to the demands generated by their interdependencies, their environmental uncertainty, and their cultural proximity? Does utilization of a cultural control system make it easier for a multinational subsidiary to adopt a low profile? Do host governments' demands to "localize" subsidiary management make it impossible to adopt cultural control systems? Is it easier to generate a geocentric orientation with a bureaucratic control system or a cultural control system?

A related area of fruitful investigation would be to determine the degree to which concerns of cultural proximity influence the foreign direct investment strategies adopted by multinational corporations; that is, are MNC executives driven more by how comfortable they feel managing a subsidiary in a country that is culturally closer to their own than by other considerations? Robinson [1978] suggests, indirectly, that the rigid preference of Japanese for cultural control in their large organizations coupled with their relative cultural distance from most foreign countries helps explain their extensive use of trading companies overseas as opposed to wholly-owned, host-country-staffed overseas subsidiaries.

There is a great potential payoff from further investigation of these issues. Results from such research could add considerably to knowledge of the functioning of multinational corporations.

In summary, this paper has focused on control and delegation issues confronting multinational corporation managers. Based on this, a conceptual framework has been advanced to assist multinational corporation managers in selecting the appropriate control system and level of delegation, essentially by stressing the notion of fit between these and the variables of interdependence, environmental uncertainty, and cultural proximity. Overall, it is most critical that multinational corporation headquarters' managers recognize the distinction between type of control and the extent of delegation, and that they refrain from treating subsidiaries similarly in terms of control systems and extent of delegation. This is no easy task, but it needs to be undertaken in order to ensure that subsidiaries are controlled in the optimum fashion.

Note

†The authors wish to thank the Graduate School and the College of Business Administration of Texas Tech University as well as the Research Committee of the Faculty of Management, McGill University, for their direct support of this research. The article benefited considerably from 3 anonymous reviewers.

References

Abegglen, J. C. *The Japanese Factory: Aspects of its Social Organization.* Free Press, 1958.

Aguilar, F. J. *Scanning the Business Environment.* Macmillan, 1967.

Allison, G. T. *The Essence of Decision: Explaining the Cuban Missile Crisis.* Little, Brown, 1971.

Ansoff, H. I. "Corporate Structure: Present and Future." Working paper, European Institute for Advanced Studies in Management, Brussels, 1974.

Barnard, C. *The Functions of the Executive.* Harvard University Press, 1951.

Beyer, J. M. and Lodahl, T. M. "A Comparative Study of Patterns of Influence in United States and English Universities." *Administrative Science Quarterly,* March 1976, pp. 104–129.

Blau, P. M.; Falbe, C. M.; McKinley, W.; and Tracy, D. K. "Technology and Organization in Manufacturing." *Administrative Science Quarterly,* March 1976, pp. 20–40.

Blau, P. M. and Schoenherr, P. A. *The Structure of Organizations.* Basic Books, 1971.

Braybrooke, D., and Lindblom, C.E. *A Strategy of Decision.* Free Press, 1963.

Burns, T., and Stalker, G. M. *The Management of Innovation.* 2nd ed. Tavistock, 1966.

Child, J. *Organization: A Guide to Problems and Practice.* Harper & Row, 1977.

——, "Strategies of Control and Organizational Behavior." *Administrative Science Quarterly,* March 1973, pp. 1–17.

——, "Organization Structure and Strategies of Control: A Replication of the Aston Study." *Administrative Science Quarterly.* June 1972, pp. 163–177.

Child, J., and Keiser, A. "Organization and Managerial Role in British and West German Companies—An Examination of the Culture-Free Thesis," In *Organizations Alike and Unlike,* edited by C. J. Lamers and D. J. Hickson. Routledge and Kegan Paul, 1978.

Child, J. and Mansfield, R. "Technology, Size, and Organization Structure." *Sociology,* September 1972, pp. 369–393.

Clark, R. *The Japanese Company.* Yale University Press, 1979.

Crozier, M. *The Bureaucratic Phenomenon,* English translation. University of Chicago Press, 1964.

Deal, Terrence E., and Kennedy, Allan A. *Corporate Cultures: The Rites and Rituals of Corporate Life.* Addison-Wesley, 1982.

Donaldson, L. "Organizational Status and the Measurement of Centralization." *Administrative Science Quarterly,* September 1975, pp. 453–456.

Doz, Yves. "Strategic Management in Multinational Companies." *Sloan Management Review,* Winter 1980, pp. 27–46.

Duncan, R. B. "Characteristics of Organizational Environments and Perceived Environmental Uncertainty," *Administrative Science Quarterly,* September 1972, pp. 313–327.

Dyas, G. P., and Thanheiser, H. T. *The Emerging European Enterprise: Strategy and Structure in French and German Industry.* Macmillan of London, 1976.

Edström, A., and Galbraith, J. R. "Transfer of Managers as a Coordination and Control Strategy in Multinational Organizations." *Administrative Science Quarterly,* June 1977, pp. 248–263.

Emery, J. *Organizational Planning and Control Systems.* Macmillan, 1969.

Etzioni, A. "Compliance Structures." in *A Sociological Reader on Complex Organizations,* 3rd ed., edited by A. Etzioni and E. Lehman. Holt, Rinehart and Winston, 1980, pp. 87–100.

Fayerweather, J. *International Business Strategy and Administration.* Ballinger, 1978.

Filley, A. C.; House, R. J.; and Kerr, S. *Managerial Process and Organizational Behavior.* Scott, Foresman, 1976.

Galbraith, J. R. *Designing Complex Organizations.* Addison-Wesley, 1973.

Greenwood, R., and Hinings, C.R. "A Research Note: Centralization Revisited." *Administrative Science Quarterly,* March 1976, pp. 151–155.

Hage, J., and Aiken, M. "Relationship of Centralization to Other Structural Properties." *Administrative Science Quarterly,* June 1967, pp. 72–92.

Hall, R. T. "Professionalization and Bureaucratization," *American Sociological Review,* February 1968, pp. 92–104.

———, *Organizations: Structure and Process.* Prentice-Hall, 1972.

Hatvany, Nina, and Pucik, Vladimir. "An Integrated Management System: Lessons from the Japanese Experience." *Academy of Management Review,* July 1981, pp. 469–480.

Hulburt, James M., and Brandt, William K. "Patterns of Communications in the Multinational Corporation: An Empirical Study." *Journal of International Business Studies,* Spring 1976, pp. 57–64.

Inkson, J. H. K.; Pugh, D. S.; and Hickson, D. J. "Organization Context and Structure: An Abbreviated Replication." *Administrative Science Quarterly,* September 1970, pp. 318–329.

Jaeger, Alfred M. "Contrasting Control Modes in the Multinational Corporation: Theory, Practice and Implications." *International Studies of Management and Organization* 12, no. 1 (1982), pp. 59–82.

———, "The Transfer of Organizational Culture Overseas: An Approach to Control in the Multinational Corporation." *Journal of International Business Studies,* Fall 1983, pp. 115–129.

Jay, A. *Management and Machiavelli.* Penguin, 1970.

Johnson, R. T., and Ouchi, W. G. "Made in America (Under Japanese Management)." *Harvard Business Review,* September–October 1974, pp. 61–91.

Kaufman, H. *The Forest Ranger: A Study in Administrative Behavior.* Johns Hopkins Press, 1960.

Keesing, R. "Theories of Culture." *Annual Review of Anthropology* 1974, pp. 73–97.

Khandwalla, P. N. *The Design of Organizations.* Harcourt Brace Jovanovich, 1977.

Kimberly, J. R. "Organizational Size and the Structural Perspective: A Review, Critique, and Proposal." *Administrative Science Quarterly,* December 1976, pp. 571–597.

Kobayashi, Noritake. "The Present and Future of Japanese Multinational Enterprises." *International Studies of Management and Organization* 12 no. 1 (1982), pp. 38–58.

Kochen, M., and Deutsch, K. W. "Decentralization by Function and Location." *Management Science,* April 1973, pp. 841–855.

Kuin, P. "The Magic of Multinational Management." *Harvard Business Review.* November–December 1972, pp. 89–97.

Lawrence, P. R. *The Changing Organizational Behavior Patterns.* Riverside Press, 1958.

———, and Lorsch, J. W. *Organization and Environment.* Irwin, 1967.

Linton, R. *The Study of Man.* D. Appleton Century Company, 1936.

Litterer, J. A. *The Analysis of Organizations.* Wiley, 1965; also 2nd ed., 1973.

Lorsch, J. W. "Introduction to the Structural Design of Organizations." In *Organizational Structure and Design,* edited by G. W. Dalton, P. R. Lawrence, and J. W. Lorsch. Irwin Dorsey, 1970.

Manns, C. Review of "Formalization and Centralization: The Case of Polish Industry" by Lena Kolarska. In *Seminars on Organizations,* edited by A. M. Jaeger. Stanford University, Palo Alto. California, Winter and Spring 1976, pp. 64–66.

Mansfield, R. "Bureaucracy and Centralization: An Examination of Organizational Structure." *Administrative Science Quarterly,* December 1973, pp. 477–488.

Mintzberg, H. *The Structuring of Organizations.* Prentice-Hall, 1979.

Ouchi, W. G. *Theory Z.* Addison-Wesley, 1981.

———, "The Relationship Between Organizational Structure and Organizational Control." *Administrative Science Quarterly,* March 1977, pp. 95–112.

Ouchi, W. G., and Jaeger, A. M. "Type Z Organization: Stability in the Midst of Mobility." *Academy of Management Review,* April 1978, pp. 305–314.

Ouchi, W. G., and McGuire, M. A. "Organizational Control: Two Functions." *Administrative Science Quarterly,* December 1975, pp. 559–569.

Pascale, R. T., and Athos, A. G. *The Art of Japanese Management.* Simon & Schuster, 1981.

Perrow, C. "A Framework for the Comparative Analysis of Organizations." *American Sociological Review,* April 1967, pp. 194–208.

———, *Organizational Analysis: A Sociological Review.* Wadsworth, 1970.

Peters, T. J., and Waterman, R. H. Jr. *In Search of Excellence.* Harper & Row, 1983.

Pugh, D. S.; Hickson, D. J.; Hinings, C. R.; Macdonald, K. M.; Turner, C.; and Lupton, T. "A Conceptual Scheme for Organizational Analysis." *Administrative Science Quarterly,* December 1963–64, pp. 289–315.

Pugh, D. S.; Hickson, D. J.; Hinings, C. R.; and Turner, C. "Dimensions of Organization Structure." *Administrative Science Quarterly,* June 1968, pp. 65–105.

Reimann, B. C. "On the Dimensions of Bureaucratic Structure: An Empirical Reappraisal." *Administrative Science Quarterly,* December 1973, pp. 462–476.

Robbins, S. P. *Organization Theory: The Structure and Design of Organizations.* Prentice-Hall, 1983.

Robinson, Richard D. *International Business Management: A Guide to Decision Making.* Dryden Press, 1978.

Rohlen, T. P. *For Harmony and Strength: Japanese White Collar Organization in Anthropological Perspective.* University of California Press, 1974.

Scharpf, F. W. "Does Organization Matter? Task Structure and Interaction in the Ministerial Bureaucracy." In *Organization Design: Theoretical Perspectives and Empirical Findings,* edited by E. H. Burack and A. R. Negandhi. Kent State University Press, 1977, pp. 149–167.

Schein, E. H. *Organizational Psychology.* Prentice Hall, 1980.

Schwartz, H. and Davis, S. M. "Matching Corporate Culture and Business Strategy." *Organizational Dynamics,* Summer 1981, pp. 30–48.

Simon, H.A. *Administrative Behavior.* 2nd ed. Macmillan, 1957.

Smircich, Linda "Concepts of Culture and Organizational Analysis." *Administrative*

Science Quarterly, September, 1983, pp. 339–358.

Stinchcombe, A. L. "Bureaucratic and Craft Administration of Production: A Comparative Study." *Administrative Science Quarterly*, September 1959, pp. 168–187.

Stopford, J. M., and Wells, L. T. Jr. *Managing the Multinational Enterprise: Organization of the Firm and Ownership of the Subsidiaries.* Basic Books, 1972.

Tannenbaum, A. *Control in Organizations.* McGraw Hill, 1968.

Thompson, J. D. *Organizations in Action.* McGraw Hill, 1967.

Vernon, R. "International Investment and International Trade in the Product Cycle." *Quarterly Journal of Economics*, May 1966, pp. 190–207.

Weick, K. E. "Educational Organizations as Loosely Coupled Systems." *Administrative Science Quarterly*, March 1976, pp. 1–19.

Wilkins, Alan L. "Organizational Stories as an Expression of Management Philosophy." Unpublished doctoral dissertation. Graduate School of Business, Stanford University, 1980.

——, and Ouchi, William G. "Efficient Cultures: The Relationship Between Culture and Organizational Performance." *Administrative Science Quarterly*, September 1983, pp. 468–481.

Woodward, J. *Industrial Organization: Theory and Practice.* Oxford University Press, 1965.

Select Bibliography

Aharoni, Y., *The Foreign Investment Decision Process* (Cambridge, Mass., Harvard Business School, 1966).

Aliber, R., "The MNE in a multiple-currency world", in J. Dunning, ed., *The Multinational Enterprise* (London, Allen and Unwin, 1971).

Andrews, K., *The Concept of Corporate Strategy* (Homewood, Ill., Richard D. Irwin, 1971).

Ansoff, I., *Corporate Strategy: An Analytic Approach to Business Policy for Growth and Expansion* (New York, McGraw-Hill, 1965).

Astley, W.G. and C. Fombrun, "Collective strategy: social ecology of organizational environments", *Academy of Management Review*, 8 (1983), pp. 576–587.

Bartlett, C. and S. Ghoshal, "Organizing for worldwide effectiveness: the transnational solution", *California Management Review*, 31 (Fall 1988), pp. 54–74.

Blau, P., "A formal theory of differentiation", *American Sociology Review*, 35 (1970), pp. 201–218.

Boddewyn, J., "Political aspects of MNE theory", *Journal of International Business Studies*, 19 (1988), pp. 341–364.

Bourgeois, L., "Strategic management and determinism", *Academy of Management Review*, 9 (1984), pp. 586–596.

Buckley, P. and M. Casson, *The Future of the Multinational Enterprise* (London, Macmillan, 1976).

Caves, R., "International corporations: the industrial economics of foreign investment", *Economica*, 38 (1971), pp. 1–27.

Caves, R. and M. Porter, "From entry barriers to mobility barriers: conjectural decisions and contrived deterrence to new competition", *Quarterly Journal of Economics*, 91 (1977), pp. 241–262.

Caves, R., M. Porter, and A. Spence, *Competition in an Open Economy* (Cambridge, Mass., Harvard University Press, 1980).

Chandler, A.D. Jr., *Strategy and Structure: Chapters in the History of Industrial Enterprise* (Cambridge, Mass., MIT Press, 1962).

Channon, D., "Strategy and structure of British enterprise" (unpublished Ph.D. dissertation, Harvard Business School, 1971).

Chrisman, J., C. Hofer and W. Boulton, "Toward a system for classifying business strategies", *Academy of Management Review*, 13 (1988), pp. 413–428.

Cyert, R. and J. March, *A Behavioral Theory of the Firm* (Englewood Cliffs, N.J., Prentice-Hall, 1963).

Doz, Y., "International industries: fragmentation versus globalization", in Bruce Guile and Harvey Brooks, eds., *Technology and Global Industry: Companies and Nations in the World Economy* (Washington, D.C., National Academy Press, 1987).

Dunning, J., *International Production and the Multinational Enterprise* (London, Allen and Unwin, 1981).

——, "A study of international business: a plea for a more interdisciplinary approach", *Journal of International Business Studies*, 20 (1989), pp. 411–436.

Egelhoff, W.G., "Strategy and structure in multinational corporations: an information-processing approach", *Administrative Science Quarterly*, 27 (1982), pp. 435–458.

Franko, L.G., *The European Multinationals* (Greenwich, CT: Greylock Press, 1976).

Galbraith, C. and N. Kay, "Towards a theory of multinational enterprise", *Journal of Economic Behavior and Organization*, 7 (1986), pp. 3–19.

Hambrick, D., "High profit strategies in mature capital goods industries: a contingency approach", *Academy of Management Journal*, 26 (1983), pp. 687–707.

Hannan, M.T. and J. Freeman, "The population ecology of organizations", *American Journal of Sociology*, 82 (1977), pp. 929–964.

Harrigan, K., *Strategies for Declining Businesses* (Lexington, Mass., Lexington Books, 1980).

——, "Exit decisions in mature industries", *Academy of Management Journal*, 25 (1982), pp. 707–732.

Hatten, K., D. Schendel and A. Cooper, "A strategic model of the U.S. brewing industry, 1952–1971", *Academy of Management Journal*, 21 (1978), pp. 592–610.

Hayes, R. and S. Wheelwright, "The dynamics of process/product life cycles", *Harvard Business Review*, 57 (March–April 1979), pp. 127–136.

Hofer, C., "Toward a contingency theory of business strategy", *Academy of Management Journal*, 18 (1975), pp. 784–810.

Hofer, C. and D. Schendel, *Strategy Formulation: Analytical Concepts* (St. Paul, MN, West Publishing Co., 1978).

Hymer, S., "The efficiency (contradiction) of multinational corporations", *American Economics Review*, 60 (1970), pp. 441–448.

Kindleberger, C., *American Business Abroad: Six Lectures on Direct Investment* (New Haven, CT, Yale University Press, 1969).

Knickerbocker, F., *Oligopolistic Reaction and Multinational Enterprise* (Cambridge, Mass., Harvard University, Graduate School of Business, 1973).

Kogut, B., "Designing global strategies; comparative and competitive value added chains", *Sloan Management Review*, 26 (Summer 1985a), pp. 15–28.

——, "Designing global strategies; profiting from operational flexibility", *Sloan Management Review*, 26 (Fall 1985b), pp. 27–38.

Lecraw, D., "Performance of transnational corporations in less developed countries", *Journal of International Business Studies*, 14 (Spring/Summer 1983), pp. 15–33.

——, "Diversification strategy and performance", *Journal of Industrial Economics*, 33 (1984), pp. 179–198.

Perlmutter, H.V., "The tortuous evolution of the multinational corporation", *Columbia Journal of World Business* (January–February 1969), pp. 9–18.

Porter, M., "Changing patterns of international competition", *California Management Review*, 28 (1986), pp. 9–40.

Prahalad, C.K., "The strategic process in a multinational corporation" (unpublished doctoral dissertation, Graduate School of Business Administration, Harvard University, 1975).

Rugman, A., *Inside the Multinationals: The Economics of Internal Markets* (New York, Columbia University Press, 1981).

Schendel, D. and C. Hofer, *Strategic Management* (Boston, Little, Brown & Co., 1979).

Scott, B., "The industrial state: old myths and new realities", *Harvard Business Review*, 51 (March–April 1973), pp. 133–148.

Stopford, M. and L. Wells, Jr., *Managing the Multinational Enterprise* (New York, Basic Books, 1972).

Teece, D., "Multinational enterprises: market failure and market power considerations", *Sloan Management Review*, 22 (1981), pp. 3–17.

——, "Transaction cost economics and the multinational enterprise", *Journal of Economic Behavior and Organization*, 7 (1986), pp. 21–45.

Vernon, R., "International investment and international trade in the product cycle", *Quarterly Journal of Economics*, 81 (May 1966), pp. 190–207.

Williamson, O., *Markets and Hierarchies: Analysis and Antitrust Implications* (New York, Free Press, 1975).

Yip, G., "Gateways to entry", *Harvard Business Review*, 60 (September–October 1982), pp. 85–92.

Name index

Subject index

action planning 366
activities, concentrated/dispersed 148–51
adaptation: corporate level 33, 34–6; and integration 31, 33–8, 39–42; in Japanese strategy 83; in matrix structures 36–7
adaptive planning 50
administrative coordination: dangers 109–11; decision-making 107–8; General Motors 105–6; smaller MNCs 101; strategy 96–7, 98
administrative managers 109
advertising 160, 248, 276
aid flows 250
aircraft industries 148, 152–3
alliances: automobile industry 352–4, 360–1,363; coordinated-activity 359; corporate 352–4; and decision-making 359, 360–3; dominant partner 363; government 252–3; minority equity 353, 359; multiple-activity 359; nonequity 353, 359, 360; organizational complexity 356–60; shared-activity 359; strategic 16; trading 359, 360; see also joint ventures; ventures
aluminium 247
America see US
antitrust laws 337
arbitrage 172, 248
area leading/product line grown matrix structure 37
area organization 32–3, 243–5, 278,

287; control systems 275; foreign sales 274, 288, 293–4; planning tasks 41; product diversity 273; and product divisions 242–3, 297–8; responsibilities in 270; strategic variables 276
automobile assembly 325
automobile industry: alliances 352–4, 360–1, 363; collaborative strategy 314; integration 99, 176; Japanese investment 328; Japanese strategy 178, 196, 198; small cars 187
autonomy: structural 310–12; subsidiaries 96, 240–2

BCG (Boston Consulting Group) 54, 55, 65–6, 68–9
behavioural perspective 4–5, 264
board of director interlocks 315, 318
bonus payments 228
brand names 125, 128, 155, 184, 329
branded foods 277, 278
broad product lines, subsidiary 290
bureaucratic control 110–11; and centralization 371; contingency factors 372–3; systems 366–7; Western MNCs 16
business–level strategy 308

cameras 203–4
Canada, and US 239, 272, 291
career development 226, 227–8, 320
cartels 159
centralization: and bureaucratization